BROADMAN

A COMMENTARY

ON

The Gospel by John

BY

DAVID LIPSCOMB

EDITED, WITH ADDITIONAL NOTES,

BY

C. E. W. DORRIS

GOSPEL ADVOCATE COMPANY
Nashville, Tennessee
1968

PREFACE.

I promised J. W. Shepherd and others to assist in preparing a complete commentary on the whole New Testament scriptures, being assigned the books of Mark and John. Since that time many untoward events have transpired to delay the fulfillment of the promise. Among the chief of these has been the lack of adequate leisure to bestow upon such an important task. But at last, I am thankful to say, that through the providence of God, I have been enabled to bring the work to a close.

In this as in the former volume, I have been handicapped in introducing subject matter and carrying it to the limit of thought for the reason space in the printed volumes was limited. For this reason much I had hoped to include in these volumes has been omitted.

I have labored to stay free from the influence of particular scholastic tenets so as to meet the wants of those who desire to know the simple truth as it is in Christ Jesus, without having it formulated in the schools, or modified by special theories of religion. Most of the commentaries examined in connection with this work were written, it seems, to defend some particular religious theory or theories to which the authors held rather than to bring out the plain truths Jesus had expressed. The result has been that in many places their works are a complete perversion of the truth and not an exhibition of it. From these writers I could derive no benefit except where their cherished doctrine was out of sight.

The work which I now send forth is an effort to supply, so far as the ability is possessed, the deficiency here complained of. I only wish I were able to feel that it is successful. But, since all present-day writers are human, and carry with them more or less the weakness of humanity, I fear, however, that the reader may find himself compelled to see in me the same fault which I have with constant reluctance seen in others. Still I am not without hope that this may not prove true for the reason that my sole aim has been to ascertain the exact sense of the scripture and to express it in terse, clear English so that the unlearned may comprehend the exact truths. How far this has been accomplished I shall not venture to say. Of what I have aimed to do, I feel that I am a perfectly competent judge, but what I have actually done, I may be a very poor one.

I hope the reader will observe that I have never at any time seemed to think whether my expositions were favoring any ism. And this is strictly true. I have been concerned solely with the sense of the scriptures, and neither the sense nor nonsense of others, for the reason that we are made free by the truth as it is in Christ Jesus. I could not feel safe in any other course.

In this volume the additional notes of the editor, added to those of David Lipscomb, are distinguished from his by being enclosed in brackets, thus [ ]. Those not thus enclosed are the writings of David Lipscomb left by him in the care of J. W. Shepherd in the form of a commentary with the request that Mr. Shepherd add to and publish them in book form. Mr. Shepherd asked me and others to aid in this work. In addition to the abovementioned notes of Mr. Lipscomb, I have included with them his comments on the Sunday Bible lessons found in the annuals as well as gleanings from his pen in the *Gospel Advocate.*

The American Revised Version has been used throughout this volume, both in the text and references to other parts of the Bible.

It remains to add only a few more items before closing this preface. The first of these is to acknowledge the valuable assistance rendered me by that godly servant of our Lord and painstaking man in all his work, J. W. Shepherd. While his head is white and his body is bending under the pressure of years and his natural strength abating, he has lost none of his ambition to render valuable assistance to all who come his way.

It is again appropriate to extend to Mrs. Sarah Deen my sincere thanks and appreciation for the valuable services she has rendered in typing the manuscript and preparing it for the printer. In this, as in the former volume, she has done her work well.

I submit this volume to the public with the prayer that it may be blessed as a means of leading men to "believe that Jesus is the Christ, the Son of God; and that believing ye may have life in his name," and that it may strengthen and increase the faith of those who already believe.

C. E. W. DORRIS.

Nashville, Tennessee, December 28, 1938.

CONTENTS.

	Page
INTRODUCTION	9
The writer	9
Source of information and its truthfulness	10
Why written	11
When written	12
Place written	12

PART FIRST.

Preliminary Ministry of Jesus (1: 1 to 4: 54).

SECTION ONE.

His Public Introduction by John (1: 1-51).

His eternal pre-existence (1: 1-14)	15
A part of John's testimony and a comment by the apostle (1: 15-18)	23
Another part of John's testimony (1: 19-28)	25
Jesus declared the Lamb of God and the Son of God (1: 29-34)	28
The last testimony repeated (1: 35-42)	29
Other disciples gained at Bethany (1: 43-51)	32

SECTION TWO.

Preparatory Work in Samaria, Galilee, and Judea (2: 1 to 4: 54).

A brief visit to Galilee and the first miracle (2: 1-12)	35
Jesus goes to the Passover (2: 13-22)	38
Signs wrought during the Passover (2: 23-25)	41
Conversation with Nicodemus (3: 1-15)	42
Remarks on the mission of Jesus and the sin of unbelief (3: 16-21)	49
Jesus at the Jordan and John at Aenon (3: 22-30)	51
Superiority of the Son and the blessing of faith (3: 31-36)	53
Jesus leaves Judea and journeys toward Galilee (4: 1-6)	54
He converses with the Samaritan woman (4: 7-26)	57
Remarks to the disciples (4: 27-38)	64
Results in Sychar and arrival in Galilee (4: 39-45)	68
Second miracle in Cana (4: 46-54)	70

PART SECOND.

Events Between the Departure into Galilee and the Last Visit to Jerusalem (5: 1 to 11: 57).

SECTION ONE.

A Miracle and a Disputation in Jerusalem (5: 1-47).

An impotent man made whole (5: 1-9)	73
Jesus accused of Sabbath breaking (5: 10-18)	75
Jesus asserts his power (5: 19-29)	77
The testimony of these claims (5: 30-40)	80
Cause of Jewish unbelief (5: 41-47)	82

Page

Section Two.

A Miracle and a Disputation in Galilee (6: 1-71).

Feeding of five thousand (6: 1-14) 85
Jesus and his disciples recross the lake (6: 15-21) 89
The multitude overtakes Jesus (6: 22-27) 91
Remarks about the bread of life (6: 28-40) 93
The people murmur and Jesus reiterates (6: 41-51) 98
More murmuring and another reiteration (6: 52-59) 101
Murmuring by the disciples (6: 60-65) 103
Jesus deserted by all but the twelve (6: 66-71) 105

Section Three.

Jesus at the Feast of Tabernacles (7: 1 to 10: 21).

After delay he goes to the feast (7: 1-13) 107
Christ teaches in the temple and refers to his first visit (7: 14-24) 110
A discussion among the people (7: 25-36) 113
Christ's speech on last day of the feast and its effect (7: 37-44) 116
Confusion among chief priests and Pharisees (7: 45-52) 118
Discussion about the woman taken in adultery (7: 53 to 8: 11) 120
Jesus declares himself the light of the world (8: 12-20) 123
He announces his departure and the inability of his enemies to follow him (8: 21-30) 127
He tells the Jews how to be free (8: 31-45) 130
He challenges the Jews to convict him of sin (8: 46-50) 134
Jesus declares the power of his work and his pre-existence (8: 51-59) 135
Jesus heals a man born blind (9: 1-12) 137
The Pharisees investigate the miracle (9: 13-34) 143
Jesus meets the man again (9: 35-41) 148
The parable of the shepherd and his speech (10: 1-6) 150
Contrast between true shepherd and the hireling (10: 7-18) 153
Division among his hearers (10: 19-21) 157

Section Four.

At the Feast of Dedication Beyond the Jordan and Recalled to Bethany (10: 22 to 11: 59).

Renewal of remarks about his sheep (10: 22-30) 159
Discussion about stoning Jesus (10: 31-39) 161
Jesus departs beyond the Jordan (10: 40-42) 164
He is recalled to Bethany (11: 1-16) 164
Lazarus raised from the dead (11: 17-44) 168
Immediate effects of the miracle (11: 45-53) 178
Jesus retires until the Passover (11: 54-57) 180

Page

PART THIRD.

Events from His Last Arrival in Jerusalem to His Resurrection (12: 1 to 21: 25).

Section One.

His Arrival and Speeches Previous to the Passover (12: 1-50).

He is anointed at a supper in Bethany (12: 1-8) 183
Curiosity about Lazarus and its effects (12: 9-11) 186
His public welcome by the people (12: 12-19) 187
A request of certain Greeks (12: 20-26) 189
The hour of his trouble (12: 27-30) 192
Jesus predicts his crucifixion (12: 31-36) 194
Jesus retires and John comments on the unbelief of the Jews (12: 37-43) 197
Other words of Jesus about belief (12: 44-50) 201

Section Two.

Conversation and Incidents at the Paschal Supper (13: 1 to 14: 31).

He washed the disciples' feet (13: 1-11) 204
He comments on the washing (13: 12-20) 209
Betrayal announced (13: 21-30) 212
Jesus announces his speedy departure (13: 31-35) 215
Peter's denial (13: 36-38) 217
He announces his final return (14: 1-6) 219
His identity with the Father (14: 7-14) 222
The promise of the Holy Spirit (14: 15-24) 226
Other works of the Spirit and words of comfort (14: 25-31) 231

Section Three.

Remarks of Jesus Between the Supper and His Arrest (15: 1 to 17: 26).

Parable of the vine and its branches (15: 1-8) 236
The disciples exhorted to abide in the love of Christ (15: 9-17) 240
Remarks on the world's hatred (15: 18-27) 244
Persecution predicted and other works of the Spirit stated (16: 1-15) 249
His departure and return (16: 16-24) 257
An end of speaking in parables (16: 25-33) 259
Jesus prays for himself and his disciples (17: 1-26) 261

Section Four.

The Arrest and Condemnation of Jesus (18: 1 to 19: 16).

Arrested and taken before Annas (18: 1-14) 272
Peter's first denial (18: 15-18) 278
Jesus is questioned and smitten (18: 19-24) 280
Peter's second and third denial (18: 25-27) 281
Proceedings before Pilate (18: 28-40; 19: 1-16) 283

Page

SECTION FIVE.

Death, Burial, and Resurrection of Jesus (19: 17-42; 20: 1-25).

Jesus bears the cross (19: 17-24) 297
Jesus commits his mother to John (19: 25-27) 300
His last suffering (19: 28-30) 301
The bodies prepared for removal (19: 31-37) 302
Jesus is buried by Joseph and Nicodemus (19: 38-42) 304
Mary, John, and Peter find the tomb empty (20: 1-10) 306
Jesus appears to Mary (20: 11-18) 309
He appears to the eleven (20: 19-23) 312
The incredulity of Thomas and its removal (20: 24-29) 314
Other signs and purposes of the record (20: 30, 31) 315
Jesus appears to seven at the lake of Tiberias (21: 1-14) 316
Remarks of Jesus to Peter (21: 15-23) 321
Conclusion of the narrative (21: 24, 25) 325

INTRODUCTION TO THE GOSPEL ACCORDING TO JOHN.

I. THE WRITER.

John was one of the twelve apostles chosen by the Lord. He was the son of Zebedee, a fisherman on the Sea of Galilee, who was prosperous enough to employ hired servants (Mark 1: 20), and was himself carrying on business with his brother James and Simon Peter as partners. He and his brother James worked with their father as fishermen until called by the Lord to follow him. Their mother's name was Salome (Matt. 27: 56; Mark 15: 40), who was probably a sister of Mary, the mother of Jesus (compare John 19: 25 with above passages). If this be true then John and Jesus were cousins. He was first a disciple of John the Baptist, followed Jesus at a hint from the former (John 1: 35-40), and he and Andrew were the first of the apostles to have an interview with Jesus. Subsequently he was one of the first four who were definitely called to the apostleship. (Matt. 4: 18-24; Mark 1: 16-20; Luke 5: 10, 11.) Peter, James, and John seem to have been nearer to the Savior than the other apostles. They are mentioned as being with him on occasions of note. John, from the order of their names and from his living later than the other disciples, is supposed to have been the younger of the two brothers, and the youngest of the apostles. He and James were called Boanerges (sons of thunder). He was distinguished as "the disciple whom Jesus loved" (John 13: 23; 19: 26; 21: 7, 20), notwithstanding which his impetuous disposition elicited rebuke from Jesus more than once (Luke 9: 49; 54, 55), and a request for high place in the kingdom excited the anger of the other apostles and was repelled by Jesus (Mark 10: 35-41).
request for high place in the kingdom excited the anger of the other apostles and was repelled by Jesus (Mark 10: 35-41).

It is supposed that it was John who leaned on the bosom of Jesus at the supper. Jesus honored him while on the cross by giving him the care of his mother. (John 19: 25-27.) John is generally regarded as gentle and effeminate in character. The facts concerning him in the scriptures do not bear this out. He and James, when the Samaritan village refused to receive them, besought the Master to call down fire. Jesus reproved them, "Ye know not what manner of spirit ye are of." (Luke 9: 55.) He stood nearest Jesus through his trials, was the first of the apostles to reach his tomb after his resurrection; and while he insisted much on love, and is called the apostle of love, no apostle has so emphasized the necessity of faithful and implicit obedience to God. He makes love the spirit of obedience and obedience the test of love. "If ye love me, ye will keep my commandments." "If a man love me, he will keep my word." "For this is the love of God, that we keep his commandments." (1 John 5: 3.) While insisting more than all on love as the essential spirit of service, he rejects all feeling or emotion or sentiment that does not lead to reverential and faithful obedience to the commands of God as love. John lived to a later date than any of the apostles and was foremost and active in all their works down to the end of his life. In addition to writing the fourth book of the gospel, he wrote first, second, and third epistles of John and also Revelation. He was a Jew. There can be no doubt that John removed from Jerusalem and settled at Ephesus, though at what time is uncertain. Tradition goes on to relate that in the persecution under Domitian he is taken to Rome, and there by his boldness, though not by death, gains the crown of martyrdom. The boiling oil into which he is thrown has no power to hurt him. He is then sent to labor in mines, and Patmos is the place of his exile. The accession of Nerva frees him from danger and he returns to Ephesus. Heresies continue to show themselves, but he meets them with the strongest possible protest. The very time of his death lies within the region of conjecture rather than of history, and the dates that have been assigned for it range from A.D. 89 to A.D. 120. It is said that he died in Ephesus and was buried there. He is the only one of the apostles who died a natural death. The others died martyrs.

II. SOURCE OF INFORMATION AND ITS TRUTHFULNESS.

The author of the gospel by John declares himself an eyewitness of the transactions recorded by him. (John 19: 35; 21: 24.) In his first epistle of John (1: 1-3; 4: 14) he again affirms that he was an eyewitness of the things done and taught by Jesus Christ. He was one of the first disciples called by our Lord and Master, and later, after he had developed sufficiently, the Lord called him to be an apostle. As a student he sat at his Master's feet for about three and a half years, being schooled and trained for the great work before him. When he, together with the other apostles, were sufficiently schooled and trained for this work, their Teacher sent them into all the world to teach and lead others to the Lamb of God. (Matt. 29: 19; Mark 16: 15.) In addition to this preparation Jesus told them that he would send them the Holy Spirit who would teach and guide them into all truth. (John 14: 16-26; 15: 26.) The Spirit came to the apostles on the day of Pentecost and spoke to the world through them. (Acts 2: 1-4.) With these facts before us no one except an infidel could deny but that John received the things he taught firsthand and that what he wrote was genuine. Further evidence is unnecessary, for the one who would not believe these facts would not believe were we to write a volume on the subject.

III. WHY WRITTEN.

It is supposed generally that John wrote after the three other records had been written, and that what he wrote was supplementary to them—to give things done and taught by Jesus that the others had omitted, and to present a phase of the Lord's character that had not been fully brought out by the others. This is true of his gospel whether it was the aim of John or not. It is thought by some that a heresy denying the divine nature of Jesus had arisen, and that John wrote to counteract and destroy this heresy. Whether this was the cause of his writing or not, he tells that Jesus was with God and was God before the world was, and that all things were created by him. Then John testifies near the close of his record: And "many other signs therefore did Jesus in the presence of the disciples, which are not written in this book: but these are written, that ye may believe that Jesus is the Christ, the Son of God; and that believing ye may have life in his name." (John 20: 30, 31.) The truth that he was the Son of God is given a prominence in the writings of John that is not given in any other of the apostolic writings. This is explained that each wrote to meet the conditions before him, and that this question had been raised before the death of John and called forth his writings.

IV. WHEN WRITTEN.

The gospel of John is held on seemingly good reasons to have been written later than the other three. It differs widely in several respects from them. It does not enter into facts and relate the same occurrences the others do. The scenes of the others are laid almost entirely in Galilee, those of John in Judea. The others say but little of the visits of Jesus to Jerusalem, or his attendance on the feasts. John lays emphasis on these. The chief data for determining the length of the ministry of Jesus after his baptism is furnished by John in giving account of his attendance on the feasts.

As to the question whether the fourth book of the gospel was written by John, there is but one denial in the second century of its authorship, and this by certain heretics, founded on its contents, because those tenets did not comport with their views. Aside from this the external testimony of the century is unanimous in affirming or implying that John is its author and that he wrote late in the first century. As to the exact time we have no fixed date. It is generally agreed by scholars that a tradition puts it while John was in exile to Patmos has no authority. Alford fixes the date between A.D. 70 and A.D. 85; Macdonald at A.D. 85 or A.D. 86; Godet between A.D. 80 and A.D. 90; and Tholuck at not far from A.D. 100.

V. PLACE WRITTEN.

The later years of John were spent in Asia Minor and principally at Ephesus. Irenaeus was educated in the same region by a disciple of John and declares that the gospel by John was written at Ephesus and with him agree Jerome and later writers. Irenaeus also tells us that it was the latest written of the gospels. It was therefore written after the departure of the apostle from Jerusalem to this portion of the country, and there can be little doubt that its place of composition was the great metropolis of this portion of the world, and for a long time after the fall of Jerusalem, the chief center of Christianity. "After the destruction of Jerusalem Ephesus became the center of Christian life in the East. Even Antioch, the original source of missions to the Gentiles, and the future metropolis of the Christian patriarch, appears for a time less conspicuous in the obscurity of early church history than Ephesus, to which Paul inscribed his epistle, and in which John found a dwelling place and a tomb. This half Greek, half oriental city, visited by ships from all parts of the Mediterranean, and united by great roads with the markets of the interior, was the common meeting place of various characters and classes of men."—*Conyheare and Hawson.*

COMMENTARY ON THE GOSPEL BY JOHN.

PART FIRST.
PRELIMINARY MINISTRY OF JESUS.
1: 1 to 4: 54.

SECTION ONE.
HIS PUBLIC INTRODUCTION BY JOHN.
1: 1-51.

1. HIS ETERNAL PRE-EXISTENCE.
1: 1-14.

1 In the beginning was the Word, and the Word was with God, and the

---

1 **In the beginning**—This is the term used in reference to the creation (Gen. 1: 1) and refers to the original creation of matter, but inchoate in what is usually known as the six days' creation. More properly the organization. [We recognize the phrase in Genesis as referring to a period antecedent to all created things, in which nothing existed but that which was self-existent and incapable of destruction. We have no doubt that John used this phrase in the same sense here and that, as we can make no periods in eternity back of time, the phrase is equivalent to "through all eternity," or "eternally."]

was the Word,—*The Word* in this place clearly refers to Jesus Christ before he was conceived and born of the Virgin Mary. [*Logos,* the Greek of "Word," was used by the Greeks to express both *reason* and *speech*, both the thought and expression, and was probably therefore selected by John as the name of the personality of which he was about to speak. For our purpose it is sufficient to know that the *logos* "became flesh," and is identified as Jesus Christ, and this Jesus, in his intercessory prayer (17: 5) is represented by John as recalling a distinct memory of the glory he had of the Father before the world was. This sets aside all idea of the *logos* as representing simply principles or attributes of deity, which were manifested in him whom he called the Son of God. Here is a Being, a Person with a continuous memory, part *antedating* time, and part *in* time.]

Word was God. 2 The same was in the beginning with God. 3 All things

and the Word was with God,—[It expresses intercourse or association with God, and therefore makes of the Word a distinct personality. Jesus was with God in the creation of all things.]

and the Word was God.—He was with the Father. He was one of the Godhead. [We here have an advance in the thought. In the first clause of the verse we had eternal existence; in the second, distinct personality; now we have *deific* personality. This eternal Being is declared to be in nature the same as he who is called God here and afterwards the Father. He therefore possesses the attributes of deity.]

There are three distinct personages presented to us as composing the Godhead—God the Father, the Word, and the Holy Spirit. These three personages, each distinct as persons, yet one in nature, being, purpose, and designs, performed distinct and different offices in the work of creation and in all the works in which they engaged. God the Father is represented as the supreme ruling power of the heavens and the earth. He ordained and provided for all things. The Word was the personage through whom the worlds were created. [The Holy Spirit organized.]

Jesus the Christ had an existence before his conception and birth of the Virgin Mary. He is nowhere called the Son of God or the son of man except prophetically before his conception and birth of the virgin. He is nowhere called Jesus or the Savior until he came to save his people from their sins, save as the Spirit in prophecy foretold this would be his mission. He is nowhere called the Christ until he was anointed "with the oil of gladness above his fellows," until he in his mission on earth received the Spirit "without measure," save as it was foretold in prophecy that he would be the anointed, the Christ of God, to save the world. These names were all bestowed as descriptive of his character and work of office.

2 **The same was in the beginning with God.**—He was one of "us" when matter was originally created. "Let us make man in our image." (Gen. 1: 26.) The Godhead is represented

were made through him; and without him [1]was not anything made that hath been made. 4 In him was life; and the life was the light of men. 5 And

[1]Or, *was not anything made. That which hath been made was life in him; and the life &c.*

as composed of God, the originator and provider of all things; the Word, the creative agent of the Godhead; and the Holy Spirit, who, when the work of creation was completed by the Word, brooded upon the face of the matter, organized it, gave laws in accordance with which the work of procreation would proceed, and in and through which the Spirit took up his abode to guide the matter forward to its predestined end.

3 **All things were made through him;**—The Word was the creative agency of the Godhead.

and without him was not anything made that hath been made.—[Without the intervention or help of any other person or being, he created all things. This language is sweeping and unevadable. The *logos* was the active agent in the whole broad work of creation.] Jesus was the active representative of the Godhead in the work of creation. Heb. 1: 1, 2: "God, having of old time spoken unto the fathers in the prophets by divers portions and in divers manners, hath at the end of these days spoken unto us in his Son, whom he appointed heir of all things, through whom also he made the worlds." John 1: 10: "He was in the world, and the world was made through him." Col. 1: 16: "In him were all things created, in the heavens and upon the earth, things visible and things invisible, whether thrones or dominions or principalities or powers; all things have been created through him, and unto him."

4 **In him was life;**—He not only created, but he imparted life to all beings, vegetable, and animal. [Having predicated of him the creation of all material things, John now turns to the sentient creation, and especially man, its crown. As it is said that God created man, and then breathed into his nostrils the breath of life, so the Word is capable of a higher work than making things; he makes them live. There has been much scientific groping to find and understand the subtle principle called life. Here is the answer and all any one can know about it. Life is an emanation from the *logos* with power of an infinite

the light shineth in the darkness; and the darkness [2]apprehended it not. 6

[2]Or, *overcame.* See ch. 12, 35 (Gr.)

series of reproductions; life in all its varieties, physical, moral, spiritual. As all objects have their present form through him so all things that *live* live by him.]

and the life was the light of men.—[In the case of man, the crown of creation distinguished from all the rest by impassable lines, the life became *light,* which, in the Bible, is put for truth, knowledge, and holiness; darkness for ignorance, error, and sin. Spiritual light and life are mainly intended in the text. Or, rather, we should say that the thought progresses to light in its highest signification.] All light comes from God. This is not only true of spiritual light, but all true light of knowledge. Science, by many, is supposed to be the enemy of revelation; but where has science ever obtained a foothold in the world where the light of the revelation of God had not gone? Where has truth on any subject gained admission unless the light of God's truth opened the way? Look at the condition of the world in all ages where the light of God's revelation has not gone and see what practical truth on any subject exists among the heathen nations.

5 **And the light shineth in the darkness;**—[This verse is a bridge to verses 7 and 8. The thought advances from the light in the abstract to the visible exhibition of the light, shining with a brilliance that men had never seen before, the incarnate *logos,* the incarnate life, the incarnate light.]

and the darkness—[The world of humanity in the condition to which sin had brought it—ignorance and sin.]

apprehended it not.—[The people rejected the light, preferred the darkness, and so the darkness was not dispelled by the light. Did not take hold of it. Did not realize what had come into its midst. The thought is in regard to the condition of the world in the years of Christ's life preceding John the Immerser's testimony. The light was already shining. It was morally impossible for Jesus to be among men and not give forth divine light. But the world knew him not, even as John the Immerser himself knew him not till he saw the sign of God at

There came a man, sent from God, whose name was John. 7 The same
came for witness, that he might bear witness of the light, that all might
believe through him. 8 He was not the light, but *came* that he might bear

his baptism. We have thus been led in the prologue from the profundity of eternity to the reality of the ministry of John. All the wonders of the opening chapters of Matthew and Luke are chronologically comprehended in these verses.]

6 **There came a man, sent from God, whose name was John.**—John the Baptizer came to prepare the way for Christ.

7 **The same came for witness,**—Christ was the light. John came to prepare for him that all, through Christ, might believe in God. [More literally "for testimony." This is the predominant character of John. All else is incidental or subordinate to this. The preaching, the baptism, the rousing men to repentance, while all in themselves useful and good, are only circumstances of the testimony, only side employments of the witness bearer.]

that he might bear witness of the light,—"He" in this verse might more naturally refer to John, but a similar expression in verses 9 and 10 shows that it refers to Jesus the light. [This sentence gives the subject of the testimony. "The light" here is not abstract, but concrete. It is the light incarnate; in other words, the Lord Jesus Christ. He was to testify to the world that "the light" had come into the world.]

that all might believe through him.—[That all might believe on Christ through the testimony of John. See verses 29-42 for the beginning of this result. This idea of testimony is one of the fundamental notions of the gospel of Christ. It is correlative to, and inseparable from, that of faith. Testimony is given only with a view to faith, and faith is impossible except by means of testimony. The only faith worthy of the name is that which fastens itself upon a divine testimony given either in act or word.]

8 **He was not the light, but came that he might bear witness of the light.**—John came to testify that others might believe in Jesus. [The apostle states that John was not the light probably in opposition to an idea of some that John himself was the Messiah. The clause is an emphatic reassertion of the statement of verse 7.]

witness of the light. 9 [1]There was the true light, *even the light* which
lighteth [2]every man, coming into the world. 10 He was in the world, and
the world was made through him, and the world knew him not. 11 He
came unto [3]his own, and they that were his own received him not. 12 But

[1]Or, *the true light, which lighteth every man, was coming*
[2]Or, *every man as he cometh*
[3]Gr. *his own things*

9 **There was the true light,**—Jesus was the only source of the light, and all who came into the world if lightened at all, must receive this light from him.

even the light which lighteth every man, coming into the world.—[Whether to connect the last clause, "coming into the world," with "the true light," or with "every man," has been a hotly disputed question among commentators. We do not think there is any reference here to an innate light belonging to every man from birth, nor to an enlightening of men before the coming of Christ, under the old dispensation, or in the various heathen religions. The apostle has to do only with the present dispensation. The true light was coming into the world, which lights every man (who receives it), that is, teaches him spiritual truth and duty, else he is not enlightened. He is the exclusive light giver.]

If God is the fountain and source of all light [and he surely is] only he who looks to God can find true light. Man is prone to look to himself for light; but in man is no light, save as he receives it from God.

10 **He was in the world,**—[John now takes a step forward. He who was coming had come. The babe had been cradled at Bethlehem, carried to Nazareth, and grown to man's estate.]

and the world was made through him,—[He was no stranger and no intruder. All the fair scenes upon which he gazed were the product of his creative power as *logos.*]

and the world knew him not.—Jesus who created the worlds was in the world, but the world did not know him. [Of all this great world, and its sentient, teeming inhabitants, there was not one being who recognized him in his divine character as Creator of the universe and Redeemer of men.]

11 **He came unto his own, and they that were his own received him not.**—We have long thought "his own" referred

as many as received him, to them gave he the right to become children of

to those prepared by John for him. They embraced a large portion of the Jewish nation, but only those who voluntarily took upon themselves the obligations by being baptized. This was a radical change in the order of God's dealings with the Jews. Hitherto those he recognized as his servants were born after the flesh. All that were born of the fleshly family of Jacob were his servants. Now the voluntary principle was introduced by John. None were his save those who through faith in John's teaching voluntarily took on themselves the obligations imposed in baptism. This principle introduced into the provisional and introductory stages of the kingdom was to be the distinguishing principle of God's government henceforth. Hence, these to whom Christ came were his own, prepared for him by John, and they were born not of blood or the will of the flesh, nor of the will of man, but of God, inasmuch as they were begotten by the word of God preached through John.

12 **But as many as received him, to them gave he the right to become children of God,**—Those of John's disciples who heard and believed in Jesus became sons of God. The Jews had been servants. Through faith in Jesus they became sons by which they could address God as "Father." (Gal. 4: 5, 6.) All moved by faith in Jesus may become sons of God. [What is meant by receiving him, how much it includes, is to be found by reading the last clause of the verse, "even to them that believe on his name." Nor is the "many" here to be confined to the Jews. John does not say *all those from among them,* but all those who in general. When Jesus is once rejected by unbelieving Israel, there is henceforth only *humanity* and in it *individual* believers or unbelievers. Observe that receiving him, that is, the believing on his name, did not make them the children of God. It only brought them into such a relationship to him that it was now their right or privilege to *become* children of God if they chose to exercise it. How they became children of God is to be learned elsewhere. (See Mark 16: 15, 16; Acts 2: 38; 8: 26-40.]

God, *even* to them that believe on his name: 13 who were [4]born, not of
[5]blood, nor of the will of the flesh, nor of the will of man, but of God. 14
And the Word became flesh, and [6]dwelt among us (and we beheld his glory,
glory as of [7]the only begotten from the Father), full of grace and truth.

[4]Or, *begotten*
[5]Gr. *bloods*
[6]Gr. *tabernacled*
[7]Or, *an only begotten from a father.* Comp. Heb. 11. 17

even to them that believe on his name:—[That is, who believe in the character belonging to him manifested by his name, "Jesus, the Christ, the Son of the living God." (20: 31; also verses 14 and 18.)]

13 **who were born, not of blood, nor of the will of the flesh, nor of the will of man, but of God.**—This relation of sons of God was not attained through the fleshly descent from Abraham or of any fleshly birth, but he is begotten of God. (3: 5.) All fleshly births are through the will of the flesh. This henceforth would not make a man a child of God. [Being a Jew did not involve the new birth or begetting. He must be born again even as others. Fleshly generation had nothing to do with it. Nor was it in any sense human in its origin. No human enactments, no human purpose, could bring it about. It was "from above." (3: 3.) The begetting is purely of God with the Holy Spirit as the agent (3: 8) and the word of God as the Spirit's instrumentality (1 Pet. 1: 23) and the birth or transfer to new relationship of the whole man becomes complete in baptism (3: 5.)]

14 **And the Word became flesh, and dwelt among us**—This Word was Immanuel—God in the flesh. He dwelt among men as a man, subject to like passions and infirmities as man, tempted in all things as we are, yet his nature and life were manifestations of divine life and truth. [The Word "became" denotes a single and complete act. His dwelling among us was not a mere transitory or momentary appearance followed by a quick vanishing. He remained with us about thirty-three and a half years so that we could study and know him.]

(and we beheld his glory, glory as of the only begotten from the Father),—In the transfiguration and works of Christ his associates saw this glory. The working of miracles was showing forth the glory of God (2: 11), full of kindness to man, teaching the truth of God. [They beheld his glory, not in any particular instance, as the transfiguration, for example, but the continuous glory of his life and character as manifested through the whole period of his active ministry and which marked him as the Son of God.]

full of grace and truth.—[Sweetness and light, or love and light. Through him both mind and heart are fed. Grace in his redemptive work; truth in his teaching. Not that there was no grace and truth before, but he is a rich storehouse of it all.]

2. A PART OF JOHN'S TESTIMONY AND A COMMENT BY THE APOSTLE.
1: 15-18.

15 John beareth witness of him, and crieth, saying, [8]This was he of whom I said, He that cometh after me is become before me: for he was [9]before me.

[8]Some ancient authorities read (*this was he that said*)
[9]Gr. *first in regard of me*

---

15 **John beareth witness of him,**—[The present, *"beareth* witness," is ordinarily explained by the *permanent* value of this testimony; but perhaps it is due rather to the fact that the author transports himself in a lifelike way backward to the moment when he heard this mysterious saying coming from such lips; he seems to himself to hear it still. We often use the present thus for the past in vivid narration.]

and crieth, saying, This was he of whom I said, He that cometh after me is become before me: for he was before me.—John was careful that they should not think he was the promised Messiah. He had already taught them that Jesus was greater than himself, and although born of the mother later than John, had existed long before John. Jesus said, "Before Abraham was born, I am." (8: 58.) John was careful that the honor which belonged to Jesus should not be bestowed on himself. [Though he is after me in point of revelation to the people, yet he at once takes position before me as the more important of the two and destined to continue in this superiority. The immerser now turns to the essential precedence both in time and rank. Though he was subsequent in revelation, yet he existed long before his revelation and long before John, his revealer, and this in such dignity that he was entitled to take precedence as soon as revealed.]

16 For of his fulness we all received, and [10]grace for grace. 17 For the law was given through Moses; grace and truth came through Jesus Christ.

[10]Or, *grace upon grace*

16 **For of his fulness we all received,**—Of the fullness and the grace of Jesus all who receive him partake. [The quotation from the immerser ceases with verse 15. It is the apostle who now speaks, having interrupted himself after verse 14 by the memory of the immerser's testimony. In verse 14 he said that the Word was "full of grace and truth." Now we, all believers who have been born again, have received from the rich stores of his fullness.]

and grace for grace.—One degree of grace leads on to a higher degree. [Ever growing supplies of grace from the fullness of Christ.]

17 **For the law was given through Moses;**—The great law of God in the Ten Commandments was given by Moses. These commandments given as the standard of right and morality were given by Moses to the children of Israel. They were given as laws with their rewards and penalties. This law given to them was good and if one kept it it fitted him for eternal life. But the kindness and love of God were not manifested in these laws.

grace and truth came through Jesus Christ.—God's character for mercy and truth was received through Jesus Christ. There was no antagonism on the part of Jesus towards the law. The law was good and right. Jesus came not to destroy the law, but to fulfill it and to introduce new features into the service of God that would enable man to obey this law and to attain to the righteousness of the law. [The grace of God was certainly exhibited in giving the Mosaic revelation, and his truth was certainly contained in it, but it sinks into insignificance by the side of the revelations of these that come through Jesus Christ. We come now for the first time to the historical name of the incarnate *logos,* but to which the apostle has been tending throughout the passage. First the Word, then Life and Light, then the Only Begotten of the Father, now Jesus Christ, who embraces all that was said of him before.]

18 No man hath seen God at any time; [11]the only begotten Son, who is in the bosom of the Father, he hath declared *him.*

[11]Many very ancient authorities read *God only begotten*

18 **No man hath seen God at any time;**—While no man hath seen God, Jesus is the only begotten Son of God and the express image of his person and the effulgence of his power and is presented to man as the best beloved of the Father and the perfect representative of God, declaring God's own fullness and perfectness and the full representative of God to the world.

the only begotten Son, who is in the bosom of the Father,—[Most intimate with him—not living, like Moses, at an infinite distance from him. This intimacy gives him such thorough knowledge of all that pertains to him as to qualify him for the next clause.]

he hath declared him.—[Revealed or manifested him. There is more in this than the mere declaration of a messenger. Jesus Christ is the visible manifestation of God. "He that hath seen me hath seen the Father." God has now been seen in the person of his Son, who was "the effulgence of his glory, and the very image of his substance."]

3. ANOTHER PART OF JOHN'S TESTIMONY. 1: 19-28.

19 And this is the witness of John, when the Jews sent unto him from Jerusalem priests and Levites to ask him, Who art thou? 20 And he confessed, and denied not; and he confessed, I am not the Christ. 21 And they

19 **And this is the witness of John, when the Jews sent unto him from Jerusalem priests and Levites**—The Jews in Jerusalem were the most zealous of the law. Jerusalem was the center of Judaism. John in the wilderness attracted the masses by his preaching.

to ask him, Who art thou?—The Jews at Jerusalem sent the priests and Levites to hear him, see what he claimed for himself as a religious teacher, and demand of him who he was.

20 **And he confessed, and denied not; and he confessed, I am not the Christ.**—Without evasion or denial he said, I am not the anointed one of God. He was not willing to claim the honor that belonged only to Christ.

asked him, What then? Art thou Elijah? And he saith, I am not. Art thou the prophet? And he answered, No. 22 They said therefore unto him, Who art thou? that we may give an answer to them that sent us. What sayest thou of thyself? 23 He said, I am the voice of one crying in the wilderness, Make straight the way of the Lord, as [12]said Isaiah the prophet. 24 [13]And they had been sent from the Pharisees. 25 And they asked him,

[12]Is. 40. 3
[13]Or, *And* certain *had been sent from among the Pharisees*

21 **And they asked him, What then? Art thou Elijah? And he saith, I am not. Art thou the prophet? And he answered, No.**—It had been foretold that a great prophet should come into the world and that before the coming of that prophet Elijah should come again. He told them that he was neither Elijah nor this great prophet that was to come. Jesus said, "And if you are willing to receive it, this [John the Immerser] is Elijah that is to come." (Matt. 11: 14.) This statement of Jesus is thought to contradict John's statement in this verse, but it is explained by Jesus when he says, "And he shall go before his face in the spirit and power of Elijah." (Luke 1: 17.) John meant that he was not the veritable Elijah. Jesus said he came "in the spirit and power of Elijah." [The Jews doubtless asked art thou literally Elijah. He said no. Art thou that prophet foretold by Moses? No, for Christ is that prophet. The difference is doubtless one speaks of the *literal* Elijah, the other who came *in the spirit* of Elijah. No contradiction here.]

22 **They said therefore unto him, Who art thou? that we may give an answer to them that sent us. What sayest thou of thyself?**—They wished him to define his mission, if neither *the* prophet nor Elijah [so that on their return to Jerusalem they could give an intelligent report to those who had sent them].

23 **He said, I am the voice of one crying in the wilderness, Make straight the way of the Lord, as said Isaiah the prophet.**—He answered that he came in the fulfillment of the prophecy of Isaiah (40: 3), of the one who should come before and prepare the way for the prophet. His work was that of preparation for the Lord.

24 **And they had been sent from the Pharisees.**—The Pharisees were the most zealous and watchful of the religious parties of the Jews.

and said unto him, Why then baptizest thou, if thou art not the Christ,
neither Elijah, neither the prophet? 26 John answered them, saying, I baptize [14]in water: in the midst of you standeth one whom ye know not, 27
even he that cometh after me, the latchet of whose shoe I am not worthy
to unloose. 28 These things were done in [15]Bethany beyond the Jordan,
where John was baptizing.

[14]Or, *with*

[15]Many ancient authorities read *Bethabarah,* some *Betharabah.* Comp. Josh. 15. 6, 61; 18. 22

25 **And they asked him, and said unto him, Why then baptizest thou, if thou art not the Christ, neither Elijah, neither the prophet?**—John gave as his reason for baptizing that he was come preparing for the Messiah and he baptized in water and the Messiah would baptize in the Holy Spirit. [The question shows that John's baptism was to them a new rite. They could understand that Christ, or Elias, or "the prophets" might establish a new ordinance by divine authority, but if John is none of these, why does he do so? Their perplexity shows that the baptismal right was new to them. This refutes the claim that Gentile proselytes to the Jewish faith were baptized by all Jewish authorities before this time.]

26, 27 **John answered them, saying, I baptize in water: in the midst of you standeth one whom ye know not, even he that cometh after me, the latchet of whose shoe I am not worthy to unloose.**—The preposition "in" is used here instead of "with." This is right, yet to say "with" does not militate against the idea of a burial. We use "with" to indicate the element used even when the thing washed is wholly submerged. We say a cloth is dyed with indigo and leather is tanned with ooze when the thing is wholly submerged. "In" is better here as placing the point contrasted beyond doubt. John told them that the one for whom he came to prepare the way was in their midst and unknown to them and probably to John at this time who was so much his superior that he was not worthy to unlatch his shoes. The servant unlatched and bound the shoes of his master.

28 **These things were done in Bethany beyond the Jordan, where John was baptizing.**—Much of John's teaching was done on the west side of the Jordan, but this was done on the east side, opposite the line between Samaria and Galilee.

4. JESUS DECLARED THE LAMB OF GOD AND THE SON OF GOD. 1: 29-34.

29 On the morrow he seeth Jesus coming unto him, and saith, Behold,
the Lamb of God, that [16]taketh away the sin of the world! 30 This is he of
whom I said, After me cometh a man who is become before me: for he was
[9]before me. 31 And I knew him not; but that he should be made manifest
to Israel, for this cause came I baptizing [14]in water. 32 And John bare
witness, saying, I have beheld the Spirit descending as a dove out of heaven;

[16]Or, *beareth the sin*

29 **On the morrow he seeth Jesus coming unto him, and saith, Behold, the Lamb of God,**—The baptism of Jesus is not mentioned by the gospel of John, but it is particularly described by the other evangelists. When he was baptized and came up out of the water the voice came from heaven saying, "This is my beloved Son, in whom I am well pleased." (Matt. 3: 17.) The Holy Spirit also in the form of a dove descended upon him and abode with him. With these assurances John testified to his disciples that he was the Lamb of God to take away the sins of the world.

that taketh away the sin of the world!—[Jesus, the Lamb, when slain, took away the sin, not of Jews only, but of the world. He died for all.]

30 **This is he of whom I said, After me cometh a man who is become before me: for he was before me.**—He again states this of whom he had spoken, as born after he was, yet existing before him.

31 **And I knew him not; but that he should be made manifest to Israel, for this cause came I baptizing in water.**—Here one of the special objects of John's baptism is said to be to make known Jesus to Israel.

32 **And John bare witness, saying, I have beheld the Spirit descending as a dove out of heaven;**—John was to know by the Spirit descending in the form of a dove which was he and then was to bear testimony to the world.

and it abode upon him.—The Spirit came in the form of a dove, abode upon him, not in this form; but its form dissolved, and took up its abode in Jesus. (Luke 3: 22.) This was when he was anointed with the Spirit above his fellows. (Heb. 1: 9.)

and it abode upon him. 33 And I knew him not: but he that sent me to baptize [14]in water, he said unto me, Upon whomsoever thou shalt see the Spirit descending, and abiding upon him, the same is he that baptizeth [14]in the Holy Spirit. 34 And I have seen, and have borne witness that this is the Son of God.

---

33 **And I knew him not: but he that sent me to baptize in water, he said unto me, Upon whomsoever thou shalt see the Spirit descending, and abiding upon him, the same is he that baptizeth in the Holy Spirit.**—John did not know Jesus. Whether it was that he was not acquainted with Jesus or that he did not know that he was the Christ has been a matter of doubt. Although their mothers were cousins, they lived eighty miles apart, and it is possible that they had not met. Or it may mean that John did not have the full assurance that he was the Christ until he was assured by the sign appointed by God and in some way revealed to John.

34 **And I have seen, and have borne witness that this is the Son of God.**—Having seen this sign from God he testified that Jesus is the Son of God.

5. THE LAST TESTIMONY REPEATED.
1: 35-42.

35 Again on the morrow John was standing, and two of his disciples;
36 and he looked upon Jesus as he walked, and saith, Behold, the Lamb

---

35 **Again on the morrow John was standing, and two of his disciples;**—This was the day after the facts stated in the preceding verses had occurred. It was some weeks at least after his baptism. He had been baptized, had been forty days in the temptation, had returned to where John was baptizing, and John had testified to his disciples what had happened at his baptism.

36 **and he looked upon Jesus as he walked,**—[Jesus, passing by or in sight, John beheld him.]

and saith, Behold, the Lamb of God!—[The lamb was slain to save the first-born of Israel when the first-born of Egypt was destroyed, and at every Passover feast a lamb was slain by every family of Israel. In the types of Judaism the lamb was slain pointing forward to "the Lamb of God, that taketh away the sin

of God! 37 And the two disciples heard him speak, and they followed
Jesus. 38 And Jesus turned, and beheld them following, and saith unto
them, What seek ye? And they said unto him, Rabbi (which is to say,
being interpreted, Teacher), where abidest thou? 39 He saith unto them,
Come, and ye shall see. They came therefore and saw where he abode;
and they abode with him that day: it was about the tenth hour. 40 One of

---

of the world." He came to die as a sacrifice to take away the sins that man had committed and to lead him to live a holy life.]

37 **And the two disciples heard him speak,**—Some of the disciples of John were jealous that Jesus gathered followers at the expense of John, but John had none of this feeling. He came to make ready a people for Jesus, bear testimony to his claims, and direct his disciples to Jesus as the Lord, and rejoiced to see him increase, while he himself decreased in followers.

and they followed Jesus.—Again at a later date he with two of his disciples saw Jesus walking and again bore witness that he was the Son of God and his disciples thus assured left John and followed Jesus.

38 **And Jesus turned, and beheld them following, and saith unto them, What seek ye?**—Jesus seems at all times to desire that those who followed him should know what they took upon themselves so he asked what they were seeking.

And they said unto him, Rabbi (which is to say, being interpreted, Teacher), where abidest thou?—He saw them coming after him and asked what they sought. They called him Rabbi, which means teacher. They declared in this they were his disciples, had come to learn of him, and asked where he dwelt that they might come unto him as learners.

39 **He saith unto them, Come, and ye shall see. They came therefore and saw where he abode; and they abode with him that day: it was about the tenth hour.**—He acknowledged himself a teacher, accepted them as learners, and asked them to come with him to his home. They did and remained with him, for it was now four o'clock in the afternoon. They spent the night with him. We may well suppose that the time was spent in discoursing of his mission and teaching. The work of Jesus in the world has been greatly hindered and marred by the unfaithfulness of his followers, yet, imperfect as that work has been, the contrast between the conditions of the world where

the two that heard John *speak,* and followed him, was Andrew, Simon
Peter's brother. 41 He findeth first his own brother Simon, and saith unto
him, We have found the Messiah (which is, being interpreted, [1]Christ).

[1]That is, *Anointed.* Comp. Ps. 2. 2

Jesus has been known and where he has not must convince the most superficial observer of the immense good Jesus has done the world. The lifting up of the common people, the provisions for the unfortunate and helpless are found only where the teachings of Jesus have gone. There is not a hospital or asylum for the unfortunate in the world that has not been built by the influence of Jesus. It would be difficult to find a country where a workingman could get more than twenty-five cents a day for labor save where Christ is known. He lifts up and helps the helpless today through the influence of his teaching as in his personal ministry.

40 **One of the two that heard John speak, and followed him, was Andrew, Simon Peter's brother.**—We may well feel sure that his stay with Jesus satisfied his desire to know and strengthened his faith in Jesus. Andrew was one of the first called of the followers of Jesus. He was Peter's brother. Their home was in Bethsaida, a city on the Sea of Galilee. This was also the home of John and James, the sons of Zebedee. They are now at Bethany—not the Bethany near Jerusalem, but a village on the east side of the Jordan, near its entrance into the Dead Sea. Simon Peter was the older of the two brothers, likely the more aggressive, and became in one sense the first leader among the disciples.

41 **He findeth first his own brother Simon,**—So moved by a natural and fleshly feeling he first sought Simon. The teaching of Jesus does not destroy the ties of the flesh, but sanctifies them. Andrew first sought his own brother. Every Christian should act on this principle. The person who is indifferent to the salvation of his own kindred and people, but who is zealous of the salvation of strangers, does not follow the example of either Jesus or his disciples. Jesus first preached to his own people then to others.

and saith unto him, We have found the Messiah (which is, being interpreted, Christ).—Messiah is the Hebrew term for

42 He brought him unto Jesus. Jesus looked upon him, and said, Thou art Simon the son of [2]John: thou shalt be called Cephas (which is by interpretation, [3]Peter).

[2]Gr. *Joanes:* called in Mt. 16. 17 *Jonah*
[3]That is, *Rock* or *Stone*

Christ in the Greek, then chiefly spoken, or anointed in English. He was anointed by the Spirit which descended upon and abode with him [at his baptism].

42 **He brought him unto Jesus. Jesus looked upon him, and said, Thou art Simon the son of John: thou shalt be called Cephas (which is by interpretation, Peter).**—His report brought Simon to Jesus, who, when he looked upon him, saw what was in him, and gave him the name of Cephas, the Hebrew of which Peter is the Greek translation, which in English means rock. It seems that Jesus gave him this name as describing in some respects his character. Andrew first came to Christ and was instrumental in bringing Peter. In their after life Peter was the more active, forward, and prominent in his work. Andrew is seldom mentioned save in the innumeration of the apostles of the Lord. It is an example of how an humble one may be instrumental in bringing forward one of more power and general effectiveness. Peter was already a disciple of John as were these others. The leading characteristics of Peter was the prompitude with which he decided and acted on questions. Jesus beheld him and knew him, for he needed not to be told what is in man.

6. OTHER DISCIPLES GAINED AT BETHANY.
1: 43-51.

43 On the morrow he was minded to go forth into Galilee, and he findeth

43 **On the morrow he was minded to go forth into Galilee, and he findeth Philip: and Jesus saith unto him, Follow me.**—Galilee was his home, and the day following that on which Peter came to him he was minded to return to Galilee and found Philip. Philip is of the same city (Bethsaida) of Peter and Andrew, James and John. They had all come down to hear the preaching of John, had been taught by him, and tarried with him until he bore testimony to Jesus. We are not to conclude that Philip and Jesus heretofore had not known each other.

Philip: and Jesus saith unto him, Follow me. 44 Now Philip was from
Bethsaida, of the city of Andrew and Peter. 45 Philip findeth Nathanael,
and saith unto him, We have found him, of whom Moses in the law, and
the prophets, wrote, Jesus of Nazareth, the son of Joseph. 46 And Nathanael said unto him, Can any good thing come out of Nazareth? Philip
saith unto him, Come and see. 47 Jesus saw Nathanael coming to him,
and saith of him, Behold, an Israelite indeed, in whom is no guile! 48

---

44 **Now Philip was from Bethsaida, of the city of Andrew and Peter.**—All of the twelve save Judas seem to have lived on the Sea of Galilee. This is not Philip, one of the seven, but the apostle Philip, which name is associated with Bartholomew.

45 **Philip findeth Nathanael, and saith unto him, We have found him, of whom Moses in the law, and the prophets, wrote, Jesus of Nazareth, the son of Joseph.**—So soon as Philip had found Jesus his first impulse seemed to be to bring others to him. This is the essential spirit of Christ. No one imbued with his spirit can know Christ and be indifferent to others, all others knowing him. First, Jerusalem, Judea, Samaria, but stops not until it reaches the uttermost parts of the earth. Converting your family stimulates the desire and leads you to convert your neighbor, your countryman—all who sit in "the valley and shadow of death." The spirit of Christ will let man enjoy no good alone. Jesus could not enjoy the glory of heaven unless man could have an opportunity to share it with him. Good is multiplied to us as we divide it with others.

46 **And Nathanael said unto him, Can any good thing come out of Nazareth? Philip saith unto him, Come and see.**—Nazareth seemed to have an ill name among the people. Philip insisted that he should come and see before deciding. He did so. Nathanael was of Cana in Galilee, and is thought to be the same as Bartholomew, with whose name Philip's is associated in the list of apostles.

47 **Jesus saw Nathanael coming to him, and saith of him, Behold, an Israelite indeed, in whom is no guile!**—The supernatural knowledge that enabled Jesus to know men and what their thoughts, purposes, and characters were enabled him to tell the character of Nathanael, whom he did not know, so announced him an Israelite in whom was no deceit or guile. This was a compliment. Such are prepared to receive the pure and guileless life of the Son of God.

Nathanael saith unto him, Whence knowest thou me? Jesus answered and
said unto him, Before Philip called thee, when thou wast under the fig tree,
I saw thee. 49 Nathanael answered him, Rabbi, thou art the Son of God;
thou art King of Israel. 50 Jesus answered and said unto him, Because I
said unto thee, I saw thee underneath the fig tree, believest thou? thou
shalt see greater things than these. 51 And he saith unto him, Verily,
verily, I say unto you, Ye shall see the heaven opened, and the angels of
God ascending and descending upon the Son of man.

---

48 **Nathanael saith unto him, Whence knowest thou me?**—He asked, "How and from what do you know me?" showing he had no acquaintance with him.

Jesus answered and said unto him, Before Philip called thee, when thou wast under the fig tree, I saw thee.—Jesus responded that he knew him as he sat under the fig tree before Philip called him. I take it that Jesus could not see him by his sight, and that Nathanael knew it required superhuman knowledge and his frank and guileless spirit, taken with what Philip had told him, he confessed that Jesus is the Son of God.

49 **Nathanael answered him, Rabbi, thou art the Son of God; thou art King of Israel.**—His knowing things that were beyond his power to learn by his senses with none to inform him satisfied the guileless spirit of Nathanael that he was superhuman. Putting it with the teaching of John and the testimony he had borne to Jesus which he learned of Philip and had likely heard of others satisfied him at once, and he acknowledged him as the Son of God, the King of Israel.

50 **Jesus answered and said unto him, Because I said unto thee, I saw thee underneath the fig tree, believest thou? thou shalt see greater things than these.**—Jesus complimented him on his ready faith in this testimony and assured him that he should see greater things than these.

51 **And he saith unto him, Verily, verily, I say unto you, Ye shall see the heaven opened, and the angels of God ascending and descending upon the Son of man.**—When this promise was fulfilled we know not unless at the ascension of Jesus. The angels ascending and descending upon him, possibly was not literal, but meant that he would be constantly watched over and guarded here in the world by the angels of God, and that their ministration to him as the Son of God would be manifested to Nathanael in the care and love God would show him.

SECTION TWO.

PREPARATORY WORK IN SAMARIA, GALILEE, AND JUDEA.

2: 1 to 4: 54.

1. A BRIEF VISIT TO GALILEE AND THE FIRST MIRACLE. 2: 1-12.

1 And the third day there was a marriage in Cana of Galilee; and the
mother of Jesus was there: 2 and Jesus also was bidden, and his disciples,
to the marriage. 3 And when the wine failed, the mother of Jesus saith
unto him, They have no wine. 4 And Jesus saith unto her, Woman, what

---

1 **And the third day there was a marriage in Cana of Galilee;**—The third day from what time is not very evident. Jesus was where John was baptizing, calling around him certain disciples whom he would teach and fit to be his apostles to teach others the words of wisdom that Jesus taught them. He had been at Bethabara, east of the Jordan; now he is in Cana of Galilee, not a great distance from Nazareth, the home of his mother Mary, and where he was chiefly brought up.

and the mother of Jesus was there:—All the circumstances show that his mother was very much at home at the marriage, and took such a personal interest and direction in the matter as to indicate it was at the home of a close personal friend or relative. The affair shows that Jesus did not even, after the beginning of his ministry, withdraw from all social relations with his friends and acquaintances, but he used the opportunities offered in these to show he was from God.

2 **and Jesus also was bidden, and his disciples, to the marriage.**—They all attended. Tradition says, John, the son of Zebedee and supposed relative of Mary and Jesus, married. I know of no ground for the tradition.

3 **And when the wine failed, the mother of Jesus saith unto him, They have no wine.**—They ran short of the accustomed quantity of wine and Mary told Jesus. It would seem that she had confidence in his ability to provide for the deficiency. This could not be because she knew his power to work miracles, for he had wrought none before. Yet her going to him is a comment upon her confidence in his ability to provide in times of

have I to do with thee? mine hour is not yet come.
5 His mother saith unto the servants, Whatsoever he saith unto you, do it.
6 Now there were six waterpots of stone set there after the Jews' manner of purifying, containing two or three firkins apiece.
7 Jesus saith unto them, Fill the waterpots with water. And they filled them up to the brim.
8 And he saith unto them, Draw out now, and bear unto the [4]ruler of the feast. And

[4]Or, *steward*

difficulty. It indicates that she had learned to rely upon him in times of need and leaves the impression that she had learned to rely upon him to aid in such emergencies. Her statement of the trouble implied a request that he should in some way remedy the deficiency.

4 **And Jesus saith unto her, Woman, what have I to do with thee?**—His response to his mother sounds to us harsh and lacking in respect, but the style of address depends on the customs of the times and place and we cannot judge by this. The response rather shows depths of feeling and earnestness in him. It was the customary style of address. Our customs differ is all.

mine hour is not yet come.—It is generally considered that he means that his hour for manifesting his power had not come. If so, it soon did come.

5 **His mother saith unto the servants, Whatsoever he saith unto you, do it.**—Her confidence that he would do something to relieve the deficiency is shown in her instructions to the servants to do his bidding.

6 **Now there were six waterpots of stone set there after the Jews' manner of purifying, containing two or three firkins apiece.**—The purification was that they should not eat without washing their hands. (See Matt. 15: 2; Mark 7: 4.) The vessels held about twenty-five gallons each. This was provided that all the guests might wash before eating.

7 **Jesus saith unto them, Fill the waterpots with water. And they filled them up to the brim.**—They had been well nigh emptied by the guests before eating the supper, and he ordered them filled to the brim to remove all doubt as to their containing wine—to show no deception was practiced.

8 **And he saith unto them, Draw out now, and bear unto the ruler of the feast. And they bare it.**—I take it only that

they bare it. 9 And when the ruler of the feast tasted the water [5]now become wine, and knew not whence it was (but the servants that had drawn the water knew), the ruler of the feast calleth the bridegroom, 10 and saith unto him, Every man setteth on first the good wine; and when *men* have drunk freely, *then* that which is worse: thou hast kept the good wine until now. 11 This beginning of his signs did Jesus in Cana of Galilee, and manifested his glory; and his disciples believed on him.

[5]Or, *that it had become*

which was drawn from the vessels full of water was changed into wine.

9 **And when the ruler of the feast tasted the water now become wine, and knew not whence it was (but the servants that had drawn the water knew), the ruler of the feast calleth the bridegroom,**—The bridegroom furnished the banquet; the governor, or friend, and one of the guests, directed the order of it. The governor, it seems, was ignorant of what had been done.

10 **and saith unto him, Every man setteth on first the good wine; and when men have drunk freely, then that which is worse: thou hast kept the good wine until now.**—The ruler was to give good wine at the beginning, then, as men got their taste satiated, they gave the inferior. But this wine made by the Savior was pronounced the best. It was pure and of the best quality of wine. There is no intimation that these guests drank to drunkenness. He speaks of the custom and says the order was changed. This was the best wine. That Jesus would make it good and pure was to be expected. Much has been said of the Savior making wine. Many think it was not intoxicating wine. Even the juice of grapes was recognized as leading to intoxication. God did not, under Christ, prohibit evils save as he prepared their hearts to voluntarily turn from the evils. So that all morality and virtue are to be from the heart. So while not prohibiting the evils, he put in operation principles that would banish all wrongs as men received them into the heart and acted on them. The governor of the feast and the bridegroom were dependent on the servants for their knowledge of this miracle.

11 **This beginning of his signs did Jesus in Cana of Galilee, and manifested his glory;**—Cana of Galilee was but a few miles from Nazareth. In Cana Nathanael lived and there Jesus healed the nobleman's son. (John 4: 46.) This was the first

12 After this he went down to Capernaum, he, and his mother, and *his* brethren, and his disciples; and there they abode not many days.

miracle wrought by Jesus. In manifesting this power to work miracles, he proclaimed the glory of God that gave such power to men.

and his disciples believed on him.—His disciples had some faith in him at this time, and this sign greatly increased their faith in him. This is called the beginning of miracles. The miracles were performed to show that God was with him and that he was imbued with divine power. The working of the miracle set forth his divinity and declared his glory. By it the disciples had their faith in him greatly strengthened. Miracles were as often wrought to strengthen the faith of his followers as to convince the unbelievers. When their faith was strengthened, they testified of him to the multitudes and caused them to believe.

12 **After this he went down to Capernaum, he, and his mother, and his brethren, and his disciples; and there they abode not many days.**—Capernaum was situated on the Sea of Galilee. Although it is said they did not remain many days, he made Capernaum his home after this. It is called his city. The greater number of his apostles were reared in Capernaum and the other cities on the Sea of Galilee.

2. JESUS GOES TO THE PASSOVER.
2: 13-22.

13 And the passover of the Jews was at hand, and Jesus went up to Jeru-

13 **And the passover of the Jews was at hand, and Jesus went up to Jerusalem.**—The Passover was the feast commemorating the passing over or sparing of the first-born of the children of Israel when the first-born of the Egyptians were slain. It was eaten on the fifteenth of the month Abib, the first month of the Jewish year, and corresponds in time to what is popularly known as "Easter." It is important that we note the Passovers during the public ministry of Jesus, as they afford one of the easiest ways of determining the length of his public ministry from his baptism until his ascension. This was the first

**salem. 14 And he found in the temple those that sold oxen and sheep and
doves, and the changers of money sitting: 15 and he made a scourge of
cords, and cast all out of the temple, both the sheep and the oxen; and he
poured out the changers' money, and overthrew their tables; 16 and to them
that sold the doves he said, Take these things hence; make not my Father's**

Passover after he began his public ministry and he went to Jerusalem to attend it.

14 **And he found in the temple those that sold oxen and sheep and doves,**—The children of Israel came to Jerusalem to observe the Passover in the temple. The law was that certain animals—oxen, sheep, goats, doves, and pigeons—must be slain at the door of the temple and offerings made on the brazen altar outside the door. Coming from distant parts in Judea, and even from distant lands, they must purchase the animals in Jerusalem. This created a demand for these animals and traders brought them here to supply the demand and they were brought into the court of the temple.

and the changers of money sitting:—They were required to make offerings of money, all in the coin of the sanctuary. This created the demand, and the traffic in these animals and coins was carried on for gain. The Jews were required to contribute the half shekel to the temple expenses. They could not contribute coin with idol images. Money of this character was in general circulation. So the money-changers exchanged with them for profit.

15 **and he made a scourge of cords, and cast all out of the temple, both the sheep and the oxen; and he poured out the changers' money, and overthrew their tables;**—When Jesus came to the temple to attend this Passover feast, he found this traffic shamelessly carried on within the sacred limits of the temple. Indignant, he made a whip of small cords and drove all the animals out. He poured out the money of the changers and overturned their tables. Jesus was now teaching. His authority, to some extent, was recognized.

16 **and to them that sold the doves he said, Take these things hence; make not my Father's house a house of merchandise.**—He now gives his reason for cleansing the temple. On a later occasion he found the same shameless profanation of the temple, and quoted Isa. 56: 7: "For my house shall be

house a house of merchandise. 17 His disciples remembered that it was
written, [1]Zeal for thy house shall eat me up. 18 The Jews therefore answered and said unto him, What sign showest thou unto us, seeing that
thou doest these things? 19 Jesus answered and said unto them, Destroy
this [2]temple, and in three days I will raise it up. 20 The Jews therefore
said, Forty and six years was this [2]temple in building, and wilt thou raise

[1]Ps. 69. 9
[2]Or, *sanctuary*

called a house of prayer for all peoples." And then adds, "But ye make it a den of robbers." (Matt. 21: 13.) He condemns and denounces their course with severity. It is a worse crime to make merchandise of the gospel of Christ, or to traffic in the privileges of the church of God—that is, to corrupt and defile the spiritual temple of God.

17 **His disciples remembered that it was written, Zeal for thy house shall eat me up.**—This zeal for his house was predicted in Psalm 69: 9, and is a little difficult to understand, but seems to apply this consuming zeal for the house of God to Jesus. He desired it kept pure and holy.

18 **The Jews therefore answered and said unto him, What sign showest thou unto us, seeing that thou doest these things?**—This seemed to use violence more than any other act save a similar one repeated on a similar occasion in his attendance of the last Passover of his ministry. (Matt. 21: 12; Luke 19: 45.) Jesus no doubt in doing it claimed he did it by the authority of God whom he represented. The Jews complained that he should exercise such authority yet work no miracles or give no proof of the authority by which he did these things.

19 **Jesus answered and said unto them, Destroy this temple, and in three days I will raise it up.**—He pointed to his death, burial, and resurrection. Spoke of his body as a temple, which, when they destroyed it, would be restored in three days. They did not understand this reference. He more than once referred those refusing to be convinced by the evidences he gave of his divine mission to his resurrection as the great sign of his being the Son of God. He "was declared to be the Son of God with power, according to the spirit of holiness, by the resurrection from the dead; even Jesus Christ our Lord." (Rom. 1: 4.)

20 **The Jews therefore said, Forty and six years was this temple in building, and wilt thou raise it up in three days?**—

it up in three days? 21 But he spake of the [2]temple of his body. 22 When
therefore he was raised from the dead, his disciples remembered that he
spake this; and they believed the scripture, and the word which Jesus had
said.

The Jews applied it to the temple in Jerusalem, while he applied it to the temple of his body. The temple had been repaired by Herod the Great, and he was forty and six years in rebuilding it.

21 **But he spake of the temple of his body.**—He called his body the temple. The misunderstanding of his meaning was the basis of the testimony borne against him in his first trial (Matt. 26: 51), and the taunts against him as he hung upon the cross (Matt. 27: 40).

22 **When therefore he was raised from the dead, his disciples remembered that he spake this; and they believed the scripture, and the word which Jesus had said.**—When it came to be understood by his disciples after his resurrection it became the ground of their believing in him more strongly.

3. SIGNS WROUGHT DURING THE PASSOVER. 2: 23-25.

23 Now when he was in Jerusalem at the passover, during the feast,
many believed on his name, beholding his signs which he did. 24 But
Jesus did not trust himself unto them, for that he knew all men, 25 and

23 **Now when he was in Jerusalem at the passover, during the feast, many believed on his name, beholding his signs which he did.**—While in Jerusalem at this Passover he wrought signs or miracles and this caused many to believe on him. What the signs were we are not told.

24 **But Jesus did not trust himself unto them, for that he knew all men,**—Jesus knew their hearts and that their faith was weak and unstable and so while he encouraged their belief, he did not trust himself to them. His infinite wisdom enabled him to know the hearts, the thoughts, and desires of all. There are many degrees of faith. It begins weak and unsteady, and by continued exercise it grows strong and steadfast. At this period Jesus trusted himself to the power of no man. He knew the uncertainty of men. Many, under the first impulse of the wonders wrought, would believe in him, but turn against him

because he needed not that any one should bear witness concerning [8]man; for he himself knew what was in man.

[8]Or, *a man; for . . . the man*

when trials and troubles came as they always do. Many in the days of the Savior were carried away by momentary excitement as now that fell away afterward.

25 **and because he needed not that any one should bear witness concerning man; for he himself knew what was in man.**—He had a divine insight into the hearts of men that enabled him to understand them without others telling of them. He gave an example of this in Nathanael. (1: 43-47.) Then he told where and what Nathanael had been doing, and understood the secret workings of his heart. He was brought to believe in Christ by this. He did the same to the woman of Samaria.

4. CONVERSATION WITH NICODEMUS.
3: 1-15.

1 Now there was a man of the Pharisees, named Nicodemus, a ruler of
the Jews: 2 the same came unto him by night, and said to him, Rabbi, we
know that thou art a teacher come from God; for no one can do these

1 **Now there was a man of the Pharisees, named Nicodemus, a ruler of the Jews:**—Nicodemus was a member of the council of the Sanhedrin. The Pharisees were the most strenuous sect of the Jews in observing the traditions of the elders. [Jesus charged that they made the commands of God of no effect by their traditions. (Matt. 15: 3.) They were the most popular sect of Judaism in the days of Christ. They believed in the resurrection. Nicodemus is mentioned (7: 51) as insisting to the Jews that "our law judge a man, except it first hear from himself and know what he doeth?" He (19: 39) brought a hundred pounds mixture of myrrh and aloes to anoint the body of Jesus. The notices we have of him indicate that he was a just and true man.]

2 **the same came unto him by night,**—[Why he came at night is a guess of no value. Possibly he desired to avoid publicity, or he found Jesus more at leisure; possibly he had more leisure himself.]

and said to him, Rabbi, we know that thou art a teacher come from God; for no one can do these signs that thou doest,

signs that thou doest, except God be with him. 3 Jesus answered and said unto him, Verily, verily, I say unto thee, Except one be born [4]anew, he

[4]Or, *from above.* See ver. 31; ch. 19. 11; Jas. 1. 17; 3. 15, 17

except God be with him.—The object of miracles was to convince the people that God was with or in those who wrought them and to give assurance to the people that when they heard him they heard God. The person acted and spoke by the authority of God. He came to Jesus that he might learn the will of God. Jesus had come and had given a number of signs or worked miracles that attracted the attention of the observant and thoughtful. Nicodemus was an honest, sincere Pharisee, a ruler and teacher among the Jews, who saw and heard these things. A person's working miracles was the token of a new message from the Father. Nicodemus came to Jesus modestly to inquire the meaning of the miracles and what truths they heralded.

3 **Jesus answered and said unto him, Verily, verily, I say unto thee,**—[Jesus at once assumes he is anxious to know of the kingdom that John had preached which was now at hand, and which Jesus came to establish, and at once tells the leading condition of entrance into that kingdom. Without entrance into it citizenship and privileges cannot be enjoyed. The condition was:]

Except one be born anew, he cannot see the kingdom of God.—God whom Jesus set forth on earth was the subject uppermost in the teachings of Jesus, and he at once responded that no person could enter into the kingdom without being born again. Jesus recognized Nicodemus as of the best of the Jews, was looking for the coming Messiah, and yet he needed to be born again to enter the kingdom of God. The kingdom of God was a more spiritual institution, a higher degree of spirituality being required to enter this kingdom than was required for membership in the Jewish kingdom. A fleshly birth introduced man into the Jewish kingdom and it was a fleshly kingdom. The kingdom introduced by Jesus was a spiritual kingdom entered by a birth of the Spirit and spiritual relations prevailed in that kingdom. Some interpreters say this means born from above. While the word translated "anew" may mean "from above,"

cannot see the kingdom of God. 4 Nicodemus saith unto him, How can a man be born when he is old? can he enter a second time into his mother's womb, and be born? 5 Jesus answered, Verily, verily, I say unto thee, Except one be born of water and the Spirit, he cannot enter into the king-

the context here shows plainly that Jesus meant "anew." Without he is born anew he cannot see the kingdom of God. The word "born" in this connection cannot be literal; but what is meant by "born anew" is essential to entrance into the kingdom of God.

4 **Nicodemus saith unto him, How can a man be born when he is old?**—He took it literally, and seeing the impossibility of such a thing he asks, "How can this be when he is old?"

can he enter a second time into his mother's womb, and be born?—This had been foretold by the prophets (Joel 3: 1-21; Jer. 31: 31), and Jesus seemed to take it for granted that Nicodemus would understand him. But his mind only recurs to the fleshly kingdom and he could not see how an old man could enter his mother's womb and be born again.

5 **Jesus answered, Verily, verily, I say unto thee, Except one be born of water and the Spirit, he cannot enter into the kingdom of God.**—Men were being baptized by John, and by way of suggestion, he added he must be born of water and the Spirit. This new birth carries with it more than is usually attached to it. It was addressed to Nicodemus and regarded as one of the truest and most faithful of the teachers under the law of Moses—one ready to accept Jesus as the teacher from God. Jesus tells him, for him or any one to enter the kingdom of heaven, he must be born anew. Nicodemus was not in the kingdom of heaven. He was a subject of the Jewish law, which only made them servants or slaves, and he must be born into a higher and better. The kingdom of heaven was to be a spiritual kingdom. In it the Spirit of God was to abide and rule. It had not done this in the Jewish kingdom. In this kingdom those who had been servants were to possess a higher measure of the Spirit of God by which they were to become sons of God. He here tells that the birth, instead of being from the mother's womb, is from the water and the Spirit. They are the agents and instruments in producing the birth. The Spirit is living, active; the water is

dom of God. 6 That which is born of the flesh is flesh; and that which is
born of the Spirit is spirit. 7 Marvel not that I said unto thee, Ye must be
born [4]anew. 8 [5]The wind bloweth where it will, and thou hearest the voice
thereof, but knowest not whence it cometh, and whither it goeth: so is

[5]Or, *The Spirit breatheth*

inanimate. The Spirit is the active agent, the water the instrument of the birth. On the day of Pentecost the Spirit spoke through the apostles—produced faith in the hearts of the people. "They then that received his word were baptized: and there were added unto them in that day about three thousand souls." The coming forth from the water of him who had believed through the teaching of the Spirit was the birth of the water and the Spirit as exemplified in the practice of the apostles. To this the whole religious world has always agreed until of late a few from partisan motives call it in question. [This last statement is sanctioned by J. R. Graves, editor, *The Tennessee Baptist,* as follows:

"If Brother Vaughn convinced us that born of water refers to anything but the baptism of one previously born of the Spirit, we never *knew* it, and we would have owned it to him and to our readers. It means nothing else, and no Baptist that we ever heard or read of ever believed otherwise until A. Campbell frightened them away from an interpretation that is sustained by the consensus of all scholars of all denominations in all ages."—(*The Tennessee Baptist,* page 5, October 30, 1886.")]

6 **That which is born of the flesh is flesh; and that which is born of the Spirit is spirit.**—It is the fleshly part of man that is born of the flesh, of his father and his mother; but it is the spirit within man that must be born or begotten of the Spirit. He is removing the difficulty in the mind of Nicodemus about the possibility of being born again.

7 **Marvel not that I said unto thee, Ye must be born anew.**—He tells him not to wonder, or think it impossible, that he said, "Ye must be born anew." All this is directing to the point that it is not the fleshly body that is to be changed and brought forth by the mother, but that it is the spirit of man that is the subject of this birth.

8 **The wind bloweth where it will, and thou hearest the voice thereof, but knowest not whence it cometh, and whither it goeth: so is every one that is born of the Spirit.**—These

every one that is born of the Spirit. 9 Nicodemus answered and said unto
him, How can these things be? 10 Jesus answered and said unto him, Art
thou the teacher of Israel, and understandest not these things? 11 Verily,
verily, I say unto thee, We speak that which we know, and bear witness
of that which we have seen; and ye receive not our witness. 12 If I told

verses have been ever of great difficulty because men try to get out of them what is not in them. Flesh in the mind of Nicodemus is the difficulty Jesus is trying to remove. He introduces the wind and its blowing which cannot be seen. It blows where it will, no one can know by seeing whence it comes or whither it goes, and then he says the one born of the Spirit is like this. That is, it is the spirit of man unseen like the wind and not the flesh, that is to be begotten of the Spirit of God. The effort was to show Nicodemus that it was the spiritual part of man, not the fleshly part that is to be born again. The man which is born, or begotten, of the Spirit is not the fleshly man that you can see, but the intangible, spiritual part of man—the spirit, invisible, like the wind. The Spirit that begets is not compared to the wind, but the invisible spirit—inner man—that is, born of the Spirit is like the wind—invisible.

9 **Nicodemus answered and said unto him, How can these things be?**—He seems not to readily take in how one must be born to enter the kingdom of God. He considered himself already in the kingdom of God. He thought he had been born into it by fleshly birth as a member of the family of Abraham. So he asked, "How can these things be?"

10 **Jesus answered and said unto him, Art thou the teacher of Israel, and understandest not these things?**—Jesus shows that he thinks a teacher of the Jews should understand these simple truths. It had been taught by the prophets of the Jewish law that a new principle would be introduced. (Jer. 31: 31-33.) Under the figure of the birth of water and the Spirit this change in the character of the subjects of the kingdom of heaven is told.

11 **Verily, verily, I say unto thee, We speak that which we know, and bear witness of that which we have seen; and ye receive not our witness.**—Jesus was a witness from God of those things he taught and yet his teaching was not received and Nicodemus is slow to accept. It had been foretold by prophets that a kingdom of higher spiritual power should be

you earthly things and ye believe not, how shall ye believe if I tell you

established on earth and a teacher like Nicodemus should know it. The great end of Jesus in this conversation was to teach Nicodemus to enter the kingdom of heaven. He must enter into a higher spiritual state than the Jews or others on earth had enjoyed. He could be a child of God, could call him Father, would have his sins forgiven once and forever, washed away by the blood of Christ, not rolled forward as was done under Moses. Among the Jews they were servants, slaves; under Christ they must be children of God, must draw near to God as a Father, and he would love and bless them as his children. He must prepare for a closer walk with God in the kingdom of heaven than men had hitherto known. This was the leading end and thought of this talk with Nicodemus. Do we read it to get this thought out of it? Or do we read it to prove that baptism is a birth, a bringing forth from the water; that baptism puts us into Christ; that without baptism we cannot enter Christ or receive the blessings to be enjoyed in Christ—the forgiveness of sins and the privileges of the Lord's blessings? This conversation illustrates and emphasizes these truths, but they do it only incidentally. The main truth he was emphasizing was the higher honors and chiefest glories of the kingdom of heaven over the honors and glories of all other kingdoms on earth, human or divine. To understand and appreciate this truth was needful to induce all, especially Jews, to leave these kingdoms of "less glory" and to seek the more glorious kingdom of heaven. Not only did Jesus hold up the transcendent beauties of the kingdom of heaven in its purer life and holier privileges and honors and insist on the purer life and more godly walk to fit them for this, but all the apostles and inspired teachers from that time forward insist on this superior life to fit them for the closer walk with God.

12 **If I told you earthly things and ye believe not, how shall ye believe if I tell you heavenly things?**—What he tells them pertains to the kingdom of God here on earth and their relation to it. If ye do not receive this how shall ye believe when I unfold to you the eternal things of the heavenly land?

heavenly things? 13 And no one hath ascended into heaven, but he that descended out of heaven, *even* the Son of man, [6]who is in heaven. 14 And as Moses lifted up the serpent in the wilderness, even so must the Son of man be lifted up; 15 that whosoever [7]believeth may in him have eternal life.

[6]Many ancient authorities omit *who is in heaven*
[7]Or, *believeth in him may have*

13 **And no one hath ascended into heaven, but he that descended out of heaven, even the Son of man, who is in heaven.**—No one else than Jesus who came down from heaven is competent to teach these things. He calls himself the Son of man, leaving his works to declare him to be the Son of God. His home or citizenship is in heaven. This was written after his ascension.

14 **And as Moses lifted up the serpent in the wilderness, even so must the Son of man be lifted up;**—When the Israelites had murmured in the wilderness against Moses and against God on account of the difficulties and trials of the way, they had as a punishment been bitten by fiery serpents and they died. The people came to Moses, confessed their sins and asked Moses to pray for them that they might be healed. Moses prayed for them and God told him to make a brazen serpent and put it on a pole and all who looked upon it should live. (Num. 21: 9.) This seems to have been given as a test of their faith in Moses. God has in all ages demanded that man's faith shall express itself in a bodily act. This was the type of Jesus being lifted up on the cross that man might be drawn to him in his service and be saved.

15 **that whosoever believeth may in him have eternal life.**—Jesus was lifted up [on the cross] and slain that he might be buried and rise again that men might believe on him. "When ye have lifted up the Son of man, then shall ye know that I am he, and that I do nothing of myself, but as the Father taught me, I speak these things." (8: 28.) "And I, if I be lifted up from the earth, will draw all men unto myself." (12: 32.) The lifting up was the killing according to the prophecies concerning him. He died [lifted from the earth to the cross] that he might rise again "Who was declared to be the Son of God with power, according to the spirit of holiness, by the resurrection from the dead; even Jesus Christ our Lord." (Rom. 1: 4.) This believ-

ing in him on these testimonies led them to so follow him as with him to enjoy life eternal. Looking upon the serpent was the expression required in this instance and it is given here as an illustration of the sinner looking to Christ for salvation. The test of his faith is that he is baptized into Christ. Being baptized into Christ was the birth of water and the Spirit into the kingdom of God.

5. REMARKS ON THE MISSION OF JESUS AND THE SIN OF UNBELIEF.
3: 16-21.

16 For God so loved the world, that he gave his only begotten Son, that whosoever believeth on him should not perish, but have eternal life. 17 For

---

16 **For God so loved the world, that he gave his only begotten Son, that whosoever believeth on him should not perish,**—God showed his love to the world, to free man, the head of the world, by giving his Son to die for the world. He showed his hatred of sin by giving his Son to die for the sins of the world that man might be delivered from the dominion and penalty of sin. God loved man despite his rebellion and sin, and so loved him that he gave his Son to die to save man from the result of his rebellion against God. That the death of Jesus so satisfied the law that God "might himself be just, and the justifier of him that hath faith in Jesus." (Rom. 3: 26.) He at the same time showed man his love to him to excite in man a corresponding love to God. "We love, because he first loved us." (1 John 4: 19.) If we love God we will keep his commandments. "For this is the love of God, that we keep his commandments." (1 John 5: 3.) "Blessed are they that wash their robes, that they may have the right to come to the tree of life, and may enter in by the gates into the city." (Rev. 22: 14.)

but have eternal life.—And being freed from sin that separates from God and brings death they become the heirs of eternal life with God. Faith in Christ leads man to follow him that he may have life eternal. It does not mean a faith alone that does not lead to obedience. A dead faith will not bring everlasting life. But faith in God through Christ is the great living principle that leads through obedience unto life everlasting.

God sent not the Son into the world to judge the world; but that the
world should be saved through him. 18 He that believeth on him is not
judged: he that believeth not hath been judged already, because he hath
not believed on the name of the only begotten Son of God. 19 And this is
the judgment, that the light is come into the world, and men loved the
darkness rather than the light; for their works were evil. 20 For every

17 **For God sent not the Son into the world to judge the world; but that the world should be saved through him.**—The world was in a state of condemnation before God on account of their sins, and God sent his Son to open the way for their return to God that they might return and be saved. God did not send his Son in the world to condemn the world—they were already in condemnation for their sins. He sent him to save them from their sins—to bring them from under the sentence of condemnation. Those who believed not in Christ were already condemned. He came as a light into the world, and men rejected him because they loved darkness and remain in condemnation or under judgment. In coming to Christ a man makes his own works manifest as wrought in God through Christ.

18 **He that believeth on him is not judged:**—When he speaks of believing on him he means an active, living faith that works through love and is perfected by obedience to him in whom he believes. Jesus having come, he has provided that through faith in him man might come to God and be saved. So those who believed in him were not under judgment.

he that believeth not hath been judged already, because he hath not believed on the name of the only begotten Son of God.—Those who refused to believe in Christ were under condemnation before he came and his coming had given better opportunities for believing and their condemnation was the more severe because of their greater opportunities.

19 **And this is the judgment, that the light is come into the world, and men loved the darkness rather than the light; for their works were evil.**—The coming of Jesus and the additional light he shed abroad showed more clearly that they loved darkness rather than the light, and he teaches that their love for darkness was because their deeds were evil and they did not wish their deeds exposed to and tested by the light.

one that [8]doeth evil hateth the light, and cometh not to the light, lest his works should be [9]reproved. 21 But he that doeth the truth cometh to the light, that his works may be made manifest, [10]that they have been wrought in God.

[8]Or, *practiseth*
[9]Or, *convicted*
[10]Or, *because*

20 **For every one that doeth evil hateth the light, and cometh not to the light, lest his works should be reproved.**—Those who do evil of choice show that they hate the light and truth and seek to cover the exposure of their deeds that the light would make.

21 **But he that doeth the truth cometh to the light, that his works may be made manifest, that they have been wrought in God.**—Those who live according to the truth love the light and rejoice in it that their works may be justified by the light of truth.

6. JESUS AT THE JORDAN AND JOHN AT AENON.
3: 22-30.

22 After these things came Jesus and his disciples into the land of Judæa; and there he tarried with them, and baptized. 23 And John also was baptizing in Ænon near to Salim, because there [1]was much water there: and they came, and were baptized. 24 For John was not yet cast into prison.

[1]Gr. *were many waters*

22 **After these things came Jesus and his disciples into the land of Judea; and there he tarried with them, and baptized.**—The foregoing conversation occurred in Jerusalem. Jesus then went into the country of Judea and tarried in the country and baptized. Jesus baptized through his disciples. (4: 2.)

23 **And John also was baptizing in Aenon near to Salim,**—There has been some dispute as to where Aenon was. It is now generally accepted that it was in Samaria, due east of the city of Samaria, about midway between it and the Jordan.

because there was much water there: and they came, and were baptized.—The water was needed for purifying the multitudes that attended the preaching of John as well as to furnish facilities for baptizing the people who came and were baptized.

24 **For John was not yet cast into prison.**—Although Jesus was now teaching, had begun his public ministry and through

25 There arose therefore a questioning on the part of John's disciples with
a Jew about purifying. 26 And they came unto John, and said to him,
Rabbi, he that was with thee beyond the Jordan, to whom thou hast borne
witness, behold, the same baptizeth, and all men come to him. 27 John answered and said, A man can receive nothing, except it have been given him
from heaven. 28 Ye yourselves bear me witness, that I said, I am not the
Christ, but, that I am sent before him. 29 He that hath the bride is the

---

his disciples was baptizing, John was not yet cast into prison and was still teaching. Both Jesus and John were teaching at the same time.

25 **There arose therefore a questioning on the part of John's disciples with a Jew about purifying.**—John taught the baptism of repentance unto the remission of sins. Jesus was teaching the same, and out of this grew some reasonings on the subject of purifying.

26 **And they came unto John, and said to him, Rabbi, he that was with thee beyond the Jordan, to whom thou hast borne witness, behold, the same baptizeth,**—The questionings were brought to John whom they addressed as Rabbi, a reverential term applied to a divine teacher, and in the conversation some of his disciples in a seemingly complaining spirit told him that Jesus whom he baptized on the east side of the Jordan and to whom he had borne witness as the Lamb of God that takes away the sins of the world was baptizing and the masses of the people were following him.

and all men come to him.—They seem to have grown somewhat jealous that the masses were leaving John to follow Jesus.

27 **John answered and said, A man can receive nothing, except it have been given him from heaven.**—However his disciples may have regarded it, there was no feeling of jealousy with him. He had to bear witness of Jesus as the Messiah that was to come so he assured them, "what I am, and he is given us from heaven, is in accordance with the will of God."

28 **Ye yourselves bear me witness, that I said, I am not the Christ, but, that I am sent before him.**—He had from the beginning testified that he was not the Christ, but is his messenger and sent before him to make ready for his coming.

bridegroom: but the friend of the bridegroom, that standeth and heareth him, rejoiceth greatly because of the bridegroom's voice: this my joy therefore is made full. 30 He must increase, but I must decrease.

29 **He that hath the bride is the bridegroom: but the friend of the bridegroom, that standeth and heareth him, rejoiceth greatly because of the bridegroom's voice:**—He explains his relation to Jesus by that of the friend of the bridegroom. He stands so related to Christ.

this my joy therefore is made full.—The friend of the bridegroom rejoices at the joy and success of the bridegroom so the joy of John was completed or filled in the success of Jesus.

30 **He must increase,**—He in this work is permanent and must continually grow. The kingdom he came to set up will become a great mountain, fill the whole earth, and stand forever. (Dan. 2: 44.)

but I must decrease.—John was preparing for Jesus, his work would soon be swallowed up in that of the greater one that he introduced.

7. SUPERIORITY OF THE SON AND THE BLESSING OF FAITH. 3: 31-36.

31 He that cometh from above is above all: he that is of the earth is of the earth, and of the earth he speaketh: [2]he that cometh from heaven is above all. 32 What he hath seen and heard, of that he beareth witness;

[2]Some ancient authorities read *he that cometh from heaven beareth witness of what he hath seen and heard*

31 **He that cometh from above is above all:**—The supremacy of Jesus over John is shown by their origin. Jesus came from heaven and was with the Father before the world was.

he that is of the earth is of the earth, and of the earth he speaketh:—John was from the earth and speaks as of the earth.

he that cometh from heaven is above all.—He who came from heaven is above all, the leader sent from God.

32 **What he hath seen and heard, of that he beareth witness; and no man receiveth his witness.**—Jesus who came from heaven testifies what he heard in heaven and the world did not believe him. The next sentence shows that this was not to be received as literally true.

and no man receiveth his witness. 33 He that hath received his witness
hath set his seal to *this,* that God is true. 34 For he whom God hath sent
speaketh the words of God: for he giveth not the Spirit by measure. 35
The Father loveth the Son, and hath given all things into his hand. 36
He that believeth on the Son hath eternal life; but he that [3]obeyeth not the
Son shall not see life, but the wrath of God abideth on him.

[3]Or, *believeth not*

---

33 **He that hath received his witness hath set his seal to this, that God is true.**—While but few received him, he who did receive him confessed in his heart that God is true.

34 **For he whom God hath sent speaketh the words of God:**—Jesus sent from God spoke the words he had heard from God. As a reason for this, he says:

for he giveth not the Spirit by measure.—God gave the Spirit in its fullness without measure to Jesus the Messiah. To all others, apostles, and prophets God gave his Spirit by measure or in modified portions.

35 **The Father loveth the Son, and hath given all things into his hand.**—God loved the Son and the Son sought only to do the will of God so he gave all things of this world into the hands of the Son. Jesus said, "All authority hath been given unto me in heaven and on earth." (Matt. 28: 18.) And "He that receiveth me receiveth him that sent me." (John 13: 20.)

36 **He that believeth on the Son hath eternal life;**—He who believes on Jesus so as to give himself up to the guidance of Jesus is an heir of eternal life because being led by the Son of God brings eternal life.

but he that obeyeth not the Son shall not see life, but the wrath of God abideth on him.—He who does not trust and follow God will never see the eternal life, but the wrath of God abides upon him.

8. JESUS LEAVES JUDEA AND JOURNEYS TOWARD GALILEE. 4: 1-6.

1 When therefore the Lord knew that the Pharisees had heard that
Jesus was making and baptizing more disciples than John 2 (although Jesus

---

1 **When therefore the Lord knew that the Pharisees had heard that Jesus was making and baptizing more disciples**

himself baptized not, but his disciples), 3 he left Judæa, and departed again
into Galilee. 4 And he must needs pass through Samaria. 5 So he cometh
to a city of Samaria, called Sychar, near to the parcel of ground that

than John—Baptism was the act in which the people declared themselves the disciples of John (Luke 7: 30), and the baptism of Christ stood in the same relation to Christ and discipleship. It is thought that this leaving Judea was to avoid conflict with the Pharisees.

2 **(although Jesus himself baptized not, but his disciples),**—What the disciples did by the command of Jesus, Jesus did through them. The disciples baptized the people in obedience to Christ, and the Holy Spirit said that Jesus baptized them. Jesus was in his disciples teaching and baptizing persons during his lifetime. If those baptized by his disciples were baptized by Jesus, all acts performed by the disciples by direction of Jesus were performed by Jesus. Jesus was in his disciples working for the salvation of the world from sin. Just as God the Father was in Christ reconciling the world unto himself so was Christ in the disciples teaching and entreating the world to be reconciled to God through Christ.

3 **he left Judaea, and departed again into Galilee.**—He left Judea where the Pharisees chiefly controlled and went back to Galilee where the religious parties were not so bitter.

4 **And he must needs pass through Samaria.**—Samaria lay between Judea and Galilee. In going from one to the other Samaria must be passed through or the person must cross the river Jordan, go on the east side, and cross over to Judea below the southern boundary of Samaria. This greatly increased the distance.

5 **So he cometh to a city of Samaria, called Sychar, near to the parcel of ground that Jacob gave to his son Joseph:**—Sychar was near the city of Samaria, in the land of Ephraim, the son of Joseph. Jacob had bought this land of Hamor, Shechem's father. (Gen. 33: 18-20.) He gave this to Joseph and Joseph's bones were brought up from Egypt and buried near to Shechem. (Josh. 23: 32, 33.)

Jacob gave to his son Joseph: 6 and Jacob's [4]well was there. Jesus therefore, being wearied with his journey, sat [5]thus by the [4]well. It was about

[4]Gr. *spring:* and so in ver. 14; but not in ver. 11, 12
[5]Or, *as he was.* Comp. ch. 13. 25

6 **and Jacob's well was there.**—This well was noted and had the reputation of having been dug by Jacob or his servants. Lieutenant Anderson in 1866 descended to the bottom, found it seventy-five feet deep, walled with stones, and dry at the time. [McGarvey says: "Jacob's well is still there, about one hundred yards from the foot of Mt. Gerizim, which rises high above it to the west. The well is a perfect cylinder, seven and a half feet in diameter, and it is walled with stones of good size, smoothly dressed, and nicely fitted together. It is an excellent piece of masonry. Its depth was stated by the earliest modern who visited it (Maundrel) at one hundred five feet, and it then contained fifteen feet of water. In 1839 it was found to be seventy-five feet deep with ten or twelve feet of water. All visitors of more recent date have found it dry and gradually filling up from the habit of throwing stones into it to hear the reverberation when they strike the bottom. [This accounts for its depth at different times.] When the writer was there in 1879 his tapeline struck the bottom at sixty-five feet. The top of the well is arched over like a cistern and a circular opening is left about twenty inches in diameter. Another opening of irregular shape has been broken through the arch, and when you look into one of these the light admitted by the other enables you to examine the walls."]

Jesus therefore, being wearied with his journey, sat thus by the well.—Jesus sat upon the stone at the well while his disciples went to the town of Sychar to buy food.

It was about the sixth hour.—The sixth hour was most probably twelve o'clock, though some place it at six in the evening.

9. HE CONVERSES WITH THE SAMARITAN WOMAN. 4: 7-26.

the sixth hour. 7 There cometh a woman of Samaria to draw water: Jesus
saith unto her, Give me to drink. 8 For his disciples were gone away into
the city to buy food. 9 The Samaritan woman therefore saith unto him,
How is it that thou, being a Jew, askest drink of me, who am a Samaritan
woman? ([6]For Jews have no dealings with Samaritans). 10 Jesus answered

[6]Some ancient authorities omit *For Jews have no dealings with Samaritans*

7 **There cometh a woman of Samaria to draw water: Jesus saith unto her, Give me to drink.**—The Samaritans were a mongrel race that had grown up in Samaria from the importation of Assyrians after the deporting of the Israelites from the land. (2 Kings 17: 24.) These imported Assyrians married with the poorer classes of the Israelites that remained in the country. At first they gave only a formal worship to the God of heaven while still worshiping the gods of Assyria. The Jews persistently refused all association with them as equals or as worshipers of their God. The Samaritans kept up the worship at the same places at which the ten tribes who forsook the house of David in the days of Jeroboam, that is, Bethel and Dan.

8 **For his disciples were gone away into the city to buy food.**—The Jews, while refusing all social and religious associations or intercourse, traded with them so the disciples had gone to this Samaritan city to buy provisions.

9 **The Samaritan woman therefore saith unto him, How is it that thou, being a Jew, askest drink of me, who am a Samaritan woman?**—The Samaritans would have been pleased to associate with the Jews, so when Jesus asked a favor of the woman and spoke in a kindly social way she was surprised and asked him how he could do so.

(For Jews have no dealings with Samaritans).—They regarded them as unclean and would not accept courtesies at their hands, although they bought from and sold to them. She did not refuse the water, but expressed a surprise that he asked it of her. Jesus came to break down all these partition walls, national and race prejudices, and to unite all who would follow him into one brotherhood.

and said unto her, If thou knewest the gift of God, and who it is that saith to thee, Give me to drink; thou wouldest have asked of him, and he would have given thee living water. 11 The woman saith unto him, [7]Sir, thou hast nothing to draw with, and the well is deep: whence then hast thou that living water? 12 Art thou greater than our father Jacob, who gave us the well, and drank thereof himself, and his sons, and his cattle? 13 Jesus

[7]Or, *Lord*

10 **Jesus answered and said unto her,**—The answer Jesus made to her shows that his purpose was to introduce the question of her spiritual condition and to direct her mind to his mission to make known the will of God to the world.

If thou knewest the gift of God, and who it is that saith to thee, Give me to drink; thou wouldest have asked of him,—The gift of God spoken of here meant the offer of eternal life to the world and that he was their Messiah to bring salvation to the world.

and he would have given thee living water.—He meant the spiritual blessings he could give to the world. Jesus did not explain his course, or argue the matter with her, but at once laid before her the great end for which he came into the world—his gift to the nations. The water of life, or living water, represents the life-giving blessings to which the teaching of Jesus leads men.

11 **The woman saith unto him, Sir, thou hast nothing to draw with, and the well is deep: whence then hast thou that living water?**—The woman failed to understand his meaning and suggested the difficulties of his getting water out of the well. Her mind was fleshly, sensual, and material. She could think of nothing but literal water, and knew of none better than that in Jacob's well. [See comments, verse 6.]

12 **Art thou greater than our father Jacob, who gave us the well, and drank thereof himself, and his sons, and his cattle?**—She gives the tradition concerning Jacob's digging and using and giving the well to his descendants. How much of this is real, how much tradition we can never tell, as the traditions never grow less as time passes concerning such things. They had come to reverence Jacob as a saint, second only to Abraham as the father of the Israelites. She felt it was presumptuous for any one to promise more in the

answered and said unto her, Every one that drinketh of this water shall
thirst again: 14 but whosoever drinketh of the water that I shall give him
shall never thirst; but the water that I shall give him shall become in him
a well of water springing up unto eternal life. 15 The woman saith unto
him, [7]Sir, give me this water, that I thirst not, neither come all the way
hither to draw. 16 Jesus saith unto her, Go, call thy husband, and come

---

way of water than that found in Jacob's well, which had slaked the thirst of their fathers for nearly two thousand years.

13 **Jesus answered and said unto her, Every one that drinketh of this water shall thirst again:**—Jesus tries again to direct her mind away from this material water to the water of spiritual life. This water gives temporary relief.

14 **but whosoever drinketh of the water that I shall give him shall never thirst; but the water that I shall give him shall become in him a well of water springing up unto eternal life.**—The water that he offered would abide with him who drank it and would give eternal life. He draws the contrast. The water which I give him will never let him thirst again. It shall be a perpetual fountain, or spring, of water within his soul, not only preventing thirst, but giving everlasting life. He is seeking to impress her with the truth that he promises not literal water, but spiritual water that gives eternal life. The blessings that bring spiritual life are frequently represented as living water. (7: 38, 39.) And then in the New Jerusalem is "a river of water of life, bright as crystal, proceeding out of the throne of God and of the Lamb." (Rev. 22: 1.)

15 **The woman saith unto him, Sir, give me this water, that I thirst not, neither come all the way hither to draw.**—The woman takes in the truth that the effects of the water he promised were permanent, but she thought it relieved from the fleshly thirst, and its possession would relieve her from coming to the well for water again.

16 **Jesus saith unto her, Go, call thy husband, and come hither.**—He has failed to reach her spiritual nature by the figure of the living water so he seeks to reach her in a different way. He knew her condition and character and opened a way to impress her with his divine knowledge by

hither. 17 The woman answered and said unto him, I have no husband.
Jesus saith unto her, Thou saidst well, I have no husband: 18 for thou hast
had five husbands; and he whom thou now hast is not thy husband: this
hast thou said truly. 19 The woman saith unto him, [1]Sir, I perceive that
thou art a prophet. 20 Our fathers worshipped in this mountain; and ye

[1]Or, *Lord*

telling the plain facts of her life. He suited his instruction to her capacities.

17 **The woman answered and said unto him, I have no husband. Jesus saith unto her, Thou saidst well, I have no husband:**—She promptly replied, "I have no husband." Jesus accedes to this and tells her important facts concerning her former life and present relations not creditable to her. She recognizes that only superhuman power could have made this known to him.

18 **for thou hast had five husbands; and he whom thou now hast is not thy husband: this hast thou said truly.**—This with his former speech and demeanor impressed her that he possessed more than human knowledge. He shows his knowledge of her past and present life and lays bare her present sinful state.

19 **The woman saith unto him, Sir, I perceive that thou art a prophet.**—The promptness of the confession shows the candor and readiness of the woman to accept the truth. His bearing and conversation, although she failed to take in the points of his instruction, had impressed her with his sincerity and high character. When he showed his knowledge of her past life, she saw and owned he was a prophet. This was the same kind of testimony he used to convince Nathanael. (2: 50.) He knew things without learning them in the ordinary way, and it at once directed the woman's mind to the subject of worship, and, as he was a Jew, to the difference between the Samaritans and the Jews.

20 **Our fathers worshipped in this mountain;**—"Our fathers" were the ten tribes that broke away from the house of David under the lead of Jeroboam. These Samaritans claimed these as their fathers, although they were a mixed race descended from them. Jeroboam set up two altars and made

say, that in Jerusalem is the place where men ought to worship. 21 Jesus saith unto her, Woman, believe me, the hour cometh, when neither in this mountain, nor in Jerusalem, shall ye worship the Father. 22 Ye worship

two calves—one in Bethel, the other in Dan. Mount Gerizim is the mount here spoken of.

and ye say, that in Jerusalem is the place where men ought to worship.—That he was a prophet and a Jew brought to her mind at once the difference between the Jews and the Samaritans. The Jews had persistently charged the Samaritans with forsaking God in leaving Jerusalem and the temple in which God had recorded his name and where he promised to meet his people at the mercy seat, and had made a calf at Bethel and met to worship at Mount Gerizim instead of Jerusalem. Moses says, "But unto the place which Jehovah your God shall choose out of all your tribes, to put his name there, even unto his habitation shall ye seek, and thither thou shalt come." (Deut. 12: 5.) He selected Jerusalem. Solomon built the temple, and God promised there to meet his children. "Jehovah said unto him [Solomon], I have heard thy prayer and thy supplication, that thou hast made before me: I have hallowed this house, which thou hast built, to put my name there for ever; and mine eyes and my heart shall be there perpetually." (1 Kings 9: 3.) From this time forward to go elsewhere to worship than to Jerusalem was to forsake God. So the prophets taught and the woman refers to this teaching.

21 **Jesus saith unto her, Woman, believe me, the hour cometh, when neither in this mountain, nor in Jerusalem, shall ye worship the Father.**—Jesus had come to supplant and swallow up this work of a merely local nature of both Jews and Samaritans and to substitute the spiritual worship of which the Jewish law and order was a material type. Jesus did not mean that in the future persons might not worship God either in Jerusalem or in this mountain. He meant that hereafter the worship of God would not be confined to either of these places, but that all who would could worship God wherever they might be. Whoever worships God according to the truth would be accepted of him. The time had come when

that which ye know not: we worship that which we know; for salvation is from the Jews. 23 But the hour cometh, and now is, when the true worshippers shall worship the Father in spirit and truth: [2]for such doth the Father seek to be his worshippers. 24 [3]God is a Spirit: and they that wor-

[2]Or, *for such the Father also seeketh*
[3]Or, *God is Spirit*

the true spiritual temple of God should be opened to all the nations of the earth, and when the worship should not be confined to Jerusalem nor to this mountain. Jesus came to introduce this era and says, "The hour cometh," or is now coming, when this shall be done. The local and external shall give way to the spiritual and eternal.

22 **Ye worship that which ye know not: we worship that which we know;**—He kept before her the truth that in forsaking God's appointments they ceased to worship God. They did not know who they were worshiping. Jesus, while seeking to open the mind of the woman to the truth, condemns the sin of the Israelites in forsaking Jerusalem and the temple worship. In doing so they forsook God, and worshiped they knew not what. They claimed to worship God, but to reject his order is to turn from him.

for salvation is from the Jews.—Salvation was to come through the family of Abraham of whom the Jews were the representatives. Salvation comes through the Jews that were true to the worship of God.

23 **But the hour cometh, and now is, when the true worshippers shall worship the Father in spirit and truth: for such doth the Father seek to be his worshippers.**—Jesus came to introduce this worship that was spiritual. The heart of man was to be enlisted. Man's spirit must lead to the service. This worship must be regulated by the truth of God. In this new covenant God said, "I will put my laws into their mind, and on their heart also will I write," and all the service must be from the heart. The introduction of it was future, now at hand. Jesus was even now introducing it. He more clearly tells them the hour now is when the true worshiper shall worship the Father in spirit and truth. This means the worship shall not be formal, local, and mechanical as it had been greatly among the Jews, but it should be from the heart.

ship him must worship in spirit and truth. 25 The woman saith unto him, I know that Messiah cometh (he that is called Christ): when he is come, he will declare unto us all things. 26 Jesus saith unto her, I that speak unto thee am *he*.

The heart shall be enlisted and the spirit molded by the truths of God, and that henceforth God will seek only the worship of those who worship him from the heart. This was bringing out the contrast between the worship under the law of Moses and of Christ.

24 **God is a Spirit: and they that worship him must worship in spirit and truth.**—He is not flesh and blood as men are. He is a Spirit and unseen by mortal eyes. The natural and seen are temporal and must pass away. The Spirit is unseen and eternal. God is Spirit and the spirit of man must worship God not simply an outward fleshly conformity to his law that seems to have satisfied the demands of the law of Moses. Although under the law of Moses a higher life of faith was possible and was accomplished by many. They who worship God must worship with the spirit or the soul and in truth. A spiritual being like God can be pleased with worship only when it comes from the heart and all worship to him must be guided by truth.

25 **The woman saith unto him, I know that Messiah cometh (he that is called Christ): when he is come, he will declare unto us all things.**—This thought seems to have been rather beyond the comprehension of the woman and she evades a direct reply. The Samaritans, in common with the Jews, looked for a coming Savior. They still maintained a nominal worship of the true God while refusing to follow his laws. He is called in the scripture Messiah. Messiah is Hebrew; Christ, Greek; Anointed, English. Both the Jews and the Samaritans looked for the prophet to come that would make known the full and perfect law of God. The bearing of Christ and the revelation that he had made to her reminded her of this promise—not that she was ready to acknowledge him as Christ, but her mind had been led out to think of Christ by what he said to her.

26 **Jesus saith unto her, I that speak unto thee am he.**—This is the most direct declaration made by Jesus to one he

was teaching that he was the Messiah, the Christ, the Son of God, the Prophet that was to come. He more frequently called himself the Son of man and left his works and teaching to declare him to be the Son of God. But this woman was a Samaritan, in many respects mentally and socially and in knowledge of the scriptures inferior to the Jews. She was fleshly, sensual, dull of perceiving spiritual truth, but frank and candid, simplehearted, ready to receive the truth, and Jesus met her in the same spirit of open and direct declaration of the truth suited to her wants. The pains and patience of Jesus to reach this woman with the stains on her character ought to be an assurance to his followers that such are open to salvation and frequently the first to be reached. Another thought worthy of consideration is when Jesus would reach the people of Samaria he did not seek the great, the noble, the intellectual. He met the humble, ignorant woman, who lived with a man not her husband and brought the truth to her heart and through her reached others. It is much more easy to reach the poor, simple-minded, open sinners than the self-righteous, who pride themselves upon their wealth, social position, or learning, and who cover and hide their sins. All who can be really reached by the word of God can be much more readily reached by Christians of this class than by those in what is called the higher circle of life. Man looks at the outward appearance; God looks at the heart. When the heart is right, God uses the person, and works his own ends.

10. REMARKS TO THE DISCIPLES.
4: 27-38.

27 And upon this came his disciples; and they marvelled that he was speaking with a woman; yet no man said, What seekest thou? or, Why

---

27 **And upon this came his disciples; and they marvelled that he was speaking with a woman;**—[Christ's disciples had left him at the well while they went to the town of Sychar to buy food.] This conversation had occurred during their absence in the city. On their return they were surprised to find him talking with the woman because of the antipathy the Jews cultivated toward the Samaritans.

speakest thou with her? 28 So the woman left her waterpot, and went
away into the city, and saith to the people, 29 Come, see a man, who told
me all things that *ever* I did: can this be the Christ? 30 They went out of
the city, and were coming to him. 31 In the mean while the disciples prayed

yet no man said, What seekest thou? or, Why speakest thou with her?—But they have learned enough of him to know remonstrance would be vain. Jesus never had a doubt or feeling of uncertainty in what he did.

28 **So the woman left her waterpot, and went away into the city, and saith to the people,**—The return of the disciples seems to have interrupted the conversation, and the woman at once bethought her of the people in the city, and in the intensity of her feeling she seems to have forgotten her mission to the well and in her haste she left the waterpot she brought and hastened to the city.

29 **Come, see a man, who told me all things that ever I did:**—She told as she went that she had found a man who could tell her all she had ever done. [He had told her some things about her life and doubtless conscience had told her the rest. She felt all was known to him and naturally exaggerates by saying, "He told me all about my life."]

can this be the Christ?—This question was suggestive and led them to believe what Jesus had directly told her. [She did not say he is the Christ—"Can this be the Christ?" Had she asserted he was the Christ probably they would not have believed her, but her modest manner excited their curiosity and made them willing to see and hear.]

30 **They went out of the city, and were coming to him.**—This aroused enough interest or curiosity to cause the people to go out and see and talk with this newly-found prophet. [Her success was immediate. I take it they were not skeptical people, but were waiting for the Deliverer.]

31 **In the mean while the disciples prayed him, saying, Rabbi, eat.**—While she was going and the people were coming from the city, the disciples prepared the food and asked him to eat. [While the woman was spreading the news, the disciples were preparing and pressing upon the Master to eat the food they had secured.]

him, saying, Rabbi, eat. 32 But he said unto them, I have meat to eat that
ye know not. 33 The disciples therefore said one to another, Hath any man
brought him *aught to eat?* 34 Jesus saith unto them, My meat is to do the
will of him that sent me, and to accomplish his work. 35 Say not ye,
There are yet four months, and *then* cometh the harvest? behold, I say unto
you, Lift up your eyes, and look on the fields, that they are [4]white already

[4]Or, *white unto harvest. Already he that reapeth &c.*

32 **But he said unto them, I have meat to eat that ye know not.**—["Man shall not live by bread alone." He had been lifted above hunger by the eagerness of his success.]

33 **The disciples therefore said one to another, Hath any man brought him aught to eat?**—They had left him when they went into the city wearied and no doubt hungry. They had returned, prepared food, and now he declines to eat. Jesus told them he had sources of strength and satisfaction of which they were ignorant.

34 **Jesus saith unto them, My meat is to do the will of him that sent me, and to accomplish his work.**—["Meat" in the scriptures means not only flesh, but any kind of food.] The doing the will of his Father supplied the place of food and refreshed and strengthened him in body as well as spirit. Here are two persons becoming so interested in spiritual truths presented that they forgot their fleshly wants and external demands. One in teaching the truth of God, and the other forgets the water for which she had gone to the well. Jesus forgets his weariness and hunger in the desire to save a soul and accomplish the work unto which he was sent.

35 **Say not ye, There are yet four months, and then cometh the harvest? behold, I say unto you, Lift up your eyes, and look on the fields, that they are white already unto harvest.**—[In Palestine harvesting began about the middle of April. Jesus spoke about the middle of December.] It is thought that this was four months before the harvest time; whether or not, it was an admonition that the spiritual harvest was always ready for the reaping. It teaches, too, that Jesus in his wisdom chose an humble, lowly sinner, one ready to confess her sins, rather than the rich and learned and self-righteous through whom to reach and influence a whole commu-

unto harvest. 36 He that reapeth receiveth wages, and gathereth fruit unto
life eternal; that he that soweth and he that reapeth may rejoice together.
37 For herein is the saying true, One soweth, and another reapeth. 38 I
sent you to reap that whereon ye have not labored: others have labored,
and ye are entered into their labor.

nity. This is so unlike the wisdom of men which seeks the wealthy, the learned, the respectable through whom to reach communities. It teaches too that we ought to improve all openings and opportunities to preach the gospel no matter how unpromising they may appear. These lowly candid sinners are much more easily reached than the self-righteous, self-satisfied classes. They are also much more effective in carrying the truth to others.

36 **He that reapeth receiveth wages, and gathereth fruit unto life eternal; that he that soweth and he that reapeth may rejoice together.**—One who improves all opportunities, who does not despise the day of small things, who is constant about the work of the Father will receive wages and in his work will bear fruit unto eternal life, both he who sows and the fruit he bears will enjoy eternal life. [They who reap a harvest of souls will receive spiritual wages; not earthly pay in money, such as reapers in harvest fields reap, nor of fame, or position, but the happiness of doing the greatest work on earth and a crown that fadeth not away in the world to come. "Gathereth fruit" means souls that are gathered as the sheaves in the heavenly garner. There saved souls and the reaper rejoice together.]

37 **For herein is the saying true, One soweth, and another reapeth.**—Jesus was now reaping what had been sown by others. He was reaping where Moses and the prophets had sown. Even this despised Samaritan woman had been prepared to look for the Messiah who would bring all things to their knowledge.

38 **I sent you to reap that whereon ye have not labored: others have labored, and ye are entered into their labor.**—Jesus sent his disciples to preach and reap what had been sown by others. This is the order of God in the natural and spiritual world. One sows; they who follow him reap.

["Sent" is a verb past and refers to an event previous to the present incident. The disciples had baptized "more than John" (4: 1), so many that John's disciples reported that "all men come to him" (3: 26). Christ's disciples who had baptized all of these (4: 2) were reaping the fruit of John's sowing, to a great degree, supplemented by the labors of Christ. John had sown; they were reaping. While on earth Christ sowed and later at Pentecost, in Judea, and in Samaria, his disciples entered into his labors. See the reaping of what he had sown in Samaria. (Acts 8: 5-8.) This principle is true now.]

11. RESULTS IN SYCHAR AND ARRIVAL IN GALILEE. 4: 39-45.

39 And from that city many of the Samaritans believed on him because of the word of the woman, who testified, He told me all things that *ever* I did. 40 So when the Samaritans came unto him, they besought him to abide with them: and he abode there two days. 41 And many more believed

---

39 **And from that city many of the Samaritans believed on him because of the word of the woman, who testified, He told me all things that ever I did.**—The woman was a dull, but candid woman. She was living a life of adultery. This was probably so common among her people as not to incur the ostracism it has in later years. Her earnest and candid statement of what had passed between her and Jesus moved many to believe on Christ through her. The fervid earnestness of a candid person causes conviction frequently. [She had borne testimony of Christ as best she could. Though an humble woman, she had not preached Christ in vain. This demonstrates what one poor soul can do for Christ.]

40 **So when the Samaritans came unto him, they besought him to abide with them:**—To converse with the woman in a social, friendly way the willingness to accept a favor as small as a drink of water, the feeling of interest in her, was matter of surprise to her and the disciples and encouraged the people to insist on his remaining with them for a time.

and he abode there two days.—The remaining with them for two days as a teacher instructing them in the truth of God was no doubt a shock to the prejudices of the disciples

because of his word; 42 and they said to the woman, Now we believe, not because of thy speaking: for we have heard for ourselves, and know that this is indeed the Saviour of the world.

---

and a surprise to the Samaritans. Yet the disciples submitted. The Samaritans felt flattered and induced them to hear him more readily. On the part of Jesus it was the beginning of breaking down the wall of separation between the different nations and peoples that would be completed in his death. [It was indeed a strange invitation for a Samaritan city to extend to a Jew, but no more strange than for a Jewish teacher to accept it.]

41 **And many more believed because of his word;**—The result of his stay was that many more believed in him through his teachings. [They heard for themselves his teaching regarding water of life and they recognized in him a divine teacher. He worked no miracle as at Jerusalem, but how different the course of the self-righteous Pharisees!]

42 **and they said to the woman, Now we believe, not because of thy speaking: for we have heard for ourselves, and know that this is indeed the Saviour of the world.**—The feeling of the people toward the woman is shown in their thinking it more creditable to believe on Jesus from hearing him than from the report she gave of him. So they rather taunt her that they believed through the teachings of the Savior. But Jesus seems to have accepted the faith of both, and I cannot resist the feeling that he was better pleased with those who the more readily believed on him, even through the poor woman. Only one point was needed to fix the faith in Christ. That is, is God with him, does he talk and act in divine authority? If so, all he says or claims to be is to be believed. The readiness to believe, like Nathanael, the Israelite without guile, like this woman on the first clear evidence of superhuman knowledge and of those who readily received her testimony, is the evidence of an artless and candid heart and soul and is more pleasing to God than those who are slower to accept the divine evidence or act on the simple instruction of the Savior.

43 And after the two days he went forth from thence into Galilee. 44
For Jesus himself testified, that a prophet hath no honor in his own country.
45 So when he came into Galilee, the Galilæans received him, having seen
all the things that he did in Jerusalem at the feast: for they also went unto
the feast.

43 **And after the two days he went forth from thence into Galilee.**—After the two days delay in his journey towards Galilee from Jerusalem he continued it.

44 **For Jesus himself testified, that a prophet hath no honor in his own country.**—Exactly what country he regarded as his own in this statement is difficult to determine. While born in Judea, he was generally regarded as a Galilean. It may possibly have been spoken to show his approbation of his reception in Samaria on his leaving it.

45 **So when he came into Galilee, the Galileans received him, having seen all the things that he did in Jerusalem at the feast: for they also went unto the feast.**—He had wrought miracles at the feast in Jerusalem. Many Galileans had been in Judea, saw the miracles he performed there and so were ready to receive him on his return to Galilee. They may have been the application of the adage stated above. These Galileans had gone to Judea to hear of his great works.

12. SECOND MIRACLE IN CANA.
4: 46-54.

46 He came therefore again unto Cana of Galilee, where he made the
water wine. And there was a certain [5]nobleman, whose son was sick at
Capernaum. 47 When he heard that Jesus was come out of Judæa into
Galilee, he went unto him, and besought *him* that he would come down, and
heal his son; for he was at the point of death. 48 Jesus therefore said

[5]Or, *king's officer*

46 **He came therefore again unto Cana of Galilee, where he made the water wine.**—Cana was not far from Nazareth where Jesus grew to manhood. There he had wrought his first miracle.

And there was a certain nobleman, whose son was sick at Capernaum.—[Probably he was connected in some way with royalty, though not certain.]

47 **When he heard that Jesus was come out of Judaea into Galilee, he went unto him, and besought him that he would come down, and heal his son; for he was at the point of death.**

unto him, Except ye see signs and wonders, ye will in no wise believe. 49
The [5]nobleman saith unto him, [1]Sir, come down ere my child die. 50
Jesus saith unto him, Go thy way; thy son liveth. The man believed the
word that Jesus spake unto him, and he went his way. 51 And as he was
now going down, his [6]servants met him, saying, that his son lived. 52 So
he inquired of them the hour when he began to amend. They said therefore unto him, Yesterday at the seventh hour the fever left him. 53 So the
father knew that *it was* at that hour in which Jesus said unto him, Thy

[6]Gr. *bondservants*

—[In some way he knew of the works of Jesus. His coming to Jesus shows that he was regarded as a prophet in Galilee.]

48 **Jesus therefore said unto him, Except ye see signs and wonders, ye will in no wise believe.**—The Jews generally sought signs and wonders. Jesus to call out a manifestation of the man's faith said, "Except ye see these things ye will not believe."

49 **The nobleman saith unto him, Sir, come down ere my child die.**—The earnestness of his entreaty and the anxiety for his son showed the sincerity and nobility of his faith.

50 **Jesus saith unto him, Go thy way; thy son liveth.**—Jesus saw in his earnest entreaty the manifestation of an earnest and humble faith, and in response to this faith Jesus did more than he asked. He healed the son without going down.

The man believed the word that Jesus spake unto him, and he went his way.—It was another manifestation of his trusting faith that he was willing to accept this assurance and to return home without Jesus.

51 **And as he was now going down, his servants met him, saying, that his son lived.**—The change for the better in the condition of the child was so marked that servants were sent out to assure him that his son was much better and doubtless that Jesus need not come.

52 **So he inquired of them the hour when he began to amend.**—That he might be sure that the healing was due to the power of Jesus, he asked the time of the change.

They said therefore unto him, Yesterday at the seventh hour the fever left him.—[Seventh hour is one o'clock—being the hour Jesus spoke and the fever left.]

53 **So the father knew that it was at that hour in which Jesus said unto him, Thy son liveth:**—They told the hour

son liveth: and himself believed, and his whole house. 54 This is again the second sign that Jesus did, having come out of Judæa into Galilee.

---

at which the fever left him. It corresponded to the time at which Jesus said he lived.

and himself believed, and his whole house.—This gave assurance to his faith, and his testimony caused the others of his household to believe with him.

54 **This is again the second sign that Jesus did, having come out of Judaea into Galilee.**—The miracle at Cana had occurred on his coming out of Galilee, and this was under the same conditions. [Jesus had worked miracles in Judea, but this was the second worked in Galilee. The first was in Cana; he was at Cana when he worked the second, but the beneficiary was at Capernaum.]

This was a physical not a spiritual healing. In spiritual healing the spirit, the soul, the heart, the inner man, must enter into the service, must be molded into the likeness of God. This is done by faith in God. Faith is the medium between the heart of man and God, who is a Spirit. Then the teacher of the word must come into, and be accepted and conformed to by, the spirit in man before his influence can be brought to bear on the spirit of man to mold and influence the man's spirit. The Spirit of God dwells in the church only to the extent that the word of God dwells in, is cherished by, and controls the heart of man. Being in the church, unless he cherishes the word of God, does not secure to him the presence of the Spirit of God. We are the temples of the Spirit of God only as the word of God dwells in and controls our hearts. The Spirit of God dwelling in the heart makes us Christians. When the Spirit of God dwells in the heart, we will obey the Lord Jesus Christ, not before. The truth saves by molding the heart, the soul, the character of man, into the likeness of Christ, into a fitness to dwell with him and his congenial spirits in the world of glory forever.

PART SECOND.

EVENTS BETWEEN THE DEPARTURE INTO GALILEE AND THE LAST VISIT TO JERUSALEM.
5: 1 to 11: 57.

SECTION ONE.

A MIRACLE AND A DISPUTATION IN JERUSALEM.
5: 1-47.

1. AN IMPOTENT MAN MADE WHOLE.
5: 1-9.

1 After these things there was [1]a feast of the Jews; and Jesus went up to Jerusalem.
2 Now there is in Jerusalem by the sheep *gate* a pool, which is called in Hebrew [2]Bethesda, having five porches. 3 In these lay a multitude of

[1]Many ancient authorities read *the feast.* (Comp. ch. 2. 13?)
[2]Some ancient authorities read *Bethsaida,* others *Bethzatha*

---

1 **After these things there was a feast of the Jews; and Jesus went up to Jerusalem.**—This feast is generally regarded as the Passover feast, although it is nowhere said to be so, and there is nothing so determining. If this be a Passover feast, it makes certain that the public ministry of Jesus lasted three and a half years. Without this there is no certainty about this. The attendance at the Passover feasts is the clearest indication of the time of his public ministry. John tells of his attendance at the feasts in Jerusalem, and of his teaching and work there much more fully than does the other gospel writers.

2 **Now there is in Jerusalem by the sheep gate**—It is thought that this is the gate through which the sheep for sacrifice were generally brought.

a pool, which is called in Hebrew Bethesda,—This pool and its qualities are not mentioned by any other writer of the Bible. Its identity and locality have not been fixed with certainty. Whether there was real curative property in the waters is not certain. Among the superstitious people imag-

them that were sick, blind, halt, withered.[3] 5 And a certain man was there,
who had been thirty and eight years in his infirmity. 6 When Jesus saw
him lying, and knew that he had been now a long time *in that case,* he
saith unto him, Wouldest thou be made whole? 7 The sick man answered
him, [4]Sir, I have no man, when the water is troubled, to put me into the

[3]Many ancient authorities insert, wholly or in part, *waiting for the moving of the water: 4 for an angel of the Lord went down at certain seasons into the pool, and troubled the water: whosoever then first after the troubling of the water stepped in was made whole, with whatsoever disease he was holden*

[4]Or, *Lord*

ination is so active that reputation for healing is frequently kept up for centuries when the imagination does all that is done for them. The record here gives no intimation that Jesus thought the healing genuine. He heals entirely independent of the waters.

having five porches.—These were five sheltered entrances to the pool called porches.

3 **In these lay a multitude of them that were sick, blind, halt, withered.**—The sick would remain waiting for the moving of the waters. Multitudes were attracted to try the efficacy of the water in healing the diseases. The fourth verse is left out of the American Revised Version. It is thought by many that it was an intermittent spring, rising and flowing at regular times, then ceasing. Such springs are known in different parts of the world. It would not be difficult to give currency to the idea that an angel did this.

5 **And a certain man was there, who had been thirty and eight years in his infirmity.**—The long affliction indicates the incurable nature and little probability of relief.

6 **When Jesus saw him lying, and knew that he had been now a long time in that case,**—Jesus knew either by inquiry or from his superhuman power of knowing things. The context does not show the source of this knowledge. His helplessness appealed to the Master.

he saith unto him, Wouldest thou be made whole?—Jesus doubtless knew he wished to be healed and asked this question by way of introduction to the sufferer.

7 **The sick man answered him, Sir, I have no man, when the water is troubled, to put me into the pool: but while I am coming, another steppeth down before me.**—This answer

pool: but while I am coming, another steppeth down before me. 8 Jesus
saith unto him, Arise, take up thy [5]bed, and walk. 9 And straightway the
man was made whole, and took up his [5]bed and walked.
Now it was the sabbath on that day. 10 So the Jews said unto him that

[5]Or, *pallet*

shows that something like the condition described in verse 4, in the Common Version, was supposed to exist. His poverty and his complete helplessness prevented his securing the benefit, whether real or supposed, of water.

8 **Jesus saith unto him, Arise, take up thy bed, and walk.**—Such a case especially commended itself to Jesus.

9 **And straightway the man was made whole, and took up his bed and walked. Now it was the sabbath on that day.**—The man made the effort to obey Jesus. Jesus supplied the power and he was relieved of the infirmity. God's help always comes to those receiving it in the effort to obey him.

2. JESUS ACCUSED OF SABBATH BREAKING. 5: 10-18.

was cured, It is the sabbath, and it is not lawful for thee to take up thy
[5]bed. 11 But he answered them, He that made me whole, the same said
unto me, Take up thy [5]bed, and walk. 12 They asked him, Who is the man
that said unto thee, Take up *thy* [5]*bed,* and walk? 13 But he that was healed

10 **So the Jews said unto him that was cured, It is the sabbath, and it is not lawful for thee to take up thy bed.**—It was contrary to the law of Moses to carry any burden on the Sabbath. The Jews raised the question of observing the Sabbath—first as to the healed man carrying his bed, and afterwards as to the sinfulness of healing on the Sabbath (verse 16). (See Neh. 13: 19; Jer. 17: 21.)

11 **But he answered them, He that made me whole, the same said unto me, Take up thy bed, and walk.**—The man wisely concluded that God was with one who could heal as he had been healed, and if he could heal he had authority to so far control him as to authorize him to carry his bed home.

12 **They asked him, Who is the man that said unto thee, Take up thy bed, and walk?**—They were somewhat incredulous about the healing and asked who had done it. It is a little singular that the man did not find out when Jesus healed him

knew not who it was; for Jesus had conveyed himself away, a multitude being in the place. 14 Afterward Jesus findeth him in the temple, and said unto him, Behold, thou art made whole: sin no more, lest a worse thing befall thee. 15 The man went away, and told the Jews that it was Jesus who had made him whole. 16 And for this cause the Jews persecuted Jesus, because he did these things on the sabbath. 17 But Jesus answered

who he was, but it was done quickly and brought great surprise to the healed man and Jesus quickly passed from his presence.

13 **But he that was healed knew not who it was; for Jesus had conveyed himself away, a multitude being in the place.**—The man had to tell them he did not know who had wrought the great cure by his word as he had gone away.

14 **Afterward Jesus findeth him in the temple, and said unto him, Behold, thou art made whole: sin no more, lest a worse thing befall thee.**—Jesus on meeting him in the temple warned him if he sinned again greater evil would come upon him. This seems to imply that this evil had come upon him as the result of his sin. The Jews believed this, yet Jesus told his disciples (9: 2, 3) that neither the blind man nor his parents had sinned to bring on his blindness.

15 **The man went away, and told the Jews that it was Jesus who had made him whole.**—On their meeting in the temple, Jesus made himself known to the healed man, and he seems to have sought the inquiring Jews at once and told them it was Jesus.

16 **And for this cause the Jews persecuted Jesus, because he did these things on the sabbath.**—The persecution of Jesus for what they claimed as breaking the Sabbath began here and it resulted in the effort to slay him.

17 **But Jesus answered them, My Father worketh even until now, and I work.**—Jesus justified his healing the man on the ground that his Father worketh hitherto or unto now, and following his example he works. It seems that "on the sabbath" is implied as the charge was for working on the Sabbath. In what sense he meant to say that God worked till that time is not clear. It is certain that he did it through all the operations of the natural universe, and it seems probable that Jesus referred to this working. The point of Jesus

them, My Father worketh even until now, and I work. 18 For this cause therefore the Jews sought the more to kill him, because he not only brake the sabbath, but also called God his own Father, making himself equal with God.

---

was that God worked on the Sabbath and that he had the same right to set aside, if need be, the Sabbath law as God had done.

18 **For this cause therefore the Jews sought the more to kill him, because he not only brake the sabbath, but also called God his own Father, making himself equal with God.**—This claim to have the right to do what God did placed himself on an equality with God and more infuriated the Jews so they now sought to kill him. [They did not undertake to put him to death at once, but began preparing the way for his death. More than two years later he was condemned to death for the claim of being the Son of God.]

3. JESUS ASSERTS HIS POWER.
5: 19-29.

19 Jesus therefore answered and said unto them, Verily, verily, I say unto you, The Son can do nothing of himself, but what he seeth the Father doing: for what things soever he doeth, these the Son also doeth in like manner. 20 For the Father loveth the Son, and showeth him all things that himself doeth: and greater works than these will he show him, that

---

19 **Jesus therefore answered and said unto them, Verily, verily, I say unto you, The Son can do nothing of himself, but what he seeth the Father doing: for what things soever he doeth, these the Son also doeth in like manner.**—Jesus disavowed any authority or power to do anything save as the Father leads and enables him to do. He doubtless referred to his healing the impotent man. He could have done this only by the power of God. His effort was to show that God worked with and through him. [In answering them Jesus retracts nothing, but reasserts his Sonship by asserting that the power of the Son comes from the Father.]

20 **For the Father loveth the Son, and showeth him all things that himself doeth: and greater works than these will he show him, that ye may marvel.**—He insists that God loves him, reveals his own works to the Son, enables him to do

ye may marvel. 21 For as the Father raiseth the dead and giveth them life,
even so the Son also giveth life to whom he will. 22 For neither doth the
Father judge any man, but he hath given all judgment unto the Son; 23
that all may honor the Son, even as they honor the Father. He that honoreth not the Son honoreth not the Father that sent him. 24 Verily, verily,
I say unto you, He that heareth my word, and believeth him that sent me,
hath eternal life, and cometh not into judgment, but hath passed out of

---

what God does, and he promises that God will enable him to do even greater works than he had yet done in their presence. [This future work would be greater than the miracle just performed.]

21 **For as the Father raiseth the dead and giveth them life, even so the Son also giveth life to whom he will.**—This verse explains the greater works promised in the preceding verse—the power to quicken the dead into life. [He gives his Father the credit of being the fountain of all life and that he can raise the dead to life and that he himself possesses the same power through the Father.]

22 **For neither doth the Father judge any man, but he hath given all judgment unto the Son;**—God has committed the work of judging and quickening the world to his Son. He gave his authority and power into the hands of the Son.

23 **that all may honor the Son, even as they honor the Father.**—The Father committing his authority and judgment to the Son and so empowering the Son to speak and act for him demands that the Son should receive the honor that the Father does.

He that honoreth not the Son honoreth not the Father that sent him.—The only method of approach to the Father is through the Son and so he who rejects the Son rejects the Father.

24 **Verily, verily, I say unto you, He that heareth my word, and believeth him that sent me, hath eternal life, and cometh not into judgment,**—The emphasis is laid on the truth that hearing Jesus and believing in God through the words of Jesus would bring them to everlasting life.

but hath passed out of death into life.—In accepting Christ and his word as our rule and guide we pass out of a state of condemnation into one of life—a state that leads to eternal life or life beyond the grave.

death into life. 25 Verily, verily, I say unto you, The hour cometh, and
now is, when the dead shall hear the voice of the Son of God; and they
that [6]hear shall live. 26 For as the Father hath life in himself, even so
gave he to the Son also to have life in himself: 27 and he gave him authority
to execute judgment, because he is a son of man. 28 Marvel not at this:
for the hour cometh, in which all that are in the tombs shall hear his voice,
29 and shall come forth; they that have done good, unto the resurrection
of life; and they that have [1]done evil, unto the resurrection of judgment.

[6] Or, *hearken*
[1] Or, *practised*

---

25 **Verily, verily, I say unto you, The hour cometh, and now is, when the dead shall hear the voice of the Son of God; and they that hear shall live.**—The knowledge of the resurrection was but slightly known. So Jesus plainly declares that the time was now coming that all the dead shall hear the voice of the Son of God, and those who heard that voice would live. [We take it that the reference is primarily to those spiritually dead. It will also be true of those in the graves at the resurrection. (Verse 28.) Jesus demonstrated his power to give life by raising Lazarus.]

26 **For as the Father hath life in himself, even so gave he to the Son also to have life in himself:**—That life would be bestowed by the Son of God, since God had given the same power to the Son to make alive as he possessed.

27 **and he gave him authority to execute judgment, because he is a son of man.**—He gave him power to execute judgment alike upon the godly and upon the ungodly. This must be executed in harmony with the laws that God committed to his hands.

28 **Marvel not at this: for the hour cometh, in which all that are in the tombs shall hear his voice,**—He more directly points out that all good and bad shall come forth from the grave.

29 **and shall come forth; they that have done good, unto the resurrection of life; and they that have done evil, unto the resurrection of judgment.**—They that have done good or kept the laws will be raised to life eternal. They that have done evil to a condemnation of eternal death or banishment from the presence of God. [Jesus makes it clear that there is a judgment beyond the grave, and that there is also a general resurrection.]

4. THE TESTIMONY OF THESE CLAIMS.
5: 30-40.

30 I can of myself do nothing: as I hear, I judge: and my judgment is
righteous; because I seek not mine own will, but the will of him that sent
me. 31 If I bear witness of myself, my witness is not true. 32 It is another
that beareth witness of me; and I know that the witness which he witnesseth of me is true. 33 Ye have sent unto John, and he hath borne
witness unto the truth. 34 But the witness which I receive is not from
man: howbeit I say these things, that ye may be saved. 35 He was the

---

30 **I can of myself do nothing: as I hear, I judge: and my judgment is righteous; because I seek not mine own will, but the will of him that sent me.**—While to Jesus had been committed the work of judging the world, he is careful that all should understand that he and his Father are one because he sought to enforce no will of his own; but his Father's will and in doing this the Father was with him.

31 **If I bear witness of myself, my witness is not true.**—If he alone bears witness of himself, the witness is not to be accepted as true. This was also the law of Moses. Every charge was to be established in the mouth of two or three witnesses. (Num. 35: 30; Deut. 19: 15.) That it does not mean the testimony is false is seen by a comparison with 8: 14.

32 **It is another that beareth witness of me; and I know that the witness which he witnesseth of me is true.**—In compliance with the law requiring two witnesses to prove a thing, Jesus announces that another beareth witness of him than himself, and Jesus knew that the testimony of this witness is true.

33 **Ye have sent unto John, and he hath borne witness unto the truth.**—These people had nearly all been baptized of John. They had gone to him as a teacher, and he had borne witness that Jesus is the Lamb of God that taketh away the sin of the world (1: 36).

34 **But the witness which I receive is not from man:**—While he presents John as a witness in whom they believed, who bore testimony for him, Jesus referred to God as witnessing in behalf of Jesus.

howbeit I say these things, that ye may be saved.—He refers to these witnesses that they might believe in Jesus and be saved.

lamp that burneth and shineth; and ye were willing to rejoice for a season
in his light. 36 But the witness which I have is greater than *that of* John;
for the works which the Father hath given me to accomplish, the very
works that I do, bear witness of me, that the Father hath sent me. 37
And the Father that sent me, he hath borne witness of me. Ye have neither
heard his voice at any time, nor seen his form. 38 And ye have not his
word abiding in you: for whom he sent, him ye believe not. 39 [2]Ye search

[2]Or, *Search the scriptures*

---

35 **He was the lamp that burneth and shineth; and ye were willing to rejoice for a season in his light.**—John was a teacher sent from God who taught the will of God and these Jews had followed him for a time.

36 **But the witness which I have is greater than that of John; for the works which the Father hath given me to accomplish, the very works that I do, bear witness of me,**—The works that Jesus did attracted the attention of the world and made the best men believe on him. Nicodemus said, "No one can do these signs that thou doest, except God be with him." (3: 2.) All that Jesus did and suffered in his mission on earth was what his Father had given him to do. The miracles he wrought, and his own triumph over death and resurrection from the dead, were the especial works that substantiated his claim to be the Son of God. He "was declared to be the Son of God with power, according to the spirit of holiness, by the resurrection from the dead." The kingdom in its unorganized elements—the head, laws, and subjects—in embryo was among [the works he was to accomplish].

that the Father hath sent me.—The works that God did through Jesus testified that Jesus was of God. The object of miracles was to prove that the person who wrought the miracles was from God and spake by the power of God.

37 **And the Father that sent me, he hath borne witness of me. Ye have neither heard his voice at any time, nor seen his form.**—When God spake, they refused to hear his voice, and they had not seen him.

38 **And ye have not his word abiding in you:**—[Proof of this fact was they did believe the testimony of John whom he had sent.]

for whom he sent, him ye believe not.—[The preaching of John bore witness of him.]

the scriptures, because ye think that in them ye have eternal life; and these are they which bear witness of me; 40 and ye will not come to me, that

39 **Ye search the scriptures, because ye think that in them ye have eternal life; and these are they which bear witness of me;**—The Jews claimed to believe and read the scriptures of the Old Testament, and thought that through them eternal life would be gained, yet they foretold of Jesus. He presents two witnesses, the works or miracles of Jesus and the fulfillment of prophecies found in the Old Testament concerning him. [The scriptures that they searched contained the testimony of Christ. All the prophets had borne witness of him. The one of whom the scriptures spoke was light and life, yet they refused to come to him that they might have life.]

40 **and ye will not come to me, that ye may have life.**—Notwithstanding these testimonies they refused to believe in him and come to him as his disciples. Jesus keeps it distinctly before them that through him alone they could receive spiritual life. [They rejected the light their own scriptures contained. "Search" implies painstaking, exhaustive examination.]

5. CAUSE OF JEWISH UNBELIEF.
5: 41-47.

ye may have life. 41 I receive not glory from men. 42 But I know you, that ye have not the love of God in yourselves. 43 I am come in my Father's name, and ye receive me not: if another shall come in his own name, him

41 **I receive not glory from men.**—Jesus did not rest his claims to glory on the testimony or witness of men.

42 **But I know you, that ye have not the love of God in yourselves.**—But their disbelief in him and his works proved that they did not have the love of God in them. "For this is the love of God, that we keep his commandments." (1 John 5: 3.) Only those who keep the commandments of God love him according to Jesus Christ, the Son of God. [He read their hearts and knew them.]

43 **I am come in my Father's name, and ye receive me not:**—Jesus came as the representative of his Father to stand in the place and do the work of his Father. This is the meaning

ye will receive. 44 How can ye believe, who receive glory one of another,
and the glory that *cometh* from [8]the only God ye seek not? 45 Think not
that I will accuse you to the Father: there is one that accuseth you, *even*
Moses, on whom ye have set your hope. 46 For if ye believed Moses, ye

[8]Some ancient authorities read *the only* one

of coming in the name of another, to take his place, do his work, and to work for and in place of another. To act for and in the name of another is to ignore self and selfish ends and to act in behalf of him whom he represents. Jesus acted in the name of and for his Father.

if another shall come in his own name, him ye will receive.—These Jews rejected Jesus, but if another was to come acting in his own name for himself, him they would receive. [They rejected Jesus, their only hope, but would accept with pleasure a deceiver. Their history shows that they did this.]

44 **How can ye believe, who receive glory one of another, and the glory that cometh from the only God ye seek not?**—One seeking the applause and praise of men and who does not seek the honor and praise of God cannot believe in Christ. His example of seeking the honor from God and not that from men would be so at war with their hearts and practices that they would not believe him as their teacher and exemplar. [Their seeking human glory and honor caused their unbelief in Jesus. They did not possess that lowly spirit needful for belief in Christ.] Whenever a church or a preacher sets out to be respectable and influential by its worldly possessions and surroundings, or when a preacher is intent on using his position as a preacher to gain worldly position or influence, they bid farewell to true usefulness to the world and would do well to cease to be churches or preachers of Christ. The honor of the world is incompatible with honor from God, and he who seeks one will forfeit the other.

The rich and fashionable and those who are unwilling to sacrifice to Christ substitute money for personal service and sacrifice. Under this spirit money has displaced self-sacrificing devotion as the chief factor in spreading the gospel. Those who rely on money seek those who have money and the poor are neglected. This spirit must be set aside or the churches

would believe me; for he wrote of me. 47 But if ye believe not his writings, how shall ye believe my words?

overloaded with money will die. Indeed, the money helps to kill them. It is utterly impossible for one who depends on money for social standing and respectability and enjoyment to be a true Christian. It is equally impossible for one seeking earthly honor and greatness, whether he seeks it in the pulpit or in the political field or the legal forum, to be an earnest and true child of God and an effective worker in saving souls. The spirit of seeking and looking to wealth and worldly honor is so antagonistic to the spirit of Jesus he asks: "How can ye believe, who receive glory one of another?" It is much easier to get the common people to do active service in the church of God than it is to get the rich, the educated, those who pride themselves on their worldly respectability.

45 **Think not that I will accuse you to the Father: there is one that accuseth you, even Moses, on whom ye have set your hope.**—They claimed to believe in Moses as their teacher and ruler. They so vitiated his law that they would fall under his condemnation and Moses in whom they claimed to believe would be their accuser.

46 **For if ye believed Moses, ye would believe me; for he wrote of me.**—Moses prophesied of Christ, and those who properly understand Moses must believe in Christ. The fact that they did not receive Christ who was the end to which the law led was evidence that they did not believe in Moses or his writings.

47 **But if ye believe not his writings, how shall ye believe my words?**—To fail to understand and believe in the writings of Moses would lead to a rejection of Christ. In this chapter the teaching of Christ [is that he regarded the Pentateuch a genuine composition of Moses. Critics who claim that these books are frauds ought to learn a lesson from Jesus]. The Jews claimed to believe in Moses, yet Moses pointed to Christ and without Christ the writings of Moses are meaningless. [Each proves the other to be true, and no one can accept the one and at the same time reject the other.]

SECTION TWO.

A MIRACLE AND A DISPUTATION IN GALILEE.
6: 1-71.

1. FEEDING OF FIVE THOUSAND.
6: 1-14.

1 After these things Jesus went away to the other side of the sea of
Galilee, which is *the sea* of Tiberias. 2 And a great multitude followed
him, because they beheld the signs which he did on them that were sick. 3
And Jesus went up into the mountain, and there he sat with his disciples.
4 Now the passover, the feast of the Jews, was at hand. 5 Jesus therefore

---

1 **After these things Jesus went away to the other side of the sea of Galilee, which is the sea of Tiberias.**—The Sea of Galilee is known as the Sea of Tiberias and the Sea of Chinneroth. Around this sea the Jews that lived in Galilee very greatly collected. Several towns or villages sprang up on its shores. The chief of these was Capernaum. Jesus, after he began his public ministry, seems to have made this his home so far as he had a home on earth. Capernaum was situated on the western shore of this sea.

2 **And a great multitude followed him,**—The eastern shore was an uninhabited wilderness and to it Jesus frequently went and the people would follow him and in the quiet of the wilderness he would teach them.

because they beheld the signs which he did on them that were sick.—They followed him, attracted by the miracles he performed; and while they did not believe in him, they brought the sick and afflicted, and he healed them. So far as the record shows, Jesus never left a soul in suffering that appealed for help to him.

3 **And Jesus went up into the mountain, and there he sat with his disciples.**—This mountain was on the east side of the Sea of Galilee.

4 **Now the passover, the feast of the Jews, was at hand.**—The feast of the Passover came on the fourteenth day of the month Abib or Nisan. If we count the feast mentioned in chapter 5: 1 as a Passover feast, this is the third Passover since the baptism of Jesus. It shows that John recorded but

lifting up his eyes, and seeing that a great multitude cometh unto him,
saith unto Philip, Whence are we to buy [4]bread, that these may eat? 6
And this he said to prove him: for he himself knew what he would do. 7
Philip answered him, Two hundred [5]shillings' worth of [4]bread is not sufficient for them, that every one may take a little. 8 One of his disciples,
Andrew, Simon Peter's brother, saith unto him, 9 There is a lad here, who
hath five barley loaves, and two fishes: but what are these among so many?

[4]Gr. *loaves*
[5]The word in the Greek denotes a coin worth about eight pence halfpenny, or nearly seventeen cents

little of what Jesus said or did in the earlier years of his public ministry. Only what is given in the fifth chapter is of what he did and taught during these years and yet Jesus was not idle.

5 **Jesus therefore lifting up his eyes, and seeing that a great multitude cometh unto him, saith unto Philip, Whence are we to buy bread, that these may eat?**—The country was dry, the temperature pleasant, and the people, accustomed to an outdoor and migratory life, followed Jesus without one idea as to how long they would remain and were detained by his teaching and became hungry. And Jesus saw fit to feed this multitude that had remained until hungry and weakened by the fasting.

6 **And this he said to prove him: for he himself knew what he would do.**—He said this to try Philip and prepare him for what he intended to do.

7 **Philip answered him, Two hundred shillings' worth of bread is not sufficient for them, that every one may take a little.**—Philip made a calculation of the number to be fed, of the amount they would eat, and of the cost. [Wisdom here for us in counting the cost before undertaking a thing. It equaled thirty dollars.]

8 **One of his disciples, Andrew, Simon Peter's brother, saith unto him,**—[Andrew's answer to the question of Jesus is recorded in Mark 6: 38. He requested them to examine and report the amount of food they had.]

9 **There is a lad here, who hath five barley loaves, and two fishes: but what are these among so many?**—They were in the wilderness where food could not be obtained, and Andrew suggested that they had these few loaves and fishes as the

10 Jesus said, Make the people sit down. Now there was much grass in
the place. So the men sat down, in number about five thousand. 11 Jesus
therefore took the loaves; and having given thanks, he distributed to them
that were set down; likewise also of the fishes as much as they would. 12
And when they were filled, he saith unto his disciples, Gather up the broken
pieces which remain over, that nothing be lost. 13 So they gathered them

only chance for bread of which he knew. [Barley was the food only of the lower classes. Probably this was the whole stock of food at the command of the disciples—no more than enough for them.]

10 **Jesus said, Make the people sit down.**—There is no doubt in the movement or purposes of Jesus. Without ostentation or boasting he proposed and effected the most stupendous and impossible things with all the assurance and composure that others undertake the most commonplace affairs of life. So he seated the multitude.

Now there was much grass in the place.—It was April, the time for grass and flowers.

So the men sat down, in number about five thousand.—["About," not exactly five thousand. Mark tells that they sat down in companies. About one loaf to every thousand men. Matthew states "besides women and children." How many of these is not stated.]

11 **Jesus therefore took the loaves; and having given thanks, he distributed to them that were set down; likewise also of the fishes as much as they would.**—He gave thanks for all he received, and gave to his disciples, most probably his apostles, and they to the multitude. In the breaking it was increased and multiplied. [It is said that the Jews considered it was stealing from God to eat without first offering thanks. Jesus always offered thanks and so should all Christians.]

12 **And when they were filled, he saith unto his disciples, Gather up the broken pieces which remain over, that nothing be lost.**—Their hunger was satisfied, and as if to teach the sin of wastefulness he commands the disciples to gather up what remained. God in all the processes of nature avoids waste. What appears to be the waste of one creature is the life of another. One would think where things come apparently so easily there would be little use for saving [but

up, and filled twelve baskets with broken pieces from the five barley loaves, which remained over unto them that had eaten. 14 When therefore the

God does not allow wastefulness at any time. Nature wastes nothing. Soil washed from the hills and mountains, God catches in the valleys and low places. It is the waste of man that brings want. It is by the waste of fragments that the great wastes occur. The waste of our nation is appalling. There is food enough for all if handled properly by man. God through nature will furnish it if man will use wisdom in producing and saving it. Christ bids us save; save the fragments.]

13 **So they gathered them up, and filled twelve baskets with broken pieces from the five barley loaves, which remained over unto them that had eaten.**—This was a miracle manifesting creative power. A miracle is the bestowing on others the power to do what God only can do. It is done to attest the presence and power of God in the person who performs the miracle to show that he acts and speaks for God, so in hearing him he hears God. There is no more power exerted in a miracle than is put forth in the ordinary provisions of nature. It did not require more power or wisdom to make this bread and these fishes than was used in devising and putting in force the processes of the material world by which men and animals have been fed through all the years of their existence. The difference is that this last is done in accordance with the fixed working, and points back to a wise Creator and Ruler, but does not definitely point out that Creator and Ruler. The miracle points out the person who represents and speaks for the Creator and Ruler of all things. This and all the miracles or signs that Jesus wrought testify to the world that he spoke and acted by the authority of God. [Simply feeding five thousand was no miracle; for the reason God fed them and the rest of the world the day before and the day following and all the time through natural laws. The way in which God did it constituted a miracle.]

14 **When therefore the people saw the sign which he did, they said, This is of a truth the prophet that cometh into the**

people saw the [6]sign which he did, they said, This is of a truth the prophet that cometh into the world.

[6]Some ancient authorities read *signs*

world.—The conclusion reached was that he was the prophet that it had been foretold would come into the world by Moses (Deut. 18: 15-19), and referred to by the delegation sent to visit John the Baptist (1: 21). This prophet was to be the king of Israel, the head of the kingdom of God on earth. They acknowledged: "This is the Christ."

2. JESUS AND HIS DISCIPLES RECROSS THE LAKE. 6: 15-21.

15 Jesus therefore perceiving that they were about to come and take him by force, to make him king, withdrew again into the mountain himself alone.

15 **Jesus therefore perceiving that they were about to come and take him by force, to make him king,**—The Jews supposed that this prophet was to be a king that would deliver them from bondage, and they went about to make him a king. The faith of these Jews seems to have been impulsive and momentary. When they saw the manifestation of power they were aroused, but when cooled down their faith passed away. They went about to make him their king, hoping that he would deliver them from bondage to the Roman rulers. Jesus felt the human love of power, was flattered by the favor shown him, and felt the human temptation to yield. Paul says that he "hath been in all points tempted like as we are, yet without sin." (Heb. 4: 15.) He resisted the temptation, sent away his disciples (Matt. 14: 22), and [he went into the mountain alone. Convinced that he was Christ, they sought to proclaim him king, to raise his standard, and establish his government.]

withdrew again into the mountain himself alone.—For a season of prayer and communion with his Father. When Jesus was tempted and tried, overcome as a human being with labor, or had important work pressing on him, he sought the seclusion of the mountain and the coming of night for continued seasons of prayer to God. (Luke 6: 12; 9: 28.)

16 And when evening came, his disciples went down unto the sea; 17
and they entered into a boat, and were going over the sea unto Capernaum.
And it was now dark, and Jesus had not yet come to them. 18 And the
sea was rising by reason of a great wind that blew. 19 When therefore
they had rowed about five and twenty or thirty furlongs, they behold Jesus
walking on the sea, and drawing nigh unto the boat: and they were afraid.

16 **And when evening came, his disciples went down unto the sea;**—[Matthew (14: 22) says Jesus sent them away by boat, then sent the multitude away, and he withdrew into the mountain to pray.]

17 **and they entered into a boat, and were going over the sea unto Capernaum. And it was now dark, and Jesus had not yet come to them.**—[It was a small fishing boat, but large enough to carry at least twelve. It was propelled by oars. Mark says to Bethsaida, but this was on the way to Capernaum. Mark specifies the first landing place and John the end of the journey.]

18 **And the sea was rising by reason of a great wind that blew.**—The Sea of Galilee, a comparatively small body of water, about six miles wide, could be quickly thrown into high waves by the winds that would come down from the surrounding mountains.

19 **When therefore they had rowed about five and twenty or thirty furlongs,**—There are eight furlongs in a mile. Had they gone in a straight course they would have been about the center of the sea. Owing to the winds and waves they were doubtless thrown out of their course. Some think they drifted along the east shore from which they started.

they behold Jesus walking on the sea, and drawing nigh unto the boat:—After they had gone this far they saw Jesus coming. Matthew (14: 25) says it was in the fourth watch, or between three o'clock and day. He walked on the sea while it was agitated by the winds and the waves rolled. Matthew (14: 26) says they thought it was "a ghost," a disembodied spirit. It is a new work in which to see Jesus.

and they were afraid.—[Mark reports that they cried out in fright.]

20 But he saith unto them, It is I; be not afraid. 21 They were willing
therefore to receive him into the boat: and straightway the boat was at the
land whither they were going.

---

20 **But he saith unto them, It is I; be not afraid.**—They were familiar with the tone of his voice and his speech allayed their fears.

21 **They were willing therefore to receive him into the boat: and straightway the boat was at the land whither they were going.**—Matthew (14: 28-33) tells of Peter's request to come to Jesus on the water, his attempt, Jesus entering into the boat, the allaying of the storm, and their landing whither they were going. [Christ was their salvation. He can also calm the troubled soul and carry it safely to heaven.]

3. THE MULTITUDE OVERTAKES JESUS.
6: 22-27.

22 On the morrow the multitude that stood on the other side of the sea
saw that there was no other [1]boat there, save one, and that Jesus entered
not with his disciples into the boat, but *that* his disciples went away alone
23 (howbeit there came [2]boats from Tiberias nigh unto the place where
they ate the bread after the Lord had given thanks): 24 when the multitude
therefore saw that Jesus was not there, neither his disciples, they themselves got into the [2]boats, and came to Capernaum, seeking Jesus. 25 And

[1]Gr. *little boat*
[2]Gr. *little boats*

---

22 **On the morrow the multitude that stood on the other side of the sea saw that there was no other boat there, save one, and that Jesus entered not with his disciples into the boat, but that his disciples went away alone**—Some of the people seem to have been at the same place the next day. They had seen the apostles leave without Jesus, and had known of no way of his leaving, so expected to find him at the place they had left him.

23 **(howbeit there came boats from Tiberias nigh unto the place where they ate the bread after the Lord had given thanks):**—The other boats that came later were those still there, and in which the people in some of them crossed over to the other side.

24 **when the multitude therefore saw that Jesus was not there, neither his disciples, they themselves got into the boats,**

when they found him on the other side of the sea, they said unto him, Rabbi,
when camest thou hither? 26 Jesus answered them and said, Verily, verily,
I say unto you, Ye seek me, not because ye saw signs, but because ye ate
of the loaves, and were filled. 27 Work not for the food which perisheth,

---

and came to Capernaum, seeking Jesus.—The people, knowing that Jesus did not go with the disciples and having no other means of going, took the boats that were there and came to Capernaum seeking him.

25 **And when they found him on the other side of the sea, they said unto him, Rabbi, when camest thou hither?**—Their curiosity to know how he crossed the sea was uppermost in their minds. The multitudes that he had fed sought him on the east side of the Sea of Galilee, where he had fed them, and not finding him they crossed over to Capernaum and found him on the west side of the sea—the other side from where they had eaten. They did not understand how he came, as they knew he did not come with his disciples, so asked the question how he came over. They addressed him as "Rabbi." This means "teacher" or master in the sense of teacher. It was applied by the Jews to their teachers, and frequently to Jesus as a recognition of his wisdom and superiority as a teacher. As applied to Jesus, it was a recognition that he was a teacher sent from God. Jesus did not answer their question but responded:

26 **Jesus answered them and said, Verily, verily, I say unto you, Ye seek me, not because ye saw signs, but because ye ate of the loaves, and were filled.**—Instead of gratifying their curiosity he sought to reprove them for seeking him for the food he gave them. While not answering their question, he tells them a truth that laid bare their hearts—that is, that they were not interested in the miracles he performed as manifestations of divine presence, but because they ate of the food and were filled. They were not interested in the great truths as was teaching as affecting their spiritual and eternal interests and God's glory and honor. That class of people exists yet and in our country. Have a meeting at which food is abundantly provided and many will attend who take no interest in the preaching, but are attracted by the dinner pro-

but for the food which abideth unto eternal life, which the Son of man
shall give unto you: for him the Father, *even* God, hath sealed. 28 They

vided. They are not specially vicious people, but fleshly people, who are satisfied with enough to fill the belly.

27 **Work not for the food which perisheth, but for the food which abideth unto eternal life, which the Son of man shall give unto you: for him the Father, even God, hath sealed.**—He diverted their minds to the great spiritual truths that he would give them as meat that would endure unto eternal life. The Father owned and confessed him as his prophet to teach the world. He makes use of this occurrence to impress the importance of seeking spiritual good that will result in eternal or imperishable blessings. The material food they ate perishes; the body sustained by this food perishes, but the spirit lives forever, and the food which sustains and promotes its well-being is spiritual food that perishes not. Jesus was drawing the distinction and contrast between the body and the spirit, and between the food that sustains the vigor of the body and that which promotes the well-being of the soul.

4. REMARKS ABOUT THE BREAD OF LIFE.
6: 28-40.

said therefore unto him, What must we do, that we may work the works
of God? 29 Jesus answered and said unto them, This is the work of God,

28 **They said therefore unto him, What must we do, that we may work the works of God?**—They recognized that when he said, "Work not for the food which perisheth, but for the food which abideth unto eternal life," he began to tell them to do the work of God that they may have life. They recognized that God's work would endure forever, and to do the work of God was to labor for the meat that will endure forever, so they asked what they should do in order that they may do that work. They understood, too, that to do what God required them to do was to do the work of God. The meaning then was: what does God require us to do that we may inherit everlasting life?

that ye believe on him whom [8]he hath sent.
30 They said therefore unto
him, What then doest thou for a sign, that we may see, and believe thee?
what workest thou?
31 Our fathers ate the manna in the wilderness; as

[8]Or, *he sent*

29 **Jesus answered and said unto them, This is the work of God, that ye believe on him whom he hath sent.**—The work that God requires of them is to believe in Jesus Christ whom God hath sent to represent him. Believing in Christ is the work of God because appointed by God. It is to be done by man, for man must believe. This is a work performed by the inner, spiritual man. A careful study of this truth will help to solve several difficulties that give trouble in the religious world. The question of salvation by works has troubled the world. A clear understanding of the different senses in which the term *works* is used would help to settle this difficulty. It is used in two distinct senses—the works of God and the works of man. Salvation is often attributed to the former; never to the latter. The works of God are those works ordained by God for man to do, not works which God himself does. The works of man are those devised by man. A work ordained by God for one dispensation or for one class of persons, taken from this and transferred to another class, becomes in this latter a work of man. The verse illustrates the truth that the works of God are works ordained by God to be performed by man.

30 **They said therefore unto him, What then doest thou for a sign, that we may see, and believe thee? what workest thou?**—They understood that he meant they were to believe in him as the Son of God. "If we are to believe on you, what sign, or miracle, do you give as evidence on which our faith in you may rest?" It was rather singular to ask this question when they had just seen the loaves and the fishes increased to feed the thousands and they had eaten of it. They ask again, "What workest thou?" What miracle, or sign, do you work that we may believe on you? This was demanding testimony while refusing to believe that already given.

it is written, He [4]gave them bread out of heaven to eat. 32 Jesus therefore
said unto them, Verily, verily, I say unto you, It was not Moses that gave
you the bread out of heaven; but my Father giveth you the true bread out
of heaven. 33 For the bread of God is that which cometh down out of
heaven, and giveth life unto the world. 34 They said therefore unto him,

[4]Neh. 9. 15; Ex. 16. 4, 15; Ps. 78. 24; 105. 40

31 **Our fathers ate the manna in the wilderness; as it is written, He gave them bread out of heaven to eat.**—They follow up this request by referring to the manna that God gave to the fathers in the wilderness. This was a work, or sign, given the fathers that they might believe on God. Now what kind of work do you do that we may believe on you? It is probable that they expected him to feed them, without labor on their part, through life as a sign.

32 **Jesus therefore said unto them, Verily, verily, I say unto you, It was not Moses that gave you the bread out of heaven; but my Father giveth you the true bread out of heaven.**—Jesus seizes this reference to the manna to show that this manna was not real spiritual bread sent down from God. He again emphasizes the truth he tells them. "It was not Moses that gave you the bread out of heaven." The bread Moses gave you came not from heaven. It was material (earthly) bread for the support of the body. "My Father giveth you the true bread." The true bread that God gave from heaven was spiritual, and will bring spiritual life. In verse 49 he tells them, "Your fathers ate the manna in the wilderness, and they died." Hence, it could not be the spiritual bread that comes from heaven. Verse 50: "This is the bread which cometh down out of heaven, that a man may eat thereof, and not die." In verse 51 he says: "I am the living bread which came down out of heaven: if any man eat of this bread, he shall live for ever." The manna that Moses gave the fathers was an earthly (perishable) food—a type of the true bread that comes from heaven in the person of Jesus Christ that brought eternal life to man.

33 **For the bread of God is that which cometh down out of heaven, and giveth life unto the world.**—He follows up this thought by the assurance that he was the true bread from

Lord, evermore give us this bread. 35 Jesus said unto them, I am the

God and he came to give life to the world. The bread that would strengthen their souls and give to them eternal life was Jesus Christ, which came down from heaven, and who giveth life to the world. Jesus Christ "brought life and immortality to light through the gospel." (2 Tim. 1: 10.) "I am the way, and the truth, and the life: no one cometh unto the Father, but by me." (John 14: 6.) Jesus came to earth to make known to man the life—the immortal life at the right hand of the Father, and to guide men into this life. He alone can give life to man.

34 **They said therefore unto him, Lord, evermore give us this bread.**—When they heard such great good would come from it they asked for this bread that they might not die, but live the fleshly life forever. This is the same effect it had upon the woman at the well in Samaria. She asked for the water that she might have to draw no more, for the well was deep. These people desired the bread that would perpetuate life without labor, but they had no conception that it meant to give up all the fleshly enjoyments and to deny self and live the life of holiness that Jesus lived. "Upon this many of his disciples went back, and walked no more with him." (Verse 66.) The desertion was so general that Jesus asked of his apostles, "Would ye also go away?" Simon Peter answered, "To whom shall we go? thou hast the words of eternal life." The meaning is, these people were willing to eat the food he provided, and to enjoy the blessings he bestowed, but when they saw that his teaching meant a denial of self to serve and honor him—a walk with Jesus in a life of humility and self-denial—they forsook him. It is yet true that the great masses of mankind are willing to enjoy the blessings of God, but not to obey him. They are willing to reign with him, but not to suffer with him. But none may reign with him unless they are willing to suffer with him. None can enjoy the blessings unless they are willing to serve him here.

bread of life: he that cometh to me shall not hunger, and he that believeth
on me shall never thirst. 36 But I said unto you, that ye have seen me,
and yet believe not. 37 All that which the Father giveth me shall come
unto me; and him that cometh to me I will in no wise cast out. 38 For I

---

35 **Jesus said unto them, I am the bread of life: he that cometh to me shall not hunger, and he that believeth on me shall never thirst.**—Jesus is the spiritual bread and will give spiritual and eternal life to all who obey him. They, like the woman of Samaria, found it difficult to rise above the thoughts of their fleshly body and its appetites and desires. This is an explanation of what is meant. Jesus himself was the bread of life. To believe on him with an earnest, living faith was to eat his flesh and drink his blood. So he that came to him by faith and submission to him would never hunger, and he that believed on him should never thirst—that is, he who comes to Jesus trusts in him, is led by him, does his will, as did the Father's will, shall have all the wants of the soul satisfied. This was an important lesson and brought the requirements of self-denial home to his followers so that all fair-weather followers forsook him and followed him no more.

36 **But I said unto you, that ye have seen me, and yet believe not.**—The reason they could not receive that life was that he had shown himself in his teachings and many works he had done in their presence, yet they refused to believe in him so refused to do the work of God.

37 **All that which the Father giveth me shall come unto me;**—There is a recognition in the scripture that certain classes of persons with honest hearts desirous to know and do the right are God's people, and will do what God desires them to do. That class is here represented as given to Christ by God. In the tenth chapter Christ speaks of having sheep not of the flock then with him, referring to the Gentiles who would receive him when he was preached to them. Again, at Corinth God told Paul, "I have much people in this city" (Acts 18: 9, 10) before any of them had confessed him. Certain persons fitted in character to receive God's word are called his people before they confess him. This explains the calling and predestination of the Bible. God has called and predestinated to eternal life all willing to receive him.

am come down from heaven, not to do mine own will, but the will of him
that sent me. 39 And this is the will of him that sent me, that of all that
which he hath given me I should lose nothing, but should raise it up at the
last day. 40 For this is the will of my Father, that every one that beholdeth
the Son, and believeth on him, should have eternal life; and [5]I will raise
him up at the last day.

[5]Or, *that I should raise him up*

and him that cometh to me I will in no wise cast out.—All that class Jesus receives. Some who are not of this class receive him temporarily, but lack depth of character and under temptation fall away. Judas was an example of this character of people.

38 **For I am come down from heaven, not to do mine own will, but the will of him that sent me.**—The end of all God's dealings with men is to bring them to do the will of God. Jesus came from heaven to earth to lead men in this way. He had no will of his own apart from the will of God. To do that will was the supreme and only object of Jesus and should be of his followers.

39 **And this is the will of him that sent me, that of all that which he hath given me I should lose nothing, but should raise it up at the last day.**—God's will was that Jesus should save all who would believe and follow him. This he does. That some start out to follow, turn back, walk with him no more, and are lost does not disprove this truth.

40 **For this is the will of my Father, that every one that beholdeth the Son, and believeth on him, should have eternal life; and I will raise him up at the last day.**—It is God's will that all who will obey Jesus should have eternal life. These Jesus will raise up at the last day. They have the faculties to see and believe that God desires them to use them in believing the truths he presents them. If they refuse they damn themselves.

5. THE PEOPLE MURMUR AND JESUS REITERATES. 6: 41-51.

41 The Jews therefore murmured concerning him, because he said, I am
the bread which came down out of heaven. 42 And they said, Is not this

41 **The Jews therefore murmured concerning him, because he said, I am the bread which came down out of heaven.**—The

Jesus, the son of Joseph, whose father and mother we know? how doth
he now say, I am come down out of heaven? 43 Jesus answered and said
unto them, Murmur not among yourselves. 44 No man can come to me,
except the Father that sent me draw him: and I will raise him up in the

Jews did not understand his meaning or see how he could be the bread of life. They looked at it all from a materialistic standpoint.

42 **And they said, Is not this Jesus, the son of Joseph, whose father and mother we know? how doth he now say, I am come down out of heaven?**—They knew his earthly origin, his reputed father and mother, and how could the claim be made? It seemed impossible and absurd to them.

43 **Jesus answered and said unto them, Murmur not among yourselves.**—[This is a rebuke. They were not honest inquirers, but cavilers.]

44 **No man can come to me, except the Father that sent me draw him: and I will raise him up in the last day.**—None could come to Jesus unless taught and drawn by the Father. [Two elements are concerned in coming to Christ. Namely, the *man's will* and the *divine drawing.* No man comes unless he *wills* to come. "Ye will not come to me, that ye may have life." (5: 40.) Jesus said to Jerusalem, "How often would I have gathered thy children . . . and *ye would not.*" Man can refuse to come and God does not compel, but he says "he that *will,* let him take the water of life freely." This is the human side. On the divine side God "draws," not so as to force man's will, but to induce the desire to come. The gospel "is the power of God unto salvation." It is the drawing power. It draws by its manifestation of the love of God, by its revelation of the crucified Savior, and his adaptation to the needs of the soul. If man's will consents, and he yields to the drawing power, he comes. If he "will not," and refuses to be drawn, he does not come. God will not force him. No one comes to Jesus unless he yields his own will and is drawn by the love of the Father manifested in the gospel. He draws men to Christ by the gospel, then Christ takes up the work and will raise them from the dead "in the last day."]

last day. 45 It is written in the prophets, [1]And they shall all be taught of God. Every one that hath heard from the Father, and hath learned, cometh unto me. 46 Not that any man hath seen the Father, save he that is from God, he hath seen the Father. 47 Verily, verily, I say unto you, He that believeth hath eternal life. 48 I am the bread of life. 49 Your fathers ate the manna in the wilderness, and they died. 50 This is the bread which

[1]Is. 54. 13; (Jer. 31. 34?)

45 **It is written in the prophets, And they shall all be taught of God.**—God through all the ages of the past had been trying and making ready a people to receive the Christ when he came. None could receive him save those who had been taught and prepared by God. [Jesus is more explicit how the Father draws men to Christ. It is by teaching men. All *taught of God,* who have heard and learned of the Father, come to Christ.]

Every one that hath heard from the Father, and hath learned, cometh unto me.—This means the same, "If ye believed Moses, ye would believe me; for he wrote of me." (5: 46.) Those who had in faith received the teachings of Moses and the prophets were prepared to receive Jesus. God drew them by the teachings he gave them. And those who had received these teachings of God received Jesus when he came. [It is what one learns from the teaching that makes him willing to come.]

46 **Not that any man hath seen the Father, save he that is from God, he hath seen the Father.**—The drawing of God was through his servants, the prophets, and teachers he had sent into the world. [We do not learn of God by seeing and hearing him personally, but we learn of his will from Jesus.]

47 **Verily, verily, I say unto you, He that believeth hath eternal life.**—Jesus came into the world to give eternal life to those who believe in him. They have it in promise, and the germs of eternal life are implanted in the heart through faith in Christ Jesus. These germs need to be treasured and cultivated that they may bear fruit in the resurrection. [Jesus affirms that faith in him is the source of life.]

48 **I am the bread of life.**—Jesus is the means and source of spiritual and eternal life as bread is the source and support of material life.

49 **Your fathers ate the manna in the wilderness, and they died.**—The manna was the bread given them to support them

cometh down out of heaven, that a man may eat thereof, and not die. 51 I
am the living bread which came down out of heaven: if any man eat of
this bread, he shall live for ever: yea and the bread which I will give is
my flesh, for the life of the world.

---

through the journey to the earthly Canaan, as Jesus was to support them in the journey to the heavenly Canaan. But the manna was not life giving, for those who ate of it died.

50 **This is the bread which cometh down out of heaven, that a man may eat thereof, and not die.**—Those who partook of the true bread of heaven should never die.

51 **I am the living bread which came down out of heaven:** —Jesus himself possessed life and could impart it to others. His life was spiritual and eternal.

if any man eat of this bread, he shall live for ever: yea and the bread which I will give is my flesh, for the life of the world. —To make his will our will and to live according to his will is to eat of his flesh and drink of his blood—make his life our life. To do this is to eat his flesh and drink his blood and his life he gave for the life of the world.

6. MORE MURMURING AND ANOTHER REITERATION. 6: 52-59.

52 The Jews therefore strove one with another, saying, How can this
man give us his flesh to eat? 53 Jesus therefore said unto them, Verily,
verily, I say unto you, Except ye eat the flesh of the Son of man and drink
his blood, ye have not life in yourselves. 54 He that eateth my flesh and
drinketh my blood hath eternal life; and I will raise him up at the last day.

---

52 **The Jews therefore strove one with another, saying, How can this man give us his flesh to eat?**—The Jews in the grossness of their nature could not perceive the spiritual truths and so murmured over the impossibility of the truths.

53 **Jesus therefore said unto them, Verily, verily, I say unto you, Except ye eat the flesh of the Son of man and drink his blood, ye have not life in yourselves.**—Insisted on the truth he had told them and that unless they made his life their life they would have no life—the life he gave—in them.

54 **He that eateth my flesh and drinketh my blood hath eternal life; and I will raise him up at the last day.**—He who makes the life of Jesus his life hath eternal life and Jesus will raise him up to the enjoyment of eternal life at the last day.

55 For my flesh is [2]meat indeed, and my blood is [3]drink indeed. 56 He that eateth my flesh and drinketh my blood abideth in me, and I in him. 57 As the living Father sent me, and I live because of the Father; so he that eateth me, he also shall live because of me. 58 This is the bread which came down out of heaven: not as the fathers ate, and died; he that eateth this bread shall live for ever. 59 These things said he in [4]the synagogue, as he taught in Capernaum.

[2]Gr. *true meat*
[3]Gr. *true drink*
[4]Or, *a synagogue*

---

55 **For my flesh is meat indeed, and my blood is drink indeed.**—The making of the life of Jesus one's life indeed or true spiritual life.

56 **He that eateth my flesh and drinketh my blood abideth in me, and I in him.**—He who makes the life of Jesus his life abides in Jesus and Jesus is in him.

57 **As the living Father sent me, and I live because of the Father;**—The Father has eternal life. He "only hath immortality," and Jesus receives life from him and lives by or through him.

so he that eateth me, he also shall live because of me.—As Jesus receives life from the Father and lives by him, so the disciples were to receive life from Christ and live by or from him. As Jesus made the Father's will his will and so lived by the Father, so we make the will of Jesus our will and live by him.

58 **This is the bread which came down out of heaven: not as the fathers ate, and died; he that eateth this bread shall live for ever.**—He as the bread from heaven possesses the eternal life and those who receive this life from him will never die, but with him live forever. [The food the fathers ate in the wilderness sustained temporary life for a season, but could not impart it, for it was dead food. The bread from heaven is endued with life, and therefore gives eternal life.]

59 **These things said he in the synagogue, as he taught in Capernaum.**—Capernaum was now the home of Jesus and these things were taught in the synagogue there.

7. MURMURING BY THE DISCIPLES.
6: 60-65.

60 Many therefore of his disciples, when they heard *this,* said, This is a
hard saying; who can hear [5]it? 61 But Jesus knowing in himself that his
disciples murmured at this, said unto them, Doth this cause you to stumble?
62 *What* then if ye should behold the Son of man ascending where he was
before? 63 It is the spirit that giveth life; the flesh profiteth nothing: the
words that I have spoken unto you are spirit, and are life. 64 But there

[5]Or, *him*

---

60 **Many therefore of his disciples, when they heard this, said, This is a hard saying; who can hear it?**—Many who claimed to be his disciples and after a kind believed in him when they heard these things were dissatisfied and turned back and no more followed him. These people really believed in him with the power of faith they possessed; but lacked depth of character or strength of character to withstand the fleshly desires and so turned back.

61 **But Jesus knowing in himself that his disciples murmured at this, said unto them, Doth this cause you to stumble?**—Jesus' knowledge of their fleshly appetites called out this question. [The disciples could not take in what had just been said. They expected an earthly king, not a crucified Savior. Hence, they murmured and were offended.]

62 **What then if ye should behold the Son of man ascending where he was before?**—Jesus knowing he would return to the Father from whom he had come asked this question to intimate that they would see or know this, and what would they think if they should see him do it?

63 **It is the spirit that giveth life;**—The trouble was in getting these people to see and understand that he was telling them great spiritual truths and not material and fleshly. The spirit in man is the permanent and abiding principle of his being. God's spirit quickens this spirit of man, giving life to it—eternal life. The flesh and fleshly relations are temporal and will pass away.

the flesh profiteth nothing:—The flesh gives no real profit. The fleshly relation to Abraham on which they relied was no profit.

the words that I have spoken unto you are spirit, and are life.—The words of Jesus were the teachings of the Spirit

are some of you that believe not. For Jesus knew from the beginning who
they were that believed not, and who it was that should [6]betray him. 65
And he said, For this cause have I said unto you, that no man can come
unto me, except it be given unto him of the Father.

[6]Or, *deliver him up*

and would bring life to them who received them. In Christ Jesus the Spirit of God dwells. He is the ever-present representative of the Godhead dwelling in his body here on earth. (Eph. 2: 2.) After man sinned and the world was sin-defiled, God found no true dwelling place on earth among men until the spiritual temple was built. Then, through the Spirit, he dwelt in that temple with his children on earth. There was a material, typical building, the earthly temple; but this was only a shadow of the heavenly power or essence. His word is full of spirit and imbued with life-giving power. "The word of God is the seed of the kingdom." In the seed the germinal, or life principle, dwells. (James 1: 18; 1 Pet. 1: 23.) The germinal principle of life dwells in the seed, and the word of God is an incorruptible seed; it never can be despoiled of its life principle. The Spirit of God dwells in and works through the laws he has given. (Rom. 8: 2.) The quickening principle dwells dormant in the seed until it comes into favorable surroundings, then it germinates or is quickened into a new being. The word of God, as the seed, is received into the heart and it germinates into life. The Spirit of God not only quickens into life, but promotes the growth of the life imparted.

64 **But there are some of you that believe not.**—Notwithstanding all the works and words of Jesus to the Jews, there were many that disbelieved, and he explains it directly to the disciples and the chosen twelve.

For Jesus knew from the beginning who they were that believed not, and who it was that should betray him.—Jesus knew who was lacking in that strength of character that would cause him, when the temptation came, to betray him.

65 **And he said, For this cause have I said unto you, that no man can come unto me, except it be given unto him of the Father.**—Because many would forsake him, and Judas would

betray him, he gave them this warning that none could come except the Father draw him. This class was not drawn by the Father in that they had not hearkened to his teachings. God had given them to him. See verses 44 and 45.

8. JESUS DESERTED BY ALL BUT THE TWELVE. 6: 66-71.

66 Upon this many of his disciples went back, and walked no more with
him. 67 Jesus said therefore unto the twelve, Would ye also go away?
68 Simon Peter answered him, Lord, to whom shall we go? thou [7]hast the
words of eternal life. 69 And we have believed and know that thou art

[7]Or, *hast words*

---

66 **Upon this many of his disciples went back, and walked no more with him.**—Many who were his disciples followed him, learning of him and believing in him, but could not endure the difficulties presented. Their faith was not strong enough to lead them to endure the teaching he presented and turned back from following him.

67 **Jesus said therefore unto the twelve, Would ye also go away?**—A feeling of depression and temporary despondency seems to have crept over the soul of Jesus when he asked this question of the twelve. It would indicate that the great number of his other disciples had left him and gone away.

68 **Simon Peter answered him, Lord, to whom shall we go?**—Peter with his accustomed boldness and frankness responds. He knew of none other who could bring eternal life. That is the only thing worth living for in this world. This indicates the depth of his thoughts and his appreciation of the teaching of Jesus.

thou hast the words of eternal life.—Only the words of Jesus can give us the words of eternal life. [The world may well ask this question. If it turns from Christ, to whom shall it go? He only has the words of eternal life.] Many followed for a time, especially when the loaves and the fishes abounded, but when self-denial was required the multitudes turned back and "walked no more with him." A feeling of discouragement seems to have crept over Jesus and he turned to his disciples and asked, "Would ye also go away?" Of the

the Holy One of God. 70 Jesus answered them, Did not I choose you the twelve, and one of you is a devil? 71 Now he spake of Judas *the son* of Simon Iscariot, for he it was that should [6]betray him, *being* one of the twelve.

multitudes that were taught by him during his mission on earth, only a few were with him at his betrayal and death. A multitude welcomed him to Jerusalem when he came to the Passover feast with shouts of "Hosanna to the King!" In a few days the multitude cried, "Crucify him, crucify him!" One of his chosen twelve betrayed him, another denied him, and all forsook him.

69 **And we have believed and know that thou art the Holy One of God.**—He here gives his full appreciation of Jesus and his mission of guiding to eternal life.

70 **Jesus answered them, Did not I choose you the twelve, and one of you is a devil?**—As Peter had confessed Christ and had given assurance of the confidence of the twelve in him, he in turn assures them he had chosen the twelve as his followers and his disciples and they had the promise of the life that he gave; but that one of the number would fail and be lost. [The shadow of sorrow is still upon his heart.]

71 **Now he spake of Judas the son of Simon Iscariot, for he it was that should betray him, being one of the twelve.**— It was not yet known among the disciples or even Judas that he would betray him. The apostle John writing this years afterward told that Judas was the man whom Jesus knew from the beginning possessed a demon and would betray him.

[Peter having made this confession for himself and the rest of the apostles that they would not depart from Jesus whom they believed to be the true Messiah, the Son of the living God; Christ intimates to Peter that his charity was something too large in promising so much for them all; for there was one traitor among them whose heart was as open to Christ as his face was to them. He meant it of Judas, of whose treachery he gave them warning at this time. Jesus knew Judas was a hypocrite at this time, but did not rebuke Peter for having a better opinion of him than he deserved.]

SECTION THREE.

JESUS AT THE FEAST OF TABERNACLES 7: 1 to 10: 21.

1. AFTER DELAY HE GOES TO THE FEAST. 7: 1-13.

1 And after these things Jesus walked in Galilee: for he would not walk
in Judæa, because the Jews sought to kill him. 2 Now the feast of the
Jews, the feast of tabernacles, was at hand. 3 His brethren therefore said

---

1 **And after these things Jesus walked in Galilee:**—After the conversation narrated in the preceding chapter, he went to Galilee. The Jews in Judea were more zealous as they thought for the law of Moses than those of other sections of the country. They misapprehended what the law taught, and in their misapprehension were bitter against Jesus to prepare for whom the law was given. A false conception of religion frequently hinders the reception of the truth more than a failure to know the truth or to be religious.

for he would not walk in Judaea, because the Jews sought to kill him.—Religion intensifies the feelings and actions of a person. If his feelings and actions are wrongly directed, it intensifies the wrong feelings and actions. So those who misunderstood the law of Moses were more embittered against Jesus than were those who were not very zealous observers of the law.

2 **Now the feast of the Jews, the feast of tabernacles, was at hand.**—The feast of tabernacles commemorated the camping out of the Jews in their journey from Egypt to Canaan. It was combined with the feast of ingathering and began on the fifteenth day of the seventh month and continued seven days.

3 **His brethren therefore said unto him,**—There is no proof that Mary and Joseph did not have other children. God ordained the marriage relation for the good of the human family and for his own glory. It is no derogation from the character of Mary as the mother of Jesus for her to have fulfilled the office of wife to Joseph and have borne other children. Nor is there the least evidence that she did not. Quite

unto him, Depart hence, and go into Judæa, that thy disciples also may
behold thy works which thou doest. 4 For no man doeth anything in secret,
[8]and himself seeketh to be known openly. If thou doest these things, manifest thyself to the world. 5 For even his brethren did not believe on him.
6 Jesus therefore saith unto them, My time is not yet come; but your

[8]Some ancient authorities read *and seeketh it to be known openly*

a number of expressions in the Bible indicate that she did fulfill the duties of wife and mother.

Depart hence, and go into Judaea,—While these brethren seem to have regarded him as something above ordinary men and were willing to see him show his powers, they yet lacked a strong faith in him and his claims to be the Son of God.

that thy disciples also may behold thy works which thou doest.—They thought if he could do anything he should show it on these occasions of the feasts when the multitudes of the Jews came together at Jerusalem. He had some disciples at Jerusalem who had been made at other visits to the city.

4 **For no man doeth anything in secret, and himself seeketh to be known openly.**—[No prophet and inspired teacher. The claim that such teachers seek the multitudes, after which, and in their presence, in the most public manner, exhibit their supernatural power.] If a man expects the world to honor him he must keep himself and his work before the world was the idea of these brethren of Jesus. This is the world's idea.

If thou doest these things, manifest thyself to the world.—["If" implies that his brethren were doubters and the following verse asserts that they were unbelievers.]

5 **For even his brethren did not believe on him.**—[Note that a clear distinction is made between his brethren and his disciples. The distinction is more clear in Matt. 12: 47. Later they became believers. (Acts 1: 14.)]

6 **Jesus therefore saith unto them, My time is not yet come;**—His time for fully manifesting himself to the world had not yet come, so he could not then go up to the feast. [He had by slow degrees and in different ways manifested himself to the people, but the time for the great and final lesson of the cross, the grave, the resurrection, and ascension had not come. His full and complete manifestation to the world

time is always ready. 7 The world cannot hate you; but me it hateth,
because I testify of it, that its works are evil. 8 Go ye up unto the feast:
I go not up [9]unto this feast; because my time is not yet fulfilled. 9 And
having said these things unto them, he abode *still* in Galilee.

[9]Many ancient authorities add *yet*

will be at his second coming when "every eye shall see him."]

but your time is always ready.—They with no special mission save to follow the world could go to the feast at any time. [He who has a mission must make ready for it. He who has a message for the world must educate it to receive it.]

7 **The world cannot hate you;**—[For it would, in that case, hate those who have its spirit and were of it. It will not hate itself. It only hates those who rebuke its sins and oppose its ways.]

but me it hateth, because I testify of it, that its works are evil.—He expected when he went to Jerusalem to call out the hatred of the world by his condemnation of the evil of the world. As they were of the world and did not condemn the world, the world would not hate them. [It has always hated those who expose and denounce its sins. Isaiah, Jeremiah, and John the Baptist all suffered because they rebuked sin in high places. When Jesus came exposing the corruptions of the priests, the hypocrisy of the Pharisees, the worldliness and debauchery of the Sadducees and Herodians, it was inevitable that he should be hated, persecuted, and put to death. But the world still hates him. The hate of such men as Voltaire, Tom Paine, and Ingersoll, and of all their followers is due to the fact that Christ and his church are a rebuke to, and condemnation of, their lives.]

8 **Go ye up unto the feast: I go not up unto this feast; because my time is not yet fulfilled.**—They could go when they pleased. There were reasons why he could not then go. His time was not fully come. [He uses the present, not future tense. The thought is, I am not *now* going. It would have doubtless defeated his purpose had he gone with those who were determined that he should make an exhibition of himself. It cannot be determined from this whether he had *yet* purposed to go at all.]

10 But when his brethren were gone up unto the feast, then went he also up, not publicly, but as it were in secret. 11 The Jews therefore sought him at the feast, and said, Where is he? 12 And there was much murmuring among the multitudes concerning him: some said, He is a good man; others said, Not so, but he leadeth the multitude astray. 13 Yet no man spake openly of him for fear of the Jews.

9 **And having said these things unto them, he abode still in Galilee.**—What the reasons were are not known, but he remained in Galilee.

10 **But when his brethren were gone up unto the feast, then went he also up, not publicly, but as it were in secret.**—His brethren went to the feast while he for the time tarried in Galilee for a day or two, and then quietly, without showing himself to the world, went up.

11 **The Jews therefore sought him at the feast, and said, Where is he?**—The report of the works of Jesus was spread abroad, and at such a gathering it was the general expectation that he would be present and do wonders. Both his enemies and his friends inquired concerning him whether he would come to the feast.

12 **And there was much murmuring among the multitudes concerning him: some said, He is a good man; others said, Not so, but he leadeth the multitude astray.**—He had impressed many of the people that he was a good man, sent from God, others that he was a deceiver. [Truth preached always stirs up the opposition and false charges.]

13 **Yet no man spake openly of him for fear of the Jews.**—This was the talk in a private way among acquaintances, none speaking publicly because the rulers of the Jews had condemned him. [They feared that open discussion would bring condemnation upon themselves from the rulers.]

2. CHRIST TEACHES IN THE TEMPLE AND REFERS TO HIS FIRST VISIT.
7: 14-24.

14 But when it was now the midst of the feast Jesus went up into the temple, and taught. 15 The Jews therefore marvelled, saying, How knoweth

14 **But when it was now the midst of the feast Jesus went up into the temple, and taught.**—About the third day of it.

this man letters, having never learned? 16 Jesus therefore answered them,
and said, My teaching is not mine, but his that sent me. 17 If any man
willeth to do his will, he shall know of the teaching, whether it is of God,
or *whether* I speak from myself. 18 He that speaketh from himself seeketh
his own glory: but he that seeketh the glory of him that sent him, the

Jesus threw off all secrecy or privacy and went into the temple and began openly to teach the people.

15 **The Jews therefore marvelled, saying, How knoweth this man letters, having never learned?**—The familiarity of Jesus with the Jewish law and his readiness in applying it and explaining the teachings were matters of wonder and surprise to all, as these things were usually learned in some of the schools. As Paul attended the school of Gamaliel, Jesus attended none of these schools, hence his teaching in these things was a surprise to all who knew it.

16 **Jesus therefore answered them, and said, My teaching is not mine, but his that sent me.**—The teaching of Jesus was not from himself. It did not originate with him. It was not derived from studying and learning of men. It was bestowed upon him by God who sent him. Jesus again brings out that he brought no theory or system or will of his own, but he came to do the will of his Father who sent him.

17 **If any man willeth to do his will, he shall know of the teaching, whether it is of God, or whether I speak from myself.**—If any one really desires to do the will of God, he shall be enabled to know that this doctrine is from God and did not originate with Jesus. Does it not involve the conclusion that if any one in the world really desires to do the will of God, he will be brought to know that will and that it is of God and not of man. Is it possible that God would give his Son to die to open the way of salvation to man and then leave one to die in ignorance of that way who would accept it if he knew it? The great hindrance to many knowing the truth is they do not desire the truth and will not walk in it when they know it.

18 **He that speaketh from himself seeketh his own glory: but he that seeketh the glory of him that sent him, the same is true,**—One reason by which he will know the truth is of

same is true, and no unrighteousness is in him. 19 Did not Moses give you
the law, and *yet* none of you doeth the law? Why seek ye to kill me? 20
The multitude answered, Thou hast a demon: who seeketh to kill thee?
21 Jesus answered and said unto them, I did one work, and ye all marvel
because thereof. 22 Moses hath given you circumcision (not that it is of
Moses, but of the fathers); and on the sabbath ye circumcise a man. 23

God is that he who speaks from himself as the author of his teaching seeks his own glory. In doing the will of God it will be so manifest that there is such a complete self-denial and glorification of God that he will know that the teaching did not originate with man.

and no unrighteousness is in him.—The one who denies self and seeks the glory of him sending him gives undeniable testimony that he did not originate his teaching, and that he is righteous.

19 **Did not Moses give you the law, and yet none of you doeth the law? Why seek ye to kill me?**—The leaders of the Jews had determined to kill him for breaking the law of Moses. Moses did not make that law. He received it from God and gave it to the Jews, as Jesus received it from God and gave it to them. None of them kept the law, yet sought to kill him on a charge of breaking the law in healing a man on the Sabbath.

20 **The multitude answered, Thou hast a demon: who seeketh to kill thee?**—At this time they were keeping their purpose to kill him secretly until an opportunity to do it should occur. Some perhaps did not know of it, and they charge him with having a demon in cherishing such a thought.

21 **Jesus answered and said unto them, I did one work, and ye all marvel because thereof.**—Jesus referred to the healing of the impotent man on the Sabbath day.

22 **Moses hath given you circumcision (not that it is of Moses, but of the fathers); and on the sabbath ye circumcise a man.**—Moses whom they claimed to honor had commanded them to circumcise their children as it had come down from Abraham. In obedience to Moses' law they circumcise a child on the eighth day, even if it fell on the Sabbath. Why should setting aside the Sabbath law to heal an afflicted man be worse than setting it aside to circumcise a child?

If a man receiveth circumcision on the sabbath, that the law of Moses may not be broken; are ye wroth with me, because I made [1]a man every whit whole on the sabbath? 24 Judge not according to appearance, but judge righteous judgment.

[1]Gr. *a whole man sound*

23 **If a man receiveth circumcision on the sabbath, that the law of Moses may not be broken; are ye wroth with me, because I made a man every whit whole on the sabbath?**—If God through Moses could set aside the Sabbath law to circumcise a child, why may not God through Jesus set aside the same law to heal an afflicted man? [The law of mercy was older than either circumcision or the Sabbath. His accusers were, therefore, inconsistent in their indignation against him because he had performed an act of mercy in healing a man. Mercy was God's eternal law.]

24 **Judge not according to appearance, but judge righteous judgment.**—Do not judge by the external appearance, but by the real standard of righteousness. [The Jews judged by "appearance" when they condemned Christ for healing the man on the Sabbath, and forgot the eternal principles of righteousness. Some times one law is broken in order to obey a higher law. They should have asked whether this was the case or not before they condemned Jesus, and then "judge with righteous judgment."]

3. A DISCUSSION AMONG THE PEOPLE.
7: 25-36.

25 Some therefore of them of Jerusalem said, Is not this he whom they seek to kill? 26 And lo, he speaketh openly, and they say nothing unto him. Can it be that the rulers indeed know that this is the Christ? 27

25 **Some therefore of them of Jerusalem said, Is not this he whom they seek to kill?**—Some from Jerusalem not of the ruling order knew of their purpose to kill him and were astonished at his boldness.

26 **And lo, he speaketh openly, and they say nothing unto him. Can it be that the rulers indeed know that this is the Christ?**—[They are bewildered. They neither condemn or approve the purpose of the rulers, but they cannot understand

Howbeit we know this man whence he is: but when the Christ cometh, no
one knoweth whence he is. 28 Jesus therefore cried in the temple, teaching
and saying, Ye both know me, and know whence I am; and I am not come
of myself, but he that sent me is true, whom ye know not. 29 I know him;
because I am from him, and he sent me. 30 They sought therefore to take
him: and no man laid his hand on him, because his hour was not yet come.
31 But of the multitude many believed on him; and they said, When the
Christ shall come, will he do more signs than those which this man hath

---

why it is not carried out. Is it possible that the rulers have found out that this is the Christ? Is this the reason for their failure to carry out their purpose?]

27 **Howbeit we know this man whence he is: but when the Christ cometh, no one knoweth whence he is.**—The difficulty came up that when Christ came none would know whence he came, and they thought they knew whence Jesus had come.

28 **Jesus therefore cried in the temple, teaching and saying, Ye both know me, and know whence I am; and I am not come of myself, but he that sent me is true, whom ye know not.**—Jesus knew what was passing in their minds and agreed that they knew in one sense whence he was, yet insisted that he had not come of his own will and they did not know him who had sent him. In that sense they did not know whence he was, or did not know God his Father.

29 **I know him; because I am from him, and he sent me.**—Jesus alone knew the Father and he had come to make known God and his will to the people.

30 **They sought therefore to take him: and no man laid his hand on him, because his hour was not yet come.**—The Jews were anxious to arrest him, but circumstances hindered. These circumstances were controlled by God. [No one could as yet do him harm, for the set time had not come.]

31 **But of the multitude many believed on him; and they said, When the Christ shall come, will he do more signs than those which this man hath done?**—His teaching, his works, his bearing convinced many that he was divine, and if not the Christ would the Messiah do more miracles than Jesus had done in his mission? [They were convinced that he was a teacher from God and were ready to follow him, yet not sure he was the Christ to come. Jesus did not proclaim himself to be the Christ. He demonstrated it by his works.]

done? 32 The Pharisees heard the multitude murmuring these things concerning him; and the chief priests and the Pharisees sent officers to take
him. 33 Jesus therefore said, Yet a little while am I with you, and I go
unto him that sent me. 34 Ye shall seek me, and shall not find me: and
where I am, ye cannot come. 35 The Jews therefore said among themselves, Whither will this man go that we shall not find him? will he go
unto the Dispersion [2]among the Greeks, and teach the Greeks? 36 What
is this word that he said, Ye shall seek me, and shall not find me; and
where I am, ye cannot come?

[2]Gr. *of*

---

32 **The Pharisees heard the multitude murmuring these things concerning him; and the chief priests and the Pharisees sent officers to take him.**—The exchange of thoughts concerning Jesus was quietly talked among the common people. The Pharisees purposed to arrest him and stop all such talk. [They did not want it to spread.]

33 **Jesus therefore said, Yet a little while am I with you, and I go unto him that sent me.**—In a short time Jesus would by his death be taken away from them, and after the crucifixion and resurrection would ascend to God who had sent him.

34 **Ye shall seek me, and shall not find me: and where I am, ye cannot come.**—After a time evil would call upon them and then they would seek him. He would be with God and to him they could never come. [This is plain to use in the light of divine history, but it is not strange that his audience on the other side of the cross did not understand his saying.]

35 **The Jews therefore said among themselves, Whither will this man go that we shall not find him? will he go unto the Dispersion among the Greeks, and teach the Greeks?**—Many Jews were scattered from Judea among the Gentiles, and it was either in ignorance or to ridicule him that they ask this question. [Would he teach them and the Greeks, as well as the Jews of Judea, and the Galileans?]

36 **What is this word that he said, Ye shall seek me, and shall not find me; and where I am, ye cannot come?**—[They could not comprehend. It seems that this bore on their minds. They were perplexed. See verse 34.]

4. CHRIST'S SPEECH ON LAST DAY OF THE FEAST AND ITS EFFECT.
7: 37-44.

37 Now on the last day, the great *day* of the feast, Jesus stood and cried,
saying, If any man thirst, let him come unto me and drink. 38 He that
believeth on me, as the scripture hath said, [3]from within him shall flow
rivers of living water. 39 But this spake he of the Spirit, which they that
believed on him were to receive: [4]for the Spirit was not yet *given;* because

[3]Gr. *out of his belly*
[4]Some ancient authorities read *for the Holy Spirit was not yet given*

---

37 **Now on the last day, the great day of the feast, Jesus stood and cried, saying, If any man thirst, let him come unto me and drink.**—The feast lasted eight days and the last day was a holy convocation, and it had come to be the greatest day of the feast. On this day he called to all who thirsted to come to him and drink the waters of salvation. [The eighth or last day of the feast probably was devoted more to rejoicing and thanksgiving for the blessings of the year and for the hope of Israel. It was called "the great day of the feast."]

38 **He that believeth on me, as the scripture hath said, from within him shall flow rivers of living water.**—The Holy Spirit would come as the representative of God on earth after his ascension to his Father and this he foretells under this figure. ["Believing" is equal to "coming" in verse 37, showing that faith is the means that brings us to Christ. It is a live, active faith; not a dead or inactive one.]

39 **But this spake he of the Spirit, which they that believed on him were to receive:**—[This makes Acts 2 the best commentary on verse 38. Luther says, "So St. Peter, by one sermon on the day of Pentecost, as by a rushing of water, delivered three thousand men from the devil's kingdom, washing them in an hour from sin, death, and Satan."]

for the Spirit was not yet given; because Jesus was not yet glorified.—[Observe (1) that the Holy Spirit was not given until after the death and ascension of Christ; (2) the disciples of Christ did not become "rivers of living water" until the Spirit was sent. This marks Pentecost as the beginning of the preaching of the gospel authoritatively by his disciples.

Jesus was not yet glorified. 40 *Some* of the multitude therefore, when they
heard these words, said, This is of a truth the prophet. 41 Others said,
This is the Christ. But some said, What, doth the Christ come out of
Galilee? 42 [1]Hath not the scripture said that the Christ cometh of the
seed of David, and from Bethlehem, the village where David was? 43 So

[1] 2 S. 7. 12 ff.; Mic. 5. 2

Peter's sermon on that day was the first sermon under the great commission, the first declaration of the condition of the gospel, the first preaching by men as the Holy "Spirit gave them utterance." It was after Jesus was glorified that he sent the Spirit, and on Pentecost it was declared, "He hath poured forth this, which ye see and hear."] The Holy Spirit would come to take up his abode in and with men only after the ascension of Jesus to his Father. Jesus said to his disciples: "It is expedient for you that I go away; for if I go not away, the Comforter will not come unto you; but if I go, I will send him unto you." (16: 7.)

40 **Some of the multitude therefore, when they heard these words, said, This is of a truth the prophet.**—[Conflicting views arose among the people. Some said he was "the prophet," spoken of in Deut. 18: 15, and referred to in John 1: 15. All agreed that a prophet was to come at the Messianic period, but some held that he was to be the Messiah himself, and others that he was to be the forerunner. Hence three questions were put to John—"Art thou Elijah? Art thou the prophet? Art thou the Christ?"]

41 **Others said, This is the Christ. But some said, What, doth the Christ come out of Galilee?**—[The opposition denied that he was the Christ, basing their opposition, not upon his character or teaching, but upon the fact that he came from Galilee. Jesus, reared at Nazareth, coming to Jerusalem from Galilee, was supposed by the Jews to have been born there, and they were well aware of the fact Christ was to be born at Bethlehem.]

42 **Hath not the scripture said that the Christ cometh of the seed of David, and from Bethlehem, the village where David was?**—[The Talmud explains Mic. 5: 2 as declaring that Bethlehem should be Christ's birthplace. The wise men

there arose a division in the multitude because of him. 44 And some of them would have taken him; but no man laid hands on him.

---

who came to Jerusalem seeking the young Babe heard the same thing from the priests. It was prophesied that he should be of the seed of David. (Isa. 11: 1; Jer. 23: 5; Psalm 89: 36.)]

43 **So there arose a division in the multitude because of him.**—[They were rent into two parties and there was sharp contention.] The teaching of Jesus impressed his hearers variously. Some thought he must be a prophet, some that he was the Christ, others could not see how he could be the Christ, for the Christ was to come out of Bethlehem. The very prophecies to which they referred to prove him not the Christ really confirmed that he was the Christ and only their ignorance of where he was born obscured the proof or what really confirmed the truth to those who knew the facts hid the truth from those ignorant of these facts. It is not infrequently so with men. Their ignorance often changes proof of what is true into evidence against the truth.

44 **And some of them would have taken him; but no man laid hands on him.**—The division among the people seems to have secured him from arrest.

5. CONFUSION AMONG CHIEF PRIESTS AND PHARISEES. 7: 45-52.

45 The officers therefore came to the chief priests and Pharisees; and they said unto them, Why did ye not bring him? 46 The officers answered,

---

45 **The officers therefore came to the chief priests and Pharisees; and they said unto them, Why did ye not bring him?**—The Pharisees had evidently sent officers to arrest Jesus. While waiting their opportunity to do it privately, they had listened to him and in common with the people were surprised and pleased with his preaching.

46 **The officers answered, Never man so spake.**—When they returned without him, they gave his teaching as the reason of failure to arrest him.

Never man so spake. 47 The Pharisees therefore answered them, Are ye
also led astray? 48 Hath any of the rulers believed on him, or of the
Pharisees? 49 But this multitude that knoweth not the law are accursed.
50 Nicodemus saith unto them (he that came to him before, being one of
them), 51 Doth our law judge a man, except it first hear from himself
and know what he doeth? 52 They answered and said unto him, Art thou
also of Galilee? Search, and [2]see that out of Galilee ariseth no prophet.

[2]Or, *see: for out of Galilee &c.*

47, 48 **The Pharisees therefore answered them, Are ye also led astray? Hath any of the rulers believed on him, or of the Pharisees?**—The Pharisees seemed to think if no Pharisee or officer was carried away with the preaching none should. These subordinates ought to defer their faith to those of the honored classes. This spirit prevails largely among religious teachers in this age. [Have any of the rulers believed? By rulers are meant the Sanhedrin. In the matter of deciding on the claims of the Messiah they hold that the judgment of the "rulers" must be decisive.]

49 **But this multitude that knoweth not the law are accursed.**—In their estimation those who did not thus defer to them were accursed. [They are ignorant of the law and are accursed. On account of their ignorance they are easily led astray.]

50 **Nicodemus saith unto them (he that came to him before, being one of them),**—Nicodemus who came to Jesus to hear of him (3: 1-15) appears upon the scene the second time. He was not one of the rulers preparing to arrest Jesus. He was a friend of Jesus, but not one of his worshipers.

51 **Doth our law judge a man, except it first hear from himself and know what he doeth?**—The law of the Jews required this fairness as all just and fair laws do and Nicodemus appeals to this law as a benefactor to Jesus.

52 **They answered and said unto him, Art thou also of Galilee? Search, and see that out of Galilee ariseth no prophet.**—Without answering his objection as to the law, they assume that he is a disciple of Jesus and object to the claims on the ground that the Christ would not come out of Galilee ignorant of the fact that Jesus was born in Bethlehem. ["Out of Galilee ariseth no prophet" is an untrue statement. Jonah

was of Galilee (2 Kings 14: 25); Elijah probably so (1 Kings 17: 1); and Nahum also (Nah. 1: 1.)]

6. DISCUSSION ABOUT THE WOMAN TAKEN IN ADULTERY. 7: 53 to 8: 11.

53 [8]And they went every man unto his own house.
1 But Jesus went unto the mount of Olives. 2 And early in the morning
he came again into the temple, and all the people came unto him; and he
sat down, and taught them. 3 And the scribes and the Pharisees bring a
woman taken in adultery; and having set her in the midst, 4 they say unto

[8]Most of the ancient authorities omit John 7. 53-8. 11. Those which contain it vary much from each other

53 **And they went every man unto his own house.**—[The session of the Sanhedrin broke up and each member went to his own home.]

1 **But Jesus went unto the mount of Olives.**—This is the earliest mention of the Mount of Olives with the visits of Jesus. The mount is situated on the east side of Jerusalem, its ascent beginning just on the suburbs of the city. From its top the city can be overlooked. It was from this mount that Jesus overlooked the city on his last visit to Jerusalem and wept over its coming ruin and desolation in terms of such tender pathos and sorrow. On its eastern slope the villages of Bethany and Bethphage are situated. The former was the home of Martha and Mary and Lazarus, the strong personal friends of Jesus, whose house seems to have been the chief stopping place of Jesus when in Jerusalem. He had strong personal friends in Bethphage as well as Bethany. He was now when in Jerusalem likely spending his nights with this family as he did during the last week of his sojourn on earth.

2 **And early in the morning he came again into the temple, and all the people came unto him; and he sat down, and taught them.**—Spending his nights at Olivet, he returned early in the morning to teach in the temple.

3 **And the scribes and the Pharisees bring a woman taken in adultery; and having set her in the midst,**—In some of the early manuscripts this account of the woman is wanting. Some conclude that it is not genuine. But it seems to have

him, Teacher, this woman hath been taken in adultery, in the very act. 5
[4]Now in the law Moses commanded us to stone such: what then sayest
thou of her? 6 And this they said, trying him, that they might have *whereof*
to accuse him. But Jesus stooped down, and with his finger wrote on the

[4]Lev. 20. 10; Dt. 22. 22f.

---

the divine stamp upon it by the spirit and wisdom in which it was treated.

4 **they say unto him, Teacher, this woman hath been taken in adultery, in the very act.**—The case was brought before Jesus by his enemies in the effort to find ground for accusing him.

5 **Now in the law Moses commanded us to stone such: what then sayest thou of her?**—The law of Moses required that one guilty of adultery should be stoned to death. (Deut. 22: 23.) The law had fallen into disuse at this time. The Roman government forbade the Jews inflicting capital punishment without the sanction of the Roman ruler. The Romans did not hold adultery a ground for capital punishment, and would not sanction the death of one for this offense. Then the character and temper of Jesus made it certain that he would not have ordered her executed if he had the power. So they imagined they could force him to set aside the law of Moses and give ground for accusing and condemning him before the people.

6 **And this they said, trying him, that they might have whereof to accuse him. But Jesus stooped down, and with his finger wrote on the ground.**—Jesus was not quick to answer. He allowed them to press the point and fully commit themselves. He knew they all had been guilty of the same sin at some time in their lives. [The dilemma they wished to get him in was somewhat like that of the tribute money. To affirm the binding validity and force of the law of Moses would be to advise a course of action contrary to the Roman law. On the other hand, if he set aside this law it would make him liable to the charge of breaking this law which would be an aid in killing his influence with the Jews. In one case they would accuse him to the Romans and place him under civil authority; in the other they could denounce

ground. 7 But when they continued asking him, he lifted up himself, and said unto them, He that is without sin among you, let him first cast a stone at her. 8 And again he stooped down, and with his finger wrote on the ground. 9 And they, when they heard it, went out one by one, beginning from the eldest, *even* unto the last: and Jesus was left alone, and the woman,

him as setting aside the law of Moses. This is the only recorded instance where Jesus ever wrote a line. What he wrote at this time no one knows for the reason it is not recorded.]

7 **But when they continued asking him, he lifted up himself, and said unto them, He that is without sin among you, let him first cast a stone at her.**—The law of Moses required the witness to cast the first stone. "The hand of the witnesses shall be first upon him to put him to death, and afterward the hand of all the people. So thou shalt put away the evil from the midst of thee." (Deut. 17: 7.) The simplicity and ease with which he caught those in the trap set for him marks the record as genuine. [They were determined to succeed so kept pressing the question, "What then sayest thou?" His answer was like a bolt of lightning. It affirmed nothing, set them back on their own hearts and bade them thus decide. It was as if he had said to them "Wherefore thou art without excuse, O man, whosoever thou art that judgest: for wherein thou judgest another, thou condemnest thyself; for thou that judgest dost practise the same things."]

8 **And again he stooped down, and with his finger wrote on the ground.**—He stooped again to write doubtless to give them opportunity to do what they desired free from restraint of observation.

9 **And they, when they heard it, went out one by one, beginning from the eldest, even unto the last: and Jesus was left alone, and the woman, where she was, in the midst.**—Jesus called into activity their own consciences and then left the conscience to direct their course. He decided according to the law and threw the responsibility of executing the law upon them. They slipped out one by one and left him and the woman alone.

where she was, in the midst. 10 And Jesus lifted up himself, and said unto her, Woman, where are they? did no man condemn thee? 11 And she said, No man, Lord. And Jesus said, Neither do I condemn thee: go thy way; from henceforth sin no more.

---

10 **And Jesus lifted up himself, and said unto her, Woman, where are they? did no man condemn thee?**—[Is there no one to prove you guilty?]

11 **And she said, No man, Lord. And Jesus said, Neither do I condemn thee: go thy way; from henceforth sin no more.**—With none to execute the law, he showed the mercy of God and told her to sin no more. To condemn her was to execute like sentence upon her. This he did not do; but in kindness condemned the sin, warned to sin no more and let the woman go. ["Go" and "sin no more" is a strong implied rebuke of the woman's past life, and charge to repent and lead a different life. It also implies an opening of the door of hope if she complied with the conditions. The Christian's mercy ought to be like that of Jesus—sorrow for the sinner but indignation for sin. It should lead him to seek to save men from sin and to open the door of hope to the fallen.]

7. JESUS DECLARES HIMSELF THE LIGHT OF THE WORLD. 8: 12-20.

12 Again therefore Jesus spake unto them, saying, I am the light of the

---

12 **Again therefore Jesus spake unto them, saying, I am the light of the world:**—Jesus lays stress on the truth, that he came to give light to the world, both intellectual, scientific, and real light on all subjects. "In him was life; and the life was the light of men." (1: 4.) He shed light when the world saw the example set in his life and actions as well as in the precepts he delivered. To follow his precepts and examples is to receive and appropriate the light he gives. [Light was considered as an accompaniment of the presence of God. Moses saw the burning bush in Horeb. When he returned from the presence of the Lord on Sinai his face was shining with heavenly radiance. The pillar of fire that lighted Israel on their journey was the emblem of the presence of

world: he that followeth me shall not walk in the darkness, but shall have
the light of life. 13 The Pharisees therefore said unto him, Thou bearest
witness of thyself; thy witness is not true. 14 Jesus answered and said
unto them, Even if I bear witness of myself, my witness is true; for I know
whence I came, and whither I go; but ye know not whence I come, or
whither I go. 15 Ye judge after the flesh; I judge no man. 16 Yea and if

God. Now Christ, in the presence of both friends and foe, makes a more stupendous claim and affirms that "I am the light of the world," not to the Jews only, but to all nations that will embrace his claims.]

he that followeth me shall not walk in the darkness, but shall have the light of life.—[As the pillar of fire lighted and guided the children of Israel on their journey toward the promised land, so shall his followers be lighted by him, and shall have not only light, but "the light of life" which is the gospel. He fills the life with light in the reception of the word of God.]

13 **The Pharisees therefore said unto him, Thou bearest witness of thyself; thy witness is not true.**—The law of Moses was that a man was not to be convicted upon the testimony of one witness. Speaking of this, it was sometimes said the witness of one man was not true. It only meant that the truth could not be established by the testimony of one witness. Again, a man must have other testimony than his own to establish his claim to a high position. This was spoken of as if a man has no witness for himself save his or his testimony is not true. The Pharisees spoke to Jesus as to his claims to be the Son of God.

14 **Jesus answered and said unto them, Even if I bear witness of myself, my witness is true; for I know whence I came, and whither I go; but ye know not whence I come, or whither I go.**—Jesus shows that even in this case his testimony could be relied on, as he knew whence he came and others did not, and they had no knowledge whence he came or whither he went.

15 **Ye judge after the flesh;**—They judged after the outward appearance. [They were fleshly—of the world and looked upon outward appearances, material forms and, like the world, judged accordingly. To such characters he is a

I judge, my judgment is true; for I am not alone, but I and the Father
that sent me. 17 Yea and in your law it is written, [6]that the witness of two
men is true. 18 I am he that beareth witness of myself, and the Father
that sent me beareth witness of me. 19 They said therefore unto him,

[6]Comp. Dt. 19. 15; 17. 6

riddle; to the "Jews a stumblingblock, and unto Gentiles foolishness."]

I judge no man.—He judged no man on such grounds. His was a righteous judgment, knowing the full truth concerning himself. [He knows the hearts of men—the most profound secret—but he lets their own works judge them. This will be true in the final judgment.]

16 **Yea and if I judge, my judgment is true; for I am not alone, but I and the Father that sent me.**—But if he should judge his judgment would be correct since God was with him and guided him in his judgment. [His mission into the world was not to judge it, but to save it. He does not refrain from judging it because of incompetence of passing just judgment, for his Father would judge in him and all hearts are "naked and laid open" unto him.]

17 **Yea and in your law it is written, that the witness of two men is true.**—"One witness shall not rise up against a man for any iniquity, or for any sin, in any sin that he sinneth: at the mouth of two witnesses, or at the mouth of three witnesses, shall a matter be established." (Deut. 19: 15.) This law was carried into the New Testament. (Matt. 18: 16; 2 Cor. 13: 1.) [The Jews accepted this law as from God. Note, that Jesus did not say *our* law, but "your law." Strange, but nevertheless true, he never classes himself with the Jews.]

18 **I am he that beareth witness of myself,**—[In addition to his own testimony that he came from the Father, there were his mighty works bearing the same testimony. "We know," said Nicodemus, "that thou art a teacher come from God; for no one can do these signs that thou doest, except God be with him.]

and the Father that sent me beareth witness of me.—He gave the two witnesses in behalf of his claims. His could be accepted inasmuch as the Father wrought through him.

Where is thy Father? Jesus answered, Ye know neither me, nor my Father: if ye knew me, ye would know my Father also. 20 These words spake he in the treasury, as he taught in the temple: and no man took him; because his hour was not yet come.

[The witness of the Father is found in all the prophets who spoke of Christ, and also given at his baptism by testimony from heaven. "And Jesus, when he was baptized, went up straightway from the water: and lo, the heavens were opened unto him, and he saw the Spirit of God descending as a dove, and coming upon him; and lo, a voice out of the heavens, saying, This is my beloved Son, in whom I am well pleased." (Matt. 3: 16, 17.)]

19 **They said therefore unto him, Where is thy Father?**—[This question shows on its face that it is full of a scornful spirit, and therefore not asked for information. Because they could not see the Father they, therefore, disputed his word.]

Jesus answered, Ye know neither me, nor my Father:—His claim was that God was his Father and that they did not know God, although they claimed to be his people. [The Pharisees clearly demonstrated that they knew not God by rejecting his Son.]

if ye knew me, ye would know my Father also.—If they knew Jesus as the Messiah who came from God they would know his Father. [Men who reject Christ prove by that act that they know not God, for "in him dwelleth all the fulness of the Godhead bodily." (Col. 2: 9.)]

20 **These words spake he in the treasury,**—The treasury was one of the apartments of the temple. [It was located in the court of the women, probably the most public part of the temple. (Mark 12: 41; Luke 21: 1.) The location of his teaching shows his boldness.]

as he taught in the temple:—[The Sanhedrin held its sessions usually in the hall Gazith, which was located between the court of women and the inner court. Jesus was therefore teaching within hearing of the headquarters of his worst enemies, from whence came the orders shortly before (7: 32, 33) for his arrest.]

and no man took him; because his hour was not yet come.—["Until the Passover, six months in the future that the plans of his enemies should all fail, and his hour should not come, was clearly known to the Lord."]

8. HE ANNOUNCES HIS DEPARTURE AND THE INABILITY OF HIS ENEMIES TO FOLLOW HIM.

8: 21-30.

21 He said therefore again unto them, I go away, and ye shall seek me,
and shall die in your sin: whither I go, ye cannot come. 22 The Jews
therefore said, Will he kill himself, that he saith, Whither I go, ye cannot
come? 23 And he said unto them, Ye are from beneath; I am from above:

---

21 **He said therefore again unto them, I go away, and ye shall seek me, and shall die in your sin:**—He turns to the same thought presented in 7:34. When distressed, and especially when they come to meet God and the judgment, they would seek to come where he is and would not be able to come. [Jesus will depart and return to heaven, and they shall seek him when it is too late and shall not find him, but die in their sins.]

whither I go, ye cannot come.—[The results of rejecting the Savior are that they shall die in their sins and therefore cannot go to heaven where he is. This, together with the next three verses, opposes the doctrine of universal salvation.]

22 **The Jews therefore said, Will he kill himself, that he saith, Whither I go, ye cannot come?**—They had previously asked: Will he go to the dispersed among the Gentiles to teach? Now they ask: Will he kill himself? [The Jews were slow to comprehend the purpose of Jesus, but surely not so dull as their question implies. Probably the question is asked in scorn. Since he had told them that he was going where they could not come, they probably meant that he was going to Gehenna, where all suicides go, rather than to heaven, where all Pharisees expect to go. They held that the darkest regions of the underworld were reserved for those who were guilty of suicide.]

23 **And he said unto them, Ye are from beneath; I am from above:**—In answer to the question of killing himself, he tells them that he is from heaven and will after his death return

ye are of this world; I am not of this world. 24 I said therefore unto you, that ye shall die in your sins: for except ye believe that I am *he,* ye shall die in your sins. 25 They said therefore unto him, Who art thou? Jesus said unto them, [1]Even that which I have also spoken unto you from the beginning. 26 I have many things to speak and to judge concerning you: howbeit he that sent me is true; and the things which I heard from him,

[1]Or, *Altogether that which I also speak unto you*

there. [They had referred to the underworld in their question to each other so Jesus in his reply to them states where each are from and that when he departs he will go to the place from whence he came.]

ye are of this world; I am not of this world.—They will tend downward in the world to come. [They will go to the place for which they are prepared, while he goes to his Father.]

24 **I said therefore unto you, that ye shall die in your sins: for except ye believe that I am he, ye shall die in your sins.**—Because of their earthly or fleshly nature, they would die in their sins and could not come to him. [The only way to escape from the doom of the wicked, either for these Jews or any one else, is here stated by the Lord. Unbelief will damn the world. A living, active faith in Christ is the only thing that leads to heaven. While they were unsaved, yet there was one ray of hope for escape, namely, believing in Christ. He who dies in unbelief dies in sin and therefore dies without hope.]

25 **They said therefore unto him, Who art thou? Jesus said unto them, Even that which I have also spoken unto you from the beginning.**—The statement that they would die in their sins and never be able to come where he will be stirred their indignation and they ask, "Who art thou?" Jesus had claimed from the beginning to be of his Father God.

26 **I have many things to speak and to judge concerning you: howbeit he that sent me is true; and the things which I heard from him, these speak I unto the world.**—Jesus had come to make known the will of God to the world. He at all times held out that what he taught was not from himself, but was the will of God, and God was true.

these speak I unto the world. 27 They perceived not that he spake to them
of the Father. 28 Jesus therefore said, When ye have lifted up the Son
of man, then shall ye know that [2]I am *he,* and *that* I do nothing of myself,
but as the Father taught me, I speak these things. 29 And he that sent me
is with me; he hath not left me alone; for I do always the things that are
pleasing to him. 30 As he spake these things, many believed on him.

[2]Or, *I am* he: *and I do*

27 **They perceived not that he spake to them of the Father.**—They did not recognize that their God was his Father. [Their minds were so full of earthly things that they did not care to heed spiritual things.]

28 **Jesus therefore said, When ye have lifted up the Son of man,**—He was to be lifted up on the cross. This foretold the manner of his death [and proved his divinity. No one but a divine being could foretell the future.]

then shall ye know that I am he,—After he was crucified they would know by the signs following that he is the Son of God, and that the Father was with and in him. Even those who failed to believe on him owned his divine power. [His resurrection would be the grounds of an increase in discipleship. Fifty days after his crucifixion about three thousand in one day obeyed the gospel and became his followers. A few weeks later other thousands did likewise. The very act that his enemies hoped would blot his name from history was the means of filling the world with obedient believers. Jesus on the cross became a badge of honor instead of a symbol of shame. It is the central act and foundation of the Christian religion. It gives spiritual life to man.]

and that I do nothing of myself, but as the Father taught me, I speak these things.—[He was his Father's agent and did nothing not authorized by him.]

29 **And he that sent me is with me; he hath not left me alone; for I do always the things that are pleasing to him.**—The ground for the Father's presence with Jesus is that he always did the will of his Father. God is with all who do his will.

30 **As he spake these things, many believed on him.**—[Their faith was produced by the testimony presented by him.]

9. HE TELLS THE JEWS HOW TO BE FREE.
8: 31-45.

31 Jesus therefore said to those Jews that had believed him, If ye abide in my word, *then* are ye truly my disciples; 32 and ye shall know the truth, and the truth shall make you free. 33 They answered unto him, We

---

31 **Jesus therefore said to those Jews that had believed him, If ye abide in my word, then are ye truly my disciples;**—The continuance in his will is the only test of true discipleship. This shows that to accept the truth and not follow it up by continuing to obey it will not save. One act of obedience does not free from sin, but a continuance in the words of God alone can free from sin and its direful results. It is a great mistake to think that one act frees us from sin. When we show our faith in God by compliance with his prescribed conditions of forgiveness he remits the penalties of past sins and places us in a condition to go forward in his service and thus secure freedom from the dominion and effects of sin; but it is only the persistent walk in keeping the words of Jesus that can free us from the bondage and condemnation of sin and fit us for companionship with God and his children in his own blessed home. Without this there can be no salvation with God. It is the continuance in the words of Jesus Christ that fits for salvation.

32 **and ye shall know the truth, and the truth shall make you free.**—To continue in the word of God is more than to obey the positive precept that brings into Christ, and now and then to attend upon the services of the Lord's house. To continue in the word of God is to take that word into our hearts, to take the spirit inspired and that dwells in that word, into our hearts and let that spirit infuse itself into our souls, so that the Spirit of Christ will dwell in us, will lead us, will be our Spirit and will inspire our feelings, will control our thoughts, mold our actions, and guide our lives in all things so that our bodies will become the temples of the Spirit of God and our lives will bear the fruits of the Spirit of God dwelling within us. To continue in his word is to make that word the supreme law of our daily lives that it may convert our souls, so that we may breathe continually an atmosphere

are Abraham's seed, and have never yet been in bondage to any man: how
sayest thou, Ye shall be made free? 34 Jesus answered them, Verily, verily,
I say unto you, Every one that committeth sin is the bondservant of sin.
35 And the bondservant abideth not in the house for ever: the son abideth

impregnated with the Spirit of God in our hearts that our souls may delight, find their joy and happiness in doing God's law.

33 **They answered unto him,**—[Probably not the believing, but the unbelieving Jews.]

We are Abraham's seed, and have never yet been in bondage to any man: how sayest thou, Ye shall be made free?—They did not understand to what the freedom applied, and insisted that since they were the seed of Abraham they were never in bondage to any man so did not need to be made free. It is just as important that we continue as Abraham did to walk in his service as it is that we enter his service; it is just as important that we follow on in faithful obedience to the will of God as it is that we believe in him. Importance is given to faith because faith leads to a continued walk in the words of God. A faith that does not lead to this is a dead faith that brings no good to man. It brings evil because it involves a degree of knowledge of God and his will. He that knows his Master's will and does it not shall be beaten with added stripes because of this knowledge. One who thinks he is helped by faith, when that faith does not lead to a continued life walk in the words of Jesus Christ, is deceived. The purpose and end of that walk is the training and schooling of the spirit of man into a oneness with the Spirit of God.

34 **Jesus answered them, Verily, verily, I say unto you, Every one that committeth sin is the bondservant of sin.**—This is the most cruel slavery. They were slow to understand his meeting, and he plainly declares it. [He who continues in sin is in slavery to Satan.]

35 **And the bondservant abideth not in the house for ever: the son abideth for ever.**—A slave is not personally connected with the family. The son is the heir and permanent member of the family.

for ever. 36 If therefore the Son shall make you free, ye shall be free
indeed. 37 I know that ye are Abraham's seed; yet ye seek to kill me,
because my word [3]hath not free course in you. 38 I speak the things which
I have seen with [4]*my* Father: and ye also do the things which ye heard
from *your* father. 39 They answered and said unto him, Our father is
Abraham. Jesus saith unto them, If ye [5]were Abraham's children, [6]ye would

[3]Or, *hath no place in you*
[4]Or, *the Father: do ye also therefore the things which ye heard from the Father*
[5]Gr. *are*
[6]Some ancient authorities read *ye do the works of Abraham*

36 **If therefore the Son shall make you free, ye shall be free indeed.**—The son, the heir, could give lasting freedom, but the servant could not make free.

37 **I know that ye are Abraham's seed;**—He knew they were Abraham's seed after the flesh but their spirit was not like Abraham's. [The civil register probably represented a genuine descent in the flesh, but there is something far more important than this, without which this is nothing.]

yet ye seek to kill me, because my word hath not free course in you.—[His word had penetrated their hearts and made them for the time being believers, but it had no further development; it had made no *advance.* On the contrary, they had, after believing for a time, again gone back. The implied conclusion is that they were not Abraham's seed in the best sense.]

38 **I speak the things which I have seen with my Father: and ye also do the things which ye heard from your father.**—Both Jesus and the Jews followed the spirit of their fathers. Jesus spoke the words of God. [He is drawing a sharp contrast between the source of their conduct and his. The devil was their father (44) and seeking to kill Jesus was evidence that they were doing their father's bidding.]

39 **They answered and said unto him, Our father is Abraham.**—They refused to own that they had any father save Abraham. Jesus was speaking of spiritual relations, and they did not receive the spirit of Abraham.

Jesus saith unto them, If ye were Abraham's children, ye would do the works of Abraham.—[They were the offspring of Abraham according to the flesh, but spiritually they had another father whom they served. (44.)]

do the works of Abraham. 40 But now ye seek to kill me, a man that
hath told you the truth, which I heard from God: this did not Abraham.
41 Ye do the works of your father. They said unto him, We were not born
of fornication; we have one Father, *even* God. 42 Jesus said unto them,
If God were your Father, ye would love me: for I came forth and am come
from God; for neither have I come of myself, but he sent me. 43 Why
do ye not [7]understand my speech? *Even* because ye cannot hear my word.
44 Ye are of *your* father the devil, and the lusts of your father it is your

[7]Or, *know*

---

40 **But now ye seek to kill me, a man that hath told you the truth, which I heard from God: this did not Abraham.**—If they were Abraham's children after the flesh, they were not after the spirit. Jesus had come into the world to elevate the spiritual man above the fleshly, and the spiritual relations above the fleshly. [Note the uncompromising assertion of Jesus as a messenger from God.]

41 **Ye do the works of your father.**—They showed the spirit of the devil so were his spiritual children.

They said unto him, We were not born of fornication; we have one Father, even God.—As they were the children of Abraham after the flesh and Abraham was a child of God, they insisted that God was their original Father. [They seem now to get a glimpse of the moral sense in which Jesus takes the notion of Sonship, and proceed to assert that they whose lineage on both sides is unimpeachable in the flesh cannot be successfully impeached in the Spirit.]

42 **Jesus said unto them, If God were your Father, ye would love me: for I came forth and am come from God; for neither have I come of myself, but he sent me.**—Jesus kept the spiritual relation before them. If God were your Father you would not oppose me.

43 **Why do ye not understand my speech? Even because ye cannot hear my word.**—Their failure to understand him was because of their fleshly, sensual nature that was cherished among them.

44 **Ye are of your father the devil, and the lusts of your father it is your will to do.**—The devil inspired their course. He is the author of all evil. The devil was their father because they desired to do his will, and while desiring to do

will to do. He was a murderer from the beginning, and standeth not in the truth, because there is no truth in him. [8]When he speaketh a lie, he speaketh of his own: for he is a liar, and the father thereof. 45 But be-

[8]Or, *When* one *speaketh a lie, he speaketh of his own: for his father also is a liar*

his will they could not understand the teachings of Jesus. No man can understand or serve God who desires to follow the devil. Those who desire to do the lust of the devil are the children of the devil.

He was a murderer from the beginning, and standeth not in the truth,—He delights in the corruption and ruin of souls as God delights in their salvation. This implies that the devil was once in the truth, was in heaven, even the atmosphere of heaven; but he loved falsehood better than truth, was cast out of heaven and was carried down to hell. "For if God spared not angels when they sinned, but cast them down to hell, and committed them to pits of darkness, to be reserved unto judgment." (2 Pet. 2: 4.) "And angels that kept not their own principality, but left their proper habitation, he hath kept in everlasting bonds under darkness unto the judgment of the great day." (Jude 6.) "And the great dragon was cast down, the old serpent, he that is called the Devil and Satan, the deceiver of the whole world; he was cast down to the earth, and his angels were cast down with him." (Rev. 12: 9.)

because there is no truth in him. When he speaketh a lie, he speaketh of his own: for he is a liar, and the father thereof. —In lying, falsehood, and deception he was speaking of his own nature and led others with him into ruin.

45 **But because I say the truth, ye believe me not.**—They being children of the devil, after the spirit like him, refuse to hear Jesus because he was of the truth and spoke the truth.

10. HE CHALLENGES THE JEWS TO CONVICT HIM OF SIN. 8: 46-50.

cause I say the truth, ye believe me not. 46 Which of you convicteth me of sin? If I say truth, why do ye not believe me? 47 He that is of God

46 **Which of you convicteth me of sin? If I say truth, why do ye not believe me?**—His works were the ground of his

heareth the words of God: for this cause ye hear *them* not, because ye
are not of God. 48 The Jews answered and said unto him, Say we not well
that thou art a Samaritan, and hast a demon? 49 Jesus answered, I have
not a demon; but I honor my Father, and ye dishonor me. 50 But I seek
not mine own glory: there is one that seeketh and judgeth. 51 Verily,

---

claim to be the Son of God, and he challenges them to convict him of any falsehood or wrong. And if they cannot convict him, why do they not believe me?

47 **He that is of God heareth the words of God: for this cause ye hear them not, because ye are not of God.**—Those who did not honor God in their hearts would not hear God's word. They would hence not listen to or accept his teaching.

48 **The Jews answered and said unto him, Say we not well that thou art a Samaritan, and hast a demon?**—The Samaritans were worse than the Gentiles in the eyes of the Jews. They were a mongrel race that claimed the privileges of the Jews, and the Jews charged that they were all possessed of demons.

49 **Jesus answered, I have not a demon; but I honor my Father, and ye dishonor me.**—Jesus insisted that he honored the Father by doing his will, and that they dishonored him by the charges brought against him.

50 **But I seek not mine own glory: there is one that seeketh and judgeth.**—As an evidence of his righteousness, he was not sent to seek honor for himself, but for another. God seeks and will judge.

11. JESUS DECLARES THE POWER OF HIS WORK AND HIS PRE-EXISTENCE.
8: 51-59.

verily, I say unto you, If a man keep my word, he shall never see death.
52 The Jews said unto him, Now we know that thou hast a demon. Abra-

---

51 **Verily, verily, I say unto you, If a man keep my word, he shall never see death.**—He makes these strong statements to draw their minds to the spiritual nature of his meaning. On account of their sensual nature, these Jews could not take in his meaning, so he made this strong statement referring to spiritual death.

52 **The Jews said unto him, Now we know that thou hast a demon. Abraham died, and the prophets; and thou sayest,**

ham died, and the prophets; and thou sayest, If a man keep my word, he
shall never taste of death. 53 Art thou greater than our father Abraham,
who died? and the prophets died: whom makest thou thyself? 54 Jesus
answered, If I glorify myself, my glory is nothing: it is my Father that
glorifieth me; of whom ye say, that he is your God; 55 and ye have not
known him: but I know him; and if I should say, I know him not, I
shall be like unto you, a liar: but I know him, and keep his word. 56 Your
father Abraham rejoiced [1]to see my day; and he saw it, and was glad. 57
The Jews therefore said unto him, Thou art not yet fifty years old, and hast

[1]Or, *that he should see*

If a man keep my word, he shall never taste of death.—They, refusing to see his meaning, feel sure that he has a demon to claim exemption for those who believed in him from the death that came to Abraham and the inspired men of old time.

53 **Art thou greater than our father Abraham, who died? and the prophets died: whom makest thou thyself?**—In their minds it was blasphemous to claim higher honor than those ancient worthies received. [Their contention is that Abraham and the prophets heard the word of God and are dead, and shall they, who hear thee, not die?]

54 **Jesus answered, If I glorify myself, my glory is nothing: it is my Father that glorifieth me; of whom ye say, that he is your God;**—To honor himself was selfish and human. But Jesus relied on him whom they claimed as their God to honor him.

55 **and ye have not known him: but I know him; and if I should say, I know him not, I shall be like unto you, a liar: but I know him, and keep his word.**—They were liars on claiming to know him, while refusing him whom God hath sent, and he having come from God and having been sent by him would be a liar to say he did not know God.

56 **Your father Abraham rejoiced to see my day; and he saw it, and was glad.**—Abraham received the promise that in his seed all the nations of the earth should be blessed and by faith he looked forward to the coming of Jesus and rejoiced in the promise. [Abraham saw it in promise by prophetic vision and rejoiced in the hope of the revelation of Christ.]

57 **The Jews therefore said unto him, Thou art not yet fifty years old, and hast thou seen Abraham?**—The Jews persisted in applying this language to Abraham in the flesh who had

thou seen Abraham? 58 Jesus said unto them, Verily, verily, I say unto
you, Before Abraham was born, I am. 59 They took up stones therefore
to cast at him: but Jesus [2]hid himself, and went out of the temple.[3]

[2]Or, *was hidden, and went &c.*
[3]Many ancient authorities add *and going through the midst of them went his way and so passed by*

been dead two thousand years. How could one who had been dead two thousand years see him now living? [They do not give the age of Jesus, but a round period that will cover it. He did not say he had seen Abraham.]

58 **Jesus said unto them, Verily, verily, I say unto you, Before Abraham was born, I am.**—Jesus was the Word that was with God in the beginning, was coexistent with God, and was the Creator of all things in the beginning. He is the same yesterday, today, and forever. Jesus existed long before Abraham did, and still exists after Abraham has died and passed away, hence he speaks of himself as existing at the present, so "Before Abraham was, I am." [Jesus does not merely assert that he *was* before Abraham, but before Abraham was "I am." He identifies himself with the "I am" of the Old Testament.]

59 **They took up stones therefore to cast at him:**—[They considered him a blasphemer. Had he been only a man, he would have been. Stoning was the penalty of blasphemy, so they, without waiting for a trial and a legal verdict, sought to inflict the punishment by mob violence.]

but Jesus hid himself, and went out of the temple.—[Disappeared in the crowd and left the temple. As Jesus and no inspired man ever worked a miracle for their own benefit, we therefore could not attribute his disappearance to a miracle.]

12. JESUS HEALS A MAN BORN BLIND.
9: 1-12.

1 And as he passed by, he saw a man blind from his birth. 2 And his

1 **And as he passed by, he saw a man blind from his birth.**—One born blind would be supposed to be more difficult to heal than one who had gone blind after he was some years of age. He left the temple, where the Jews sought to stone

disciples asked him, saying, Rabbi, who sinned, this man, or his parents, that he should be born blind? 3 Jesus answered, Neither did this man sin, nor his parents: but that the works of God should be made manifest in him.

---

him, and saw a man blind from birth. The presence of the afflicted and suffering seems at all times to have excited the interest and sympathy of Jesus. He was touched with a sense of our infirmities and sympathized with human suffering. So he showed that he was willing to help this blind man.

2 **And his disciples asked him, saying, Rabbi, who sinned, this man, or his parents, that he should be born blind?**—The Jews cherished the idea that since affliction came as the result of sin, every afflicted one, or his parents, had been guilty of sin. The idea seems to have prevailed among the Jews that all bodily afflictions came as the result of the sins of the person afflicted or of his parents. Often men were miraculously smitten with affliction on account of sins. Uzziah was smitten with leprosy for assuming priestly functions. Zacharias was made dumb because he doubted the angel. Sins were visited upon the children to the third and fourth generations. The Jews concluded that affliction is the result of the sin of the person afflicted or of his parents. The Jews had clear ideas of punishment for sin only in this world. In a very general sense all affliction—all suffering—came as the result of sin. Without sin no suffering would have been known on earth. Yet sin once introduced, and mortality inflicted, discord prevailing, disease and affliction have come upon man through his surroundings without moral guilt or sin upon his part. The disciples shared the common belief of the Jews on this subject and asked Jesus whether this blindness was for his own sin or that of the sins of his parents. The Jews said to the blind man (34): "Thou wast altogether born in sins, and dost thou teach us?" This may mean that they thought he was blind because of the sins of his parents so he was altogether born in sin.

3 **Jesus answered, Neither did this man sin, nor his parents:**—A little thought would have convinced them that he could not have been born blind for any sin he had committed. If such an affliction was the result of sin, it must have been

the sin of his parents or his ancestors. All affliction comes as the result of sin. But there is such a long line of ancestors before us all guilty of sin, and the lines of transmission may have become so complicated that infirmity and affliction may come upon us as the result of sins of others than our immediate parents transmitted through the law of transmission from parent to child. The meaning is that neither he nor his parents have sinned that brought this blindness upon him. Jesus knew that when discord had been introduced into the world, and mortality had come upon man, that as a result of weakness in the parents the child might be born blind without sin on the part of parents or child. So he says neither has sinned to bring this blindness.

but that the works of God should be made manifest in him. —So this person had not been born blind for either his or for the sins of his parents, but the result would be to manifest the power and glory of God by Jesus healing him. He said he was blind to this end or purpose. We do not understand that he was afflicted just to afford an opportunity of Jesus healing him. Such for examples are given. There is a similar expression. Speaking of the death of Lazarus Jesus said, "This sickness is not unto death, but for the glory of God, that the Son of God may be glorified thereby." (11: 4.) I do not understand that God directed that this man should be born blind to afford Jesus an opportunity to heal him, nor that Lazarus sickened and died only to give Jesus an opportunity to restore him to life, and so show his power; but in the providence of God these things had happened to these men through the workings of God's laws. The weaknesses and infirmities of the parents, or the surroundings of the persons, had been such as resulted in blindness to the child. He having been born blind, Jesus used the opportunity presented to open his eyes to show forth the glory of God—his power and kindness—and the power of God made known to the world. This was not a denial of the truth that all suffering and disorder came as the result of sin and violation of the divine law. But this blindness was not the direct result of sins in the parents or the child.

4 We must work the works of him that sent me, while it is day: the night cometh, when no man can work. 5 When I am in the world, I am the light

4 **We must work the works of him that sent me, while it is day:**—Jesus declares that he must improve the opportunities of doing the work the Father sent him to do while he lived. God had sent Jesus that in him the works of God should be manifested. Miracles are intended to declare that God is with the man who works the miracle. He works the miracle that declares God is with and speaks through him, then men believe the message is from God. The miracle assures the world the message delivered is a message from God. The miracle is the attestation that the message the man speaks is from God. (4: 34; 5: 19, 26.) "While it is day" means while life is granted, for death would come when he would cease to work. (11: 9; 12: 35; 17: 4.) Jesus must be doing the work of God while life lasted.

the night cometh, when no man can work.—He industriously, yet with no haste, did the work God sent him to do, conscious that his death would soon come when he would cease his work on earth, or the night of death would come when no man worketh.

5 **When I am in the world, I am the light of the world.**—His teaching by precept and example would enlighten the world while he was in it. He came as the light of the world. Jesus is the only light of the world to chase away the gloom and darkness of eternal night and lift up and enlighten the world. This has proved true in the history of the world. There has been no light of science, of religion, of morality save where the will of God is made known through Christ. The fundamental principle of all science is: there is one great first cause and overruling power that directs everything in accordance with fixed and unchangeable laws. Without these as a starting point there can be no science. But this truth has never prevailed save where the Bible is known. Jesus Christ is the great central truth of the Bible, both in the Old and the New Testaments. Without him both are meaningless. Jesus brought the light of divine wisdom to the world. His

of the world. 6 When he had thus spoken, he spat on the ground, and made clay of the spittle, [4]and anointed his eyes with the clay, 7 and said unto him, Go, wash in the pool of Siloam (which is by interpretation, Sent). He went away therefore, and washed, and came seeing. 8 The neighbors

[4]Or, *and with the clay thereof anointed* his *eyes*

teaching consisted in both precept and example. The life of Jesus was his precepts put into practice. This much he said preparatory to opening the eyes of the blind that they might appreciate the lesson taught in the miracle. Jesus is called the Son of righteousness. As the sun gives light to the material world so Jesus gives light to the moral and spiritual world. His business was to dispense light while he lived.

6 **When he had thus spoken,**—What he spoke was explanatory of what he proceeded to do. He had so explained that they could see the miracle was evidence that God was working through him. Jesus desired no honor to himself. He desired them to understand the work was of God.

he spat on the ground, and made clay of the spittle, and anointed his eyes with the clay,—He spat on the ground, mixed dirt with the spittle, so as to make a paste, or clay, and anointed the eyes of the blind man with it. Jesus used means to accomplish this that had no virtue in them to open the blind eyes. This kind of means was used to show that the power and virtue came from God, and not from the means used. [The smaller and more insignificant the means used, the greater was the display of the power of God. Why use means at all when he could speak the word and it would be done? To show that God works through means and will bestow his favors when the means he orders are used or the conditions complied with. Those conditions are often tests of faith. There is nothing in them that reason would show fitted to produce the results, so must be accepted and used in faith. The use of them showed faith in God. The result showed the presence of God.]

7 **and said unto him, Go, wash in the pool of Siloam (which is by interpretation, Sent). He went away therefore, and washed, and came seeing.**—The man was restored to sight.

therefore, and they that saw him aforetime, that he was a beggar, said, Is not this he that sat and begged? 9 Others said, It is he: others said, No, but he is like him. He said, I am *he*. 10 They said therefore unto him, How then were thine eyes opened? 11 He answered, The man that is

There was no healing power in the spittle, in the clay, in the water, nor in the application of the clay or the water. The healing was done by Jesus. In him was the power and virtue to heal. The reception of the clay, the going to the place, and washing were acts of the man, showing his willingness to obey Jesus, and in the obedience Jesus healed him of his blindness.

8 **The neighbors therefore, and they that saw him aforetime, that he was a beggar, said, Is not this he that sat and begged?**—The man was well known, as he had all his life, now forty years old, sat in a public place and begged. The multitude saw him now a healed man, and it created wonder and talk among them. [The change in this man was so great that they could hardly believe their own eyes.]

9 **Others said, It is he: others said, No, but he is like him. He said, I am he.**—Some men are never certain of anything. They are vacillating in their minds and deficient in will power and are never positive as to anything; others reach positive and definite conclusions and can be relied on to be true to them. The healed man seems to have been of this character. Those who knew him best said, "It is he." Those not knowing him so well, or not willing to appear or to be too bold, said, "He is like him." But the blind man said, "I am he." I am the same person who was born blind and sat and begged.

10 **They said therefore unto him, How then were thine eyes opened?**—This was the one question of interest to all. All those persons who knew him and had seen him, satisfied now that he was the same man born blind that had begged amongst them, asked, "How then were thine eyes opened?" It was a wonderful and an unheard-of thing that one should open the eyes of the blind. The demons could exercise some miraculous powers. (10: 21.) When the question as to who Jesus was, and by what power he could work such a miracle, was asked, "Can a demon open the eyes of the blind?" The devil could

called Jesus made clay, and anointed mine eyes, and said unto me, Go to
Siloam, and wash: so I went away and washed, and I received sight. 12
And they said unto him, Where is he? He saith, I know not.

---

do miracles of hurt and destruction to man, but not healing and blessedness.

11 **He answered, The man that is called Jesus made clay, and anointed mine eyes, and said unto me, Go to Siloam, and wash: so I went away and washed, and I received sight.**—He seems not to have known much about Jesus, but tells plainly what was done and the effect. This implied that Jesus possessed miraculous power. [Note the growth in this man's apprehension of Jesus; here he is "the man"—in verse 17 "a prophet," in verse 33 "from God." Thus he gropes toward the final truth.]

12 **And they said unto him, Where is he? He saith, I know not.**—During the excitement produced by finding that the blind man could see Jesus had quietly withdrawn, the blind man knew not whither. [This question probably was asked out of curiosity. Those asking the question were the neighbors of the man born blind.]

13. THE PHARISEES INVESTIGATE THE MIRACLE. 9: 13-34.

13 They bring to the Pharisees him that aforetime was blind. 14 Now
it was the sabbath on the day when Jesus made the clay, and opened his

---

13 **They bring to the Pharisees him that aforetime was blind.**—The Pharisees were the most active of the sects of Judaism. They were the most learned and pretentious, and so the blind man was brought by the executive command to them for further explanation of the occurrence.

14 **Now it was the sabbath on the day when Jesus made the clay, and opened his eyes.**—The Sabbath day was to be kept holy under the law of Moses. The keeping of this holy was the test of loyalty to God under the Mosaic law. Jesus had healed this man on this day, and they concluded that God would not be with a man that would heal on the Sabbath.

eyes. 15 Again therefore the Pharisees also asked him how he received
his sight. And he said unto them, He put clay upon mine eyes, and I
washed, and I see. 16 Some therefore of the Pharisees said, This man is
not from God, because he keepeth not the sabbath. But others said, How
can a man that is a sinner do such signs? And there was a division among
them. 17 They say therefore unto the blind man again, What sayest thou
of him, in that he opened thine eyes? And he said, He is a prophet. 18
The Jews therefore did not believe concerning him, that he had been
blind, and had received his sight, until they called the parents of him that
had received his sight, 19 and asked them, saying, Is this your son, who

---

15 **Again therefore the Pharisees also asked him how he received his sight. And he said unto them, He put clay upon mine eyes, and I washed, and I see.**—Not satisfied, they again question the man. He quietly, but with positiveness, gave the conditions of the healing.

16 **Some therefore of the Pharisees said, This man is not from God, because he keepeth not the sabbath.**—Some thought it a violation of the Sabbath law to heal a man on the Sabbath and that a good man could not violate that law.

But others said, How can a man that is a sinner do such signs? And there was a division among them.—The fact of the healing stared them in the face, and could a sinner heal the blind? The Sabbath law was strict among the Jews. Jesus from the beginning of his ministry began to rebuke the severity of the requirements of this law. In the New Testament there is not an expression imposing the Sabbath law.

17 **They say therefore unto the blind man again, What sayest thou of him, in that he opened thine eyes?**—In the dispute they again appeal to the man who was healed to know what he thought of Jesus who had healed him.

And he said, He is a prophet.—His response was prompt; he is inspired of God a prophet, a divine teacher.

18 **The Jews therefore did not believe concerning him, that he had been blind, and had received his sight, until they called the parents of him that had received his sight,**—Some in their doubt as to the man appealed to his parents. [They now begin scheming to get around Jesus working the miracle. They insisted that the man was not born blind. They undertook to prove it by his parents.]

19 **and asked them, saying, Is this your son, who ye say was born blind? how then doth he now see?**—They ques-

ye say was born blind? how then doth he now see? 20 His parents answered and said, We know that this is our son, and that he was born blind:
21 but how he now seeth, we know not; or who opened his eyes, we know
not: ask him; he is of age; he shall speak for himself. 22 These things
said his parents, because they feared the Jews: for the Jews had agreed
already, that if any man should confess him *to be* Christ, he should be put
out of the synagogue. 23 Therefore said his parents, He is of age; ask
him. 24 So they called a second time the man that was blind, and said
unto him, Give glory to God: we know that this man is a sinner. 25 He

---

tioned them as to the identity of the man as their son and of his having been born blind.

20 **His parents answered and said, We know that this is our son, and that he was born blind:**—["We know" these two facts to be true. They were very positive in this.]

21 **but how he now seeth, we know not; or who opened his eyes, we know not: ask him; he is of age; he shall speak for himself.**—But as to or by whom he was made to see, his parents had only his word and they referred all parties to him. [He is of age and competent to testify in the case.]

22 **These things said his parents, because they feared the Jews: for the Jews had agreed already, that if any man should confess him to be Christ, he should be put out of the synagogue.**—While what the parents said was strictly true, they did not care to incur the persecution of the Pharisees. They clearly believed the statement of their son, but spoke evasively to avoid trouble.

23 **Therefore said his parents, He is of age; ask him.**—[The parents did not wish to be excommunicated from the privileges of the synagogue, so they were noncommittal concerning how their son received his sight. The decision of these rulers that if any confessed Jesus as the Christ they should be put out of the synagogue shows that the people were considering the question and that it was rapidly developing in their minds. They, therefore, hoped to nip the sentiment in the bud by their decree.]

24 **So they called a second time the man that was blind, and said unto him, Give glory to God: we know that this man is a sinner.**—They were unable to explain the facts, and in the face of the probable miracle, to use wisdom on the man that was healed, they say this man that did the healing was a sinner be-

therefore answered, Whether he is a sinner, I know not: one thing I know,
that, whereas I was blind, now I see. 26 They said therefore unto him,
What did he to thee? how opened he thine eyes? 27 He answered them, I
told you even now, and ye did not hear; wherefore would ye hear it again?
would ye also become his disciples? 28 And they reviled him, and said,
Thou art his disciple; but we are disciples of Moses. 29 We know that

---

cause he had healed on the Sabbath. [Having failed to get any satisfaction from the parents they again call the son for a conference. This time they try to force an acknowledgment from him that there was some deception or mistake about Jesus restoring his sight. Their evidence of deception was "we *know* that this man is a sinner." Their proof that he was a sinner was he healed on the Sabbath day.]

25 **He therefore answered, Whether he is a sinner, I know not: one thing I know, that, whereas I was blind, now I see.** —The man refused to enter into the casuistry or the ethics of the case, but stood to the stern facts that I was blind and now I see. [He refused to be drawn into a dispute over the matter or to participate in their deceptive scheme. He was firm and held fast to the truth.]

26 **They said therefore unto him, What did he to thee? how opened he thine eyes?**—To entangle him and justify themselves, they again ask him to recount what was done to heal him. [Hoping to find something with which to strengthen their scheme of deception, they now begin to cross-examine the man.]

27 **He answered them, I told you even now, and ye did not hear; wherefore would ye hear it again? would ye also become his disciples?**—The blind man pressed the conclusion: would you recognize him as a prophet and become his disciples. He knew when men are determined to disbelieve the truth repeating the evidence will not convince, but rather infuriate them. [His "also" implies that he was inclined to be a disciple.]

28 **And they reviled him, and said, Thou art his disciple; but we are disciples of Moses.**—They claimed to be disciples of Moses, while the man whose eyes were opened owned himself ready to accept the man who had opened his eyes as a prophet of God.

God hath spoken unto Moses: but as for this man, we know not whence
he is. 30 The man answered and said unto them, Why, herein is the
marvel, that ye know not whence he is, and *yet* he opened mine eyes. 31
We know that God heareth not sinners: but if any man be a worshipper
of God, and do his will, him he heareth. 32 Since the world began it was
never heard that any one opened the eyes of a man born blind. 33 If this
man were not from God, he could do nothing. 34 They answered and said

---

29 **We know that God hath spoken unto Moses: but as for this man, we know not whence he is.**—They believed Moses was sent from God, but the origin of this man they did not know. [They felt that they were on safe ground in clinging to Moses, but refused to be disciples of "this man" on the ground that "we know not whence he is."]

30 **The man answered and said unto them, Why, herein is the marvel, that ye know not whence he is, and yet he opened mine eyes.**—How singular that a man able to open the eyes of the blind in the name of God should be unknown to the defenders of the faith of God! [He declares it a "marvelous thing" that these Jewish defenders of the scriptures did not know after this wonderful miracle that the one performing it was from God. He had a better knowledge of the scriptures than they.]

31 **We know that God heareth not sinners: but if any man be a worshipper of God, and do his will, him he heareth.**—It was a well-known truth among all the disciples of Moses and the servants of God that God heareth not those who rebel against him, and that he only enabled those who obey him to work miracles in his name. How then could this man who opened his eyes be a sinner? [Nicodemus said, "No one can do these signs that thou doest, except God be with him." (3: 2.) Both he and the healed man affirm that God only heard true worshipers and those who did his will.]

32 **Since the world began it was never heard that any one opened the eyes of a man born blind.**—Such a case had never been known. [Certain kinds of blindness have been and may be cured, but this unheard-of cure—one born blind—he insisted could be attributed only to the power of God.]

33 **If this man were not from God, he could do nothing.**—No man could do this work except God was with him.

unto him, Thou wast altogether born in sins, and dost thou teach us? And they cast him out.

34 **They answered and said unto him, Thou wast altogether born in sins, and dost thou teach us?**—Chagrined and provoked that this man withstood them, they taunt him with the idea that he was born blind in consequence of his own or his parents' sins and now you presume to teach us regarding the teachers of God.

And they cast him out.—They ordered him out of the synagogue. [It may mean that they cast him out not only from their presence, but also from their sympathy and intercourse with them and their people. Note, that the avowed enemies of Jesus investigate a miracle of Jesus in repeated hearings and that they could find no flaw. Also observe that the people refer the case to a great religious order composed of enemies of Christ; that members of this order first examine the facts; then the case is referred to a higher tribunal, the official representatives of the nation, who cross-examine the parents, as well as the subject of the miracle. This judicial investigation shows by the testimony of both that the man was born blind, that he now saw, and his own testimony was given that he was healed by Jesus. The attempt to disprove the miracle was an utter failure and the court sought to discredit it by excommunicating the chief witness.]

14. JESUS MEETS THE MAN AGAIN.
9: 35-41.

35 Jesus heard that they had cast him out; and finding him, he said, Dost thou believe on [1]the Son of God? 36 He answered and said, And who

[1]Many ancient authorities read *the Son of Man*

35 **Jesus heard that they had cast him out; and finding him, he said, Dost thou believe on the Son of God?**—Jesus was not unmindful of one so true to him, after he was driven out of the synagogue, sought him, and gave him further instruction and help. He wished to lead him up to believe that he (Jesus) was the Son of God. [The poor man, through faithfulness to the truth, lost the world, but Jesus is ready to give him heaven.]

is he, Lord, that I may believe on him? 37 Jesus said unto him, Thou hast
both seen him, and he it is that speaketh with thee. 38 And he said, Lord,
I believe. And he [2]worshipped him. 39 And Jesus said, For judgment
came I into this world, that they that see not may see; and that they that
see may become blind. 40 Those of the Pharisees who were with him heard
these things, and said unto him, Are we also blind? 41 Jesus said unto

[2]The Greek word denotes an act of reverence, whether paid to a creature (as here) or to the Creator (see ch. 4. 20)

36 **He answered and said, And who is he, Lord, that I may believe on him?**—He already believed that he was sent of God and that God was with him. But he did not know that he was the Son of God. So he was ready to believe whatever Jesus would tell him.

37 **Jesus said unto him, Thou hast both seen him, and he it is that speaketh with thee.**—Jesus then assured the man that he himself was the Son of God.

38 **And he said, Lord, I believe. And he worshipped him.**—The man at once accepted the truth of the statement and confessed his faith in Jesus by worshiping him as the divine Being. [The believer believes with his heart, confesses Christ with his mouth, and shows his faith by obedience.]

39 **And Jesus said, For judgment came I into this world, that they that see not may see; and that they that see may become blind.**—Those who are thought by others to be fools and claim no wisdom of their own may be made wise with the wisdom of God, and those who think they are wise after the world's wisdom may be made to realize that they are fools before God. [Jesus came into the world, not to condemn it, but to save it; but the effect of his coming is to reveal every man's true condition. The light reveals the stains of sin on the heart that would otherwise be unseen. Jesus is the touchstone. He not only gave sight to the blind, but opened the eyes of those who were in the darkness of ignorance. Publicans and sinners were enabled to see, while Jews and Pharisees, who claimed to be enlightened, were left in darkness, because they closed their eyes and would not hear.]

40 **Those of the Pharisees who were with him heard these things, and said unto him, Are we also blind?**—The Pharisees saw that he classed them as blind and spoke to him of it.

them, If ye were blind, ye would have no sin: but now ye say, We see: your sin remaineth.

[Jesus had mentioned two classes—those who did not see who should see and those who saw or had the greatest spiritual opportunities—who should become blind by willfully closing their eyes.]

41 **Jesus said unto them, If ye were blind, ye would have no sin: but now ye say, We see: your sin remaineth.**—If ye were really blind ye would not be guilty as you are now in claiming that you are not blind and so refuse to be taught. Because you refuse to acknowledge your blindness and turn to Jesus, you remain in your sins. [If they were blind, that is, entirely without knowledge and means of enlightenment, they would have no moral responsibility, but they claimed to see and had the greatest opportunities for knowing. Therefore, when they closed their eyes against the truth and thus willfully refused to see, they were guilty. Our responsibility is measured by our opportunities and will thus be judged at the last day.]

15. THE PARABLE OF THE SHEPHERD AND HIS SHEEP. 10: 1-6.

It is doubtful whether the teaching that follows was spoken in connection with the preceding chapter. Some think the former chapter was spoken at the feast of tabernacles (chapter 7) and this at the feast of dedication (verse 22) in the winter. They are distinct enough to have been spoken on different occasions, and yet enough similarity to be a continuation of the same discourse.

There are two parables presented here that are often combined as one. This creates some confusion. Again, persons frequently conclude that because a person or fact represents one thing in a parable it must do it in all parables. This produces confusion. The first parable here spoken concludes with verse 6. A second and distinct parable begins with verse 7 and concludes with verse 10. In the first parable, Jesus is the Shepherd entering into the fold and calling his sheep. In the second, Jesus is the door by or through which the

1 Verily, verily, I say unto you, He that entereth not by the door into
the fold of the sheep, but climbeth up some other way, the same is a thief
and a robber. 2 But he that entereth in by the door is [3]the shepherd of
the sheep. 3 To him the porter openeth; and the sheep hear his voice: and

[3]Or, *a shepherd*

sheep enter into the fold of God. After the conclusion of the two parables, he presents truths drawn from them.

1 **Verily, verily, I say unto you, He that entereth not by the door into the fold of the sheep, but climbeth up some other way, the same is a thief and a robber.**—He explains in this who is the true Shepherd or Christ and who are false christs. The true Christ enters by the door. This parable is based on what is said to be the practice of the shepherds in the east. The different flocks of sheep are gathered at night into one common fold, the door is closed, a porter keeps the door, and in the morning the shepherds come, the porter opens the door to him as he comes, he calls his sheep by name, and the sheep know their shepherd's voice, and follow him. This is to show that Christ the true Shepherd comes to the door; the porter opens to him, he enters, calls his sheep, and they follow him. All who come claiming to be christs that do not enter the open door are false christs, are thieves and robbers.

2 **But he that entereth in by the door is the shepherd of the sheep.**—The door, it seems to me, is the entering into the way pointed out by the prophets. To come as they foretold is to enter by the door into the work of saving the world. [The prophecies pointing to the coming of Christ was the door through which he passed. He fulfilled all of them. He who claims to be the shepherd of the sheep, failing to fulfill these prophecies, has climbed up some other way than going through the door, and is therefore a thief and a robber.]

3 **To him the porter openeth;**—[The gatekeeper. One man was left in charge of the fold who spent the night there on watch against thieves and wild beasts. When the hour arrived for leading out the flocks in the morning, the shepherd came to the door and being recognized was admitted by the porter.] The porter that is to admit and bear testimony to

he calleth his own sheep by name, and leadeth them out. 4 When he hath
put forth all his own, he goeth before them, and the sheep follow him: for
they know his voice. 5 And a stranger will they not follow, but will flee
from him: for they know not the voice of strangers. 6 This [4]parable spake
Jesus unto them: but they understood not what things they were which he
spake unto them.

[4]Or, *proverb*

Christ the Shepherd, it seems to me, is John the Baptist. He was the forerunner of Jesus to bear witness to him and introduce him as the Shepherd of the fold of God.

and the sheep hear his voice:—["Hear" is used in the sense of intelligent hearing. They recognize and give heed to his voice. They could "hear" simply a rabbi's voice as well as the shepherd's.]

and he calleth his own sheep by name,—[This corresponds exactly with the facts of eastern shepherd life. They give names to sheep as we do to our tame animals. It denotes Christ's individual interest in each soul.]

and leadeth them out.—[To pasture where there is plenty to feed upon.] Those ready to receive the spiritual shepherd and hear his voice are led by him out into green pastures of the children of God.

4 **When he hath put forth all his own,**—[Has separated his sheep from those of his neighbors.]

he goeth before them, and the sheep follow him:—[This is in accordance with oriental custom to this day. Sheep are not driven but led, the shepherd walking in front occasionally uttering a peculiar voice.]

for they know his voice.—[Distinct from that of all other voices.] Jesus leads by his teaching and example, and those willing to hear follow out of the fold of Judaism into the privileges of Christ.

5 **And a stranger will they not follow, but will flee from him: for they know not the voice of strangers.**—[An eastern sheep will not follow a strange voice.] One whose voice is not attended by the divine teaching a true disciple will not hear. All who came claiming to be christs were thieves and robbers who came to steal and rob.

6 **This parable spake Jesus unto them: but they understood not what things they were which he spake unto them.**—This

was a completed parable that the people did not understand what he meant to teach. They had not understood and believed those who had gone before him.

16. CONTRAST BETWEEN TRUE SHEPHERD AND THE HIRELING.
10: 7-18.

7 Jesus therefore said unto them again, Verily, verily, I say unto you,
I am the door of the sheep. 8 All that came [5]before me are thieves and
robbers: but the sheep did not hear them. 9 I am the door; by me if any

[5]Some ancient authorities omit *before me*

7 **Jesus therefore said unto them again, Verily, verily, I say unto you, I am the door of the sheep.**—He then introduces another parable to show how the sheep may enter into the fold of God and find the care and protection they need to protect them from the thieves and robbers that would destroy them for their selfish ends. Jesus himself is the door into the fold. We enter into the fold of God by entering in or through Christ. [The prophecies were the door through which Christ came and Christ is the door through which we go into the church of Christ. There is but one door or entrance. All who enter the church must go through this door. Baptism is the completing act that puts us through the door into Christ or the church. (Matt. 28: 19; Gal. 3: 27; John 3: 5.) The "door" here represents Jesus beyond doubt, but how? In the fold is shelter by night, in the pasture is sustenance by day. Through the door they pass to one at night, to the other in the morning. The door then represents the gateway to all our spiritual blessings.]

8 **All that came before me are thieves and robbers:**—All that came before him claiming to be christs in and through whom they could enter the fold of God were thieves and robbers [for the reason they did not fulfill the prophecies relating to Christ. Instead of entering in through the door, they climbed up some other way].

but the sheep did not hear them.—[Those who were prepared for Christ came to him in spite of them as did the blind man of the previous chapter. They are goats, not true sheep, that wander off after false teachers.]

man enter in, he shall be saved, and shall go in and go out, and shall find
pasture. 10 The thief cometh not, but that he may steal, and kill, and destroy: I came that they may have life, and may [6]have *it* abundantly. 11

[6]Or, *have abundance*

9 **I am the door; by me if any man enter in, he shall be saved,**—[From all the skulkers of the night, the hosts of evil, that would fain destroy the sheep.] If any one enters the fold of God through Christ as the door, he shall be saved.

and shall go in and go out, and shall find pasture.—As the shepherd leads his sheep in for protection and out for pasture and water so Christ will give these protection and food. This is a reference to the shepherd leading his flock out to the pasture and into the cote or fold for protection. It means that God affords his children food and protection. No parable is intended to apply in all its parts, but one leading point or feature represents the lesson intended to be taught. [Jesus is at once the door, the shepherd, and the pasture. His pasture is the bread of life and the water of life. All who enter by him in the way ordained by God are saved and shall never be lost unless they cease to continue to hear and obey his voice. This is a picture of the happy, contented life of the sheep folded by night and fed by day. So may those who have entered into Christ rest in peace sure that he will lead them by day and protect them by night.]

10 **The thief cometh not, but that he may steal, and kill, and destroy:**—The false christ comes only for selfish purposes and will kill and destroy others for his selfish ends. [All those who enter otherwise than by the door wish to prey upon the flock. Their object is not to save the flock, but to destroy it. False religion robs men; true religion blesses and enriches them. After having served for the satisfaction of their pride, ambition, and cupidity they will perish morally, and at least even externally by the effect of this pernicious guidance. The false and selfish teacher is not only a thief who steals the substance and the opportunities of the flock, but a destroyer. This is a universal truth that any person of wide observation has seen illustrated too often. He destroys the spiritual life of the flock, leads it away from God, fills it

I am the good shepherd: the good shepherd layeth down his life for the
sheep. 12 He that is a hireling, and not a shepherd, whose own the sheep
are not, beholdeth the wolf coming, and leaveth the sheep, and fleeth, and
the wolf snatcheth them, and scattereth *them:* 13 *he fleeth* because he is a

---

with false doctrines, destroys the faith that is in men's hearts, and scatters the flock abroad until the sheep can no longer be found at the Lord's house. My observation is that this is, sooner or later, the picture of the pastor system. Too many preach to satisfy the money and popular sides.]

I came that they may have life, and may have it abundantly.—[Overflowingly; richfulness of nourishment (Comp. Psalm 23); abundance of spiritual possessions (grace and truth) (1: 14) in which the life consists.] Jesus the true Shepherd will lay down his life to save the sheep and for their growth to a higher good.

11 **I am the good shepherd: the good shepherd layeth down his life for the sheep.**—He distinctly announces that he himself is the good Shepherd who came from heaven to earth to give his life to save those who would trust and follow him.

12 **He that is a hireling, and not a shepherd, whose own the sheep are not, beholdeth the wolf coming, and leaveth the sheep, and fleeth, and the wolf snatcheth them, and scattereth them:**—Others who are hirelings or work for selfish ends forsake the sheep and flee when they see danger approaching and leave the sheep to be destroyed. ["The laborer is worthy of his hire," and hence it is not the bare fact of a man receiving pay that makes him a hireling. He is a hireling who would not work were it not for the money he receives. He only cares for his own selfish ends. He will lead the flock away from hope with false doctrines when popularity lends its influence in that direction. Those he described above as thieves and robbers, he now describes as hirelings. Thus true and false shepherds are described.]

13 **he fleeth because he is a hireling,**—He whose labor is for selfish ends flees when danger threatens, and when the chances are he will lose instead of gain by the danger. [All his care and love is centered on his pay and self-interest, and none on the church. It is said that "when yellow fever struck Memphis the hireling shepherds fled to the north."]

hireling, and careth not for the sheep. 14 I am the good shepherd; and I
know mine own, and mine own know me, 15 even as the Father knoweth
me, and I know the Father; and I lay down my life for the sheep. 16
And other sheep I have, which are not of this fold: them also I must [7]bring,
and they shall hear my voice; and [8]they shall become one flock, one shepherd. 17 Therefore doth the Father love me, because I lay down my life,

[7]Or, *lead*
[8]Or, *there shall be one flock*

and careth not for the sheep.—He works for his own selfish good and not for the good of others.

14 **I am the good shepherd; and I know mine own, and mine own know me,**—There is a recognition that certain persons, when they hear the truth, will accept and follow it. Jesus recognizes that these are his before they hear the gospel and accept it. In this sense he is known of his own and knows them. In verse 16 he speaks of those who are his own, but not of this fold. The Lord told Paul at Corinth, "I have much people in this city" (Acts 18: 10) before they had heard or believed the gospel. They loved the truth, and were of that frame of mind that when they heard it would accept and follow it.

15 **even as the Father knoweth me, and I know the Father; and I lay down my life for the sheep.**—The Father knew Jesus would lay down his life for the sheep and because he loved the truth himself, and so loved that he was willing to die to lead all willing to follow truth.

16 **And other sheep I have, which are not of this fold: them also I must bring, and they shall hear my voice; and they shall become one flock, one shepherd.**—Among the Gentiles were many who, when they heard the truth, would accept and follow Jesus. These he calls his sheep of another fold. He would call them and of the two he would make one fold under one Shepherd.

17 **Therefore doth the Father love me, because I lay down my life, that I may take it again.**—The reason God loved Jesus and sent him to save sinners was because he had no will save to do the will of God and was willing to die to save all who would serve God. He gave his life with the full assurance that he would take it up again.

that I may take it again. 18 No one [9]taketh it away from me, but I lay it down of myself. I have [10]power to lay it down, and I have [10]power to take it again. This commandment received I from my Father.

[9]Some ancient authorities read *took it away*
[10]Or, *right*

18 **No one taketh it away from me, but I lay it down of myself.**—While the Father desired that Jesus should give his life for the world, no necessity was laid on him to do it against his own will. Indeed he was chosen of the Father to make this sacrifice because he designed to give his life for the world.

I have power to lay it down, and I have power to take it again. This commandment received I from my Father.—While wicked men took his life by violence, he could have called twelve legions of angels to his deliverance had he desired. While he drew back from the bitter cup of death offered him, it was only momentarily so, for he came for this end, and pursued it to the bitter end. While it was his will, yet in doing it, he acted according to the commandment of God. [He laid down his life at the cross and took it again at the resurrection.]

17. DIVISION AMONG HIS HEARERS.
10: 19-21.

19 There arose a division again among the Jews because of these words.
20 And many of them said, He hath a demon, and is mad; why hear ye him?

19 **There arose a division again among the Jews because of these words.**—The teachings of Jesus always produced division among those who heard. Some were willing to hear and believe, others would reject it. It is so now. As much depends upon the condition of the heart of the hearers as upon the amount of the testimony given. Those not willing to believe are influenced and embittered by additional testimony.

20 **And many of them said, He hath a demon, and is mad; why hear ye him?**—Some attributed his speech and works to a demon. [The Jews believed that demons could produce

21 Others said, These are not the sayings of one possessed with a demon. Can a demon open the eyes of the blind?

supernatural effects. (Matt. 12: 24.) They used this as a foundation in explaining the miraculous power of Christ.]

21 **Others said, These are not the sayings of one possessed with a demon. Can a demon open the eyes of the blind?**—Others insisted that demons did not talk in this way, and especially that a demon could not open the eyes of the blind. Demons could sometimes do supernatural works, but they were never good works or helpful to man. [Their question suggests that demons could not do miraculous good works like healing the blind. It had never been known that demons could open the eyes of the blind.]

[Here the historian shows what different effects the teaching of Jesus had upon the Jews. Many of them calumniate and slander him as one possessed of a demon and mad, and therefore not to be heard and obeyed; others of calmer thoughts and more levelheaded said that the doctrine he taught, and the late miracle which he had wrought in curing the blind man, were abundantly sufficient to confute such a groundless slander. Note, that the teaching of Christ meeting with diversity of dispositions—it is no wonder it occasions different effects to the softening of some and hardening of others; even as the same sun that melts the wax hardens the clay; yet this is not to be attributed to the teaching of Jesus, but to men's corruptions which oppose the truth and the maintainers of it.]

SECTION FOUR.

AT THE FEAST OF DEDICATION BEYOND THE JORDAN AND RECALLED TO BETHANY.
10: 22 to 11: 59.

1. RENEWAL OF REMARKS ABOUT HIS SHEEP.
10: 22-30.

22 [1]And it was the feast of the dedication at Jerusalem: 23 it was winter;
and Jesus was walking in the temple in Solomon's [2]porch. 24 The Jews
therefore came round about him, and said unto him, How long dost thou
hold us in suspense? If thou art the Christ, tell us plainly. 25 Jesus answered them, I told you, and ye believe not: the works that I do in my
Father's name, these bear witness of me. 26 But ye believe not, because ye

[1]Some ancient authorities read *At that time was the feast*
[2]Or, *portico*

22 **And it was the feast of the dedication at Jerusalem:**—Herod the Great had rebuilt the temple—was forty-six years in restoring it—and a feast celebrating that dedication was observed to perpetuate it.

23 **it was winter;**—Near the time when the people in this country celebrate Christmas. [This feast came in December, but the day is not certain.]

and Jesus was walking in the temple in Solomon's porch.—This was a large portion of the temple, four hundred feet long, in which numbers could congregate.

24 **The Jews therefore came round about him, and said unto him, How long dost thou hold us in suspense?**—The Jews clearly saw that there was something above the ordinary human being in speech and works of Jesus and persuaded themselves that they desired to know and do the truth.

If thou art the Christ, tell us plainly.—They desired that he should make a plain declaration as to whether he was the Christ.

25 **Jesus answered them, I told you, and ye believe not: the works that I do in my Father's name, these bear witness of me.**—While Jesus occasionally told those to whom he spoke that he was the Christ, generally he left the works that he did to make the impression, and when he saw a willingness to promptly accept the truth, he told them that he was the

are not of my sheep. 27 My sheep hear my voice, and I know them, and they follow me: 28 and I give unto them eternal life; and they shall never perish, and no one shall snatch them out of my hand. 29 [3]My Father, who hath given *them* unto me, is greater than all; and no one is able to snatch

[3]Some ancient authorities read *That which my Father hath given unto me*

Christ. But when they caviled about his work and showed a desire to reject him, he refused to tell them. He chided them here with having refused to believe either his word or the works the Father had done through him. These people had seen many works performed at Jerusalem on his frequent visits to the city and had seen the blind mentioned in the ninth chapter healed. Matthew (11: 5) gives an enumeration of the miracles he performed in their midst.

26 **But ye believe not, because ye are not of my sheep.**—They in that state of heart were determined not to believe, so he refused not to recognize them as his sheep. You are not of that class who are willing to receive the truth.. He had tried them. (John 12: 39, 40; Matt. 13: 14, 15.)

27 **My sheep hear my voice, and I know them, and they follow me:**—He and those willing to hear him both loved truth and were naturally drawn to each other.

28 **and I give unto them eternal life; and they shall never perish,**—As a result of their hearing and following him, they should never perish.

and no one shall snatch them out of my hand.—None could separate them from Christ while they were anxious to do his will. No one can separate one anxious to follow Christ from him. Only the person himself can separate from Christ, and he can do this only by refusing to hear him.

29 **My Father, who hath given them unto me, is greater than all;**—God the Father is the provider and protector of all. He had given to Christ all who were willing to follow him. "No man can come to me, except the Father that sent me draw him: and I will raise him up in the last day. It is written in the prophets, And they shall all be taught of God. Every one that hath heard from the Father, and hath learned, cometh unto me." (6: 44, 45.) Which shows that God gave to Jesus those who had heard and learned of the prophets and were willing to receive him as the Christ.

[4]*them* out of the Father's hand. 30 I and the Father are one. 31 The Jews

[4]Or, aught

and no one is able to snatch them out of the Father's hand.—[No man is able to do it, but the Father can and will if we cease to follow Jesus. (15: 2.) None shall ever fall away from want of divine grace, or the power of adversaries, but because they cease to hear and follow Jesus. By our own sins we are separated from God. (Isa. 59: 2.)]

30 **I and the Father are one.**—They are one in nature, character, and purpose, and worked in perfect harmony in saving men. His doing the will of God his Father was the evidence he was from God, that he was the Son of God, and that he was in the Father and the Father in him.

2. DISCUSSION ABOUT STONING JESUS.
10: 31-39.

took up stones again to stone him. 32 Jesus answered them, Many good works have I showed you from the Father; for which of those works do ye

31 **The Jews took up stones again to stone him.**—To make himself one with God was regarded by the Jews as blasphemy. And blasphemy was to be punished by death by stoning. (Lev. 24: 14-16.)

32 **Jesus answered them, Many good works have I showed you from the Father; for which of those works do ye stone me?**—Jesus hindered the stoning by appealing to the good works he had done—works of mercy and love—in healing the afflicted in their midst. Jesus knew they could not deny them so he confidently referred to them as known by the Jews about to stone him. It was unto these people that Peter boldly affirmed that Jesus of Nazareth was "a man approved of God unto you by mighty works and wonders and signs which God did by him in the midst of you, even as ye yourselves know." (Acts 2: 22.) Judas testified (Matt. 27: 4) that he was innocent and sealed his testimony with his own blood; Pilate testified that he found no fault in him (Luke 23: 4, 14); the centurion who crucified him testified, "This was the Son of God" (Matt. 27: 54); and here those who sought his life testify that they knew he did many miracles of good works in their midst.

These testimonies show that Jesus never did evil to a living soul. He was persecuted and crucified; but while receiving evil from many, he never returned evil. When the fleshly body passed away, the church of God as his spiritual body took its place in which his Spirit dwells. The spiritual body is nearer to the Son of God than his fleshly body ever was. Jesus is persecuted and stoned in the spiritual body as unjustly and as cruelly as he ever was in the fleshly body. He still returns only good for evil. Jesus the Christ in the spiritual body has never brought evil to a single soul, and this challenge still comes to those who turn from him and neglect and abuse and divide and sever his spiritual body. "Many good works have I showed you from the Father; for which of those works do ye stone me?" All the good things of a material, intellectual, and spiritual nature we enjoy in this age of the world come from God and are the fruits borne by the tree planted by God two thousand years ago. They came to us through the spiritual body of Christ. It often exposes the evil, but it never produces it. It exposes it that its evil influences may be counteracted and destroyed. Jesus Christ came as a Savior to man, and neither in the fleshly nor the spiritual body did he ever injure or harm a living soul.

Churches claiming to be churches of God have injured and done harm to mortals, but it was the human grafts upon that tree planted by God that did the evil and bore the bitter fruit of humanity. Human grafts and trees of human planting always bear bitter fruit. They can bear no other because man, their author and founder, is evil. An evil tree cannot bear good fruit any more than the good tree can bear evil fruit. A stream cannot rise higher than its fountain. All human kingdoms and all human grafts upon the divine tree can bear only evil and bitter fruit to humanity, and every friend of man and of God must set his face firmly against all human grafts upon the divine tree.

33 **The Jews answered him, For a good work we stone thee not, but for blasphemy; and because that thou, being a man,**

but for blasphemy; and because that thou, being a man, makest thyself God.
34 Jesus answered them, Is it not written in your law, [5]I said, Ye are gods?
35 If he called them gods, unto whom the word of God came (and the
scripture cannot be broken), 36 say ye of him, whom the Father [6]sanctified
and sent into the world, Thou blasphemest; because I said, I am *the* Son
of God? 37 If I do not the works of my Father, believe me not. 38 But
if I do them, though ye believe not me, believe the works: that ye may
know and understand that the Father is in me, and I in the Father. 39
They sought again to take him: and he went forth out of their hand.

[5]Ps. 82. 6
[6]Or, *consecrated*

makest thyself God.—Here those anxious to kill Jesus are made to bear testimony to the many good works he did in their midst. They admitted that he had done these works, but insisted that they did not stone him for these works, but for making himself the Son of God when he was only a man.

34-36 **Jesus answered them, Is it not written in your law, I said, Ye are gods? If he called them gods, unto whom the word of God came (and the scripture cannot be broken), say ye of him, whom the Father sanctified and sent into the world, Thou blasphemest; because I said, I am the Son of God?**—Jesus quotes this to show that their own law recognizes those as gods who executed the law of God that came to them. As God's servants, they enforced his law and the Psalmist calls them gods. If this be so, why should it be regarded as blasphemy when one specially sent from God into the world calls himself the Son of God? [The word "sanctify" means to make holy or set apart. It is here used in the latter sense.]

37 **If I do not the works of my Father, believe me not.**—He presents the works he did in their midst as the witness that he was from God and that God was with him.

38 **But if I do them, though ye believe not me, believe the works: that ye may know and understand that the Father is in me, and I in the Father.**—Independent of the words and claims of Jesus, the works that he did ought to prove to them that the Father was with and in Jesus doing the works and so approving him as sent of God. To this there was no reply. [If they had personal prejudices against Jesus, they ought to consider his works without prejudice.]

39 **They sought again to take him: and he went forth out of their hand.**—They sought to arrest him, and still even by

physical force. How he escaped we are not told. [Here ends the three months of stormy ministry in the life of Jesus in Jerusalem. Twice they attempted to mob him (8: 59; 10: 31); twice efforts were made to arrest him (7: 32, 45; 10: 39); and also secret plans to assassinate him had been laid (7: 19; 8: 37).]

3. JESUS DEPARTS BEYOND THE JORDAN.
10: 40-42.

40 And he went away again beyond the Jordan into the place where John
was at the first baptizing; and there he abode. 41 And many came unto
him; and they said, John indeed did no sign: but all things whatsoever
John spake of this man were true. 42 And many believed on him there.

---

40 **And he went away again beyond the Jordan into the place where John was at the first baptizing; and there he abode.**—He left Judea because they would not believe him, and went to the east side of the Jordan to Bethabara where John had baptized and remained there for a time.

41 **And many came unto him; and they said, John indeed did no sign: but all things whatsoever John spake of this man were true.**—The teaching and miracles of Jesus brought many to see him wherever he abode.

42 **And many believed on him there.**—It is likely that the testimony of John at his baptism had a favorable influence in his behalf and his testimony and works caused many to believe on him at this place. [John's preparatory work there was so thorough that they readily received and believed on Jesus. His work here was fruitful, due to the fact that "all things whatsoever John spake of this man were true."]

4. HE IS RECALLED TO BETHANY.
11: 1-16.

1 Now a certain man was sick, Lazarus of Bethany, of the village of
Mary and her sister Martha. 2 And it was that Mary who anointed the

---

1 **Now a certain man was sick, Lazarus of Bethany, of the village of Mary and her sister Martha.**—Mary and Martha seem to have been better known than Lazarus They seem to have been prominent persons of the city. Bethany was

Lord with ointment, and wiped his feet with her hair, whose brother
Larazus was sick. 3 The sisters therefore sent unto him, saying, Lord,
behold, he whom thou lovest is sick. 4 But when Jesus heard it, he said,
This sickness is not unto death, but for the glory of God, that the Son of
God may be glorified thereby. 5 Now Jesus loved Martha, and her sister,

---

on the east of Mount Olivet, a little less than two miles from Jerusalem. [John is the only one of the sacred writers that mentions the name of Lazarus, though his family is spoken of by Matthew, Mark, and Luke.]

2 **And it was that Mary who anointed the Lord with ointment, and wiped his feet with her hair, whose brother Lazarus was sick.**—This anointing is most likely that mentioned in chapter 12: 1 which occurred after the raising of Lazarus, but this was written by John after that occurred and he refers to it to distinguish this Mary from other Marys mentioned in connection with Jesus. [There was Mary the mother of Jesus, Mary Magdalene, Mary the mother of Mark, and Mary the wife of Cleophas.]

3 **The sisters therefore sent unto him, saying, Lord, behold, he whom thou lovest is sick.**—There seems to have been no effort upon the part of Jesus or of the sacred writers to conceal the special love that Jesus had for this family, for the apostles, and for John above others of his followers and friends. Jesus is absent at this time in Bethabara, and when Lazarus sickens, the minds of the sisters turn toward Jesus as one able to relieve in time of sickness. It was two days' journey from Jerusalem to Bethabara. They appeal to the love Jesus bore to Lazarus to induce him to come to their relief. [The disease is not stated, but it proved fatal.]

4 **But when Jesus heard it, he said, This sickness is not unto death,**—[That is, death was not its object. It had been permitted for another reason as follows:]

but for the glory of God, that the Son of God may be glorified thereby.—Jesus made up his mind as to his course and so told his disciples that he would be glorified through this sickness. [Jesus was glorified through the manifestation of miraculous power in raising Lazarus from the dead as well as the lessons surrounding the case furnished.]

and Lazarus. 6 When therefore he heard that he was sick, he abode at
that time two days in the place where he was. 7 Then after this he saith
to the disciples, Let us go into Judæa again. 8 The disciples say unto him,
Rabbi, the Jews were but now seeking to stone thee; and goest thou thither
again? 9 Jesus answered, Are there not twelve hours in the day? If a
man walk in the day, he stumbleth not, because he seeth the light of this

---

5 **Now Jesus loved Martha, and her sister, and Lazarus.**—Martha seems to have been the head of the household, possibly from her energy and business habits. [Probably this explains why the sisters sent for him and that his delay in coming was not from indifference.]

6 **When therefore he heard that he was sick, he abode at that time two days in the place where he was.**—Jesus had often healed the sick, but had not raised one buried and time was given for the decay of the body to begin. He intends now to give an example of this so remains until he is dead and buried. [He did not allow personal sympathy and friendship to interfere with his work, so he did not hasten away. Then, too, the longer the interval between his burial and resurrection, the more convincing would the miracle be, and greater means to silence his enemies who might claim that Lazarus was not really dead. He left no room for doubt and a charge of fraud.]

7 **Then after this he saith to the disciples, Let us go into Judaea again.**—The matter had passed from the minds of the disciples as he had told them that his sickness was not unto death.

8 **The disciples say unto him, Rabbi, the Jews were but now seeking to stone thee; and goest thou thither again?**—When he speaks of returning to Judea, they do not seem to think of Lazarus, but of the danger to Jesus since the Jews sought to stone him at the feast of dedication, the time of his last visit. (10: 31.) [They did not want him to return to the locality of his enemies for fear they would stone him.]

9 **Jesus answered, Are there not twelve hours in the day? If a man walk in the day, he stumbleth not, because he seeth the light of this world.**—To walk in the day here means to walk in the allotted time.

**world. 10 But if a man walk in the night, he stumbleth, because the light
is not in him. 11 These things spake he: and after this he saith unto them,
Our friend Lazarus is fallen asleep; but I go, that I may awake him out of
sleep. 12 The disciples therefore said unto him, Lord, if he is fallen asleep,
he will [7]recover. 13 Now Jesus had spoken of his death: but they thought
that he spake of taking rest in sleep. 14 Then Jesus therefore said unto**

[7]Gr. *be saved*

10 **But if a man walk in the night, he stumbleth, because the light is not in him.**—If he walks after the time allotted for life passes, he will stumble and come to his end. [Jesus often expressed himself by simile as in this case. It means that he is not walking in darkness, but in light for the reason he knows what he is going to do. He is not stumbling in darkness. He is not groping in the night or walking uncertainly. He has a clear pathway on which the sun is shining. Whether it leads him to Judea, to Jerusalem, to his enemies, or to death, in either case he will walk in the light, for the reason all his purposes and plans are made out and he is walking accordingly. What was dark and mystified to the disciples was clear to him.]

11 **These things spake he: and after this he saith unto them, Our friend Lazarus is fallen asleep; but I go, that I may awake him out of sleep.**—He now directs their minds to Lazarus and his affliction as causing him to return to Judea. Sleep is often used to represent death. [The term sleep is used as a symbol of death in scripture. (See 2 Chron. 14: 1; Psalm 3: 13; Jer. 51: 57; Job 14: 12; Dan. 12: 2; Matt. 27: 52; Acts 7: 60; 1 Cor. 7: 39; 1 Thess. 4: 13.)]

12, 13 **The disciples therefore said unto him, Lord, if he is fallen asleep, he will recover. Now Jesus had spoken of his death: but they thought that he spake of taking rest in sleep.**—His disciples took his language as literal, and to sleep in sickness rests the system and restores vigor. [They also took it that since Lazarus was resting well that his case was hopeful, and lessens the Master's reason for going into the community where his enemies, who desired to stone him, would be. So they use the fact that Lazarus was sleeping as an argument for Jesus not going.]

them plainly, Lazarus is dead. 15 And I am glad for your sakes that I was not there, to the intent ye may believe; nevertheless let us go unto him. 16 Thomas therefore, who is called [1]Didymus, said unto his fellow-disciples, Let us also go, that we may die with him.

[1]That is, *Twin*

14, 15 **Then Jesus therefore said unto them plainly, Lazarus is dead. And I am glad for your sakes that I was not there, to the intent ye may believe; nevertheless let us go unto him.** —Jesus tells them plainly his condition and was glad that he was not there, as now he will have the opportunity of raising him from the grave after the time for decay to set in, that they may see a more striking manifestation of God's presence with and in him, and so their faith in him may grow stronger. [It is implied that if Jesus had been present, on account of the friendship existing between him and the family, he would have been constrained to restore his health. Such a miracle would be less effective than the one now to be performed in raising him from the dead. To raise one from the dead after he had been in the grave four days, and after decomposition began, was as great a manifestation of divine power as was in creating the world.]

16 **Thomas therefore, who is called Didymus, said unto his fellow-disciples,**—Thomas is Hebrew, Didymus is the corresponding name in Greek and means twin.

Let us also go, that we may die with him—The characters drawn in the scriptures always harmonize. Thomas was a doubting man that looked on the dark side and saw the difficulties that threatened. He anticipated the death of Jesus, but proposed to the other disciples to go with him and share his fate. Thomas was faithful to his Master, although anticipating the worst.

5. LAZARUS RAISED FROM THE DEAD.
11: 17-44.

17 So when Jesus came, he found that he had been in the tomb four days

17 **So when Jesus came, he found that he had been in the tomb four days already.**—Lazarus had died about the time the message of his sickness reached Jesus. He remained two

already. 18 Now Bethany was nigh unto Jerusalem, about fifteen furlongs
off; 19 and many of the Jews had come to Martha and Mary, to console
them concerning their brother. 20 Martha therefore, when she heard that
Jesus was coming, went and met him: but Mary still sat in the house.
21 Martha therefore said unto Jesus, Lord, if thou hadst been here, my
brother had not died. 22 And even now I know that, whatsoever thou shalt
ask of God, God will give thee. 23 Jesus saith unto her, Thy brother shall
rise again. 24 Martha saith unto him, I know that he shall rise again in

---

days and spent two days in the journey, making four days from his death until the arrival of Jesus.

18 **Now Bethany was nigh unto Jerusalem, about fifteen furlongs off;**—[A little less than two miles and located on the eastern slope of Mount Olivet.]

19 **and many of the Jews had come to Martha and Mary,**—Martha and Mary were known to and esteemed by many of the Jews in Jerusalem. The Jews, as most of the eastern nations, were demonstrative in their sorrow and made much show of mourning. The formal mourning lasted thirty days. The first three days were called the "days of weeping."

to console them concerning their brother.—Their friends from Jerusalem came to sympathize and sorrow with them.

20 **Martha therefore, when she heard that Jesus was coming, went and met him: but Mary still sat in the house.**—Martha, the stirring active one of the sisters, naturally heard of the coming of Jesus first and went out to meet him. Mary, ignorant of his coming, sat in the house.

21 **Martha therefore said unto Jesus, Lord, if thou hadst been here, my brother had not died.**—Jesus had healed many sick, and the thought first expressed was that if Jesus had been there before his death he could have saved him from death.

22 **And even now I know that, whatsoever thou shalt ask of God, God will give thee.**—The thought occurred to her that even now he was able to restore him to life. We often accept a truth as a theory that we cannot realize in practice.

23 **Jesus saith unto her, Thy brother shall rise again.**—Jesus promptly assured her that her thoughts should be realized.

24 **Martha saith unto him, I know that he shall rise again in the resurrection at the last day.**—Martha, unable to fully be-

the resurrection at the last day. 25 Jesus said unto her, I am the resurrection, and the life: he that believeth on me, though he die, yet shall he live;
26 and whosoever liveth and believeth on me shall never die. Believest
thou this? 27 She saith unto him, Yea, Lord: I have believed that thou
art the Christ, the Son of God, *even* he that cometh into the world. 28
And when she had said this, she went away, and called Mary [2]her sister
secretly, saying, The Teacher is here, and calleth thee. 29 And she, when
she heard it, arose quickly, and went unto him. 30 (Now Jesus was not

[2]Or, *her sister, saying secretly*

lieve the promise, evasively says, "I know that he shall rise at the last day." [All the Jews, except the Sadducees, looked forward to, and believed in, a resurrection. Mary was not a skeptic.]

25 **Jesus said unto her, I am the resurrection, and the life: he that believeth on me, though he die, yet shall he live;**—It is through Christ that all shall rise. He will call them forth from the grave. [He means that he is the power which will open every grave, that will give life to every sleeper, and will call them forth from the tomb to a new existence, that the life that endows men with eternal being is in him and proceeds from him. In the light of his own resurrection, he means that when he opens the tomb he does it for all men and that they may have won the victory over death.]

26 **and whosoever liveth and believeth on me shall never die. Believest thou this?**—He here speaks of spiritual life and death. He who believes in Jesus shall never die spiritually. He saw Martha's inability to realize the truths he was teaching, and pointedly asked if she believes his teaching.

27 **She saith unto him, Yea, Lord: I have believed that thou art the Christ, the Son of God, even he that cometh into the world.**—She confesses her faith in him as the Christ, but evades the expression of her faith in the resurrection. She accepted the theory, but found it difficult to accept the reality.

28 **And when she had said this, she went away, and called Mary her sister secretly, saying, The Teacher is here, and calleth thee.**—Jesus failed to get a clear conception of himself and of his proposed work of raising her brother and asked for Mary. So Martha notified Mary of the Master's call.

29 **And she, when she heard it, arose quickly, and went unto him.**—Mary, less active and energetic in worldly affairs,

yet come into the village, but was still in the place where Martha met him).
31 The Jews then who were with her in the house, and were consoling her,
when they saw Mary, that she rose up quickly and went out, followed her,
supposing that she was going unto the tomb to [8]weep there. 32 Mary
therefore, when she came where Jesus was, and saw him, fell down at his
feet, saying unto him, Lord, if thou hadst been here, my brother had not

[8]Gr. *wail*

was much devoted to the Master, and when his presence was made known to her she quickly responded without making it known to her company and went out to meet the Master.

30 **(Now Jesus was not yet come into the village, but was still in the place where Martha met him).**—Jesus had come from beyond Jordan, where John at first did baptize. (10: 39, 40.) He heard of the sickness of Lazarus at Bethany, two miles from Jerusalem, and had now come to the place, but was yet without the town where Martha had met him.

31 **The Jews then who were with her in the house, and were consoling her, when they saw Mary, that she rose up quickly and went out, followed her, supposing that she was going unto the tomb to weep there.**—They thought she was going to the grave to give greater expression to her grief. Mary, less active and self-reliant, likely gave way to grief over the loss of her brother more than Martha did. A number of her Jewish friends were with her in the house to console and comfort her, and saw her rise up hastily and go out—not knowing that Martha had called for her—supposed she arose to go to the grave to weep so they followed her. In deep grief and sorrow, persons alone are liable to give way to excess that may work injury to them, so their friends dislike to leave them alone. The Jews followed Mary to console her.

32 **Mary therefore, when she came where Jesus was, and saw him, fell down at his feet, saying unto him, Lord, if thou hadst been here, my brother had not died.**—Concentrating her feelings on the object of her grief when she saw Jesus, she fell on her face before him to worship him. Like Martha, the thought occurred to her that if Jesus had been there before the death of her brother, he had not died. She showed her reverence for him by falling at his feet upon her knees and "saying unto him, Lord, if thou hadst been here, my brother

died. 33 When Jesus therefore saw her [4]weeping, and the Jews *also* [4]weep-
ing who came with her, he [5]groaned in the spirit, and [6]was troubled, 34
and said, Where have ye laid him? They say unto him, Lord, come and
see. 35 Jesus wept. 36 The Jews therefore said, Behold how he loved

[4]Gr. *wailing*
[5]Or, *was moved with indignation in the spirit*
[6]Gr. *troubled himself*

had not died." She knew of his kindly feeling toward her brother and sister, of his power and willingness to heal sickness and relieve from suffering, and believed his love would have led him to heal her brother, so she said, if thou had been here, you could and would have healed him, that he had not died. This was the language of Martha when she met him. Mary gives no expression to a thought that he could raise him as Martha did, so he did not speak of the resurrection to Mary as he did to Martha.

33 **When Jesus therefore saw her weeping, and the Jews also weeping who came with her, he groaned in the spirit, and was troubled,**—Jesus was troubled at her excessive grief, and sympathized with the sisters and people and groaned in spirit out of deep sympathy for others. This is a characteristic trait of Jesus worthy of being kept in memory. Mary had less self-reliance and gave way to grief more than Martha did. Jesus had more than a human sympathy for human suffering and sorrow. God sympathizes with man, and the sympathy of Jesus was more tender and strong than any mere human sympathy can be; so, touched with the grief and sorrow of Mary and the Jews weeping with her, "he groaned in the spirit, and was troubled." His sympathy for their sorrow disturbed his feelings.

34 **and said, Where have ye laid him? They say unto him, Lord, come and see.**—He asked that he might go to the grave and call him forth. They showed him the grave, that he might see the place where one he loved was laid that he might look upon it with affection. But his purpose was fixed before he left beyond the Jordan.

35 **Jesus wept.**—[The shortest verse in the Bible, but one of the most touching. How precious those tears which assure the real, tender, loving, sympathizing humanity of Jesus in

him! 37 But some of them said, Could not this man, who opened the eyes
of him that was blind, have caused that this man also should not die? 38

the very moment in which he is preparing to exert his omnipotence!] This was an overflow of sympathy for the sorrow of the sisters. The grief and sorrow shown on this occasion must have grown out of sympathy for the grieving sisters, not from sorrow for the dead brother. He knew, even before he came that he was dead, and that he would raise him to life, and he was glad for the sake of his apostles that he was not there before he died. He had often shown his power to heal sickness. He now wishes to show his power to raise the dead—his power over death—"I am glad for your sakes . . . to the intent ye may believe." (15.) [Jesus had both sorrow and gladness in the death of his friend.] "This sickness is not unto death, but for the glory of God, that the Son of God may be glorified thereby." (4) His weeping shows his kind sympathetic nature. He did not weep because Lazarus was dead and he would see him no more, for he knew he would restore him to life, but in sympathy for the sorrows of others. Only on one other occasion is it said that Jesus wept, then he wept over wickedness and sins and consequent sorrow that must come upon the city of Jerusalem. (Luke 19: 41-44.) On Jerusalem God had bestowed his most abundant blessings and sought its good, but the Jews of the city had rejected him and brought upon themselves his direct curses.

36 **The Jews therefore said, Behold how he loved him!**—The Jews who saw his tears interpreted them as signs of his love for Lazarus.

37 **But some of them said, Could not this man, who opened the eyes of him that was blind, have caused that this man also should not die?**—These Jews, although they did not believe in and follow him, yet knew of the miracles and signs he had wrought on the afflicted and suffering. And it occurred to them, as it had to the sisters that he might have saved the man from death. All seemed to have recognized that it would require greater power to raise the dead than to heal one while yet alive.

Jesus therefore again [7]groaning in himself cometh to the tomb. Now it was a cave, and a stone lay [8]against it. 39 Jesus saith, Take ye away the stone. Martha, the sister of him that was dead, saith unto him, Lord, by this time [9]the body decayeth; for he hath been *dead* four days. 40 Jesus saith unto her, Said I not unto thee, that, if thou believedst, thou shouldest

[7]Or, *being moved with indignation in himself*
[8]Or, *upon*
[9]Gr. *he stinketh*

38 **Jesus therefore again groaning in himself cometh to the tomb. Now it was a cave, and a stone lay against it.**—With deep sorrow of heart, he approached the grave, the mouth to which was closed by a heavy stone placed over it. Many of the Jewish burying places were caves in the rocky hill-side rather what we would call a vault than a grave.

39 **Jesus saith, Take ye away the stone.**—Rock vaults were closed with large stones. The sepulcher in which the body of Jesus was placed was one the women could not move, and on the way to anoint his body were troubled to know who would remove the stone for them. Jesus saw it would take some power to remove this stone. He had the fixed purpose to raise him from the dead, and the removing of the stone was preliminary to it.

Martha, the sister of him that was dead, saith unto him, Lord, by this time the body decayeth; for he hath been dead four days.—Martha knew he had been dead long enough for decay to set in, and in her practical, direct way objected to opening the grave. He had been dead four days and in that time the body would be offensive. She took it for granted the common course of nature was followed, and to take away the stone would cause a stench offensive to those present, and unpleasant to be remembered of a beloved brother, so her practical common sense, coupled with her failure to believe Jesus would raise him from the dead, led her to oppose the removing of the stone from the grave.

40 **Jesus saith unto her, Said I not unto thee, that, if thou believedst, thou shouldest see the glory of God?**—The raising of Lazarus could glorify and magnify God through him. So when he told Martha her brother should rise, he told her she should see the glory of God. He reminds her of his promise,

see the glory of God? 41 So they took away the stone. And Jesus lifted
up his eyes, and said, Father, I thank thee that thou heardest me. 42 And

and that what she expected to be fulfilled only at the resurrection at the last day would be manifested now. He would raise Lazarus from the grave. This was not a resurrection to immortality. It was restoring him to temporal life to die again. But it showed his power over death and gave a strong assurance that he would call all the sleeping dead from the grave. "The hour cometh, in which all that are in the tombs shall hear his voice, and shall come forth." (5: 28, 29.) This is a manifestation of that power, and it set forth the glory, the power, and the presence of God with Jesus. It showed his power over death.

41 **So they took away the stone. And Jesus lifted up his eyes, and said, Father, I thank thee that thou heardest me.**— Jesus had such assurance that God heard him that before the people knew his purpose, he in their hearing thanked God that he had heard him and would give life to the dead body. Jesus was one with God and did the will of God in all things. He knew then that God would hear him. In obedience to the command of Jesus the stone was taken away from the mouth of the cave in which the body was laid. There was something in the manner of Jesus that commanded the respect of those around him. Who did this we are not told, but it was likely the friends of Martha and Mary present. It may have been his disciples. When this was done, and the material obstacles to resurrection were removed, he then looked up to God. It is worthy of note that Jesus used miraculous power only when the result could not be effected by natural or ordinary means. He could have removed the stone by a miracle, but as this could be done by ordinary means, he did not exert extraordinary power to do it. Only when supernatural or extraordinary ends were to be accomplished did he use extraordinary power. The power used corresponded to the end to be accomplished. Jesus looked up to God as a declaration that all of his power came from him.

I knew that thou hearest me always: but because of the multitude that standeth around I said it, that they may believe that thou didst send me.
43 And when he had thus spoken, he cried with a loud voice, Lazarus,

42 **And I knew that thou hearest me always: but because of the multitude that standeth around I said it, that they may believe that thou didst send me.**—He wished all to know that it was God who did through him what would be done that all might believe that he was sent of God. Jesus prayed only for the things that would bring honor and glory to God—only for those things that were well-pleasing to the Father. God always hears prayers that are made in accord with his will and for his honor and glory. "If any man be a worshipper of God, and doeth his will, him he heareth." (John 9: 31.) Jesus gave to him a pure, holy, undivided worship, and did his will with faultless obedience. It was his meat and drink to do his Father's will. He hungered to do his will as the hungry man desires to eat and drink. Doing the will of God brought strength to him as meat and drink bring strength to the weary. Jesus knew God would hear him at all times. "But because of the multitude that standeth around I said it." That is, he wanted to let them know he raised the dead by the power of God, and that all might know that he was sent by God and spoke only the words of God, hence that the people might believe that God sent him.

43 **And when he had thus spoken, he cried with a loud voice, Lazarus, come forth.**—After preparing them to understand what was about to be done, he called on Lazarus to come forth. He spoke these things that those who heard him might know God sent him, and his power was from God. Then he cried with a loud voice, "Lazarus, come forth." At the command of Jesus life came into the dead body, and warmth and vigor flowed to the extremities. He arose and came forth from the grave. Jesus said, "The hour cometh, and now is, when the dead shall hear the voice of the Son of God; and they that hear shall live." (5: 25.) This referred to the final resurrection from the dead. But this calling up of Lazarus required the same power, and he adopts the same means that will call the sleeping dead forth at the last day. The dead

come forth. 44 He that was dead came forth, bound hand and foot with [10]grave-clothes; and his face was bound about with a napkin. Jesus saith unto them, Loose him, and let him go.

[10]Or, *grave-bands*

hear the voice, awake to life, and come forth. His loud speaking let all the people see the connection between his calling and the coming forth that they might know one produced the other. This shows what power is exerted through the word of God.

44 **He that was dead came forth, bound hand and foot with grave-clothes; and his face was bound about with a napkin. Jesus saith unto them, Loose him, and let him go.**—His body had been prepared for the grave as bodies usually were, so he came forth so clothed. Adam Clarke says: "This binding was with long strips of linen, in which the body was wrapped from head to foot, binding the arms close to the body and the legs and feet together." The mummies found in the ancient tombs are so swathed, leaving only the head and face exposed. One could rise and walk with difficulty thus wrapped up. So he walked but little until Jesus said to them, "Loose him, and let him go." This shows that he could walk but little, and with difficulty, while bound; and he could not well unloose himself, as his hands were bound to his body. Who unloosed him we do not know, but any would have gladly obeyed such directions. Probably it was the disciples. Those who thus handled him were made to realize more fully his resurrection, and could bear testimony that they handled him and took his graveclothes off him. Jesus used human agencies where they could do the work. [Jesus just before his own death and burial and in the face of his enemies works a crowning miracle. He demonstrates that he is "the resurrection and the life." It is worked under such circumstances that the most captious cannot question the reality of either the death or the resurrection.]

6. IMMEDIATE EFFECTS OF THE MIRACLE.
11: 45-53.

45 Many therefore of the Jews, who came to Mary and beheld [11]that which he did, believed on him. 46 But some of them went away to the Pharisees, and told them the things which Jesus had done.
47 The chief priests therefore and the Pharisees gathered a council, and said, What do we? for this man doeth many signs. 48 If we let him thus

[11]Many ancient authorities read *the things which he did*

45 **Many therefore of the Jews, who came to Mary and beheld that which he did, believed on him.**—It would seem singular that any who saw this could doubt, but saying that many believed shows that some did not. Those who followed Mary to the grave were present, and heard and saw what was said and done, and many of them believed on Jesus. The evidence was such that no honest-hearted man could doubt that Jesus was of God, that God was with him, and spoke and acted through him. The strange thing is that any should fail to believe on him.

46 **But some of them went away to the Pharisees, and told them the things which Jesus had done.**—The facts were told the Pharisees doubtless to see what explanation they would give of the occurrence. Many then as now exercise no faith of their own until their leaders tell them what to believe. The Pharisees themselves, instead of being softened in their feelings toward him by this manifestation of the presence of God with him, were hardened, and took counsel to kill him. "So from that day forth they took counsel that they might put him to death. Jesus therefore walked no more openly among the Jews, but departed thence into the country near to the wilderness, into a city called Ephraim; and there he tarried with the disciples." (53, 54.) This shows how much the fruits borne by the gospel depend upon the condition of the heart of him who hears it. It is "to the one a savor from death unto death; to the other a savor from life unto life." While faith rests on testimony, testimony will not produce faith in all hearts alike. Some will not believe, though one arose from the dead. Much of unbelief arises from an evil heart.

alone, all men will believe on him: and the Romans will come and take away both our place and our nation. 49 But a certain one of them, Caiaphas, being high priest that year, said unto them, Ye know nothing at all, 50 nor

47 **The chief priests therefore and the Pharisees gathered a council, and said, What do we? for this man doeth many signs.**—They gathered the Jewish Sanhedrin together to consult of the matters. They admitted that many signs were wrought by Jesus. In this they admitted that Lazarus was raised from the dead. Testimony that cannot be questioned infuriates the hearts of those determined not to believe.

48 **If we let him thus alone, all men will believe on him:**—Jesus had foretold the destruction of Jerusalem in consequence of their sins and the scattering of the Jewish nation. They connect the success of Jesus with the triumph of the Roman powers, and so to arouse one another and the people against Jesus tell that his success would be the complete destruction of Jerusalem and the carrying away of the people as was done by Nebuchadnezzar when the people were taken into captivity into Babylon.

and the Romans will come and take away both our place and our nation.—[Judea was a Roman province; there was a Roman governor; there was a Roman garrison located in the tower of Antonia overlooking the temple itself. So the Romans were already there. But they still had their "place"—there were priests with great revenues, or members of the Sanhedrin with great power. If sedition arose on account of faith in Christ they might lose their "place," as they did a few years later. To take away their "place," I take it, would be to destroy their ecclesiastical organization, and take away the "nation" would be to destroy their civil organization.]

49 **But a certain one of them, Caiaphas, being high priest that year, said unto them,**—This is the same Caiaphas that sat in judgment on Jesus and urged his condemnation. He was not a believer in Jesus, but was high priest and spoke by virtue of his office.

Ye know nothing at all,—[Not even the simplest rule of statesmanship—that one must be "sacrificed to the many."

do ye take account that it is expedient for you that one man should die for the people, and that the whole nation perish not. 51 Now this he said
not of himself: but being high priest that year, he prophesied that Jesus
should die for the nation; 52 and not for the nation only, but that he might
also gather together into one the children of God that are scattered abroad.
53 So from that day forth they took counsel that they might put him to death.

He was highly sarcastic and charges the Sanhedrin with blindness to its own interest.]

50 **nor do ye take account that it is expedient for you that one man should die for the people, and that the whole nation perish not.**—Whether there was prophetic power connected with the office or not, he foretold that Jesus would die for the nation. He was anxious for the death of Jesus and the wish was the father of the thought. This was spoken to suggest the death of Jesus to them.

51 **Now this he said not of himself: but being high priest that year, he prophesied that Jesus should die for the nation;**—[He thought he spoke it of himself, but unwittingly he announced a prophecy, like Balaam, while wickedly counseling the death of Christ interprets the results of his death.]

52 **and not for the nation only, but that he might also gather together into one the children of God that are scattered abroad.**—This verse is the comment of the apostle John on the prophecy of Caiaphas. The children of God here means all among all nations who would believe in Jesus when the gospel should be preached to them. It was a recognition that there were people among all nations who would believe in Jesus, and that not any fleshly family as such would be blessed of God.

53 **So from that day forth they took counsel that they might put him to death.**—The irresistible testimony that God was in him, given by raising one from the dead, was the time from which the more determined purpose to destroy Jesus dates. If we cannot confute his claims we will kill him is the demoniacal spirit that prompts them.

7. JESUS RETIRES UNTIL THE PASSOVER.
11: 54-57.

54 Jesus therefore walked no more openly among the Jews, but departed

54 **Jesus therefore walked no more openly among the Jews,**—Jesus had done his duty to them; they were infuriated by

thence into the country near to the wilderness, into a city called Ephraim;
and there he tarried with the disciples. 55 Now the passover of the Jews
was at hand: and many went up to Jerusalem out of the country before
the passover, to purify themselves. 56 They sought therefore for Jesus, and
spake one with another, as they stood in the temple, What think ye? That
he will not come to the feast? 57 Now the chief priests and the Pharisees
had given commandment, that, if any man knew where he was, he should
show it, that they might take him.

---

the evidence; he withdraws from them and leaves them to their fate. He can do them no good. His presence would inflame their feelings and draw abuse upon himself.

but departed thence into the country near to the wilderness, into a city called Ephraim; and there he tarried with the disciples.—Ephraim is supposed to be the place called Ephron (2 Chron. 13: 19), called also Ephrata, near Bethel, and about twenty miles from Jerusalem. It is supposed that he went to this place soon after the feast of the Passover.

55 **Now the passover of the Jews was at hand: and many went up to Jerusalem out of the country before the passover,**—When the Passover drew nigh many people from all the country where Jesus dwelled went up to the feast. They naturally expected Jesus who had created such a stir wherever he went, and who claimed to be a teacher sent from God, to be present. These people went up and after reaching Jerusalem prepared themselves to eat the passover.

to purify themselves.—[This explains why they came in advance of the time of the Passover—to purify themselves from ceremonial uncleanness before the feast. While there were no special rites of purification required of the Jews before the Passover, yet they were expected to purify themselves before participating in any important event (Ex. 19: 10, 11), and were accustomed to go through certain special rites of purification before the Passover (2 Chron. 30: 13-20).]

56 **They sought therefore for Jesus, and spake one with another, as they stood in the temple, What think ye? That he will not come to the feast?**—There was general conversation concerning him and an interest among the people, each asking to know of the others if they thought he would come.

57 **Now the chief priests and the Pharisees had given commandment, that, if any man knew where he was, he should**

show it, that they might take him.—The chief priests and Pharisees expected him to be present and had come to the fixed determination to kill him at this feast, so had given the direction that they might be aided in their work. Other scriptures say that they required his presence to be made known to them when in a retired and quiet place that they might take him without exciting the multitude. [Bear in mind that it was the Sanhedrin that published the edict commanding any man who knew of his whereabouts to reveal it in order that he might be arrested.]

[Note here—1: How baneful and destructive evil counsel is, especially out of the mouths of leading men, and how soon embraced and followed. Caiaphas no sooner propounds the putting of Christ to death, but from that day forward they lie in wait to take him. The high priests had satisfied their consciences, and now they made all possible speed to put their malicious designs and purposes in execution. Note 2: The prudential care and means which Jesus used for his own preservation, to avoid their fury he withdraws himself privately. Observe 3: When the time was come that he was to expose himself; when the time of the Passover drew near, in which he, being the true Paschal lamb, was to be slain, to put an end to that type; he withdraws no more, but surrenders himself to the rage and fury of his enemies and dies a shameful death for sinners, as the next chapter more at large informs us.]

[Observe from these latter verses that the spirit of prophecy did fall sometimes upon very bad men and that God has been pleased to reveal some part of his mind to the worst of men. Thus Pharaoh and Nebuchadnezzar had in their dreams a revelation from God—what things he intended to do. It is consistent with the holiness of God sometimes to make use of the tongues of the worst of men to publish and declare his will. Caiaphas, though a vile and wicked man, was, it is thought by many, influenced by God to prophesy and speak as an oracle. God may, when he pleases, employ wicked men this way without any prejudice to his holiness.]

PART THIRD.

EVENTS FROM HIS LAST ARRIVAL IN JERUSALEM TO HIS RESURRECTION.

12: 1 to 21: 25.

SECTION ONE.

HIS ARRIVAL AND SPEECHES PREVIOUS TO THE PASSOVER.

12: 1-50.

1. HE IS ANOINTED AT A SUPPER IN BETHANY.

12: 1-8.

1 Jesus therefore six days before the passover came to Bethany, where Larazus was, whom Jesus raised from the dead. 2 So they made him a supper there: and Martha served; but Lazarus was one of them that [1]sat

[1]Gr. *reclined*

---

1 **Jesus therefore six days before the passover came to Bethany, where Lazarus was, whom Jesus raised from the dead.**—The Passover began on the fourteenth day of the month of Abib or Nisan, the first month of the Jewish year. Six days before would be on the eighth day of the month. The most marked thing that had occurred at Bethany so far is that he raised Lazarus from the grave. The raising of Lazarus made him the most distinguished person in the village. [Bethany was the scene of the resurrection of Lazarus (11: 44) and of Christ's own ascension (Luke 24: 50). These two great events gave the village its notoriety.]

2 **So they made him a supper there: and Martha served; but Lazarus was one of them that sat at meat with him.**—The supper was made on what we would call Saturday evening; but, according to their division of time, the beginning of the first day of the week, Saturday night, after six o'clock. It is not said that this supper was served at the house of Lazarus. Matthew (26: 6, 7) says that a feast was made for him at Bethany in the house of Simon the Leper, and that a woman poured on him an alabaster box of ointment. There has

at meat with him. 3 Mary therefore took a pound of ointment of [2]pure nard, very precious, and anointed the feet of Jesus, and wiped his feet with her hair: and the house was filled with the odor of the ointment. 4 But Judas Iscariot, one of his disciples, that should [3]betray him, saith, 5 Why was not this ointment sold for three hundred [4]shillings, and given to the

[2]Or, *liquid nard*
[3]Or, *deliver him up*
[4]See marginal note on ch. 6. 7

been diversity of opinion as to whether there were two occurrences of this kind at Bethany the last week of his life. There is no means of definitely determining this question. There is no incompatibility in the idea that Martha with her talent for serving would serve at a feast at a neighbor's house, or that Mary with her tender and earnest devotion should anoint his head, or that Lazarus should be a guest of honor at the table with Jesus who had raised him from the dead.

3 **Mary therefore took a pound of ointment of pure nard, very precious,**—The ointment was pure, costly, and of exquisite odor. [It was the most expensive anointing oil of that date.]

and anointed the feet of Jesus,—Matthew (26: 7) and Mark (14: 3) say that it was poured upon his head. Both head and feet and the exposed parts of the body were all anointed. To anoint him for his burial would suggest this.

and wiped his feet with her hair: and the house was filled with the odor of the ointment.—John who alone tells who did the anointing says that the loving humility of Mary led her to anoint the feet and to wipe them with the hair of her head.

4 **But Judas Iscariot, one of his disciples,**—Judas was a lover of money, carried the purse kept by Jesus and his apostles, and, as with other men, it required evil surroundings to call the evil disposition into activity. His love of money now caused him to grumble at the wasteful expenditure of Mary.

that should betray him, saith,—When the prospects of Jesus grew darker still, and the evil passions were aroused, this evil spirit led him to betray his Lord.

5 **Why was not this ointment sold for three hundred shillings, and given to the poor?**—Evil desires in men often clothe themselves under pretense of good. It is possible that Judas

poor? 6 Now this he said, not because he cared for the poor; but because
he was a thief, and having the [5]bag [6]took away what was put therein. 7
Jesus therefore said, [7]Suffer her to keep it against the day of my burying.

[5]Or, *box*
[6]Or, *carried what was put therein*
[7]Or, *Let her alone:* it was *that she might keep it*

persuaded himself that he cared for the poor; but John, after seeing the full manifestation of his course, saw that he did not. It was selfish greed. [Judas, through his selfish motive, gives us an insight as to the worth of the ointment used by Mary in anointing Jesus. It was worth, according to his statement, around three hundred dollars. He was so narrow and covetous that he could see nothing in the gift but a "waste." He cared nothing for the poor. His plea was only a greedy pretext. It is a well-known fact to close observers that those who love Jesus most will do most for the poor.]

6 **Now this he said, not because he cared for the poor; but because he was a thief, and having the bag took away what was put therein.**—He wished to get possession of the money and keep control of it. [Jesus and his disciples had a common treasury from which they drew money to defray their expenses. Judas was treasurer. He carried the money around with them in a "bag"—purse. Being a thief, he desired the ointment to be sold and the money turned into the treasury so that he could steal it. The fact that a few days later he sold his Lord and Master for about seventeen dollars shows his greed for money. But the Judases are not all dead. He is a good type of all those treasurers, cashiers, and managers of business institutions who steal trust funds and money entrusted to them. He will have plenty of company at the resurrection and beyond the judgment, many like himself claiming to be very religious and friends of the poor.]

7 **Jesus therefore said, Suffer her to keep it against the day of my burying.**—Jesus reproved his complaint at her and told him that this was anointing him for his burial. Not that he expected to die then and be buried, but he knowing his end was near said it could serve as the anointing for his burial. [Judas virtually accused Mary of robbing the poor. So Jesus came forward in her defense and complimented her, saying

8 For the poor ye have always with you; but me ye have not always.

---

she has anointed my body before death and prepared it for burial. This was the only anointing the body of Jesus received from the hands of his female friends since he arose from the grave before they reached the sepulchre with their spices. Mary did not know the full import of her act of love at the time she bestowed it.]

8 **For the poor ye have always with you; but me ye have not always.**—Jesus knew that it was not care for the poor that moved Judas, so he told him that he could at all times help the poor, but these acts of kindness could not be always extended to him [for the reason he would shortly return to his Father, and what is done to my fleshly body must be done now.]

2. CURIOSITY ABOUT LAZARUS AND ITS EFFECTS. 12: 9-11.

9 The common people therefore of the Jews learned that he was there: and they came, not for Jesus' sake only, but that they might see Lazarus also, whom he had raised from the dead. 10 But the chief priests took counsel that they might put Lazarus also to death; 11 because that by reason of him many of the Jews went away, and believed on Jesus.

---

9 **The common people therefore of the Jews learned that he was there:**—Jews here refer to the inhabitants of Judea as distinguished from the Galileans. The twelve apostles were all Galileans save probably Judas. The Jews in a self-righteous way held aloof from Jesus, but he now by the miracles he had done wrought up the idea of making him their king and hence gave him that royal reception of a king.

and they came, not for Jesus' sake only, but that they might see Lazarus also, whom he had raised from the dead.—His most noted miracle was raising Lazarus from the dead. He, as one who had been in the grave until the fourth day, was an object of curiosity to all.

10 **But the chief priests took counsel that they might put Lazarus also to death;**—The presence of Lazarus alive was a continual reminder of the power of Jesus over death and the grave, and the chief priests, seeing this, felt the neces-

sity of putting him out of the way. It is singular that they did not see that if Jesus had restored him to life once he could easily do it again, and their madness gives added testimony to the claims of Jesus to be the Christ the Son of God.

11 **because that by reason of him many of the Jews went away, and believed on Jesus.**—The sight of Lazarus alive after he had been four days in the grave was a striking proof of the claims of Jesus as the sent of God.

3. HIS PUBLIC WELCOME BY THE PEOPLE.
12: 12-19.

12 On the morrow [8]a great multitude that had come to the feast, when
they heard that Jesus was coming to Jerusalem, 13 took the branches of the
palm trees, and went forth to meet him, and cried out, Hosanna: Blessed
is he that cometh in the name of the Lord, even the King of Israel. 14

[8]Some ancient authorities read *the common people*. See ver. 9

12 **On the morrow a great multitude that had come to the feast, when they heard that Jesus was coming to Jerusalem,**—[Josephus tells us that from two to three millions attended a passover. All four of the divine writers of the gospel give an account of his entry into Jerusalem. (See Matt. 21: 1-11; Mark 11: 1-11; Luke 19: 29-44.)]

13 **took the branches of the palm trees, and went forth to meet him, and cried out, Hosanna: Blessed is he that cometh in the name of the Lord, even the King of Israel.**—It had been the expectation of the Jews that a king would arise to deliver them from their bondage to the Roman Empire. The miracles and wonders wrought by Jesus drew their minds to him as the deliverer, so they work themselves into a state of enthusiasm over him as their king. They came out to Bethany to meet him, and they treated him as their coming king. They cast their garments in the way and when these did not suffice they cut the branches off the palm trees and cast them in the way that the king and even the ass on which he rode might not be defiled by walking upon the earth. [They literally carpeted the Master's pathway with leaves of the palm trees. He is not seeking privacy now. He is now publicly forcing the issue.]

And Jesus, having found a young ass, sat thereon; as it is written, 15 [9]Fear not, daughter of Zion: behold, thy King cometh, sitting on an ass's colt. 16 These things understood not his disciples at the first: but when Jesus was glorified, then remembered they that these things were written of him, and that they had done these things unto him. 17 The multitude therefore that was with him when he called Lazarus out of the tomb, and raised him

[9]Zech. 9. 9

14 **And Jesus, having found a young ass, sat thereon; as it is written,**—It had been foretold that the king would come as here described. He came in fulfillment of these promises and was the King, but they misunderstood the nature of his kingdom, and when a few days later, the prospects of an earthly kingdom having vanished, it is likely that many of those who honored him as a King, joined them in the cry, "Crucify him, crucify him."

15 **Fear not, daughter of Zion: behold, thy King cometh, sitting on an ass's colt.**—He found the young ass, as related by Matthew (21: 1-11) and Mark (11: 1-9) and rode upon this ass to the city of Jerusalem as foretold by the prophet: "Rejoice greatly, O daughter of Zion; shout, O daughter of Jerusalem: behold, thy king cometh unto thee: he is just, and having salvation; lowly, and riding upon an ass, even upon a colt the foal of an ass." (Zech. 9: 9.)

16 **These things understood not his disciples at the first: but when Jesus was glorified, then remembered they that these things were written of him, and that they had done these things unto him.**—His disciples did not at this time understand that these things had been foretold of the Messiah by the prophets, but after he ascended to his Father, they remembered these things had been written concerning Christ and that they had been done as foretold.

17 **The multitude therefore that was with him when he called Lazarus out of the tomb, and raised him from the dead, bare witness.**—The raising of Lazarus and the fact that he was present in their midst kept it fresh in their minds, and many who were present and saw him come forth from the grave were now in Jerusalem and testified to the facts and so caused added honor to be bestowed on Jesus. [The mir-

from the dead, bare witness. 18 For this cause also the multitude went
and met him, for that they heard that he had done this sign. 19 The Pharisees therefore said among themselves, [1]Behold how ye prevail nothing; lo,
the world is gone after him.

[1]Or, *Ye behold*

acle, raising Lazarus to life, had its effects on this great demonstration.]

18 **For this cause also the multitude went and met him, for that they heard that he had done this sign.**—On account of these witnesses, the interest of the people in Jesus was greatly increased.

19 **The Pharisees therefore said among themselves, Behold how ye prevail nothing; lo, the world is gone after him.**—These Pharisees were determined not to believe, and to such then as now added testimony excited wrath and bitterness rather than produced faith and repentance toward God. So in wrath they say the world is going after him. But they persist in a course that would have done them honor if they had been in a good cause. [These opposers had joined the Sanhedrin to put Jesus to death, and were astounded when they thought that practically the whole nation had gone over to him and demonstrated his popularity.]

4. A REQUEST OF CERTAIN GREEKS.
12: 20-26.

20 Now there were certain Greeks among those that went up to worship
at the feast: 21 these therefore came to Philip, who was of Bethsaida of
Galilee, and asked him, saying, Sir, we would see Jesus. 22 Philip cometh

20 **Now there were certain Greeks among those that went up to worship at the feast:**—It has been a question of doubt as to who these Greeks were. The Jews dwelling in Greece were called Grecians. All the texts call them Greeks. They were proselyte Greeks most likely. As strangers they desired to see Jesus and came to Philip.

21 **these therefore came to Philip, who was of Bethsaida of Galilee, and asked him, saying, Sir, we would see Jesus.**—As strangers, and since isolated by their nationality, they desired to see Jesus, and sought the interview through Philip

and telleth Andrew: Andrew cometh, and Philip, and they tell Jesus. 23
And Jesus answereth them, saying, The hour is come, that the Son of man
should be glorified. 24 Verily, verily, I say unto you, Except a grain of
wheat fall into the earth and die, it abideth by itself alone; but if it die,

himself, a Grecian Jew, as his name indicates. He doubtless understood their language and was approachable on this ground. ["See" is used in the sense we desire a conversation with him. Surely they could see Jesus with the natural eye without any intervention with Philip.]

22 **Philip cometh and telleth Andrew: Andrew cometh, and Philip, and they tell Jesus.**—[Andrew takes the lead. The request of these Greeks evidently assumed importance, for it is the occasion of a remarkable discourse. These men represented the Gentile world in its unrest, its hopelessness, its deep yearning for some divine Redeemer, to lift the helpless race out of its imbecility and despair, and guide it into nobler life.]

23 **And Jesus answereth them, saying, The hour is come, that the Son of man should be glorified.**—Jesus tells them that the time of his glorification is now at hand. He calls himself usually the Son of man, leaving it to his teachings and works to declare him the Son of God. In a few instances when they were disposed to doubt, he called himself the Son of God. [The disciples had always had inadequate ideas of what his kingdom was to be, and the pathway through which it was to be reached. Doubtless their faces at once lit up with the radiance of expectation, that the time was close at hand for the high places of the kingdom to be distributed. But Jesus has a lesson for them they little expect. Glory is coming, through a pathway of which they would never have dreamed, a pathway of tears, and sorrow, and pain and death.]

24 **Verily, verily, I say unto you, Except a grain of wheat fall into the earth and die, it abideth by itself alone; but if it die, it beareth much fruit.**—Preceding his glorification, his humiliation, his sufferings, his death, and his burial must come. Naturally must the humiliation precede the glorification, but his death and resurrection would result in bringing many into his service and so to eternal life. He compares

it beareth much fruit. 25 He that loveth his [2]life loseth it; and he that hateth his [2]life in this world shall keep it unto [3]life eternal. 26 If any man

[2 3]*life* in these places represents two different Greek words

himself to a grain of wheat. If the grain is not planted and does not die, it will remain alone. But if it die in the ground, it gives its life to the production of many seeds. So if he preserved his life, his disciples would not multiply; but if he died, out of his death would come a multitude of disciples. [A grain of wheat might lie on a hard, smooth, dry surface a long time and never be anything but a grain of wheat with large possibilities of fruitfulness within it; they would never be developed into realities. Falling into the ground, covered over, exposed to soil, and warmth, and moisture, the grain dies and decays; the germ within is released; it feeds upon the very decay of the enveloping grain, and lo, the plant; and not another grain, but thirty, sixty, a hundredfold. Life comes out of death and more abundantly. It is almost certain that even yet the disciples did not understand him, but it is equally evident, in the light of after events, that he meant to tell them that his glorification was to come through his death. From this the coming of the Greeks could not save him, but was valuable as a symbolic indication of how, in the end, he would draw all men unto him.]

25 **He that loveth his life loseth it;**—If Jesus had so loved this present life that he had refused to give it up, he would have gained no future life for others. He gives as a general truth of all beings that love this life so as not to sacrifice it to honor God and bless men could not gain the life that is eternal. [Indicating thus the joyousness with which he went forth to sacrifice in view of its results, he now proceeds to give the principle a general application to his disciples. A selfish love of life that keeps a man from duty only entails its ultimate loss.]

and he that hateth his life in this world—To hate this life is to be willing to surrender it, or to hold it in less esteem than the spiritual life in the future. ["Hates" it, only as its careful preservation interferes with duty; "hates" it, in this sense, that he will ever make it subordinate to high and holy

serve me, let him follow me; and where I am, there shall also my servant be: if any man serve me, him will the Father honor. 27 Now is my soul

aims, to generous devotion to the glory of God and the good of men.]

shall keep it unto life eternal.—[What seems to be its loss is only apparent. It never can be lost in that way.]

26 **If any man serve me, let him follow me;**—To follow Jesus is to do his will, to be actuated by the same principles that moved him. In living like him, we will be made like him in character and so will be fitted to dwell with him. [Follow me in the pathway of self-abnegation and self-sacrifice to which I have already alluded.]

and where I am,—[The present tense used for the future. He would be with his Father in heaven.]

there shall also my servant be:—[Having followed me in self-sacrifice, he shall be with me in glory.]

if any man serve me, him will the Father honor.—As God honored his Son so will he honor all who serve his Son. [How little does modern Christendom realize the lesson of this passage! On what miserable foundations of self-indulgence and self-saving are men building hope of glory and honor at God's right hand, which can find a solid foundation only on self-denial and self-sacrifice.]

5. THE HOUR OF HIS TROUBLE.
12: 27-30.

troubled; and what shall I say? Father, save me from this [4]hour. But

[4]Or, *hour?*

27 **Now is my soul troubled;**—[The full shadow of the awful experience through which he is so soon to pass falls across his pathway and overwhelms him with its darkness. The humanity shuddered with a horror that only proved its humanity, and brought into clearer relief the grandeur of its final victory over itself.]

and what shall I say?—What prayer shall I offer to my Father and with what words shall it be clothed? In anticipation of the sufferings and death, he in his human feelings

for this cause came I unto this hour. 28 Father, glorify thy name. There came therefore a voice out of heaven, *saying,* I have both glorified it, and will glorify it again. 29 The multitude therefore, that stood by, and heard

shrank back from it, and pondered whether he should ask God to save him from the sufferings that were before him.

Father, save me from this hour.—He now thought of his having come into the world to endure the very sufferings from which he now shrank so he did not make the prayer. [A footnote has the interrogative "hour"? Some think this to be the only form that can be reconciled with the character of Jesus, and the outcome of the struggle. Passing through the profound trouble of his soul, he soliloquizes in the presence of those surrounding him: "Oh, what shall I do? Shall I yield to my human shrinking, and ask my Father to save me from this supreme hour which is approaching?"]

But for this cause came I unto this hour.—[All that has preceded, the incarnation, the life, the teachings, the miracles, leading up to this hour, were important because of their relations to this hour. The atonement is the climax of all that has preceded.]

28 **Father, glorify thy name.**—Instead of praying for deliverance from that hour, he prayed that God would do that which would promote his glory regardless of the suffering of himself. This was equivalent to the prayer, "Not my will, but thine be done." (Luke 22: 42.) [The struggle is over. This is the victor's cry. Glorify thy name! No matter what it costs me, no matter through what pathway it leads me, no matter what self-denial or self-sacrifice it requires, yet glorify thy name through me!]

There came therefore a voice out of heaven, saying, I have both glorified it,—[Jesus had ever ascribed his mighty works to God, and, as the Father thus heard and answered his prayer, as so recently in the case of Lazarus, he glorified his own name in these displays of power.]

and will glorify it again.—God glorified himself in sending Jesus into the world to die for sinners. He would glorify it again in glorifying Jesus at his right hand as Lord of lords and King of kings. [This was to be accomplished in that

it, said that it had thundered: others said, An angel hath spoken to him.
30 Jesus answered and said, This voice hath not come for my sake, but for

wondrous series of events, culminating in the resurrection and ascension, upon whose threshold they now stood.]

29 **The multitude therefore, that stood by, and heard it, said that it had thundered: others said, An angel hath spoken to him.**—This voice most likely spoke in the Hebrew or Aramaic tongue as the voice to Saul did. The people hearing the sound and not understanding what was said, thus concluded from the temperament of the hearers. [They heard it as well as Jesus, but their ears were not attuned to heavenly speech. Others realized that it was more than a sound, that it was a "voice," but were not able to distinguish it from a clap of thunder.]

30 **Jesus answered and said, This voice hath not come for my sake, but for your sakes.**—This voice came from heaven to convince the people that God was in Jesus and spake through him. It was for the profit of the hearers, not for that of Jesus. [He needed nothing to strengthen and confirm his faith, for the victory was gained before the voice spoke, but they did need much.]

6. JESUS PREDICTS HIS CRUCIFIXION.
12: 31-36.

your sakes. 31 Now is [5]the judgment of this world: now shall the prince

[5]Or, *a judgment*

31 **Now is the judgment of this world:**—He warned them that the contest between him and this prince of the world, the evil one, was close at hand. This contest was to take place in the grave. Jesus surrendered himself into the power of the evil one. He was carried down into the grave by the evil one—"him that hath power over death and the grave." "Since then the children are sharers in flesh and blood, he also himself in like manner partook of the same; that through death he might bring to nought him that had the power of death, that is, the devil." (Heb. 2: 14.) Jesus in his flesh and blood went down into the grave as a prisoner of the devil.

of this world be cast out. 32 And I, if I be lifted up [6]from the earth, will
draw all men unto myself. 33 But this he said, signifying by what manner
of death he should die. 34 The multitude therefore answered him, We have

[6]Or, *out of*

["Now" is the vivid presentation of the near future. The world's crisis is just at hand. Calvary will inaugurate it, and tremendous consequences flow from it.]

now shall the prince of this world be cast out.—In the grave he contended with the devil, overcame him in his own dark domain, and was a victor over him. The prince of this world was overcome, cast out of his authority by the resurrection of Jesus from the grave. In the grave the battle was fought; in the grave the victory was won that freed the world from the domain of the evil one. [His dominion is to cease. And this is to be accomplished through that very death of Jesus which Satan is now scheming to bring about, but which, unwittingly to him, is but the prelude to the resurrection and glorification of Jesus, and the rescue of humanity. Satan, like Samson, pulled his own pillar from under his building.]

32 **And I, if I be lifted up from the earth, will draw all men unto myself.**—He again refers to the fact that his dying on the cross and his burial would be the means of drawing men to him by his resurrection from the dead. He "was declared to be the Son of God with power, according to the spirit of holiness, by the resurrection from the dead; even Jesus Christ our Lord." (Rom. 1: 4.) So men were drawn to him by his being lifted up on the cross. [He will draw all kinds of men —men of all nations. The relation of what has preceded, to the coming of the Greeks, comes out in this verse. As one king is dethroned, another and mightier one takes his place who invites all men to him by persuasion of the cross.]

33 **But this he said, signifying by what manner of death he should die.**—His lifting up referred to his death upon the cross. [This passage in which Jesus, after having shuddered in view of the cross, strengthened himself by tracing in broad outlines the picture of the immense revolution which it will effect, may be compared with that of Paul (Col. 2: 14, 15), where he represents Jesus as making a spectacle of the in-

heard out of the law that the Christ abideth for ever: and how sayest thou, The Son of man must be lifted up? who is this Son of man? 35 Jesus therefore said unto them, Yet a little while is the light [7]among you. Walk

[7]Or, *in*

fernal powers, despoiling them of their power, and triumphing over them on the cross.]

34 **The multitude therefore answered him, We have heard out of the law that the Christ abideth for ever:**—They referred to the language of David: "Jehovah hath sworn, and will not repent: Thou art a priest for ever after the order of Melchizedek." (Psalm 110: 4.) And to such other prophecies as: "Of the increase of his government and of peace there shall be no end, upon the throne of David, and upon his kingdom, to establish it, and to uphold it with justice and with righteousness from henceforth even for ever. The zeal of Jehovah of hosts will perform this." (Isa. 9: 7.) "And there was given him dominion, and glory, and a kingdom, that all the peoples, nations, and languages should serve him: his dominion is an everlasting dominion, which shall not pass away, and his kingdom that which shall not be destroyed." (Dan. 7: 14.) All the Old Testament scriptures are classed as the law. It is true that he was to abide forever, but not in the flesh.

and how sayest thou, The Son of man must be lifted up? who is this Son of man?—[Jesus had frequently applied this term to himself, which they quote also from Dan. 7: 13, 14. Realizing that he refers to death in the "lifting up," they exclaim against the incongruity of this with the Jewish idea of a glorified, victorious Messiah.]

35 **Jesus therefore said unto them, Yet a little while is the light among you.**—Jesus was the light of the world. While he was with them they should listen to his teaching and walk by the light of his wisdom. When he was gone they would have none to give light. This is the same as he told his disciples, "A little while, and ye behold me no more; and again a little while, and ye shall see me." (16: 16.)

Walk while ye have the light,—[Turn your footsteps into the path of faith which it marks out while the light is shining.]

while ye have the light, that darkness overtake you not: and he that walketh in the darkness knoweth not whither he goeth. 36 While ye have the light, believe on the light, that ye may become sons of light.
These things spake Jesus, and he departed and [8]hid himself from them.

[8]Or, *was hidden from them*

that darkness overtake you not:—[Out of the pathway of duty, for it will then be so difficult to find it. The thought is—seek the light and walk in it while you have an opportunity, for the opportunity may soon pass away and you be left in the dark unsaved.]

and he that walketh in the darkness knoweth not whither he goeth.—[He stumbles over the many obstacles in his path. Since the rejection of Jesus by the Jews, Israel has wandered in the wilderness of this world, as a caravan without a goal and without a guide.]

36 **While ye have the light, believe on the light, that ye may become sons of light.**—While Jesus was with them, they should believe in him that they may be children of the light—practice the truths taught as constituting the truth. To walk in the light we must appropriate the opportunity as it is offered to us.

These things spake Jesus, and he departed and hid himself from them.—[He withdrew from them so they could not find him. He departed from the temple, where he was never seen again. They never saw him again in the city until he was a prisoner in the hands of the Sanhedrin. It is a sad dark day when Jesus departs either from an individual, a city or a nation for the reason destruction is sure to follow. Unbelief closed their spiritual eyes against the truth Jesus presented and was the cause of his departing from them. Unbelief will damn the world today.]

7. JESUS RETIRES AND JOHN COMMENTS ON THE UNBELIEF OF THE JEWS.
12: 37-43.

37 But though he had done so many signs before them, yet they believed

37 **But though he had done so many signs before them, yet they believed not on him:**—Additional testimony does not

**not on him: 38 that the word of Isaiah the prophet might be fulfilled,
which he spake,**

°Lord, who hath believed our report?
And to whom hath the arm of the Lord been revealed?

39 For this cause they could not believe, for that Isaiah said again, 40

°Is. 53. 1

produce faith where the heart is wicked and bitter. Jesus said: "If they hear not Moses and the prophets, neither will they be persuaded, if one rise from the dead." (Luke 16: 31.) [John only records seven of these miracles, but often refers to a great number of them. (2: 23; 4: 45; 7: 31; 20: 30.) Some of them had a sort of faith in Jesus as a man of God, or as the "prophet of Galilee," but they did not confess that faith which believes, trusts, obeys, and devotes one's life to his service.]

38 **that the word of Isaiah the prophet might be fulfilled, which he spake, Lord, who hath believed our report? And to whom hath the arm of the Lord been revealed?**—In view of the fact so few would believe in Jesus, notwithstanding his many miracles, Isaiah asked, "Lord, who hath believed our report," and who have recognized the power of God in the miracles performed? [This quotation is found in Isa. 53: 1. The prophet predicted such a condition as we here find existing among the Jews.]

39 **For this cause they could not believe, for that Isaiah said again,**—In their condition of heart, no amount or degree of signs could produce faith. [The cause of their failing to believe is not the fact that God, through Isaiah, said thus and thus, but he simply points out the cause of their unbelief in what he said. The reason why they could not believe was not that God had decreed their unbelief and destroyed their free agency, but that, in the exercise of their free agency, they had made themselves, by the operation of God's moral laws, incapable of belief. Then, too, the same means that God uses, the gospel of Christ, to save the world, will soften the heart of one and lead him to heaven and at the same time harden the heart of another and cause him to be banished away from God at the last day. The gospel will either lift

[10]He hath blinded their eyes, and he hardened their heart;
Lest they should see with their eyes, and perceive with their heart,
And should turn,
And I should heal them.

[10]Is. 6. 10

a man to heaven or else send him to hell. It all depends upon whether one opens his heart and cooperates with God as to which place he goes.]

40 **He hath blinded their eyes, and he hardened their heart; lest they should see with their eyes, and perceive with their heart, and should turn, and I should heal them.**—Because they loved sin and rebellion, God hardened their hearts and stiffened their necks to lead them on to their ruin. Isaiah foretold that they could not believe so as to be healed or saved by God, but he meant in the disposition of heart they were cultivating they could not do these things. ["This explains why they could not believe. Whether they were morally responsible for their unbelief depends on how God blinded their eyes and hardened their hearts. If he did it by a direct act, regardless of their moral condition, then they were not responsible. If, however, he did it by a law of the universe that whoever turns from the light shall become blind, and whosoever steels his heart against the truth shall find his heart hardened, then they were morally responsible if they had turned from the light and hardened their hearts. It is a physical as well as a moral law that he who turns from the light and seeks to abide in darkness will become blinded until he will 'believe a lie and be damned.' The men who are the champions of unbelief, such men as Voltaire, Paine, and Ingersoll, are unbelievers because they did not wish to believe. Their moral condition was such that they could not justify their course of life only by refusing to believe on the Christ. They sought the darkness, and as a result finally they became so blinded that they could not believe. They blinded their own eyes because they brought upon themselves the penalty. God blinded their eyes because their blindness resulted from the action of his universal law. Thus it is said

41 These things said Isaiah, because he saw his glory; and he spake of him.
42 Nevertheless even of the rulers many believed on him; but because of
the Pharisees they did not confess [11]*it,* lest they should be put out of the

[11]Or, him

of Pharaoh that 'God hardened his heart,' but it is also said that Pharaoh hardened his heart. He chose, in the exercise of his voluntary agency, to harden his heart, but it is God's law that those who harden their hearts shall be hardened, and hence God, by this law, hardened his heart. By reference to Matt. 13: 14 the reader will find this passage from Isaiah quoted and applied by the Savior to the Jews. In the application he shows how they were blinded, 'Their eyes have they closed.' The Savior's words settle how God blinded their eyes. It was by the application of his invariable law to their own acts. French says: 'The Lord, having constituted as the righteous law of moral government, that sin should produce darkness of heart and moral insensibility, declared that he would allow the law to take its course.' "—Johnson. The means God used to touch and tender the hearts of the children of Israel and cause them to follow Moses, their leader, also hardened the heart of Pharaoh.]

41 **These things said Isaiah, because he saw his glory; and he spake of him.**—Isaiah foresaw the glory of the works and power of Jesus and foretold of these, and yet how few would believe him.

42 **Nevertheless even of the rulers many believed on him;**—Notwithstanding the general unbelief and hardness of heart, some of the leading men believed in him, who did not as yet confess him. Among this number were some who for the time seem not to have openly confessed him. Nicodemus and Joseph of Arimathea were among these. But these did not love the praise of men more than the praise of God, for they in the darkest hours do confess him and so could not have been of the class to which reference is here made.

but because of the Pharisees they did not confess it, lest they should be put out of the synagogue:—The Jews had threatened that any who would confess that he was the Christ should be put out of the synagogue. This must refer to

synagogue: 43 for they loved the glory *that is* of men more than the glory *that is* of God.

---

physical or bodily exclusion from attendance in the service of the synagogue. It involved the forfeiture of all rights pertaining to membership in the synagogue. Here faith failed to bring the salvation from God because those who believed had not courage to act on the faith; they did not exercise the faith; faith did not perfect itself in works of obedience. This faith left the man a poor, helpless, self-condemned outcast sinner. A faith that fears man, that loves the praise of men more than the praise of God, engulfs itself in deeper ruin, leaves the soul without excuse in the hands of an insulted, outraged, and angry God, who whets the sword of his wrath to execute vengeance on those who refuse the gospel of his Son. He who knows his Master's will and so believes and yet refuses to do it will be beaten with many stripes.

43 **for they loved the glory that is of men more than the glory that is of God.**—This class here mentioned must have been of that class of which Jesus spoke when he said: "He that denieth me in the presence of men shall be denied in the presence of the angels of God." (Luke 12: 9.) [The fact that these rulers did not confess Christ openly for fear shows their cowardly spirit and only added to their sin. They were dishonest and the worst hypocrites. There is no hope for such characters.]

8. OTHER WORDS OF JESUS ABOUT BELIEF.
12: 44-50.

44 And Jesus cried and said, He that believeth on me, believeth not on me, but on him that sent me. 45 And he that beholdeth me beholdeth him

---

44 **And Jesus cried and said, He that believeth on me, believeth not on me, but on him that sent me.**—He does not believe in Jesus as the author and founder of the good that he did and taught, but in God who sent him and gave him all power and whose will he came to do.

45 **And he that beholdeth me beholdeth him that sent me.**—He was only the representative of the Father who sent him,

that sent me. 46 I am come a light into the world, that whosoever be-
lieveth on me may not abide in the darkness. 47 And if any man hear my
sayings, and keep them not, I judge him not: for I came not to judge the
world, but to save the world. 48 He that rejecteth me, and receiveth not
my sayings, hath one that judgeth him: the word that I spake, the same

and in hearing and seeing him they saw the Father who sent him.

46 **I am come a light into the world, that whosoever believeth on me may not abide in the darkness.**—The world as created was enveloped in darkness—physical and spiritual—and Jesus came in his life and teaching to become a moral and spiritual light to the world. [It was the work of Jesus to make all things clear. He illuminates the mysteries of our being and destiny when we grasp them in their fullness. Those who walk in his light will have their doubts solved, mysteries cleared up, and the clouds rolled away from the future.]

47 **And if any man hear my sayings, and keep them not, I judge him not: for I came not to judge the world, but to save the world.**—Jesus in person was not to judge or condemn, but to save the world. He spoke the words of God that through these words the world might be saved. [It is not the office of Jesus to judge those who keep not his sayings. While he will sit upon the throne in the day of judgment, yet he will not judge and condemn the world that he came to save. Each individual will be either saved or condemned on his arrival at the judgment. His word that he left in the world will decide the destiny of every one. The work assigned to Jesus in that day is to consign each to the place for which they are prepared.]

48 **He that rejecteth me, and receiveth not my sayings, hath one that judgeth him: the word that I spake, the same shall judge him in the last day.**—One who was not saved by the word of God, made known through Christ, would be condemned by that word. These words will be the standard by which in the last day all shall be judged. The great trouble with most religious people is that they desire to be religious, they desire to honor God, but they desire to do it in their

shall judge him in the last day. 49 For I spake not from myself; but the Father that sent me, he hath given me a commandment, what I should say, and what I should speak. 50 And I know that his commandment is life eternal: the things therefore which I speak, even as the Father hath said unto me, so I speak.

---

own way. They have confidence in their ability to invent ways that will please God. This is a fatal mistake.

[Christ and his doctrine are inseparable; to receive his doctrine is to receive him; and to reject his doctrine is to reject him. Such rejecters of Christ and the doctrine of the gospel shall not escape the judgment of Christ in the last day. The word is now the rule of living, and it shall be hereafter the rule of judging.]

49 **For I spake not from myself; but the Father that sent me, he hath given me a commandment, what I should say, and what I should speak.**—What Jesus spoke did not originate with him, but came from God. God gave the rule by which the world must be judged. Jesus as the Son of God, sent by him into the world, delivered no message or command of his own, but only the things given him of God. [The Son was the Father's agent and he spake through him.]

50 **And I know that his commandment is life eternal: the things therefore which I speak, even as the Father hath said unto me, so I speak.**—Jesus knew the commandment was from God and that it would give or lead all who followed it to life everlasting. The following teaches the same thing: "And the witness is this, that God gave unto us eternal life, and this life is in his Son. He that hath the Son hath the life; he that hath not the Son of God hath not the life." (1 John 5: 11, 12.) The laws that God gave to Jesus grew out of the principles that moved God. Jesus was God in the flesh, showing what the principles and life of God would be in the flesh. For man to receive these principles into his heart and to live them is to make him like God in character and will fit him to live with God forever. [Jesus said, "My words are spirit and they are life." There are life-giving principles in the word of God when received in the heart and become the law of life. John here closes his record of the revelation of Jesus to the world.]

SECTION TWO.

CONVERSATION AND INCIDENTS AT THE PASCHAL SUPPER.

13: 1 to 14: 31.

1. HE WASHED THE DISCIPLES' FEET. 13: 1-11.

1 Now before the feast of the passover, Jesus knowing that his hour was come that he should depart out of this world unto the Father, having loved his own that were in the world, he loved them [1]unto the end. 2 And

[1]Or, *to the uttermost*

1 **Now before the feast of the passover,**—[How long before is not specified. I take it to mean *just* before. This feast refers to the eating of the paschal lamb.]

Jesus knowing that his hour was come—[The exact hour was close at hand—the time was come. The preliminaries had already begun.]

that he should depart out of this world unto the Father,—[Calvary was no accident. Jesus knew that he would die on the morrow.]

having loved his own that were in the world, he loved them unto the end.—[I take "his own" here to mean his disciples. They were "in the world," and were to remain in the world, exposed to its temptations and trials. He is filled with a tender sympathy for them, knowing that they are soon to be deprived of his presence and counsel. Having given them abundant proofs of his love in word and deed heretofore, now at the close of his intercourse he will give them a crowning proof in the acts and words of this memorial night.] The Passover was approaching when he knew that he must suffer and die. The knowledge of his approaching sufferings did not destroy his interest in his disciples, but rather increased unto the end. Indeed all the sufferings that he endured were for the sake of these disciples—not the world. He suffered all for them and his desire for their happiness increased as the end approached. This was said in view of what follows.

during supper, the devil having already put into the heart of Judas Iscariot,
Simon's *son,* to [2]betray him, 3 *Jesus,* knowing that the Father had given
all things into his hands, and that he came forth from God, and goeth

[2]Or, *deliver him up*

2 **And during supper, the devil having already put into the heart of Judas Iscariot, Simon's son, to betray him,**—This is Thursday evening as is generally believed. On the day previous, Judas had bargained with the chief priests and elders to betray him. It was to be done in the absence of the crowds without strife or confusion. The Common Version reads: "After supper"; the Revised, "During supper." A better rendering than either is the Bible Union Version, which renders it, "Supper being served, ready to be eaten." It was after it was served, ready to be eaten, knowing all things about to occur, after they had seated themselves at the table, Jesus arose and washed the feet of his disciples. [The fact that the devil put into Judas' heart to betray Jesus does not exculpate or excuse Judas. It is true that Satan may cast darts of temptation into the heart, but we need not allow them to rankle. We are not responsible for the evil thought suggested by the devil, but we are responsible for harboring it and acting upon it.]

3 **Jesus, knowing that the Father had given all things into his hands, and that he came forth from God, and goeth unto God,**—To understand this, we must look at the circumstances attending. It was the Passover to which no unclean person could approach. When the Jews came up to Jerusalem to observe the Passover, they purified themselves: "Now the passover of the Jews was at hand: and many went up to Jerusalem out of the country before the passover, to purify themselves." (10: 55.) These disciples of the Lord had thus prepared themselves when they came to the city of Jerusalem; but in passing to and from the city were liable to have their feet contaminated by the touch of something unclean, and to avoid this, after they approached the supper, their feet were washed. This was the occasion of the washing at this time, hence the language of Jesus to Peter: "He that is bathed needeth not save to wash his feet, but is clean every whit."

unto God, 4 riseth from supper, and layeth aside his garments; and he took a towel, and girded himself. 5 Then he poureth water into the basin, and began to wash the disciples' feet, and to wipe them with the towel wherewith he was girded. 6 So he cometh to Simon Peter. He saith unto him, Lord, dost thou wash my feet? 7 Jesus answered and said unto

(Verse 10.) They had been purified when they came to the city and now only needed the washing of the feet to be clean entirely so they could partake of the Passover supper. Another fact that should not be overlooked is that "there arose also a contention among them, which of them was accounted to be greatest." (Luke 22: 24.) This was after they came to the table. The washing of one another's feet, it seems probable, gave rise to this contention. The humbler should wash the feet of the greater was the rule among the Jews. While they were disputing over this and to reprove them for their untimely contention, Jesus prepared himself to wash their feet. This gives significance to Peter's language: "Thou shalt never wash my feet." While contending with his fellow disciples that some of them should do it, the emphasis was that Jesus should not. The presence of the basin and towels at the place indicate the correctness of this statement. [Here Jesus asserts anew his divinity and anticipates his ascension. He did not allow the treachery working in the heart of Judas to prevent him from doing what follows. He did not wash Judas' feet in ignorance that he would betray him, but with full knowledge of it.]

4 **riseth from supper, and layeth aside his garments; and he took a towel, and girded himself.**—While they were contending who should wash the feet of the others, Jesus laid aside his outside robe and girdle as a servant does and tied the towel around his waist.

5 **Then he poureth water into the basin, and began to wash the disciples' feet, and to wipe them with the towel wherewith he was girded.**—He then proceeded to perform the office of a servant.

6 **So he cometh to Simon Peter. He saith unto him, Lord, dost thou wash my feet?**—With whom he began it is not certain. It may mean, in beginning to do the work, he came to

him, What I do thou knowest not now; but thou shalt understand hereafter. 8 Peter saith unto him, Thou shalt never wash my feet. Jesus answered him, If I wash thee not, thou hast no part with me. 9 Simon

---

Peter first. If he did not begin with Peter, the one with whom he began seems to have made no remonstrance. This question of Peter, with the reply of Jesus, seems to show that he came first to Peter with water before he had washed any others.

7 **Jesus answered and said unto him, What I do thou knowest not now; but thou shalt understand hereafter.**—What Jesus did Peter did not now understand, but when he came to know the true spirit and mission of Jesus he would understand the significance of the service he rendered them. Connect with this the teaching recorded by Luke (22: 24-27) in reproof of the strife as to who is greatest: "And there arose also a contention among them, which of them was accounted to be greatest. And he said unto them, The kings of the Gentiles have lordship over them; and they that have authority over them are called Benefactors. But ye shall not be so: but he that is the greater among you, let him become as the younger; and he that is chief, as he that doth serve. For which is greater, he that sitteth at meat, or he that serveth? is not he that sitteth at meat? but I am in the midst of you as he that serveth." [This is not a mere foot washing, for then another and not I ought to have performed it. It is a symbol. Peter ought to have realized the meaning of these words, but, with his usual rashness, answers hastily.]

8 **Peter saith unto him, Thou shalt never wash my feet.**—Peter with his impulsiveness and promptness, in deciding and acting, told Jesus he could never submit to so dishonoring Jesus as to permit him to wash his feet. [He is stupid. He does not realize that Jesus must have a lofty reason. He only sees the humiliation of the Master he loves and he cannot bear it.]

Jesus answered him, If I wash thee not, thou hast no part with me.—This response of Jesus may have a deeper and more far-reaching meaning than we are in the habit of seeing in it. If I wash thee not, if I cleanse thee not, thou hast no

Peter saith unto him, Lord, not my feet only, but also my hands and my head. 10 Jesus saith to him, He that is bathed needeth not [3]save to wash his feet, but is clean every whit: and ye are clean, but not all. [2]11 For he

[3]Some ancient authorities omit *save,* and *his feet*

part with me. [Your part is submission to my will. It is not for you to question—only to obey. Make your choice, submission or exclusion.] The reply of Jesus had a double meaning. The question of purification was brought out again: If I purify you not, you have no part with me. While this literal washing was primarily referred to, the deeper significance of a spiritual purification was implied. (Rev. 1: 5, 6.)

9 **Simon Peter saith unto him, Lord, not my feet only, but also my hands and my head.**—Peter with the same quick and decisive spirit asks him to wash his face and his hands also. [Here is the same Peter who rushes upon the water and a moment afterwards cries, "I perish!" Who strikes with the sword and who takes to flight, who enters into the presence of the high priest and yet denies his Master. The loyalty of heart which was under all this insubordination speaks out here. If it is a question of union with thee, wash me completely. Consecrate my whole body. He still does not enter fully into the thought. He is imagining something efficacious in the physical act.] Peter, with his earnestness and impulsiveness, seeing his favor with Jesus depended on his being washed by him runs to the other extreme and asks him not only to wash his feet, but his hands and head also. "Wash me all over," in other words.

10 **Jesus saith to him, He that is bathed**—[He who has washed his whole body once for the day.]

needeth not save to wash his feet,—[Which may have become soiled from the defilements of the road.] But since they had been purified and only the feet had been exposed to contamination, only the feet needed to be washed and the whole person was cleansed.

but is clean every whit:—[In all other particulars. So he who, by earnestly attaching himself to Christ, has broken with sin once for all has no need at each particular defilement to begin anew this general consecration; he has only to

knew him that should betray him; therefore said he, Ye are not all clean.

cleanse himself from the stain by confession and recourse to Christ.]

and ye are clean, but not all.—Here he gives a spiritual significance to his language and says that not only the body was clean, but they were all spiritually clean, save one, whom he knew would betray him. [There was one of the little crowd who had not spiritually bathed himself, to whom mere foot washing would do no good.]

11 **For he knew him that should betray him;**—Jesus already knew that Judas had bargained to betray him.

therefore said he, Ye are not all clean.—After the service had been performed, he asked if they knew the significance of it. [By expressing in this way the grief which they thought his crime caused him to feel, Jesus makes a last effort to bring Judas to repentance. And if he does not succeed, he will at least have shown to his disciples that he was not the dupe of his hypocrisy. (Verse 19.)]

2. HE COMMENTS ON THE WASHING.
13: 12-20.

12 So when he had washed their feet, and taken his garments, and [4]sat
down again, he said unto them, Know ye what I have done to you? 13 Ye
call me, Teacher, and, Lord: and ye say well; for so I am. 14 If I then,

[4]Gr. *reclined*

12 **So when he had washed their feet,**—[Peter therefore submitted, and his feet were washed with the rest.]

and taken his garments, and sat down again, he said unto them,—[The object lesson is over. Now comes the explanation of its teaching.]

Know ye what I have done to you?—[You know the literal act, but do you understand its significance, the spiritual application?]

13 **Ye call me, Teacher, and, Lord: and ye say well; for so I am.**—They all recognized him as their Teacher and Ruler. [Jesus exalts his relationship to them in order that the lesson to be drawn from his act of humility may be the stronger.]

the Lord and the Teacher, have washed your feet, ye also ought to wash one another's feet. 15 For I have given you an example, that ye also should do as I have done to you. 16 Verily, verily, I say unto you, A [5]servant is not greater than his lord; neither [6]one that is sent greater than

[5]Gr. *bondservant*
[6]Gr. *an apostle*

The word "Lord" has a distinct meaning, and in reading the word of God that meaning should be kept in mind. You call me your Ruler and Teacher. "And ye say well [or rightly]; for so I am." He had come from God to teach them. They had left all to follow him, as his servants and pupils. He impresses the relationship and his superiority upon them, for, without feeling this, they could not understand the lesson he was teaching them.

14 **If I then, the Lord and the Teacher, have washed your feet, ye also ought to wash one another's feet.**—I have performed the office of a servant for you and you ought to do such acts for one another.

15 **For I have given you an example,**—He is enforcing on this occasion the great lesson of his mission—that the true end of the servant of God is to serve and not to be served, that men and angels will find their highest and best good in helping others. Man can bless himself only by blessing others.

that ye also should do as I have done to you.—This washing of the feet was the cleansing that they might eat the passover supper. The special service could not again occur save on a similar occasion. As the Passover passed away or was swallowed up in Christ, our Passover, the same service might occur. But the principle taught in this by example was: let him that would be greatest be servant of all. There is nothing in this that could indicate a special ordinance or formal observance to be perpetuated in the church. The feet washing of both the Old Testament and the New were acts of helpful kindness when needed. [To take these words as a command to establish the church ordinance of foot washing, as some have done, is to utterly miss the spirit of the whole scene, and the great lesson it was intended to convey.]

16 **Verily, verily, I say unto you, A servant is not greater than his lord; neither one that is sent greater than he that**

he that sent him. 17 If ye know these things, blessed are ye if ye do
them. 18 I speak not of you all: I know whom I [7]have chosen: but that
the scripture may be fulfilled, [8]He that eateth [9]my bread lifted up his heel
against me. 19 From henceforth I tell you before it come to pass, that,

[7]Or, *chose*
[8]Ps. 41. 9
[9]Many ancient authorities read *his bread with me*

sent him.—If the Master could perform such acts for the servants, the servants should not object to doing it for one another. I send you—do not think you are better than I. If you are my servants, as you are sent by me, you should not feel yourselves above doing what I do; you should follow my footsteps and be led by the Spirit that moves me.

17 **If ye know these things, blessed are ye if ye do them.**—If they understood the lessons taught it would add much to their happiness if they would do them. The spirit that is willing to serve is one that will always bring happiness, and without which true happiness cannot be attained. A person that is always expecting and exacting deference will be unhappy. Seek to show deference, let such esteem others better than themselves, is the spirit that Christ inculcates and is one that will bring happiness in time and eternity. What will bring true happiness in time will also bring it in eternity and vice versa. Then if you have understood these things, you shall be blessed if you do them. The principle of helping the helpless, of weeping with those that weep, and of encouraging the lowly and encouraging the sinful to sin no more is the essential and fundamental spirit of Jesus Christ and his holy religion, and to cultivate the spirit and practice of doing good to others is the work that fits mortals for the home with him forever.

18 **I speak not of you all:**—In these commendatory remarks he embraces all save Judas.

I know whom I have chosen: but that the scripture may be fulfilled, He that eateth my bread lifted up his heel against me.—He fulfilled the prophecy of Psalm 41: 9. The action of Judas fulfilled this scripture rather than he did it to fulfill it. The scripture foretold it because it would be done.

19 **From henceforth I tell you before it come to pass, that, when it is come to pass, ye may believe that I am he.**—Jesus

when it is come to pass, ye may believe that I am *he*. 20 Verily, verily, I
say unto you, He that receiveth whomsoever I send receiveth me; and he
that receiveth me receiveth him that sent me.

---

foretold the treason of Judas as of other things that would occur at once to prepare them for what would be done, and that after they came to pass as he foretold they would, they might see his divine foreknowledge and believe in him as the Son of God.

20 **Verily, verily, I say unto you, He that receiveth whomsoever I send receiveth me; and he that receiveth me receiveth him that sent me.**—In connection with the assertion of his authority he tells them that those he might send out would go clothed with his authority as he was clothed with the authority of him who sent him, and the treatment given them and their message would be received as done to himself. [Those who received the apostles not only received the messengers of Christ, but Christ himself. To receive Christ would be to receive the Father who sent him.]

3. BETRAYAL ANNOUNCED.
13: 21-30.

21 When Jesus had thus said, he was troubled in the spirit, and testified,
and said, Verily, verily, I say unto you, that one of you shall [10]betray me.
22 The disciples looked one on another, doubting of whom he spake. 23

[10]Or, *deliver me up*

---

21 **When Jesus had thus said, he was troubled in the spirit, and testified, and said, Verily, verily, I say unto you, that one of you shall betray me.**—After saying these things, his mind recurred to the treason of Judas, and the sufferings before him and this troubled him. Jesus had all the repugnance of a strong sensitive nature to suffering and he shrank from it, as his prayer "remove this cup from me" indicates, and he repeats in sorrowful tones "that one of you shall betray me."

22 **The disciples looked one on another, doubting of whom he spake.**—The disciples, save Judas did not know to whom he referred. So wondering and inquiring glances were exchanged in doubt as to whom he referred. There seems to have been nothing in the conduct of Judas heretofore that

There was at the table reclining in Jesus' bosom one of his disciples, whom
Jesus loved. 24 Simon Peter therefore beckoneth to him, and saith unto
him, Tell *us* who it is of whom he speaketh. 25 He leaning back, as he
was, on Jesus' breast saith unto him, Lord, who is it? 26 Jesus therefore
answereth, He it is, for whom I shall dip the sop, and give it him. So
when he had dipped the sop, he taketh and giveth it to Judas, *the son* of
Simon Iscariot. 27 And after the sop, then entered Satan into him. Jesus

---

directs suspicion or attention to him as the person to whom reference was made, notwithstanding it had been said that he was a thief in carrying the bag.

23 **There was at the table reclining in Jesus' bosom one of his disciples,**—It is said that the persons at the table reclined on couches placed around the table, each resting on the left elbow, leaving the right hand free for use. One in front of the other could easily turn the head and rest on the bosom of the person behind.

whom Jesus loved.—John who is known as the beloved of Jesus occupied this position nearest Jesus.

24 **Simon Peter therefore beckoneth to him, and saith unto him, Tell us who it is of whom he speaketh.**—Peter, always prompt and forward in every case that arose, beckoned to John to ask which it was that should betray him.

25 **He leaning back, as he was, on Jesus' breast saith unto him, Lord, who is it?**—[John complied with the request of Peter and asked, "Who is it?" All innocent parties were interested in knowing who he was.]

26 **Jesus therefore answereth, He it is, for whom I shall dip the sop, and give it him. So when he had dipped the sop, he taketh and giveth it to Judas, the son of Simon Iscariot.**—He dipped the sop and gave it to Judas Iscariot and in this way pointed him out as the person. This exposed Judas to the disciples as the traitor. It let him know that Jesus knew that he had already bargained to betray him.

27 **And after the sop, then entered Satan into him.**—[Up to this time he had doubts and impulses to do better, but now he gives himself up wholly to Satan's work. He was already under his influence, but now he plunges headlong into the bottomless pit.] Satan had entered into Judas and led him

therefore saith unto him, What thou doest, do quickly. 28 Now no man at the table knew for what intent he spake this unto him. 29 For some thought, because Judas had the [1]bag, that Jesus said unto him, Buy what things we have need of for the feast; or, that he should give something

[1]Or, *box*

to go to the priests to bargain for his betrayal, now he enters to prompt him to put his purpose into execution.

Jesus therefore saith unto him, What thou doest, do quickly.—The time had come and Jesus desired that what he did should be done and completed. [Judas was now fully exposed. Christ knew he had covenanted to betray him, and bids him do it at once. He desired the wicked deed to be done that night and for the traitor to leave the little band at once so that he might be alone to give a last charge to the faithful disciples.]

28 **Now no man at the table knew for what intent he spake this unto him.**—Those at the table did not understand the significance of the language.

29 **For some thought, because Judas had the bag, that Jesus said unto him, Buy what things we have need of for the feast; or, that he should give something to the poor.**—Judas kept the treasury that the apostles had, and out of it things were bought for the feast and the poor were helped. They expected something would be done promptly. There is difficulty in harmonizing all the facts connected with the Passover by Jesus. He had partaken of the Passover at this time, but he speaks of the feast yet future. Again on the next day the priests that accused Jesus did not go into Pilate's judgment hall "that they might not be defiled, but might eat the passover." (18: 28.) This would imply that the passover was not yet eaten. Two explanations are offered for this. One is that Jesus ate the passover at the appointed hour, but that throughout the week of the feast there were other meals to be eaten, and as no unleaven bread could be used during the week so all had to keep themselves clean for this eating during the week, and this language refers to some feasting at a later day of the week. The other theory is that Jesus ate the passover as is attested (Matt. 26: 17-19; Mark 14: 12-18; Luke

to the poor. 30 He then having received the sop went out straightway: and it was night.

22: 7-15), but that he ate it the evening before the regular time, and he himself was slain at the hour of slaying the paschal lamb, intended to typify the slaying of Jesus. This latter seems to me probable. He could not be slain at the time for slaying the passover lamb and eat the passover at the accustomed time too. He chose to die at the appointed hour and so was compelled to anticipate the time of eating it.

30 **He then having received the sop went out straightway: and it was night.**—Judas having been pointed out as the person who should betray him and admonished to do it at once, immediately left the table and went out on his mission.

4. JESUS ANNOUNCES HIS SPEEDY DEPARTURE. 13: 31-35.

31 When therefore he was gone out, Jesus saith, Now [2]is the Son of man glorified, and God [2]is glorified in him; 32 and God shall glorify him in

[2]Or, *was*

31 **When therefore he was gone out, Jesus saith, Now is the Son of man glorified, and God is glorified in him;**—Judas, leaving on this mission, brought more vividly to his mind that the time was now come for the tragedy that would end in his resurrection, ascension, and glorification at the right hand of God. He looks beyond the sorrows to this end. God would be glorified in glorifying Jesus. [The hour has come and Jesus is about ready to go through his bloody pathway into the presence of his Father. The disciples will be left without him to meet the trials and persecutions of the earth. The time has arrived for him to pour forth the deepest feelings of his soul in their behalf. In the discourse that follows he comforts, consoles, instructs, and points them to the glory, power, and grace of their Lord. He strives as never before to reveal himself to the disciples so fully that every doubt of his divinity shall pass away when the darkness and gloom that gathered around his tomb shall have been dispelled by a deep knowledge of his glory.]

himself, and straightway shall he glorify him. 33 Little children, yet a little
while I am with you. Ye shall seek me: and as I said unto the Jews,
Whither I go, ye cannot come; so now I say unto you. 34 A new commandment I give unto you, that ye love one another; [3]even as I have loved
you, that ye also love one another. 35 By this shall all men know that ye
are my disciples, if ye have love one to another.

[3]Or, *even as I loved you, that ye also may love one another*

32 **and God shall glorify him in himself, and straightway shall he glorify him.**—The glorification is mutual. God glorifies himself in exalting and glorifying Jesus. So Jesus is glorified in glorifying those who honor him.

33 **Little children, yet a little while I am with you.**—He spoke to them tenderly because they were but children in their ignorance of what was before them. He had often told them that he must die, be buried, and rise the third day, but in their weakness and blindness they failed to take it in.

Ye shall seek me: and as I said unto the Jews, Whither I go, ye cannot come; so now I say unto you.—He tells his disciples, as he had told the Jews before, that soon he would leave them and they could not come to him while he was absent. He would die, they would be scattered, and for a little while be in distress and doubt over their condition. [He would be in the grave and while there they could not come to him; but he comforts them by assuring them that he would come to them again.]

34 **A new commandment I give unto you, that ye love one another;**—This was given in anticipation of what would befall them. Moses had said unto them, "Thou shalt love thy neighbor as thyself." (Lev. 19: 18.)

even as I have loved you, that ye also love one another.—Jesus introduced a higher order of love—a love that caused him to leave heaven, come to earth, and suffer and die for them. His disciples must partake of the same degree or measure of love, and give up earthly and temporal good for their spiritual and eternal good. [The commandment to love was not new, but such love as Jesus commanded was. This love demands that we give up all as Jesus did.]

35 **By this shall all men know that ye are my disciples, if ye have love one to another.**—By this self-denying love for

one another, partaking of the love he manifested all men should know that they were his disciples. [The presence of such love does more than cause those who see it working in others to marvel. It points them to Christ as its author, for all must admit, when it shines forth in its excellency, that it is of heavenly origin. When it is fully exhibited men know that those who possess it are the disciples of Christ.]

5. PETER'S DENIAL.
13: 36-38.

36 Simon Peter saith unto him, Lord, whither goest thou? Jesus answered, Whither I go, thou canst not follow me now; but thou shalt follow afterwards. 37 Peter saith unto him, Lord, why cannot I follow thee even now? I will lay down my life for thee. 38 Jesus answereth, Wilt thou lay

---

36 **Simon Peter saith unto him, Lord, whither goest thou? Jesus answered, Whither I go, thou canst not follow me now; but thou shalt follow afterwards.**—[Peter does not yet comprehend the Lord's death. We now come to one of the saddest points recorded by John, that is, the last moments the Lord spent with his own before his suffering, a moment in which he speaks words full of tenderness and heavenly meaning. The Lord's way was to the cross, the sepulchre, the ascension, and to heaven. Peter might follow in due time, but the Lord had other work for him now. The Lord does not answer his question directly. Tradition says that Peter did follow Christ to the cross in death. He was also crucified.]

37 **Peter saith unto him, Lord, why cannot I follow thee even now? I will lay down my life for thee.**—Peter felt mortified by Jesus saying that they could not follow him now. He felt that Jesus had implied that they had not the courage and fidelity to follow him, and Peter really felt that he was ready to die for and with Jesus, and why could he not go with Jesus wherever he went. Peter was in this claiming the same love for Jesus that Jesus had for them. Peter was sincere and thought he was ready to die with Jesus, but he did not understand himself. He was rashly bold and courageous, but when the conditions called for discreet and patient endurance without display Peter failed. Jesus knew

down thy life for me? Verily, verily, I say unto thee, The cock shall not crow, till thou hast denied me thrice.

what was in Peter. He knew the good and he knew also his weakness.

38 **Jesus answereth, Wilt thou lay down thy life for me? Verily, verily, I say unto thee, The cock shall not crow, till thou hast denied me thrice.**—John refers to but one cock crowing. The other writers refer to two. There are two times for cockcrowing. At midnight the cock crows, but only a little. At three o'clock in the morning the principal cock-crowing takes place. When only one is spoken of as the cockcrowing, the three o'clock, when the chief crowing occurs, is meant. When two are spoken of, both the twelve o'clock crowing and the main one at three o'clock are referred to. When Jesus said to Peter, "The cock shall not crow, till thou hast denied me thrice," he meant before the second or time for the main crowing, or as we would say, "Before three o'clock you will deny me." When John says, "The cock shall not crow, till thou hast denied me thrice," he means the chief crowing of the cock will not take place till thou hast denied me thrice. Both mean you will deny me before three o'clock. ["The Lord reveals to him his weakness. It was then night. Before the cock shall crow for the dawn of the next morning he will have thrice denied his Lord. For the fulfillment of this prediction, see Luke 22: 54-60. Peter had bravely attempted to defend his Master with a sword when the company came, led by Judas, but when Christ was led away, he 'followed afar off.' His courage was departing. First, in the hall of the high priest, he denied to the maidservant that he knew Christ, then a little while later he denied to another. About an hour later another said, 'Of a truth this man also was with him; for he is a Galilean.' And Peter denied with oaths, declaring, 'Man, I know not what thou sayest.' Just then the cock crowed for the approach of day."]

6. HE ANNOUNCES HIS FINAL RETURN.
14: 1-6.

1 Let not your heart be troubled: [4]believe in God, believe also in me.
2 In my Father's house are many [5]mansions; if it were not so, I would have
told you; for I go to prepare a place for you. 3 And if I go and prepare

[4]Or, *ye believe in God*
[5]Or, *abiding-places*

1 **Let not your heart be troubled:**—Jesus had impressed them with the truth that he would leave them; that Judas had gone to bring a band of soldiers to arrest him; that Peter, the boldest of the disciples would deny that he knew him, and more or less discouragement took possession of the hearts and minds of the disciples. Jesus under these circumstances spoke words of comfort and assurance to them. [There was everything to fill their hearts with gloom, and doubtless a silence like death had settled upon the little company, and they needed the comforting words spoken by Jesus.]

believe in God,—[Have confidence in God! Do not let your faith fail because of these earthly troubles! God is still your Father, still supreme. He can, and will, overrule all for good.]

believe also in me.—He and God are one. As they believed in God, so they were to have confidence in him. So listen to the words of assurance which Jesus speaks. [If God seems so far off and your troubles so near, here am I in your midst. He that hath seen the Father. You know that I love you; you know my power with the Father. But their hearts kept saying, "Thou art going away from us."]

2 **In my Father's house are many mansions;**—[Many "abiding-places" in the footnote; many *homes;* in short, besides this one we call earth. Leaving earth, there are other places to which to go, places all radiant with beauty.]

if it were not so, I would have told you;—[I would not have allowed you to give up the things of this world if I had not had better things to offer you. I would have told you frankly that it was all sacrifice and no reward.]

for I go to prepare a place for you.—[This separation that makes you so sad is only a step toward providing you with a better home than earth can furnish.] He had told them

**a place for you, I come again, and will receive you unto myself; that where
I am, *there* ye may be also. 4 [6]And whither I go, ye know the way. 5**

[6]Many ancient authorities read *And whither I go ye know, and the way ye know*

that he would be separated from them for a time; that he would go where for a while they could not come, but afterward they would be with him. The assurance he gave them was that there was ample room in his house for them to dwell with him, and that he went before to prepare a place for them. When Jesus went to prepare for them the Holy Spirit came to earth to guide and direct them, to prepare and fit them to dwell in the place he prepared for them. Had there not been ample place he would have told them. He could not deceive them.

3 **And if I go and prepare a place for you,**—[What a thought is this that beautiful as the mansions of God must be, they are not beautiful enough; that Jesus goes to *prepare* them, make them fit for his followers! What must a home be when prepared by omnipotence and omniscience, moving at the dictate of infinite love.]

I come again,—[(See Acts 1: 11; 3: 21; 1 Thess. 4: 13-17.) Let no one rob you of your confidence in the return of your Lord in glory. Some refer this coming to the resurrection of Christ; others refer it to the death of the believer as in the case of Stephen; and still others refer it to the coming of the Holy Spirit. We think these positions inadmissible. The reference is not to Christ's return from the grave, but a return from heaven, the second coming of the Lord, which is a part of the Christian faith.]

and will receive you unto myself; that where I am, there ye may be also.—[Connected directly with the coming again. Evidently the condition of final glory. Evidently, also, heaven is a locality as well as a state, and we have the most substantial joys to which to look forward. To be so purified as to be able to dwell where Jesus is, and to be so ennobled as to share his life and glory is to reach the most exalted destiny of which created intelligences are capable.] He would go as their forerunner to make ready for them. He

Thomas saith unto him, Lord, we know not whither thou goest; how know we the way? 6 Jesus saith unto him, I am the way, and the truth, and the

would come again before the close of the earthly affairs. God always fits his creatures with honor suited for them. When the disciples were fitted to dwell with Jesus, they would have a home with him.

4 **And whither I go, ye know the way.**—He had told them of the place and that he was the way. They ought to have understood this. [Jesus probably uttered these words to provoke questions such as follow. He was going to his Father from whom he came and the way by which he would go was the cross, the tomb, the resurrection, and the exaltation. (Matt. 16: 21; 17: 22; 20: 17.)]

5 **Thomas saith unto him, Lord, we know not whither thou goest; how know we the way?**—Thomas was of a doubting and despondent disposition and found many difficulties in the way, so he was slow to take in what Jesus said, and especially the spiritual truths he spoke. [Thomas was a plain, honest, and plain-spoken disciple. He lost all faith and hope when Jesus died. He did not believe the Lord had risen until he saw with his own eyes. Now he affirms, "We know not whither thou goest." We expected you to stay with us and reign as our king in an earthly kingdom. We cannot understand your going away and dying nor whither thou goest. Then how can we know the way?]

6 **Jesus saith unto him, I am the way,**—To enter into Christ and continue in him is the way. [Jesus only answers his difficulties in part. He is the exemplar, the living embodiment of what is needful to impart immortality. He who walks in his footsteps will travel the same road.]

and the truth,—He was the embodiment of the truth of God, and embodied that truth in his life and words. [He was not merely truth, but *the* truth—the key of all truth—the revelation of all truth necessary to elevate man to God.]

and the life:—He taught true and real life to the world. He brought life and immortality to light both by revealing the existence of both and revealing the conditions on which

life: no one cometh unto the Father, but [7]by me. 7 If ye had known me,

[7]Or, *through*

they could be enjoyed. [He is life itself—the bread of life—the living waters—the source from which the germ from which immortal life is imparted to the soul. Without him there would be no way revealed, no saving truth, nor immortal life.]

no one cometh unto the Father, but by me.—[No one can enter heaven without him, neither can he come close enough to the Father to enjoy the spiritual blessings of Christ Jesus. All must hold to Jesus to be saved. "For neither is there any other name under heaven, that is given among men, wherein we must be saved." "By me," that is, walk in the way I map out.]

7. HIS IDENTITY WITH THE FATHER.
14: 7-14.

ye would have known my Father also: from henceforth ye know him, and

7 **If ye had known me, ye would have known my Father also:**—Jesus was the most complete and perfect representation of God that could be revealed to man. He was God "manifested in the flesh." Man is so fleshly that he cannot apprehend or appreciate true spirit. [After associating with Jesus as their teacher for about three and a half years they did not yet know, only in part. The central truth here is to know God is to know Christ. The universe which he created reveals his grandeur, the Old Testament his moral government, but it is only in Christ that he reveals his surpassing love, mercy, and solicitude for the salvation of man. Through him he reveals himself as a Father. Previous to his coming men were not authorized to address God in prayer as "Our Father who art in heaven."]

from henceforth ye know him, and have seen him.—So God clothed himself as humanity that man might live and know him. Jesus was this manifestation. So to know Jesus is to have the most complete knowledge of God that it is possible for him to know, and no man can come to God save

have seen him. 8 Philip saith unto him, Lord, show us the Father, and it
sufficeth us. 9 Jesus saith unto him, Have I been so long time with you,
and dost thou not know me, Philip? he that hath seen me hath seen the
Father; how sayest thou, Show us the Father? 10 Believest thou not that
I am in the Father, and the Father in me? the words that I say unto you
I speak not from myself: but the Father abiding in me doeth his works.

---

through Jesus Christ. [They would see Jesus crucified the next day and from the cross they would know him. From the grave would burst forth upon their minds a new revelation of the character and mission of Jesus whom they had up to this time thought to be only an earthly, temporal king.]

8 **Philip saith unto him, Lord, show us the Father, and it sufficeth us.**—Philip failed to take in the truth, and still asked to see the Father. [He perhaps expected such a manifestation as Moses saw on the holy mount. (Ex. 33: 8.) He, like many now, wanted to walk by sight instead of by faith.]

9 **Jesus saith unto him, Have I been so long time with you, and dost thou not know me, Philip? he that hath seen me hath seen the Father; how sayest thou, Show us the Father?** —[He, like the rest of the apostles, did not comprehend that the Son came to reveal the Father. He wanted a literal sight of God with the natural eyes. Natural eyes cannot behold God who is a "Spirit" no more than they can see the soul of man. Man "cannot see God and live," but he can see and understand "God manifested in the flesh." Christ was not an ambassador from God, but "Immanuel, God with us," the "Godhead in bodily form."]

10 **Believest thou not that I am in the Father, and the Father in me?**—Jesus entered into a more minute statement of the oneness of himself with the Father.

the words that I say unto you I speak not from myself: but the Father abiding in me doeth his works.—The oneness is so complete that the words of Jesus came from the Father and God dwelling in Jesus did the works done by Jesus. Jesus was the human body in which God dwelled and through which he spoke and worked. [The personalities of the Son and the Father was perfect union, and we may never on earth comprehend fully its nature, but we can understand it to be

11 Believe me that I am in the Father, and the Father in me: or else believe me for the very work's sake. 12 Verily, verily, I say unto you, He that believeth on me, the works that I do shall he do also; and greater *works*

so complete that he was the manifestation of God in the flesh.]

11 **Believe me that I am in the Father, and the Father in me: or else believe me for the very works' sake.**—If he could not believe on the teachings of Jesus as from God, the works that he did through Jesus ought to convince him that God was in Jesus. Both the mercy and power shown in the works of Jesus proclaimed him divine. [The works Jesus did were never done by man, and they ought to convince them that he was divine.]

12 **Verily, verily, I say unto you, He that believeth on me, the works that I do shall he do also;**—Jesus advances another step in his instruction. Not only did God work through Jesus, but he would work through all those that believe in him. Through the believers after his return to his Father's throne he would send the Spirit that would guide the apostles into all truth and would abide with his church forever.

and greater works than these shall he do; because I go unto the Father.—During the life of Jesus on earth his work was restricted to the limitations of his physical presence. After he ascended to his Father and the Holy Spirit came in his name, a greater and more extended work would be done by the fuller inspiration of the apostles, and the more extended mission they would fill. Then when miraculous gifts should cease altogether, the church through its members would enter upon its world-wide mission of carrying the truth of God to the world. This last, performed through the regular working of the laws of the Spirit, would be more far reaching than the miraculous manifestations. It is comparable to the works of God in the natural world. Jesus by the exercise of miraculous power created food to feed the multitudes; but this, while more showy and calculated to attract attention, was not so effective as the regular workings of God through the laws of nature. [At the time he was cru-

than these shall he do; because I go unto the Father. 13 And whatsoever ye
shall ask in my name, that will I do, that the Father may be glorified in
the Son. 14 If ye shall ask [8]anything in my name, that will I do. 15 If

[8]Many ancient authorities add *me*

cified Jesus had, so far as we know, only about five hundred disciples; but on the day of Pentecost the apostles converted three thousand. It was necessary that the Son return to the Father to enable his disciples to do these "greater works."]

13 **And whatsoever ye shall ask in my name, that will I do,**—To do anything in the name of Christ one must be in his name; become a part of his spiritual body and ask as the representative of Christ and for him. It means more than to ask by his authority. Asking as a member of his body, we must ask in accordance with his will. The prayer of Jesus in Gethsemane—"Father, if thou be willing, remove this cup from me: nevertheless not my will, but thine, be done" (Luke 22: 42)—should teach what prayer in the name and spirit of Christ means. We attach to our prayers, and properly so, "in the name of Christ." This implies an absolute self-sacrifice, and a prayer that our very prayers may not be answered except in so far as they are in accordance with the divine will. [To enjoy these promises, we must (1) believe; (2) we must ask in his name; (3) we must approach him with a complete submission to the Father's will.]

that the Father may be glorified in the Son.—[God is honored and glorified in his Son now through Christians. They are his representatives on earth. He works with and through them. He is glorified only when they work in harmony with his will.]

14 **If ye shall ask anything in my name, that will I do.**—This was to make the spiritual body on earth, and as the Father who sent him worked through him, so he would work through his body, the church on earth. After the passing of the fleshly body of Jesus, his disciples entered into a closer spiritual relation to him than they had hitherto been able to do. His spirit entered into and dwelt in them.

8. THE PROMISE OF THE HOLY SPIRIT.
14: 15-24.

ye love me, ye will keep my commandments. 16 And I will [9]pray the Father, and he shall give you another [10]Comforter, that he may be with

[9]Gr. *make request of*
[10]Or, *Advocate* Or, *Helper* Gr. *Paraclete*

15 **If ye love me, ye will keep my commandments.**—He gives here the fruit and test of their love to him. If they loved him as their Lord and Master, they would cherish and obey his commandments. This is the divine test of love. Love as God views it is practical and embodies the actions of the whole man. And the test and proof of love is the desire to do the will and seek the honor of the one whom we love. To do God's will, to do it because it is the will of God, is God's test. Let us apply it. [Christ's own test of love was keeping the Father's commandments.]

16 **And I will pray the Father, and he shall give you another Comforter,**—In response to their love manifested by keeping his words, he would pray the Father and he would send them another comforter. This was addressed directly to his apostles, and had a more direct application to them than to others. Yet it presents a truth and a principle applicable to all servants of God. If these disciples would keep his words, the Father would send them another comforter. Jesus had been their teacher and comforter while he was on earth; he was about to leave them. They felt bereft and disappointed, and to comfort and assure them he makes this promise of the Father.

that he may be with you for ever,—[Not to be with you a few years, as I, and then be taken away. He is to be the perpetual counselor of the church.] The Spirit was to be the guiding, directing power of the spiritual world as he is of the material world. He gave the law; he dwells in and guides through the law. "It is the spirit that giveth life; the flesh profiteth nothing: the words that I have spoken unto you are spirit, and are life." (6: 63.) "The seed is the word of God." (Luke 8: 11.) The seed is the dwelling place of the life principles. It is the body in which the life

you for ever, 17 *even* the Spirit of truth: whom the world cannot receive;

germ abides. The seed is placed in the soil to bring the life germ into contact with the juices of the soil. We take the word in the heart to bring the Spirit that dwells in the word into contact with the warm affections of the heart that the germ in all principle may spring forth and bear fruit in the life. "Having been begotten again, not of corruptible seed, but of incorruptible, through the word of God, which liveth and abideth." (1 Pet. 1: 23.) The word of God in the heart is in the mind, the affections, the will. It leads to prompt action so that its entrance into the heart leads to immediate obedience to Christ. No principle of life is imparted by birth. The principle of life is imparted in the believing [the begetting] or taking the word in which the Spirit which gives life dwells into the heart. The old state is left. The new principle of life, imparted through faith, is brought into a new state by being baptized. In that new state it may develop a higher spiritual life. If the Spirit imparts life, he does it before birth; and without this imparting life there is nothing to be born. Yet without birth there can be no development or manifestation of distinct life. The life that is not brought to the birth perishes.

17 **even the Spirit of truth:**—The Spirit whose special mission is to guide them into all truth, to call to their remembrance all things that Jesus had taught them, and to enable them to record and teach all truth to the world. He is hence called the Spirit of truth. He approves all truth, rejects all falsehood.

whom the world cannot receive;—The disciples who kept his word could receive this Spirit, but the world, as distinguished from the disciples or who rejected that truth, could not receive this Spirit. [He cannot enter into men of the world as distinguished from the church, and all theological theories that teach the opposite contradict Christ. "Because ye are sons [not to make you sons], God sent forth the Spirit of his Son into our hearts, crying, Abba, Father." (Gal. 4: 6.)]

for it beholdeth him not, neither knoweth him: ye know him; for he abideth with you, and shall be in you. 18 I will not leave you [11]desolate: I come unto you. 19 Yet a little while, and the world beholdeth me no more; but

[11]Or, *orphans*

for it beholdeth him not, neither knoweth him:—[The reasons why the world cannot receive the comforter: It does not observe him, does not give that sympathetic attention to him which results in knowledge; it had treated Jesus with contempt who was the only one through whom the Holy Spirit could be seen and known. Some had even ascribed his miracles to Beelzebub. Such a world was incapable of receiving him.]

ye know him; for he abideth with you,—[Present tense. It is something which they then have, and yet something less than they are yet to receive. It refers to Jesus being in their midst, he being filled with the Holy Spirit.]

and shall be in you.—[Ultimately they are to have what Jesus then has. They, too, are to be filled with the Holy Spirit, and the beginning of the fulfillment of this was on the following Pentecost, and in this they were but the representatives and forerunners of all those who love Jesus and keep his commandments.] The Spirit up to this time had not, as representatives of God, abode with his servants on the earth. He had made visits and revelations to men, but had not entered into and remained with them. But he would come to them after Jesus ascended to his Father. (Verse 20.) In Christ the disciples would enter into a closer relationship to God than his servants had ever held toward him. They would become sons of God, and the measure of the Spirit that pertains to a son would enter in and abide with them.

18 **I will not leave you desolate: I come unto you.**—When Jesus left them, he would send the Spirit to dwell with them forever, so they would have a divine aid and comforter. Jesus and his Father would come to them and dwell with them forever.

19 **Yet a little while,**—[Less than twenty-four hours Jesus would be crucified.]

ye behold me: because I live, [12]ye shall live also. 20 In that day ye shall know that I am in my Father, and ye in me, and I in you. 21 He that hath my commandments, and keepeth them, he it is that loveth me: and he

[12]Or, *and ye shall live*

and the world beholdeth me no more;—[None but his disciples saw him after his burial.]

but ye behold me:—[The present use of the future.]

because I live, ye shall live also.—[The mind of Jesus sweeps on in its outlook to the glorious consequences of the resurrection. Not only shall they see him for the few weeks between the resurrection and ascension, but they, too, will conquer death, and they, in their restored and eternal life, will continue to behold him.] In a short time he would be crucified. This was spoken on the day preceding his crucifixion. The world could see him till his burial. Then the world would see him no more. But his disciples would see him after his resurrection and would be with him through eternity. The world did not see Jesus after his resurrection, only his brethren.

20 **In that day ye shall know that I am in my Father, and ye in me, and I in you.**—After his resurrection, the disciples would know his union with the Father, and their union and oneness with Jesus. [Beginning, at least, on Pentecost, if not confined to it, for then began that clearness of spiritual perception which goes on through the ages to the final glory. They shall realize the divine personality of Christ as never before. But they shall also realize, through the Holy Spirit, a divine exaltation for themselves which shall bring them into the most intimate spiritual relations with him.]

21 **He that hath my commandments, and keepeth them, he it is that loveth me:**—Love as presented by Jesus is not a mere sentiment, but it is a living, active principle. "For this is the love of God, that we keep his commandments." (1 John 5: 3.) So he makes the keeping of the commandments of God the test of their love for him. Man needs a test to try his love for God. .When do I love him sufficient to be accepted of him is a question that will frequently come up to the believer. Jesus gives the test: If we are willing to do

that loveth me shall be loved of my Father, and I will love him, and will manifest myself unto him. 22 Judas (not Iscariot) saith unto him, Lord, what is come to pass that thou wilt manifest thyself unto us, and not unto the world? 23 Jesus answered and said unto him, If a man love me, he will keep my word: and my Father will love him, and we will come unto

---

what he commands us to please him, he will accept us. He gives commands that man can see no wisdom in, and that are humiliating that he may be sure he keeps the command from a desire to obey God. [Jesus repeats his crucial test of love. It is of the highest importance to us that we shall not overlook this pregnant utterance and substitute for obedience emotional ecstasies.]

and he that loveth me shall be loved of my Father,—To those who show their love to God by obedience to his commands, the Father will both love and manifest himself to them.

and I will love him, and will manifest myself unto him.—Jesus will be with and in them as feeling and bearing their weaknesses, temptations, and sins; and they would be in him as partaking of his strength and comfort and sharing his blessings and honors.

22 **Judas (not Iscariot) saith unto him,**—Judas was the brother of James and is the same person as "Lebbaeus" and "Thaddaeus" and is the author of the Epistle of Jude.

Lord, what is come to pass that thou wilt manifest thyself unto us, and not unto the world?—He failed as yet to understand the spiritual nature of Christ's kingdom or the condition of his disciples after the resurrection; he expected an earthly, temporal rule and did not see how Jesus could manifest himself to the disciples and fail to do the same to the world. [This reveals again the carnal inability of the disciples at this time to comprehend the spiritual revelations of Christ. The spiritual manifestation in the heart they knew nothing about. They thought only of external, visible manifestation in Messianic glory, and they supposed, and rightly, that this would be to the whole world.]

23 **Jesus answered and said unto him, If a man love me, he will keep my word:**—Jesus declares that the rule he had laid down, or the test given, applied not only to his immediate

him, and make our abode with him. 24 He that loveth me not keepeth not my words: and the word which ye hear is not mine, but the Father's who sent me.

---

disciples, but it was one that applied to all men. If any one loves him, he must believe in him as the Son of God, infinite in wisdom, goodness, and power, and one who so believes and loves him will keep his words. All pretenses to believe in him, and trust him, while refusing to keep his words, are false and misleading.

and my Father will love him, and we will come unto him, and make our abode with him.—This abode will be through the Holy Spirit as their representative. "In whom ye also are builded together for a habitation of God in the Spirit." (Eph. 2: 22.) The Spirit as the representative of God dwells in his church.

24 **He that loveth me not keepeth not my words:**—On the other hand, he who does not love God will not keep his words—will not obey and follow him. To keep his words is to cherish and ponder them in the heart, and to obey them because they have been commanded by God. One may do the very thing commanded by God, and yet not keep the words of God. He may do it from some other motive than to please and honor him. All service to God must be with the desire to please and honor him. [No other evidence of the want of love is necessary. This is conclusive.]

and the word which ye hear is not mine, but the Father's who sent me.—All things spoken by Jesus were from God, hence to hear Jesus was to hear God. [He thus adds the final sanction to all that he has been saying. In refusing to keep my words, they are refusing to keep the Father's word, and, thus rejecting all divine instruction, they are unworthy of all divine presence.]

9. OTHER WORKS OF THE SPIRIT AND WORDS OF COMFORT. 14: 25-31.

25 These things have I spoken unto you, while *yet* abiding with you. 26

---

25 **These things have I spoken unto you, while yet abiding with you.**—Jesus knew the hour of his departure was now at

But the [1]Comforter, *even* the Holy Spirit, whom the Father will send in my name, he shall teach you all things, and bring to your remembrance all

[1]Or, *Advocate* Or, *Helper* Gr. *Paraclete*

hand. This was spoken the very night of his betrayal. Judas had already gone to bring the band to arrest him.

26 **But the Comforter, even the Holy Spirit, whom the Father will send in my name,**—The disciples were now distressed that Jesus was about to leave them. The coming of the Holy Spirit to teach and strengthen them would be an especial comfort to them so he is called the Comforter. The Father would send him in his name to take the place as the representative of Jesus.

he shall teach you all things, and bring to your remembrance all that I said unto you.—He was to teach all things needful to their well-being and to guide them into all truth, and to recall to their remembrance his teaching. Man is forgetful and a divine Monitor is sent to them to call to their memory all things he had taught them. The ground for their reliance on the certainty of the word of God is that the Spirit of God guided into the truths stated. All departure from the word of God concerning entrance into the church and into Christ come from the idea that the Spirit teaches outside of the word of God. All additions to the church in its order, organization, and work come from the idea that the Spirit dwells in, guides, and directs the church apart from his teaching in and through the word of God. To give up the word of God as the only direction and guidance of the Spirit is to give loose reign to the dreams and imaginations, the reasonings, and philosophies of men as the directions of the Holy Spirit. It is to substitute these for the revelations of God when "men spake from God, being moved by the Holy Spirit." (2 Pet. 1: 21.) There used to be a dilemma about creeds. If a creed has more than is in the Bible, it has too much; if it has less than is in the Bible, it has too little; if it differs from the Bible, it is wrong; if it has just what the Bible has, it is the Bible, and not a human creed. So if the Spirit teaches more than the Bible teaches, he teaches too

that I said unto you. 27 Peace I leave with you; my peace I give unto you: not as the world giveth, give I unto you, Let not your heart be troubled, neither let it be fearful. 28 Ye heard how I said to you, I go away, and I come unto you. If ye loved me, ye would have rejoiced, because I go unto

---

much; if he teaches less, he teaches too little; if he teaches different from the word of God, he teaches wrong; if he teaches what the word teaches, he teaches through the word, for no uninspired soul ever learned a spiritual truth save through the words of the Bible.

27 **Peace I leave with you; my peace I give unto you:**—The peace that Jesus gave them was not peaceable and pleasant surroundings. It was not an outward or external peace, but it was a composure and peace of mind and spirit that no external surroundings or troubles can destroy or disturb. This is the only sure and true peace on earth. Disturbances, trials, and troubles will arise in the world, and the mind that is dependent upon the external surroundings for peace will never find peace on earth. One who believe and trusts in Jesus, the Spirit of God dwells with and imparts to him the Spirit of Jesus, and he becomes a partaker of the peace that Jesus possesses. With the peace of Jesus in our hearts, we may look without fear on all the troubles and disturbances of life. This is unlike the peace the world proposes.

not as the world giveth, give I unto you,—[Either in quantity or quality. I give richly, abundantly, my presence and my Father's presence in the most intimate communion.]

Let not your heart be troubled, neither let it be fearful.—[Neither caring for what has come, nor dreading that which may still come. Thus he returns to the beginning of the lesson begun at the opening of the chapter. Believe in God, believe also in me, and rest in perfect peace!]

28 **Ye heard how I said to you, I go away, and I come unto you.**—It was for the good of the disciples and of all who keep his words that Jesus should go away. The Holy Spirit would not come unless he went away, and it was as needful that the believers in Jesus should enjoy the presence and offices of the Spirit as that they should those of Jesus.

If ye loved me, ye would have rejoiced, because I go unto the Father:—An intelligent love of Jesus would desire that

the Father: for the Father is greater than I. 29 And now I have told you before it come to pass, that, when it is come to pass, ye may believe. 30 I will no more speak much with you, for the prince of the world cometh:

he should go unto the Father that he might send the Spirit. "Nevertheless I tell you the truth: It is expedient for you that I go away; for if I go not away, the Comforter will not come unto you; but if I go, I will send him unto you." (16: 7.)

for the Father is greater than I.—His returning to the Father would be the occasion of God bestowing greater or fuller blessing in sending the Spirit. The blessings of the Spirit were greater than those of Jesus only in the sense that the Spirit completed and perfected the work begun by Jesus.

29 **And now I have told you before it come to pass, that, when it is come to pass, ye may believe**—In knowing beforehand what was coming to pass would give them composure and endurance in passing through the trials, and be an assurance to them, after they had taken place as Jesus foretold. The object and purpose of prophetic foretellings were not to produce a completed faith in the things foretold in those to whom the announcements were made, but that when the fulfillment did come, the people then seeing the fulfillment of the announcements, would believe the matter was prearranged and under the direction of God, and hence provided and inspired of God.

30 **I will no more speak much with you, for the prince of the world cometh:**—The prince of the world was Satan. He was embodied in the wicked rulers, Jewish and Gentile, that were compassing the death of Jesus.

and he hath nothing in me;—As the rulers of the kingdoms of this world, instigated by the prince of this world, they found nothing in Jesus for them to uphold, defend, or cherish. His works and spirit were antagonistic to theirs. [There was then, as now, nothing in common between the prince and spirit of the world and Christ, and hence had no sympathy for him. The devil never did, and never will, capture a man unless he finds something in him common with himself. If he finds a sinful ambition or lust in him, he seizes upon it and makes it the means of his ruin.]

and he hath nothing [2]in me; 31 but that the world may know that I love the Father, and as the Father gave me commandment, even so I do. Arise, let us go hence.

[2]Or, *in me.* 31 *But that &c. . . . I do, arise &c.*

31 **but that the world may know that I love the Father, and as the Father gave me commandment, even so I do.**—The test of love is the keeping or obeying the commandments of God. This is the test of love in all the relations of life. The child shows its love for the parents by keeping the commands of the parents, so of the wife to the husband, the citizen to the earthly ruler. The dependent or subject shows love to those over them by keeping their commandments. The superior shows love for the inferior by sacrifice and condescension to help the inferior. The test of Christ's love was to do the commandments of God, even unto the giving up of his life to please and honor him. This speech, beginning at chapter 13: 21 and continuing through this chapter, was spoken while they were still at the table.

Jesus not only abode in his Father's love by keeping his Father's commandments, but he showed this love for the Father to the world by keeping his commandments. He knew of no better way to show his love to his Father than by doing his Father's commandments. Are we wiser than he? Can we show our love to God in any better way, in any other way, than by doing the commandments of God? "He that hath my commandments, and keepeth them, he it is that loveth me. . . . If a man love me, he will keep my word. . . . He that loveth me not keepeth not my words." (14: 21-24.) "He that saith, I know him, and keepeth not his commandments, is a liar, and the truth is not in him; but whoso keepeth his word, in him verily hath the love of God been perfected. Hereby we know that we are in him." (1 John 2: 4, 5.) "Hereby we know that we love the children of God, when we love God and do his commandments. For this is the love of God, that we keep his commandments." (1 John 5: 2, 3.)

Arise, let us go hence.—They arose and went toward the Mount of Olives. On the way this discourse was completed, embracing the fifteenth and sixteenth chapters.

SECTION THREE.

REMARKS OF JESUS BETWEEN THE SUPPER AND HIS ARREST.

15: 1 to 17: 26.

1. PARABLE OF THE VINE AND ITS BRANCHES.

15: 1-8.

1 I am the true vine, and my Father is the husbandman. 2 Every branch in me that beareth not fruit, he taketh it away: and every *branch* that

---

1 **I am the true vine,**—Jesus often illustrated spiritual relations and things by natural ones. As they walked it is probable that they passed a vine with its spreading branches growing out of the vine. The intimate union existing between the vine and its branches suggested to his mind the intimate relations between himself and his disciples. Jesus with the twelve apostles as the teachers of the truths of the Bible constitute the vine.

and my Father is the husbandman.—His Father as the husbandman dresses, trims, and keeps the vine and its branches.

2 **Every branch in me that beareth not fruit, he taketh it away:**—The language was spoken directly to the apostles and in a special manner illustrated his and their relationship to each other. The disciples grew out of him, are dependent upon him for life and strength, development and growth. He is the source of life and growth to them, and if they fail to receive life and growth from him and to bear worthy fruit, the Father as the vinedresser takes away the barren branch. [There is no such thing as "turning one out of the church" nor "joining the church" in the New Testament. We can neither vote him in nor out of the church. He obeys the gospel and the Lord adds him to the church (Acts 2: 47), and if he fails to bear spiritual fruit the Lord will pluck him out. This he will do in the end of this world. (Matt. 13: 40-47.) We may withdraw fellowship from one (2 Thess. 3: 6), but this does not put him out of the church.]

and every branch that beareth fruit, he cleanseth it, that it may bear more fruit.—The twelve apostles were the

beareth fruit, he cleanseth it, that it may bear more fruit. 3 Already ye
are clean because of the word which I have spoken unto you. 4 Abide in
me, and I in you. As the branch cannot bear fruit of itself, except it abide
in the vine; so neither can ye, except ye abide in me. 5 I am the vine, ye

---

branches. Judas had ceased to bear fruit. He had him taken away. The other of the twelve were chastened and purified by the trials through which they passed at the time of the death of Jesus, and they were better fitted for the reception of the Holy Spirit, and so for bearing better and more fruit unto the Lord. [What we exist for as Christians is spiritual fruit; without it we are spiritual failures.]

3 **Already ye are clean because of the word which I have spoken unto you.**—The disciples were cleansed and prepared through the word that Jesus had spoken to them. They were brought to believe and obey this word, and through obedience they were made clean and holy. [The teaching of Jesus and their associating with him had placed them as branches. They belonged to the fruit bearers, and they had been partially pruned. But Jesus well knew that they would need much additional pruning to load them with the glorious clusters of richest fruit which they were one day to bear. We should not overlook the fact that the fruit grows on the branches, not on the vine.]

4 **Abide in me, and I in you. As the branch cannot bear fruit of itself, except it abide in the vine; so neither can ye, except ye abide in me.**—There was the same mutual dependence between Jesus and his apostles that exists between the vine and the branches. The branches can live only through the life they draw from the vine, so the disciples of Christ can live only through their union with him and the life they draw from him. So, too, the vine produces its fruit through the branches. Jesus would exert his influence to do good through the apostles. He teaches the world through them. A higher glory was to come to Jesus when he ascended to his Father and the apostles endued with the Spirit preached the gospel. [The prime necessity of the branch is to remain attached to the vine. But there can be no abiding in the spiritual vine except by a continued attention to the word

are the branches: He that abideth in me, and I in him, the same beareth much fruit: for apart from me ye can do nothing. 6 If a man abide not

of Christ. That which grafts us in continues us there. This being true of us, the abiding in him necessarily involves his abiding in us through his word. The moment a branch is cut or torn from the vine the conditions of life have ceased. There can be no more production of fruit. For a few hours there may be a semblance of life, but it is soon gone. The theme here formulated is not that of the moral powerlessness of the natural man for any good; it is that of the unfruitfulness of the believer left to his own strength, when the question is of producing or advancing the spiritual life, the life of God, in himself or others.]

5 **I am the vine, ye are the branches:**—[The only "branches" recognized in the word of God are individual Christians. "Branch churches are denominational organizations" presents a thought utterly foreign to the New Testament. Every Christian is a branch of the vine. His life is drawn from the vine. No denominationalism is warranted here.]

He that abideth in me, and I in him, the same beareth much fruit:—[It is absolutely impossible for the Christian who is in vital union with Christ to be fruitless. The life within him will *force* itself out in holy words and actions. There is no such thing as a do-nothing real Christian. Not only fruit, but *much* fruit and *good* fruit.]

for apart from me ye can do nothing.—The disciples apart from Jesus were as lifeless and unable to bear fruit as the branches separated from the vine. [Here is the explanation of so much of the inefficiency of the church today. Men and women are not living in vital union with Christ. They go where Christ cannot go with them. They do what Christ cannot see with allowance, and say what he ought not to hear. They drive him away from them. Therefore there are no spiritual fruits.]

6 **If a man abide not in me,**—This expression—"a man"—is a statement of a general truth. It applies to any and all men. A person must be in Christ before he can be or abide in him. [A Christian neglecting the means of grace.]

in me, he is cast forth as a branch, and is withered; **and they gather them,
and cast them into the fire, and they are burned. 7 If ye abide in me, and
my words abide in you, ask whatsoever ye will, and it shall be done unto**
you. 8 Herein [3]is my Father glorified, [4]that ye bear much fruit; and *so* shall

[3]Or, *was*
[4]Many ancient authorities read *that ye bear much fruit, and be my disciples*

he is cast forth as a branch, and is withered;—If he abides not in him he loses his life, withers, and dies, is unworthy of Christ, or of any good and is fit only for destruction. [This is true whether what is called "church action" is taken or not. We can see such branches all around us. But well may we tremble as we read the next words. They are words of doom, but they cannot be set aside.]

and they gather them, and cast them into the fire, and they are burned.—This indicates the manner of their destruction. ["The Son of man shall send forth his angels, and they shall gather out of his kingdom all things that cause stumbling, and them that do iniquity, and shall cast them in the furnace of fire: there shall be the weeping and the gnashing of teeth." (Matt. 13: 41, 42.)]

7 **If ye abide in me, and my words abide in you,**—To be in Christ, he must be in us. If he is in us, his words must abide in us. None can enter Christ save through his teachings, or receiving, believing and obeying his word. So if we abide in Christ, his word must be in and abide with us and mold our thoughts and feelings, and control our lives, and form our characters.

ask whatsoever ye will, and it shall be done unto you.—If his words abide in us, we will ask according to his will, and he will grant what we ask. [We do not understand this sentence to apply to prayer in general, as though *anything* we might ask for would be granted, but to pray for spiritual strength and blessing, pray with the view of bearing spiritual fruit. The next verse shows this. A prevailing prayer must be in the name of Christ (John 1: 13); according to his will (1 John 5: 14); in faith (James 1: 6); followed by obedience to his commandments (1 John 3: 22; James 4: 3).]

8 **Herein is my Father glorified, that ye bear much fruit;**—God is glorified by his servants doing his will, keeping his

words, and so bringing themselves fully under his guidance. [There are therefore the most cogent reasons why he should grant such a prayer. Temporal blessings given to us might not inure to his glory, but quite to the contrary, but spiritual strength must always promote the glory of God. Bearing much fruit is the test of true discipleship.]

and so shall ye be my disciples.—In this course we bear much fruit unto him, and so become more and more the disciples of Jesus who came to do his Father's will.

2. THE DISCIPLES EXHORTED TO ABIDE IN THE LOVE OF CHRIST.
15: 9-17.

ye be my disciples. 9 Even as the Father hath loved me, I also have loved
you: abide ye in my love. 10 If ye keep my commandments, ye shall abide

---

9 **Even as the Father hath loved me, I also have loved you:** —The love that God bestowed on Jesus, Jesus bestowed upon his disciples.

abide ye in my love.—They continued in his love by continuing to do his will. [By natural transition he now passes from the manifestations of spiritual life to the cardinal principle thereof, that is, love. If we may be allowed the expression, this is the divine sap which runs from the vine through the branches, and from the branches back through the vine, keeping up the divine circulation which is essential to divine life. But *how* shall we abide in his love?]

10 **If ye keep my commandments, ye shall abide in my love;**—God is the Ruler of the universe. Everything in the universe continues in harmony with God by complying with the laws God gives to govern the universe. Everything in harmony with God and so with the laws of the universe will receive God through the workings of the laws of the universe. Everything not in harmony with the laws of the universe must be brought to ruin by the workings of the laws God has given to control the universe. [How different is Christ's teaching all through this evening from the vague rhapsodies of many so-called spiritual lights of today! How intensely practical! "Keep my commandments" is the ever-recurring

in my love; even as I have kept my Father's commandments, and abide in
his love. 11 These things have I spoken unto you, that my joy may be in
you, and *that* your joy may be made full. 12 This is my commandment,

refrain of this divine music. It is the product, but it is also the condition of spiritual life.]

even as I have kept my Father's commandments, and abide in his love.—Jesus was the most highly blessed and honored of all the spirits in the universe, because he more than any other being kept the laws of God. Jesus showed his love for the Father and remained in that love by keeping his commandments, so we can show our love to Jesus by keeping his commandments. This is the rule by which God tested his Son, and all his disciples are tested by the same rule. It is vain, a mockery of God, to claim to be his disciple, or to believe in him, while we refuse to keep his commandments. [Jesus has thus reached the climax of his exhortation, and now presents the blessed result of heeding it.]

11 **These things have I spoken unto you, that my joy may be in you,**—Jesus spoke these things to them before he left them, that the joy that he possessed in keeping his Father's commandments might remain with them. Jesus possessed a joy and a peace that no sufferings or evil surroundings, not even the sufferings of the cross could disturb. Paul, in speaking of the sufferings of Jesus, says: "Who for the joy that was set before him endured the cross, despising shame, and hath sat down at the right hand of the throne of God." (Heb. 12: 2.) [Thoughtfully he thinks back over the address and states why it was delivered. The exquisite joy that he feels in the consciousness of obedience to his Father, and the Father's approving love on account of that obedience produced that joy.]

and that your joy may be made full.—Jesus wished that they might be filled with the same joy and comfort to bear them up in the distress that would come upon them in his death and the persecutions that would come upon them for his sake. [That a corresponding joy on their part may be made complete in their consciousness that they are sincerely and constantly endeavoring to do his will.]

that ye love one another, even as I have loved you. 13 Greater love hath no man than this, that a man lay down his life for his friends. 14 Ye are my friends, if ye do the things which I command you. 15 No longer do I

12 **This is my commandment, that ye love one another,**—Jesus had so loved them that he gave up heaven for a time, took upon himself the nature and sufferings of the world, and the death of the cross for them. [Not my *only* commandment, but my *great* commandment. He had said to the lawyer in regard to the Mosaic law that its very essence was to love God and love your neighbor.]

even as I have loved you.—While they would not equal him in the strength of his love, they must cultivate the same love one for another, and be willing to deny self and suffer one for another. [Not only as certainly as I have loved you, but as intensely as I have loved you.]

13 **Greater love hath no man than this, that a man lay down his life for his friends.**—The strongest love for one's friends is that he would lay down his life for them. Jesus was about to lay down his life for them. [This is the very acme of self-sacrificing love as between friends. Damon and Pythias have become immortal on its account. This was precisely what Jesus was about to do for his friends and which he did do the next day. But, more astounding still, for his *enemies,* though that is not introduced here. As the greater includes the less, this new exhortation of verse 12 includes all the offices that love can render and, we can readily understand, would transform the earth.]

14 **Ye are my friends,**—That they might know whether they came within the bounds of his love, he tells them who are his friends.

if ye do the things which I command you.—Jesus loved the whole world and shed his blood for it, but only they who accepted the benefits of his death by doing his will appropriated that love and received the benefits from it. Those who obeyed were his friends and so only his friends received and appropriated the benefits of his love. While he loved his enemies and provided for their happiness, they could enjoy it only by keeping his commandments. [Again he

call you [5]servants; for the [6]servant knoweth not what his lord doeth: but I have called you friends; for all things that I heard from my Father I have made known unto you. 16 Ye did not choose me, but I chose you, and

[5]Gr. *bondservants*
[6]Gr. *bondservant*

brings out the oft-repeated divinely appointed test of relationship to Christ—obedience to his command. We ought not to overlook this constantly repeated lesson.]

15 **No longer do I call you servants;**—The people of God under the Jewish dispensation had been servants. Only Abraham through faith had become a friend of God. But Jesus came to lift them out of their state of servitude and make them, as later revealed, children of God. [Greek, *slaves,* as in chapters 12: 26; 13: 13. There is no disagreement here with verse 20, or with the apostles afterwards calling themselves servants. He does not say they are not servants under solemn obligations to serve, but he *calls* them friends. Just as a master having great confidence in, and intense love for, a slave, might call him friend and treat him as such without for a moment weakening his claim upon him as a slave.]

for the servant—[Treated only as such.]

knoweth not what his lord doeth:—The master does not make known to the servants his plans. He commands what the servant must do.

but I have called you friends;—[I have treated you as friends—given you my confidence.]

for all things that I heard from my Father I have made known unto you.—To a friend he makes known his purposes, plans, and will, and advises with him. Jesus had treated them as friends in making known to them all the will and purposes of his Father. [See Matt. 13: 11. Not *all* absolutely, for there was still a great deal to be learned by them, but all that the most intimate friendship would demand up to that time; all that was proper to be communicated; for even to our friends we do not tell everything at once.]

16 **Ye did not choose me, but I chose you, and appointed you,**—Jesus had chosen the apostles to be his witnesses, and to this end he had made known to them the will of God and

appointed you, that ye should go and bear fruit, and *that* your fruit should abide: that whatsoever ye shall ask of the Father in my name, he may give it you. 17 These things I command you, that ye may love one another.

commissioned them to teach all things he had taught them. [A wholesome memento after the lofty things he had just said about their mutual indwelling, and the unreservedness of the friendship to which they had been admitted. The initiative of their present relationship was with him. They were still under the highest obligations to him. He had set them apart to the apostolate.]

that ye should go and bear fruit,—[The purpose for which they were set apart. The great object of the apostleship, as of all Christian activity, is to garner fruit for heaven.]

and that your fruit should abide:—His choosing them brought them into a closer relationship to him; he taught them more fully and they were enabled to bear much more fruit as his friends, and in doing his will he again assures them that the Father will hear them.

that whatsoever ye shall ask of the Father in my name, he may give it you.—[That is, in all that appertains to the accomplishment of the work given into their hands.]

17 **These things I command you, that ye may love one another.**—The end of these teachings was that they must love one another, be ready to suffer for the good of each other, and work for each other's good as brethren.

3. REMARKS ON THE WORLD'S HATRED. 15: 18-27.

18 If the world hateth you, [7]ye know that it hath hated me before *it hated* you. 19 If ye were of the world, the world would love its own: but because

[7]Or, *know ye*

18 **If the world hateth you, ye know that it hath hated me before it hated you.**—The hatred of the world for Jesus was seen in the treatment the people gave him. They rejected his words, refused to obey him, and persecuted him. If they were true followers, they might expect the same treatment.

19 **If ye were of the world, the world would love its own:**—To be of the world was to reject Jesus and his teaching and

**ye are not of the world, but I chose you out of the world, therefore the
world hateth you. 20 Remember the word that I said unto you, A [6]servant
is not greater than his lord. If they persecuted me, they will also persecute you; if they kept my word, they will keep yours also. 21 But all these**

---

to cling to the ways of the world. Jesus chose them, not to take them out of the material world, but that, while in the world, they might not follow the ways of the world, but his teachings, which are out of harmony with the world. The world seeks happiness and good in the world by gratifying the desires, lusts, and ambitions of the flesh. Jesus so directs his disciples that they find good and happiness in denying self and seeking the good of others. Find good in doing good to others and find happiness in making others happy is the essence of the teaching of Jesus.

but because ye are not of the world, but I chose you out of the world, therefore the world hateth you.—This principle condemns the world and the world opposes those who practice this divine principle. The end of God's training of man is to make man like God—like him in thought, purpose, and character. Man needs to be assimilated to God in character that he may be fitted to live with him and find pleasure with God and in his companionship. Man cannot enjoy the presence of God and his angel hosts unless he is educated and trained in character to dwell with them. The wicked, transported to heaven in their wickedness, with their wicked spirit, would be out of harmony and sympathy with God, Christ, and all the associations of heaven, and would find no joy or peace in heaven.

20 **Remember the word that I said unto you, A servant is not greater than his lord.**—The servant need not expect better treatment than the Master received. Those who persecuted him will persecute his disciples. Those who kept the word of Jesus will keep the words of his apostles.

If they persecuted me, they will also persecute you; if they kept my word, they will keep yours also.—[Those who would persecute the Lord will persecute his followers also. Those who would receive the Lord's words will also receive and keep their words. Some will persecute; others will accept

things will they do unto you for my name's sake, because they know not him that sent me. 22 If I had not come and spoken unto them, they had not had sin: but now they have no excuse for their sin. 23 He that hateth

the gospel. Christians must expect both results, persecution and glad reception, and be not disappointed in the persecution. This has been true since apostolic days. (Acts 13: 42-45.)]

21 **But all these things will they do unto you for my name's sake,**—All the opposition of the world and the persecution of the servants will be done because of their fidelity to the teachings of Jesus.

because they know not him that sent me.—The rejection of Jesus arose from their not knowing God who sent him. These Jews now trying to destroy Jesus claimed to know and worship God, but Jesus says they did it because they really did not know God who sent Jesus.

22 **If I had not come and spoken unto them, they had not had sin:**—[Here are three principles involved: (1) The degree of sin is determined by the measure of our opportunities. They who are in darkness cannot be blamed for not seeing unless they are responsible for being in the darkness. Those who have had no light from heaven will be lightly judged for breaking laws for which they could have no knowledge. (2) Increased opportunities bring the consciousness of sin. A ray from the noonday sun in the parlor reveals, but does not create, the cobweb. It was there before. So, too, the motions of sin in the soul are imperfectly recognized until the spiritual light shines in, but in that light sin is seen to be sin, and the conscience is alive to it. "Apart from the law sin is dead. And I was alive apart from the law once: but when the commandment came, sin revived, and I died." (Rom. 7: 8, 9.) So the knowledge of Christ, filling the soul with light, brings sin into full view and takes away all excuse for continuance therein. (3) The sin of all sins is the rejection of Christ. He who refuses him deliberately chooses sin. He not only willfully retains all past sins, but he adds to them the sin of rejecting Christ's offer of mercy as embodied in the gospel.]

me hateth my Father also. 24 If I had not done among them the works
which none other did, they had not had sin: but now have they both seen
and hated both me and my Father. 25 But *this cometh to pass,* that the

but now they have no excuse for their sin.—[There is no excuse for it, no shelter, no covering, nothing that can extenuate sin. Ignorance might be an excuse, but when the offer of pardon is made and refused, ignorance cannot be pleaded. Christ's offer takes away every excuse and leaves the sinner at the judgment day to the sentence of condemnation.] It is frequently said that all were sinners and Jesus came to redeem them from sin. The language here must mean: If Jesus had not come as a messenger from God and spoken the words to them, they would not have been guilty of the sin of rejecting the one sent of God. But since he came and did these works of God, there is no cloak with which to hide themselves.

23 **He that hateth me hateth my Father also.**—Love and hate in the Bible are practical words, and mean to do good or evil. To hate means to reject or oppose. And he who rejects or opposes Jesus does the same to his Father. They are one. Jesus is in the Father and the Father is in Jesus. The only way of approach to the Father is through the Son.

24 **If I had not done among them the works which none other did, they had not had sin:**—Jesus had done among them works of a character impossible to be done by man. These works showed that God was with him. If he had not done these works they would not have been guilty of the sin of rejecting Christ—the greatest sin of all sins.

but now have they both seen and hated both me and my Father.—These works which showed God's presence having been performed before their eyes, there was no excuse for their sins. They were the greater sinners for rejecting these works. Their rejecting him while the Father was working through him manifested their hatred of both him and his Father. To reject Jesus as the Christ is the greatest hatred of sin.

word may be fulfilled that is written in their law, [1]They hated me without a cause. 26 But when the [2]Comforter is come, whom I will send unto you from the Father, *even* the Spirit of truth, which [3]proceedeth from the Father, he shall bear witness of me: 27 [4]and ye also bear witness, because ye have been with me from the beginning.

[1]Ps. 35. 19; 69. 4
[2]Or, *Advocate* Or, *Helper* Gr. *Paraclete*
[3]Or, *goeth forth from*
[4]Or, *and bear ye also witness*

25 **But this cometh to pass, that the word may be fulfilled that is written in their law, They hated me without a cause.**—This is quoted from Psalm 35: 19. This condition of things showed that the scripture was true which foretold that "They hated me without a cause." (Psalm 35: 19.)

26 **But when the Comforter is come, whom I will send unto you from the Father,**—Jesus had said, "If ye love me, ye will keep my commandments. And I will pray the Father, and he shall give you another Comforter, that he may be with you for ever." (14: 15, 16.) "Nevertheless I tell you the truth: It is expedient for you that I go away; for if I go not away, the Comforter will not come unto you; but if I go, I will send him unto you." (16: 7.) The meaning of all the teachings of the fourteenth to the sixteenth chapters is that Jesus was about to leave his disciples here in this world. It distressed their hearts and this promise of another heavenly Guest, another divine Person, another representative of the Godhead to dwell with, instruct, go with, and comfort them in their sorrow over the departure of Christ is promised them. He gives the qualities of the Spirit. He will comfort for the absence of the Son; he is a Spirit that brings truth, lives truth, and dwells in truth, never in a falsehood.

even the Spirit of truth, which proceedeth from the Father, he shall bear witness of me:—He comes from God. Has received the truth from God in heaven, brings that truth to earth, makes it known to man, and will testify of the truth concerning Jesus, and his mission and his home with his Father.

27 **and ye also bear witness, because ye have been with me from the beginning.**—These disciples that now were so dis-

heartened and disconsolate over his leaving them, in the days when the Holy Spirit should come to bear witness of him, would with gladness and joy join with the Spirit in bearing witness to the world of him and his works. Here the specific work of the Holy Spirit is said to bear witness of Jesus, and this witness of the Spirit is in and through the witness of the apostles themselves.

4. PERSECUTION PREDICTED AND OTHER WORKS OF THE SPIRIT STATED.
16: 1-15.

1 These things have I spoken unto you, that ye should not be caused to
stumble. 2 They shall put you out of the synagogues: yea, the hour cometh,
that whosoever killeth you shall think that he offereth service unto God.
3 And these things will they do, because they have not known the Father,

---

1 **These things have I spoken unto you, that ye should not be caused to stumble.**—Jesus foretold that these things would come to pass so that when they did happen his disciples might not be discouraged and caused to fall by appalling things coming upon them. To tell them beforehand would assure them that he was divine and would insure confidence in him. To stumble in the Bible generally means to fall into sin.

2 **They shall put you out of the synagogues: yea, the hour cometh, that whosoever killeth you shall think that he offereth service unto God.**—He told them these things to prepare them for the trials, persecutions, and afflictions to which they would be subjected. [Not merely a physical driving forth, but excommunication and deprival of all synagogue privileges. All this was to be the bitter ingredient in the cup. It is one thing to be persecuted by those whom we not only know to be wicked, but who know themselves to be wicked. But to be persecuted by those who, like Saul of Tarsus, means to do right, and think they are serving God in making us suffer is quite another thing. It is calculated to make the sufferer wonder whether he is doing right himself.]

3 **And these things will they do, because they have not known the Father, nor me.**—All these persecutions and afflictions they would bring upon the disciples because they neither

nor me. 4 But these things have I spoken unto you, that when their hour is come, ye may remember them, how that I told you. And these things I said not unto you from the beginning, because I was with you. 5 But now

knew the Father nor Christ. Their failure to know God and his Christ causes men to hate those who obey the laws of God. [This was to prepare them against the persecutions they would be called upon to endure. He assures them that though the zeal of their persecutors might be a "zeal of God," yet it would not be according to knowledge. Their religious education and training gave them no real knowledge of the Father or himself. Consequently the disciples need not waver or be uncertain about their own religious status on account of persecution.] "These things" are the persecutions even unto death which Jesus had just told his disciples that they would suffer. This was evidently spoken by way of explaining why the world would so severely persecute them. It is but another way of saying there is eternal and uncompromising enmity on the part of those who know not God and his Son Jesus Christ against those who walk with God and believe on the Lord.

4 **But these things have I spoken unto you, that when their hour is come,**—[The hour of their fulfillment.]

ye may remember them, how that I told you.—[Remembering thus that he had predicted the sorrows, they would also remember the joys beyond and be comforted and upheld.]

And these things I said not unto you from the beginning, because I was with you.—These afflictions that would come upon them, he did not tell them in the beginning of his ministry because he was abiding with them. But now he is about to leave them, he forewarns them that when the trials come upon them they will remember them and not be driven from faith in God and in him. [He advanced in his instruction just as they were prepared to receive it. By degrees had he revealed to the disciples the dark, rugged, and bloody pathway that they should be called upon to travel. In the beginning of his ministry he did not teach of these things for the reason they were not prepared to receive it. In the second year of his ministry he began to gradually unfold them, but

I go unto him that sent me; and none of you asketh me, Whither goest thou? 6 But because I have spoken these things unto you, sorrow hath filled your heart. 7 Nevertheless I tell you the truth: It is expedient for

only in the hour of his departure does he reveal to them the trials that are to come upon them. The greatest of all their trials, unless the promised comforter came, would be the departure of the Lord. While he was with them the bolts of hatred and malice would be thrust at him, but when he was gone and they represented him on the earth these bolts would hit them. As long as Jesus was with them these personal trials of the apostles would not begin, and therefore he saw no necessity of burdening their hearts prematurely with their anticipation. But *now* he was to be taken from them, so he unfolds it.]

5 **But now I go unto him that sent me;**—[Jesus shows himself conscious of pre-existence, of having come from another world to which he was to return by the way of the cross. (17: 5.)]

and none of you asketh me, Whither goest thou?—The Father had sent Jesus into the world to perform a work; when he has reached the time to finish that work he will return to his Father. [They had asked this question (15: 36; 14: 5), but they had become so preoccupied with themselves and the desolate condition in which his going would leave them that they had ceased to ask him. His human yearning for sympathy shows itself in this tender reproach.]

6 **because I have spoken these things unto you, sorrow hath filled your heart.**—Peter (13: 36) and Thomas (14: 5) had both asked this question, but now when his going away is at hand, none ask "whither goest thou"? but sorrow fills their hearts. [They were entirely given up to their gloomy forebodings.]

7 **Nevertheless I tell you the truth:**—The Father provides for all things; the Son creates or embodies the purposes and provisions of the Father; and the Spirit then gives life and order to this creation, gives law to guide and promote and perfect and multiply the order created by the Father. [This is not an assertion of his veracity, as though they had doubted

you that I go away; for if I go not away, the [2]Comforter will not come unto you; but if I go, I will send him unto you. 8 And he, when he is come,

it, but an intimation of the necessity of its communication, and of the necessity of his departure. And now he proceeds to give grounds for the latter point.]

It is expedient for you that I go away;—[With their false ideas of an earthly political kingdom with Jesus their king, nothing could have seemed harder to receive than this. They *might* submit to the inevitable, but that the departure of Jesus should be expedient—desirable—this was too hard to receive.]

for if I go not away, the Comforter—[The Holy Spirit, called in the footnote "Advocate or Helper."]

will not come unto you;—[Jesus evidently holds this up as a supereminent gift to obtain which might well justify any sacrifice on their part, even giving up the precious companionship with him which had been the joy of their hearts.]

but if I go, I will send him unto you.—[The death of Christ was necessary to his glorification. For some reason not revealed even Jesus, here upon earth in his natural human condition, could not, or at least did not, confer upon them supereminent gifts of the Holy Spirit. While he was with them

the Holy Spirit reached them *through* him. In the future the Holy Spirit is to reach the world *through* them.] The work that Jesus had begun in the disciples could not be completed and perfected unless the Spirit came and completed his work. The work of the Spirit was needed to complete and perfect them to dwell with God and to do the work he had chosen them to do and to fit them to enjoy the home and blessings of God forever. If they had understood these things they would have rejoiced at Jesus leaving them since he left to send the Spirit that they might receive the greater blessings.

8 **And he, when he is come,**—[It is strange in the light of these words, and, indeed, this whole conversation, that any can be found to deny the personality of the Holy Spirit, and to speak of him as a mere abstract influence. Here, as in regard to Satan, Jesus made a very uncertain use of words,

will convict the world in respect of sin, and of righteousness, and of judgment: 9 of sin, because they believe not on me; 10 of righteousness, because

---

if he did not know, and mean to assert, the personality of the Holy Spirit.]

will convict the world—[Not by *direct* work upon their hearts, but as the event shows (Acts 2: 37), through the life of the apostles, declaring the wonderful works of God. He came not to the world, but "unto you," the disciples. The world could not receive him directly (14: 17), and never can, *as the world*. But the apostles received him, and through their testimony he reaches the world.]

in respect of sin,—[This convicting and convincing work of the Holy Spirit is entirely in relation to Jesus Christ. The world had no consciousness of sin in regard to him, believing him either fanatic or impostor in the claims which he made. The Holy Spirit is to show them that they are sinners against Christ.] When the Spirit came on the day of Pentecost, his first work was to bear witness that Jesus was from God, that the world had rejected and crucified him; but that God had raised him from the dead and had made him both Lord and Christ. The Spirit did this work of bearing witness of Christ through the apostles, who, under the guidance of the Spirit, bore witness themselves of the works he had done, of his death, burial, resurrection, and ascension to his Father, and the descent of the Holy Spirit who was directing the works they saw.

and of righteousness,—He not only convicted the world of sin in crucifying the Lord, but they presented him as the Holy One, through whose mission the sinner could be made righteous.

and of judgment:—Judgment in which the wrath of God against sin and the reward of righteousness would be executed. [The power with which Jesus is to be clothed to judge the world.]

9 **of sin, because they believe not on me;**—The greatest, because the sin of all sins, without which no sin could be blotted out, is the sin of unbelief in the Son of God. [He

I go to the Father, and ye behold me no more; 11 of judgment, because the prince of this world hath been judged. 12 I have yet many things to

proceeds to describe the *method* of the Holy Spirit's mission to the world. It is logical in character. The sin, the supreme sin, the acme of the world's sin, is to be shown in the rejection of Jesus Christ. If the world had no other sin to answer for, this will be enough to destroy it if it shall persist in it after the Spirit has done his work.]

10 **of righteousness, because I go to the Father, and ye behold me no more;**—His righteousness in himself doing the full righteous will of God, and through his death making others righteous he went to his Father where they would no more see him on earth. [The death of Jesus, had it been perpetual, would have been a tremendous argument against his claims. But when the Holy Spirit demonstrated his resurrection and ascension to the Father, and his power in the invisible world for good, it establishes the truth of those claims, and his consequent righteousness, beyond a peradventure.]

11 **of judgment,**—[That is, of impending judgment of the world by Christ.]

because the prince of this world hath been judged.—The evil one is the prince of this world. He became so when man, the ruler in Eden, chose to follow Satan rather than obey God. All in this world had been intrusted to man, and he transferred his allegiance of the world to him instead of God. Jesus came into the world to rescue man and the world from the rule of the devil. The final conflict was now at hand. He would surrender himself to the power of the devil, go down into the grave, and there in the devil's own prison house overcome him, burst the bonds of death, and condemn him as a usurper of the prerogatives of God. The prince of this world used the rulers of the kingdoms of the world to bring Jesus to the grave. [Satan's great power was death. The world had ever been in bondage to him through death. (Heb. 2: 14, 15.) This power he had exercised even over Jesus; but this only temporarily and by per-

say unto you, but ye cannot bear them now. 13 Howbeit when he, the Spirit of truth, is come, he shall guide you into all the truth: for he shall not speak from himself; but what things soever he shall hear, *these* shall

---

mission. The resurrection of Jesus broke his sceptre and announced his judgment. He was a criminal at the bar instead of a mighty lord. But he who had power to judge the universal conqueror of humanity would certainly have power to judge the world. Thus complete and logical is the argument of the divine advocate of Jesus as predicted by Jesus. For its fulfillment read Acts 2 and indeed the whole line of the apostolic ministry, which was and is the ministry of the Holy Spirit to the world.]

12 **I have yet many things to say unto you, but ye cannot bear them now.**—Jesus could teach only as they were able to understand and appreciate. Their dullness precluded his teaching them now. He could transfer it to the coming of the Spirit who would qualify them for, and guide them into, all truth. [The death of Christ would have a wonderful clarifying effect upon their spiritual vision, and also to give a great uplift to their moral strength, and an indescribable intensification to their faith. Under these changed conditions revelations, which now would be beyond their comprehension, would be clear to them, and doubtless the "forty days" (Acts 1: 3) were full of these sayings.]

13 **Howbeit when he, the Spirit of truth, is come, he shall guide you into all the truth:**—The mission of the Spirit to them was to complete the revelation of God's will to them. Notwithstanding their inability to receive all the truth then, the Holy Spirit would complete the revelation to them, would guide them into all the truth. [The "you" here is specific to the apostles. "All the truth" comprehends redemption through the death of Christ, the relation of grace to the law, the conversion of the Gentiles without any Mosaic legal condition. In a word, the contents of the epistles and the apocalypse so far as they pass beyond those of the teaching of Jesus.]

for he shall not speak from himself; but what things soever he shall hear, these shall he speak:—The Spirit, like Jesus

he speak: and he shall declare unto you the things that are to come. 14
He shall glorify me: for he shall take of mine, and shall declare *it* unto
you. 15 All things whatsoever the Father hath are mine: therefore said I,

himself, would not originate what he spoke, but would speak what he heard from the Father. The Spirit would become the representative of the Godhead on earth.

and he shall declare unto you the things that are to come.—[*All* the things that are revealed. This is confined to the apostles. It opens up no place for modern visionaries with their claims of new and advanced revelations. He was to declare to them not only what might be necessary for their guidance (Acts 20: 22, 23), but for the benefit of the church.]

14 **He shall glorify me:**—[His mission is to exalt or glorify Christ. It pertains entirely to him. It is to advance his glory that he comes.]

for he shall take of mine,—[He has nothing to communicate of his own. He takes up the work where Christ stops and carries it to completion.]

and shall declare it unto you.—He will from the Father receive the full and perfect knowledge of the Son of God, and make it known to the disciples. This was done on Pentecost when the Spirit revealed the full mission and character of Christ to the apostles, and through them to the world. [This verse is decisive against all additions and pretended revelations subsequent to and besides Christ, it being the work of the Spirit to testify and declare the things of Christ, not anything new and beyond him.]

15 **All things whatsoever the Father hath are mine: therefore said I, that he taketh of mine, and shall declare it unto you.**—Jesus and his Father are one in their character and possessions. As the Son of God, he was heir to all things, therefore in revealing the things of God, they made known those of Christ the Lord. [We are here shut up to two alternatives, either that Jesus of Nazareth is not only the Christ, but the Son of the living God, in all that those words can imply of deific attributes and essence, or that he was the most arrogant pretender that the world has ever seen.]

5. HIS DEPARTURE AND RETURN.
16: 16-24.

that he taketh of mine, and shall declare *it* unto you. 16 A little while,
and ye behold me no more; and again a little while, and ye shall see me.
17 *Some* of his disciples therefore said one to another, What is this that
he saith unto us, A little while, and ye behold me not; and again a little
while, and ye shall see me: and, Because I go to the Father? 18 They
said therefore, What is this that he saith, A little while? We know not
what he saith. 19 Jesus perceived that they were desirous to ask him, and
he said unto them, Do ye inquire among yourselves concerning this, that I
said, A little while, and ye behold me not, and again a little while, and ye
shall see me? 20 Verily, verily, I say unto you, that ye shall weep and
lament, but the world shall rejoice: ye shall be sorrowful, but your sorrow

---

16 **A little while, and ye behold me no more; and again a little while, and ye shall see me.**—In a little while he would be taken from them and go into the grave where they could not see him and, in a little while he would appear again and they could see him. These things would be brought about as preparatory to his return to his Father.

17 **Some of his disciples therefore said one to another, What is this that he saith unto us, A little while, and ye behold me not; and again a little while, and ye shall see me: and, Because I go to the Father?**—The apostles were still ignorant of his coming death, burial, and resurrection. He had told them, but it differed so far from their ideas of what his cause would be that they could not perceive by dying and rising again.

18 **They said therefore, What is this that he saith, A little while? We know not what he saith.**—They say among themselves that they cannot understand the meaning and desired to ask him to explain it.

19 **Jesus perceived that they were desirous to ask him, and he said unto them, Do ye inquire among yourselves concerning this, that I said, A little while, and ye behold me not, and again a little while, and ye shall see me?**—Jesus, without being told, knew their thoughts and their desire to ask him and himself asked if they wished him to explain his meaning. [This power to read their thoughts proves he was more than human.]

20 **Verily, verily, I say unto you, that ye shall weep and lament, but the world shall rejoice: ye shall be sorrowful, but**

shall be turned into joy. 21 A woman when she is in travail hath sorrow, because her hour is come: but when she is delivered of the child, she remembereth no more the anguish, for the joy that a man is born into the world. 22 And ye therefore now have sorrow: but I will see you again, and your heart shall rejoice, and your joy no one taketh away from you.

your sorrow shall be turned into joy.—The results of their grief and sorrow would be followed by joy and gladness. [This was in a few hours fulfilled. His disciples were broken-hearted and wept at the grave. "We trusted that he would restore the kingdom of Israel" was the wail of buried hopes. At the same time his enemies were rejoicing over what they thought was a glorious victory. But soon all was changed. The glad news came, "The Lord is risen." They heard him exclaim "all authority hath been given unto me in heaven and on earth," then they saw him ascend into heaven, then they "returned to Jerusalem with great joy." Their sorrow, indeed, was turned into joy.]

21 **A woman when she is in travail hath sorrow, because her hour is come: but when she is delivered of the child, she remembereth no more the anguish, for the joy that a man is born into the world.**—He illustrates by the pain and anguish of a woman in travail chased away by the joy that a man is born into the world. [The figure of a woman in travail was used to illustrate sudden sorrow and anguish. (Isa. 21: 3; Hos. 13: 13; Mic. 4: 9.) But here Jesus gives it a new application by asserting that joy comes out of the pains of travail.]

22 **And ye therefore now have sorrow: but I will see you again, and your heart shall rejoice,**—So now in his going away sorrow will fill their hearts to be succeeded by joy when they see him again.

and your joy no one taketh away from you.—Their joy shall be permanent; none shall deprive them of it. The resurrection of Christ foretokens the resurrection to eternal life of all who believe in him. [Jesus refers to his own appearance to the disciples after his sufferings and resurrection, which would turn their sorrow into joy. That joy would be permanent. All enemies on earth combined with those of

23 And in that day ye shall [6]ask me no question. Verily, verily, I say unto you, If ye shall ask anything of the Father, he will give it you in my name. 24 Hitherto have ye asked nothing in my name: ask, and ye shall receive, that your joy may be made full.

[6]Or, *ask me nothing* Comp. ver. 26; ch. 14. 13, 20

the underworld might assail them, but "no man could take it" away.]

23 **And in that day ye shall ask me no question. Verily, verily, I say unto you, If ye shall ask anything of the Father, he will give it you in my name.**—Then they shall be brought into immediate union with God the Father and in that state they could approach him directly without the intervention of a mediator. He will gladly answer them himself.

24 **Hitherto have ye asked nothing in my name:**—As yet they had not regarded Jesus as the mediator through whom they must approach God. He had not entered upon his mediatorial work, and so they had asked nothing in his name.

ask, and ye shall receive, that your joy may be made full.—When he had suffered and died as a sacrifice for the sins of the world and ascended to his Father as the Great High Priest and Advocate with the Father, then they must ask in his name, as his servants and representatives, purchased by him, and the fullness of the blessings would make their joy full.

6. AN END OF SPEAKING IN PARABLES. 16: 25-33.

25 These things have I spoken unto you in [1]dark sayings: the hour cometh, when I shall no more speak unto you in [1]dark sayings, but shall tell you plainly of the Father. 26 In that day ye shall ask in my name:

[1]Or, *parables*

25 **These things have I spoken unto you in dark sayings: the hour cometh, when I shall no more speak unto you in dark sayings, but shall tell you plainly of the Father.**—These things he teaches now in parables or illustrations, but when his death and resurrection were accomplished, he would speak plainly and they would then have learned enough to understand.

and I say not unto you, that I will [2]pray the Father for you; 27 for the
Father himself loveth you, because ye have loved me, and have believed
that I came forth from the Father. 28 I came out from the Father, and am
come into the world: again, I leave the world, and go unto the Father.
29 His disciples say, Lo, now speakest thou plainly, and speakest no [3]dark
saying. 30 Now know we that thou knowest all things, and needest not
that any man should ask thee: by this we believe that thou camest forth
from God. 31 Jesus answered them, Do ye now believe? 32 Behold, the
hour cometh, yea, is come, that ye shall be scattered, every man to his own,
and shall leave me alone: and *yet* I am not alone, because the Father is

[2]Gr. *make request of*
[3]Or, *parable*

26, 27 **In that day ye shall ask in my name: and I say not unto you, that I will pray the Father for you; for the Father himself loveth you, because ye have loved me, and have believed that I came forth from the Father.**—After his resurrection and ascension they were to ask in his name. Then he does not say he will ask the Father for them because by their faith in him as sent of God and their love and obedience to him God would of his own love bless them.

28 **I came out from the Father, and am come into the world: again, I leave the world, and go unto the Father.**—He had been with God, had been sent forth by God into this world. Soon he would leave the world and return to God.

29 **His disciples say, Lo, now speakest thou plainly, and speakest no dark saying.**—They thought they comprehended his plain statement and so claimed; but it is very doubtful if they grasped its meaning, or if they did, it slipped from them, for after his crucifixion they still did not understand that he was to die, be buried, and rise again.

30 **Now know we that thou knowest all things, and needest not that any man should ask thee: by this we believe that thou camest forth from God.**—By virtue of his knowing their thoughts and answering their difficulties they claim to know that he is from God and knows all things. These impressions seemingly clear at times would often vanish and their hearts would be beclouded with doubts and uncertainty.

31 **Jesus answered them, Do ye now believe?**—This was asked in view of their lack of steadfastness in their faith.

32 **Behold, the hour cometh, yea, is come, that ye shall be scattered, every man to his own, and shall leave me alone:**—

with me. 33 These things have I spoken unto you, that in me ye may have peace. In the world ye have tribulation: but be of good cheer; I have overcome the world.

He here presents the trials that they would be called upon to undergo by which their faith would be tested. They would forsake him—all of them leave him alone. The feeling of loneliness seems to creep over him.

and yet I am not alone, because the Father is with me.—He was not alone, for God never forsakes his children that are faithful to him in the darkest hour.

33 **These things have I spoken unto you, that in me ye may have peace. In the world ye have tribulation: but be of good cheer; I have overcome the world.**—He transfers his own source of joy to them. In the world tribulation, persecution, and sorrow would come; but he had overcome the world. He had done it for them, and the Father would be with them as he had been with Jesus. They could overcome the world, too.

7. JESUS PRAYS FOR HIMSELF AND HIS DISCIPLES.
17: 1-26.

1 These things spake Jesus; and lifting up his eyes to heaven, he said, Father, the hour is come; glorify thy Son, that the Son may glorify thee:

1 **These things spake Jesus; and lifting up his eyes to heaven, he said,**—When Jesus had concluded the discourse contained in chapters 14 to 16, at the close of the passover supper at which he had instituted the Lord's Supper, he offered the prayer recorded in this chapter. He was then expecting the return of Judas with his band to arrest and deliver him into the hands of the chief priests and scribes.

Father, the hour is come;—[The hour for which all the other hours had existed, the hour for the consummation of the great work of redemption. All of the coming day is comprehended in this "hour."]

glorify thy Son, that the Son may glorify thee:—This petition was made in view of the trials through which he was to pass. He asked the Father to give him strength to be

2 even as thou gavest him authority over all flesh, that [4]to all whom thou hast given him, he should give eternal life. 3 And this is life eternal, that

[4]Gr. *whatsoever thou hast given him, to them he &c.*

able to bear it all. In this way God would glorify him, that in his faithfulness he might glorify God before the world. [The hour of suffering and death has come, but Jesus looks through this to what is beyond. He has not come to this hour for the mere purpose of suffering, but that the suffering may bring glory to himself and his Father. The resurrection, the ascension, the coronation—these are what he prays for because through these the glorification of him and the Father, together with eternal life to the race, comes.]

2 **even as thou gavest him authority over all flesh,**—God had given into his hands the rule and destiny of all flesh. He came to redeem all by his death. "But we behold him who hath been made a little lower than the angels, even Jesus, because of the suffering of death crowned with glory and honor, that by the grace of God he should taste of death for every man." (Heb. 2: 9.) [All human beings is meant. The authority came by the appointment of the Father because of his purpose to redeem man by sacrifice. As he knew that the purpose held, and that he would carry it out, he speaks as though it were already accomplished, though the authority was not fully asserted till after the resurrection. (Matt. 28: 18-20.)]

that to all whom thou hast given him,—[The significance of this phrase, and the number it embraces, can only be settled by ascertaining the full number of believers in Christ, using "believers" in the correct sense as meaning those who have definitely committed themselves to him. A select number is not here meant by this.]

he should give eternal life.—[The design of the creation of the world is the glorification of God and Christ in the blessedness of men—such, likewise, is the design of the redemption. The Father is to be glorified by the diffusion of salvation in Christ, the dissemination of eternal life.] God had given him all who would believe in him and be led by him. So he gives eternal life to all who obey him.

they should know thee the only true God, and him whom thou didst send, *even* Jesus Christ. 4 I glorified thee on the earth, having accomplished the work which thou hast given me to do. 5 And now, Father, glorify thou me with thine own self with the glory which I had with thee before the world

3 **And this is life eternal, that they should know thee the only true God, and him whom thou didst send, even Jesus Christ.**—To know God as the ruler and maker of the universe and his Son Jesus Christ as the Redeemer and Savior of the world is to obtain eternal life. To know them in the sense of obeying him.

4 **I glorified thee on the earth,**—In doing the work of his Father he had glorified him. [Jesus stands upon an elevation from which he looks back over his whole earth life as well as that of the few hours remaining. He sees in it only the glorification of the Father. He does not see in his life at this supreme moment either any evil committed or any good omitted. The duty of every hour had been fulfilled.]

having accomplished the work which thou hast given me to do.—God had sent Jesus into the world to manifest God's love, and this work he had finished. [He has laid down the principles of his church. He is about to shed the blood which shall cement together, and upon these principles the living stones of that institution.]

5 **And now, Father, glorify thou me with thine own self with the glory which I had with thee before the world was.**—Jesus was in heaven with God before the world was. To show the way for man's return to God he gave up that glory, came to earth, took upon himself the nature of man, became subject to mortality and death to save man. The end of this work on earth now approaches and he prays that he might be delivered from these earthly trials and be restored to his original position of honor in heaven. [Jesus here goes back of history, back of creation itself, and speaks of the glory which he then had with the Father. This can be understood only in the light of the opening verses of the first chapter of John, where not only pre-existence, but *deific and eternal pre-existence* is predicated of him.]

was. 6 I manifested thy name unto the men whom thou gavest me out of the world: thine they were, and thou gavest them to me; and they have kept thy word. 7 Now they know that all things whatsoever thou hast given me are from thee: 8 for the words which thou gavest me I have given unto them; and they received *them,* and knew of a truth that I came forth from thee, and they believed that thou didst send me. 9 I [5]pray for them: I [5]pray not for the world, but for those whom thou hast given me;

[5]Gr. *make request*

6 **I manifested thy name unto the men whom thou gavest me out of the world:**—Among those who were given to him by the Father were the twelve apostles or chosen witnesses. [It is by revealing himself as Son that Jesus has revealed God to them as the Father.]

thine they were, and thou gavest them to me;—[Probably this refers to a spiritual relationship to and knowledge of God on the part of these men, brought about by the preaching of John the Baptist, which marked them out as belonging to God. (1: 35-39.) They were true "Israel" in whom was "no guile."]

and they have kept thy word.—Jesus had given to them the word of God, and they had kept it. Judas is excepted as failing to keep the word of God. (Verse 12.) [Notwithstanding all the temptations to unfaithfulness which have assailed them during these years (Luke 22: 28) and before which others have fallen, they have kept in their heart the teaching of Jesus.]

7 **Now they know that all things whatsoever thou hast given me are from thee:**—These, through the teachings of Jesus, had come to know that what Jesus taught was from God the Father. Jesus taught only as God gave him to teach.

8 **for the words which thou gavest me I have given unto them; and they received them, and knew of a truth that I came forth from thee, and they believed that thou didst send me.**—Jesus gave the words of God to the disciples and through these they came to know that Jesus came from God and that God sent him.

9 **I pray for them: I pray not for the world,**—[At this time. Jesus does not mean to say that the world is excluded from his sympathy, for the reason he was dying to save the world.]

for they are thine: 10 and all things that are mine are thine, and thine
are mine: and I am glorified in them. 11 And I am no more in the world,
and these are in the world, and I come to thee. Holy Father, keep them in
thy name which thou hast given me, that they may be one, even as we *are*.

---

but for those whom thou hast given me; for they are thine:—Jesus first prays for those who had believed on him and so were given to him of God. [Jesus intimates that they occupy a relationship to God, also, which he will doubtless recognize as giving them special claims to his blessings. They have not ceased to be thine by becoming mine.]

10 **and all things that are mine are thine, and thine are mine:**—The oneness of Jesus and the Father is again emphasized and the truth Jesus had taught these disciples had kept them.

and I am glorified in them.—He was glorified in their holy lives and in the work they would do in his name.

11 **And I am no more in the world, and these are in the world, and I come to thee.**—Jesus would leave the world and go to God, but he would leave these chosen witnesses in the world.

Holy Father, keep them in thy name which thou hast given me,—He had kept them while he was with them in the world; but as he leaves them he prays God to keep them in his own name, that they may be one as God and Jesus are one. To keep them in the name of God was to keep them as his servants doing his work and looking to God for help and strength. [The disciples would not have his visible presence to encourage, strengthen, and bless and he intercedes for them. We cannot overestimate the sympathy that breathes in every word of this prayer. His heart's desire was that the apostles be kept in the spiritual sphere into which they had entered by accepting him as their Teacher and believing the truths he had presented.]

that they may be one, even as we are.—[The only security for the unity of the disciples of Christ is in answering fidelity to his word. Abiding thus in his word, in his name which is the symbol of his truth, they will be as closely united in

**12 While I was with them, I kept them in thy name which thou hast given
me: and I guarded them, and not one of them perished, but the son of perdition; [6]that the scripture might be fulfilled. 13 But now I come to thee;
and these things I speak in the world, that they may have my joy made
full in themselves. 14 I have given them thy word; and the world hated
them, because they are not of the world, even as I am not of the world.**

[6]Ps. 41. 9?

sympathy and work as the Father and the Son. All departures from unity have been departures from the word.]

12 **While I was with them, I kept them in thy name which thou hast given me: and I guarded them, and not one of them perished, but the son of perdition; that the scripture might be fulfilled.**—When he was in the world he acted in the name of the Father. By the power and for the service of God he kept his disciples, and only the son of perdition was lost, as the scriptures foretold. [Judas had the same care bestowed on him that was bestowed on the others, and was lost because he would not be saved. What scripture is referred to here is somewhat doubtful. Some say Psalm 109: 8; others Psalm 41: 9.]

13 **But now I come to thee; and these things I speak in the world, that they may have my joy made full in themselves.**—Before leaving the world to go to God he spoke these things to his disciples yet in the world, that they might possess the joy in this world that filled Jesus, "who for the joy that was set before him endured the cross, despising shame, and hath sat down at the right hand of the throne of God." (Heb. 12: 2.) The sufferings and shame of the cross could not dispossess him of his joy. [Jesus was leaving these words in the world as a legacy to the apostles that they might have the same certainty of the protection and love of the Father that he had.]

14 **I have given them thy word;**—[Looking back over, and summing up, the teaching of the past years, which was the word of God.]

and the world hated them, because they are not of the world, even as I am not of the world.—The words of God received into the heart, cherished and obeyed, would separate them from the world as he was separated from the world, and

15 I [6]pray not that thou shouldest take them [7]from the world, but that
thou shouldest keep them from [8]the evil *one*. 16 They are not of the world,
even as I am not of the world. 17 [9]Sanctify them in the truth: thy word

[7]Gr. *out of*
[8]Or, *evil*
[9]Or, *consecrate*

would cause the world to hate them as it hated Christ; but it would secure to them the joy that he possessed, of which nothing could deprive them. [The world as opposed to God, or caring nothing for him, are trampling his divine will under foot, or making his word of no effect by their traditions. Necessarily, those whose thoughts were centered upon God would be the antipodes of these and would excite their antipathy.]

15 **I pray not that thou shouldest take them from the world,**—[For the reason that then one of the great objects of his would be defeated. They have a mission to be fulfilled; they are to be the salt of the earth and the light of the world. The world is to be blessed through them, but not by their departure.]

but that thou shouldest keep them from the evil one.—To keep them from being led into the sins of the world and so from its sorrows.

16 **They are not of the world,**—His disciples, guided by his words, were not of this world, but by this were made partakers of his nature and sharers of his spiritual kingdom. [Not of the world because they have different hopes and aims from the world. They are living in a sphere of holiness into which Christ through his teaching has brought them with himself.]

even as I am not of the world.—[Like their Master, they are to be separate from sinners, and undefiled, but to remain in the world that they may carry forward the saving work established by Jesus.]

17 **Sanctify them in the truth: thy word is truth.**—To sanctify to a sacred and holy use or purpose. The prayer was separate them and set them apart (from the world) to God through the truth. Lest men should misapprehend what he regards as truth, he adds, "Thy word is truth." No one can

is truth. 18 As thou didst send me into the world, even so sent I them
into the world. 19 And for their sakes I [9]sanctify myself, that they themselves also may be sanctified in truth. 20 Neither for these only do I [5]pray,

---

be separated from the world, or sanctified to God by the truth, save as he makes that truth the rule of his life and is led away from all other paths into the path marked out by this.

18 **As thou didst send me into the world, even so sent I them into the world.**—The disciples taught and sent by Jesus stood related to him as he stood related to the Father who sent him. [Jesus has raised them up into his own sphere of divine thought and feeling, and from this sent them forth as messengers to the world, even as he himself had been sent from a higher sphere to the low-lying grounds of the world. They are to take up and carry on his mission. They have, therefore, the highest claims upon our reverence.]

19 **And for their sakes I sanctify myself,**—For the sake of them he sanctified himself to death and shed his blood to seal the truth. [This covers the entire consecration of Jesus to his mission, including all he was to do and suffer on the next day. He sacrificed everything, even his own life, to the fulfillment of his mission.]

that they themselves also may be sanctified in truth.—That these disciples might be led by that truth, devoted to it, and sanctified by it. The only way of sanctification is through the truth of God. The only union possible is in the truth as God has delivered it. He who turns from the truth of God—sets aside any of that truth for the sake of union with others—not only sets at naught the authority of God, but he places himself upon ground upon which union is impossible. Union is not only undesirable, but impossible, save as men are sanctified by the word of God. A union in any other way save as we are sanctified by and in the truth would be a union out of and against God. If this were possible, it would only be the presage of swift and widespread destruction from God.

20 **Neither for these only do I pray,**—The apostles were the chosen witnesses to testify the things done and taught by Christ. They were guided by the Holy Spirit in this work.

but for them also that believe on me through their word; 21 that they may
all be one; even as thou, Father, *art* in me, and I in thee, that they also
may be in us: that the world may believe that thou didst send me. 22 And

Their testimonies or words were the foundation of faith in Christ.

but for them also that believe on me through their word;—When he had prayed for the witnesses, he extends the prayer in behalf of those who would believe on him through their words. All faith in Jesus in the years since his death came through the words of the apostles.

21 **that they may all be one;**—The oneness of the children of God as God and Jesus are one was a question near the heart of the Son of God.

even as thou, Father, art in me, and I in thee, that they also may be in us: that the world may believe that thou didst send me.—One reason of this earnest desire for this oneness was that through this oneness the world might be brought to believe in Jesus as the Son of God and be saved. The belief and salvation of the world depends upon the children of God being one. They can be one only by adhering faithfully to the word of God. Through all the ages to come man can believe in God through Christ in the words of the apostles. [The Father and Son have no separate will, kingdom or interest. Such a union is here demanded of the disciples of Christ. It is impossible to convert and save the world to Christ as long as they who claim to be his followers are divided into various denominations, each having a different doctrine, property and interest, separate churches, colleges, papers, and missions. Denominationalism is utterly opposed to this prayer, and every apologist for it is disloyal to the spirit of the prayer and working against the salvation of the world. Nor is it fulfilled in any church where there are factions, where all are not "perfected together in the same mind and in the same judgment." If Christ abides in the heart, the one life will draw all who have Christ formed within them into one family. This union is needful and the world will never believe in the Christ until it is accomplished. Sectarian divisions is the most fruitful source of skepticism

the glory which thou hast given me I have given unto them; that they may be one, even as we *are* one; 23 I in them, and thou in me, that they may be perfected into one; that the world may know that thou didst send me, and lovedst them, even as thou lovedst me. 24 Father, [1]I desire that they also whom thou hast given me be with me where I am, that they may behold my glory, which thou hast given me: for thou lovedst me before the foundation of the world. 25 O righteous Father, the world knew thee

[1]Gr. *that which thou hast given me, I desire that where I am, they also may be with me, that &c.*

that can be found. The union of Christendom would soon convert the world; but this union must be on the word of God.]

22 **And the glory which thou hast given me I have given unto them;**—The power and wisdom God had given the Son when he sent him into the world, he thus gives to his apostles that through this power they might show that God was with them as he had been with Jesus.

that they may be one, even as we are one;—God's Spirit in Christ makes them one. This same Spirit ruling in the disciples will make them one with God and one with each other. All persons guided by the one Spirit will be one with each other.

23 **I in them, and thou in me, that they may be perfected into one; that the world may know that thou didst send me, and lovedst them, even as thou lovedst me.**—Jesus loved those he died to redeem. He loved them while they were yet sinners and rebels against God. That love was intensified and strengthened by their response to his love and sacrifice.

24 **Father, I desire that they also whom thou hast given me be with me where I am, that they may behold my glory, which thou hast given me: for thou lovedst me before the foundation of the world.**—When they became the children of God, this love was intensified and he desired that they should be with him, see his glory in the world of glory bestowed upon him by his Father, and share that glory with him. The Father loved him before the world was, and gave him the glory that he now desired them to behold and share.

25 **O righteous Father, the world knew thee not,**—The world had been created by God; but it lost sight of him and

not, but I knew thee; and these knew that thou didst send me; 26 and I made known unto them thy name, and will make it known; that the love wherewith thou lovedst me may be in them, and I in them.

turned from him. "And the light shineth in the darkness; and the darkness apprehended it not." (1: 5.)

but I knew thee; and these knew that thou didst send me;—While the world did not know him, Jesus who had been with him did know him, and the disciples through his works and teaching had come to know that God had sent him and was with him.

26 **and I made known unto them thy name, and will make it known;**—By the name of God is meant more than by the simple term by which he is known; but person, character, and mission of God in his dealings with man. "And Jehovah descended in the cloud, and stood with him there, and proclaimed the name of Jehovah. And Jehovah passed by before him, and proclaimed, Jehovah, Jehovah, a God merciful and gracious, slow to anger, and abundant in lovingkindness and truth; keeping lovingkindness for thousands, forgiving iniquity and transgression and sin; and that will by no means clear the guilty, visiting the iniquity of the fathers upon the children, and upon the children's children, upon the third and upon the fourth generation." (Ex. 34: 5-7.) [I have made known unto them thy nature, attributes, counsels, will, and commandments, and I will continue the manifestation of the same unto the end. The saving knowledge of God was not attainable by natural abilities, but cometh to us by the special revelation of Christ.]

that the love wherewith thou lovedst me may be in them, and I in them.—Jesus had declared the work, mission, character, and office of the Creator and Ruler of the world; he would still do it in person till his final ascension; then he would do it through the Spirit that the Father would send in his name, that the apostle acting as he acted, living as he lived, might be the object of God's love as he (Jesus) was loved by his Father. [It is not enough for the people of God that they are beloved of him, and that his love is towards them; but they must endeavor to have it in them.]

SECTION FOUR.

THE ARREST AND CONDEMNATION OF JESUS.
18: 1 to 19: 16.

1. ARRESTED AND TAKEN BEFORE ANNAS.
18: 1-14.

1 When Jesus had spoken these words, he went forth with his disciples over the [2]brook [3]Kidron, where was a garden, into which he entered, himself and his disciples. 2 Now Judas also, who [4]betrayed him, knew the place: for Jesus oft-times resorted thither with his disciples. 3 Judas then,

[2]Or, *ravine* Gr. *winter-torrent*
[3]Or, *of the Cedars*
[4]Or, *delivered him up*

1 **When Jesus had spoken these words,**—The preceding speech, embracing chapters 14 to 16, with prayer and conclusion in chapter 17, occurred after the eating of the passover supper before the crossing over of the brook Kidron in going out toward Bethany, the place where Jesus spent the nights during his last week before his crucifixion.

he went forth with his disciples over the brook Kidron,—This brook is a rivulet, dry in the later centuries except during the rainy season. It is noted on account of its relations to the city of Jerusalem, the capital city of the Jewish people, and the transactions associated with it. It had to be crossed in going to Mount Olivet, Bethany, and Bethphage.

where was a garden, into which he entered, himself and his disciples.—The garden was Gethsemane, a garden of olive trees. Matthew (26: 36-46) gives the account of his entrance into this garden, his leaving his disciples, save Peter, James, and John, near the entrance; he went with these three further into the garden and went through the agonies and the three prayers that the cup might pass from him, if in accordance with the Father's will. John passes over this without mention, probably because of the fullness with which the record is made by the other biographies of Jesus.

2 **Now Judas also, who betrayed him, knew the place: for Jesus oft-times resorted thither with his disciples.**—This garden of Gethsemane was a retired, quiet spot which Jesus and his disciples in passing from the city to Mount Olivet seem

having received the [5]band *of soldiers,* and officers from the chief priests and the Pharisees, cometh thither with lanterns and torches and weapons.

[5]Or, *cohort*

often to have entered and enjoyed a season of instruction and prayer. So Judas knew his custom and seems to have selected his visit to this place as the time in which he would betray Jesus into the hands of the priests and scribes away from the multitude as they had stipulated should be done.

3 **Judas then, having received the band of soldiers, and officers from the chief priests and the Pharisees,**—Judas had gone from the passover supper, the washing of the feet, before the institution of the Lord's Supper, at the suggestion of Jesus to do "What thou doest, do quickly" (13: 27), when he disclosed to Judas that he knew of the contracted treason to the chief priests and the Pharisees, who had agreed to furnish him a band of soldiers to arrest Jesus and bring him to them. The number constituting the band has been a matter of much and diverse conjecture. Some think there was an army of Roman soldiers. Others, that it was an irregular mob of loose men gathered and paid by the Jews to make the arrest. They wished to make the arrest, bring him before the Jewish rulers, and get the trial and condemnation well under way before the masses generally should know of it. So as few as could be intrusted to accomplish the work without tumult or confusion among the people was desired. So the band was an irregular mob gathered to do this work. ["Band" in Greek is *cohort,* which was the garrison of the fort, Antonia, distinguished from the *officers* of *justice* appointed by the Sanhedrin. It does not follow that the whole cohort (600 men) was present, but a number representative of them. The "officers from the chief priests and the Pharisees" were a part of the temple guard (Luke 22: 52), "Jewish policemen."]

cometh thither with lanterns and torches and weapons.—It was after night, probably after nine o'clock. It was the fourteenth of the month. The moon was at its full. But the garden was on the west side of the Mount of Olives that cut off the light of the moon, and especially the deep shades of

4 Jesus therefore, knowing all the things that were coming upon him, went
forth, and saith unto them, Whom seek ye? 5 They answered him, Jesus
of Nazareth. Jesus saith unto them, I am *he*. And Judas also, who
betrayed him, was standing with them. 6 When therefore he said unto
them, I am *he*, they went backward, and fell to the ground. 7 Again there-

the garden of olive trees would make it so dark that without lights it would be impossible to identify Jesus. So they brought the lanterns and torches and the swords and clubs to enforce their authority. [These elaborate preparations are a clear indication of the estimate of the power and popularity which his enemies held.]

4 **Jesus therefore, knowing all the things that were coming upon him,**—Jesus had gone through the fearful struggle of the agonies as the hour approached, the angel had appeared strengthening him, and a composure of mind and determination to drink the cup followed. So as the band approached, he went forth to meet them. [Jesus had just aroused the sleeping disciples for the last time. (Mark 14: 42.) Note the fullness and freeness of his sacrifice.]

went forth, and saith unto them, Whom seek ye?—With this determination, too, he knew the sufferings through which he would pass and went forth composedly to meet the coming sufferings. [Probably he stepped in front of the mob to protect the disciples. His face may have been still shining from the spiritual victory which ended the passion and therefore may have been inexpressibly majestic.]

5 **They answered him, Jesus of Nazareth. Jesus saith unto them, I am he. And Judas also, who betrayed him, was standing with them.**—The other writers tell us that he kissed Jesus as the sign by which he would designate him. John does not mention this. It must have occurred at this time. Jesus made no effort to conceal himself, but stepped forward to let them know that he was the person whom they sought. [This is the only mention of Judas' presence during the scene made by John.]

6 **When therefore he said unto them, I am he, they went backward, and fell to the ground.**—This going backward and falling to the ground, though singular, is not mentioned by

fore he asked them, Whom seek ye? And they said, Jesus of Nazareth. 8
Jesus answered, I told you that I am *he;* if therefore ye seek me, let these

Matthew, Mark, or Luke. Its cause and meaning are difficult to see. Commentators usually attribute it to the exercise of divine power by Jesus, executed to show them his power to protect himself and destroy them, that all might understand that he surrendered his life himself and none could take it from him. While this was true of Jesus, this reads as though the act was voluntary on the part of those doing it. If it had been done through the exercise of the power of Jesus, it must have created a feeling of consternation and terror among the soldiers that would have been manifested and it would have been difficult to have induced them to proceed in arresting him. There was already a degree of apprehension on the part of the leaders in this work. But if it was voluntary, I know nothing to indicate what prompted it or what it signified. [I take it that being overwhelmed by the sudden appearance and boldness in identifying himself, coupled with the majesty of his presence, was such a shock to their cowardly spirits that they could not, for the moment, do otherwise than fall to the earth. Jesus could easily, while they were prostrate, have walked from their midst unharmed, as he had done more than once before (8: 59; footnote; Luke 4: 30; 7: 44-46; 10: 39), but he had purposed to make a complete self-sacrifice.]

7 **Again therefore he asked them, Whom seek ye? And they said, Jesus of Nazareth.**—Whatever may have been the cause and meaning of the performance, it seems to have created a hesitation on their part that caused Jesus to repeat this question to them.

8 **Jesus answered, I told you that I am he;**—He seems to be impatient at delay, and as the time had come, and he had been strengthened by the appearance of the angel to drink the cup, all signs of dread or trepidation had vanished, and, as he had told Judas while at the passover supper, "What thou doest, do quickly," he now urges them forward in their work.

if therefore ye seek me, let these go their way:—The words and manner of Jesus were not those of a person in

go their way: 9 that the word might be fulfilled which he spake, Of those
whom thou hast given me I lost not one. 10 Simon Peter therefore having
a sword drew it, and struck the high priest's [6]servant, and cut off his right
ear. Now the [6]servant's name was Malchus. 11 Jesus therefore said unto

[6]Gr. *bondservant*

dread; but while respectful and courteous, he spoke as though conscious of his authority and power. [If they had not made motions looking to the seizure of the disciples, Jesus had probably, by his divine insight, perceived their purpose, and designed by his repeated question to remind them of the limits of their commission, and by this, secure the escape of the disciples.]

9 **that the word might be fulfilled which he spake, Of those whom thou hast given me I lost not one.**—This refers to what is said in chapter 17: 12. [We have here an illustration of the freeness of scriptural methods of quotation, a very striking one as being a quotation by the writer from his own work but a paragraph before.]

10 **Simon Peter therefore having a sword drew it, and struck the high priest's servant, and cut off his right ear.**—The presence of the sword and Peter's use of it has been singular in the life of Jesus. The whole teaching and practice of Christ is against violence, offensive or defensive. Luke (22: 36) says that Jesus told his disciples to sell their garments and buy a sword. Two were bought and he said they were enough. Peter on this occasion used one of them in cutting off the ear of the servant of the high priest. This was done in the defense of Jesus, but was an act of rashness. [During the evening Peter had boasted that he would die for his Master, but now remembering his boast and the reply of Jesus he proceeds to show that his words were not mere boasts. Probably he intended to cleave his head from his body.]

Now the servant's name was Malchus.—[From verse 15 we learn that John (who doubtless speaks of himself) knew the high priest, and would therefore probably know the name of the servant.]

11 **Jesus therefore said unto Peter, Put up the sword into the sheath:**—Jesus reproves him and asks:

Peter, Put up the sword into the sheath: the cup which the Father hath given me, shall I not drink it?

12 So the [5]band and the [7]chief captain, and the officers of the Jews, seized

[7]Or, *military tribune* Gr. *chiliarch*

the cup which the Father hath given me, shall I not drink it?—Matthew (26: 52) says: "Then saith Jesus unto him, Put up again thy sword into its place: for all they that take the sword shall perish with the sword." His condemnation of its use in his defense is strong and clear. Some have thought that Jesus desired the presence of the sword that he might have the occasion to strongly condemn its use among his followers, or in defense of himself and his teachings. [At this point Luke mentions the complete healing of Malchus' ear, not recorded by any other writer, the last miracle of Jesus, and wrought upon an enemy. We can imagine, however, a motive additional to compassion in removing every trace that carnal weapons had been used, both for Peter's sake, and to leave him free to say to Pilate, "If my kingdom were of this world, then would my servants fight." How utterly has professed Christians, in numberless instances, departed from this implied principle of Christ, that his cause is not to be sustained, defended or advanced by physical force nor at the mouth of the cannon.]

12 **So the band and the chief captain, and the officers of the Jews, seized Jesus**—The captain here was the chiliarch or captain of a thousand men, corresponding to colonel in the army order in this country. It is not probable that all his command were present. How many is a matter of conjecture. Jesus desired to complete his work on earth and submitted to them.

and bound him,—How they bound him, we are not told. An ordinary method among the Romans was to bind the prisoner with a chain on one arm and to pass the other end of the chain around the body of a soldier. While they were binding him, the disciples "all left him, and fled." (Mark 14: 50.) [They all had a hand in it, as though some mighty desperado were being captured, instead of a meek, unresisting sufferer.]

Jesus and bound him, 13 and led him to Annas first; for he was father in law to Caiaphas, who was high priest that year. 14 Now Caiaphas was he that gave counsel to the Jews, that it was expedient that one man should die for the people.

---

13 **and led him to Annas first; for he was father in law to Caiaphas, who was high priest that year.**—Annas had been high priest and still acted sometimes in that capacity, although Caiaphas, his son-in-law at the time, was acting high priest. It is said that Annas had five sons, who in succession filled the high priest's place in addition to his son-in-law. He was of great influence. It is likely that Jesus was first brought before him to inquire into the matter as a court of inquiry to see what charges should be formulated against him. [Annas was about sixty years old. While the synoptics all speak of the leading away of Jesus, only John mentions Annas, and he alone gives an account of the examination before Annas (verses 19-23), which preceded his appearance before Caiaphas. Annas was a smooth, cunning intriguer, and ruled at this time through his son-in-law; and such was his overpowering influence as head of the Sadducean party that it was deemed an act of policy to take Jesus first to him before presenting him to Caiaphas.]

14 **Now Caiaphas was he that gave counsel to the Jews, that it was expedient that one man should die for the people.**—Caiaphas had first suggested to the Jews the death of Jesus as the end of the contention concerning him. (11: 48-50.) There seems to have been something of prophecy connected with the office of the high priest. Now Jesus is sent to him to be put on trial for his life. The Jewish Sanhedrin had the power to sit in judgment on Jesus and to sentence him to death. This sentence could not be executed without the approval of the Roman governor. Caiaphas sits to judge him.

2. PETER'S FIRST DENIAL.
18: 15-18.

15 And Simon Peter followed Jesus, and *so did* another disciple. Now

---

15 **And Simon Peter followed Jesus, and so did another disciple.**—"Another disciple" here is generally understood to

that disciple was known unto the high priest, and entered in with Jesus into the court of the high priest; 16 but Peter was standing at the door without. So the other disciple, who was known unto the high priest, went out and spake unto her that kept the door, and brought in Peter. 17 The maid therefore that kept the door saith unto Peter, Art thou also *one* of this

be John. It seems that Peter and John recovering from their fright at his first arrest, now returned, and followed the band having him in charge to the courtroom of the high priest.

Now that disciple was known unto the high priest, and entered in with Jesus into the court of the high priest;—John was known to the high priest and went in with Jesus as his friend to be present at his trial. The rashness of Peter in striking off the ear of the servant likely made him the more fearful now.

16 **but Peter was standing at the door without. So the other disciple, who was known unto the high priest, went out and spake unto her that kept the door, and brought in Peter.** —"The other disciple" obtained permission likely from the high priest, went out, spoke to the woman who seemed to guard the door, and brought Peter in. It seems that women were frequently employed in such positions as janitress to a building. Others speak of Peter following afar off. (Matt. 26: 58.) [The damsel who guarded the door suffered John, who was an acquaintance, to pass in; but probably seeing Peter was a stranger refused to admit him. John went in, evidently expecting Peter to follow, but when he did not he returned and requested the maid to allow him to enter and she did so.]

17 **The maid therefore that kept the door saith unto Peter, Art thou also one of this man's disciples? He saith, I am not.** —This woman, damsel, had doubtless seen Peter at some time and now as he came in she asked him if he was not one of the company that followed Jesus. Peter, completely demoralized and disheartened in the presence of John, said, "I am not." [He is not so keen now to use his sword since his Master is arrested and now before the court. Many, like Peter now, weaken and fail to declare the truth when it is not popular to do so.]

man's disciples? He saith, I am not. 18 Now the [8]servants and the officers were standing *there,* having made [9]a fire of coals; for it was cold; and they were warming themselves: and Peter also was with them, standing and warming himself.

[8]Gr. *bondservants*
[9]Gr. *a fire of charcoal*

18 **Now the servants and the officers were standing there, having made a fire of coals; for it was cold; and they were warming themselves: and Peter also was with them, standing and warming himself.**—It was now about midnight, growing cold, and the servants of the priests and those who waited in the court had built a fire to warm and Peter stood with them warming himself.

3. JESUS IS QUESTIONED AND SMITTEN.
18: 19-24.

19 The high priest therefore asked Jesus of his disciples, and of his teaching. 20 Jesus answered him, I have spoken openly to the world; I ever taught in [10]synagogues, and in the temple, where all the Jews come together; and in secret spake I nothing. 21 Why askest thou me? ask them that have heard *me,* what I spake unto them: behold, these know the things

[10]Gr. *synagogue*

19 **The high priest therefore asked Jesus of his disciples, and of his teaching.**—It is not customary in our courts to require a man to testify concerning himself or to convict himself of any wrong. This custom did not obtain in the courts generally of that day. So they question him.

20 **Jesus answered him, I have spoken openly to the world; I ever taught in synagogues, and in the temple, where all the Jews come together; and in secret spake I nothing.**—[Jesus replies to their question as relating to himself, but ignores that pertaining to the disciples, doubtless for the reason that he, not they, is on trial. He had taught publicly in the synagogue and temple. He had entered into no conspiracies as Annas himself had done.] Jesus recognized that the fair and just way was to prove by others if he were guilty of wrong. So he answered that the Jews have had ample and frequent opportunity to know all that he taught, so he said:

21 **Why askest thou me? ask them that have heard me, what I spake unto them: behold, these know the things which I said.**—[All his life and teaching could be learned by in-

which I said. 22 And when he had said this, one of the officers standing by
struck Jesus [1]with his hand, saying, Answerest thou the high priest so?
23 Jesus answered him, If I have spoken evil, bear witness of the evil: but
if well, why smitest thou me? 24 Annas therefore sent him bound unto
Caiaphas the high priest.

[1]Or, *with a rod*

quiring of those who had heard him, so let those who seek information ask them. He had no secret clique, but "taught the world." His reply seems to be a rebuke to those trying him. Jesus claims that the examination may proceed in the regular order by calling witnesses. "Ask them"; "Why askest thou me?" He wanted all the facts brought out.]

22 **And when he had said this, one of the officers standing by struck Jesus with his hand, saying, Answerest thou the high priest so?**—The answer was construed as impertinent and one of the officers struck him on the mouth, and reproved him for so answering the high priest. [To hear a prisoner stand upon his rights and boldly defend them was new to the officer so he struck Jesus.]

23 **Jesus answered him, If I have spoken evil, bear witness of the evil: but if well, why smitest thou me?**—Jesus plead, if there is evil in what he said, point it out, if no evil why should he be smitten. Moderation, self-control, and courage marked all that Jesus said or did. He was never excited or thrown into a temper. [Paul under similar circumstances (Acts 23: 3) answers like a man, but Jesus like the Prince of Peace. Usually those who are in the wrong resort to violence.]

24 **Annas therefore sent him bound unto Caiaphas the high priest.**—This verse tells what had before been implied.

4. PETER'S SECOND AND THIRD DENIALS.
18: 25-27.

25 Now Simon Peter was standing and warming himself. They said

25 **Now Simon Peter was standing and warming himself.**—Peter, chilled by standing without, now crowded himself up to the fire, kindled by the servants of the high priest and the officers of the court.

therefore unto him, Art thou also *one* of his disciples? He denied, and said, I am not. 26 One of the [2]servants of the high priest, being a kinsman of him whose ear Peter cut off, saith, Did not I see thee in the garden with him? 27 Peter therefore denied again: and straightway the cock crew.

[2]Gr. *bondservants*

They said therefore unto him, Art thou also one of his disciples?—Either from his appearance or the fact that he was an acquaintance of John, those standing around the fire asked him the second time if he was not one of them. More than one seems to have joined in asking this question. It is probable that a number had spoken of his being one of the disciples of Jesus and together approached him on the subject. Luke (22: 58) says, "After a little while another saw him, and said, Thou also art one of them. But Peter said, Man, I am not." John says "they," implying more than one.

He denied, and said, I am not.—[He simply lied, which shows that poor weak human beings do not know in advance what course they will take under extreme test of their faith and loyalty. But the Lord knew, and told Peter in advance just what he would do and the time of doing it.]

26 **One of the servants of the high priest, being a kinsman of him whose ear Peter cut off, saith, Did not I see thee in the garden with him?**—He saw and recognized him [and knew that he had lied. Matthew reports that Peter made his denial with an oath, even cursing and swearing. He grew desperate.]

27 **Peter therefore denied again: and straightway the cock crew.**—There have been questions raised about the cockcrowing and contradictions charged. There certainly was no effort made by the different writers to show exact agreement. Each told what occurred in his own way and in his own style and from his own standpoint. There are two periods of cockcrowing. The crowing at the latter hour is much more profuse than that at twelve o'clock. Hence that at three o'clock is the cockcrowing when only one is mentioned. When two are mentioned that at twelve o'clock is the first cockcrowing; that at three, the second. Some of the writers speak of only one, that at three o'clock; others of the two. The last denial of Peter occurred just before three o'clock. Peter was a man

of courage even to rashness, as his smiting off the ear of the servant of the high priest proved. When he cut off his ear he doubtless expected a resistance on the part of Jesus and his disciples. The healing of the servant, his enemy, and the reproof of Peter for using the sword discouraged and disheartened him, took from him his courage and left him despondent. He knew not what to do. He in common with the other disciples then fled. His courage was renewed sufficiently to return with John; but "followed him afar off." (Matt. 26: 58.) This is a dangerous position. John entered as a friend of Jesus. Peter in his fear after what had passed sought to pass as a stranger. The temptation came upon him much stronger than if he had at once declared himself the friend of Jesus. The man who declares himself as the friend of Jesus and walks closest to him finds fewer temptations to deny him and greater help to stand with him. Luke says that when the last denial was made, "The Lord turned, and looked upon Peter." The reproving look was more than he could bear; he broke down and "went out, wept bitterly." (Luke 22: 61, 62.) [Following this, at dawn of day, Jesus was tried before the Sanhedrin, as recorded in Luke (22: 66-71); and all attempts to prove him guilty of some crime or violation of the law had failed. In spite of false witnesses Jesus was called upon to answer, and upon his affirmation of divine majesty they condemned him to die as guilty of blasphemy. To carry the sentence into effect the sanction of the Roman governor was necessary. Therefore he is next sent to Pilate.]

5. PROCEEDINGS BEFORE PILATE.
18: 28-40; 19: 1-16.

28 They lead Jesus therefore from Caiaphas into the [3]Prætorium: and it

[3]Or, *palace*

---

28 **They lead Jesus therefore from Caiaphas into the Praetorium:**—The Jewish council determined that Jesus should be put to death. The Jews were permitted to try and inflict any punishment save that of death on their subjects. When the sentence was death, they were compelled to have the sanc-

was early; and they themselves entered not into the [8]Prætorium, that they
might not be defiled, but might eat the passover. 29 Pilate therefore went
out unto them, and saith, What accusation bring ye against this man? 30
They answered and said unto him, If this man were not an evil-doer, we
should not have delivered him up unto thee. 31 Pilate therefore said unto

---

tion of the Roman governor. This sentence then necessitated the trial of Jesus before the Roman governor. The praetorium was what we would call the courtroom. Courts were frequently in session at night in that country to avoid the heat of day. Then, too, the Jews were pressing this to the end that there might be no reaction in the public mind or opportunity of the common people to interfere in behalf of Jesus.

and it was early; and they themselves entered not into the Praetorium, that they might not be defiled, but might eat the passover.—The Gentile houses, courts, and everything they touched were defiled to the Jews. This was the passover week and these priests and scribes were especially anxious to avoid defilement that they might eat the passover, so they did not go in to make their accusations.

29 **Pilate therefore went out unto them,**—It was an act of condescension on the part of Pilate that, to accommodate them, he went out of his courtroom to hear their accusation and proof against Jesus.

and saith, What accusation bring ye against this man?—The accusation had not been sent up with the prisoner, so he asks them for their charge.

30 **They answered and said unto him, If this man were not an evil-doer, we should not have delivered him up unto thee.**—It is clear that they had no thought of a regular legal trial. They had not given him this in their own council. Nicodemus very pointedly asked the Sanhedrin: "Doth our law judge a man, except it first hear from himself and know what he doeth?" (7: 51.) There must be a specific charge and clear proof of guilt in the thing charged. They give to Pilate an indefinite and evasive answer, which shows that they expected him to give his judgment to please them regardless of facts. The results show that they did not misjudge him.

31 **Pilate therefore said unto them, Take him yourselves, and judge him according to your law.**—Since he was an evil-

them, Take him yourselves, and judge him according to your law. The Jews said unto him, It is not lawful for us to put any man to death: 32 that the word of Jesus might be fulfilled, which he spake, signifying by what manner of death he should die.

33 Pilate therefore entered again into the [3]Prætorium, and called Jesus, and said unto him, Art thou the King of the Jews? 34 Jesus answered,

---

doer according to their law and they desired Pilate to act on their judgment of their law, he naturally suggested that they take him and judge him according to their law.

The Jews said unto him, It is not lawful for us to put any man to death:—They had determined to put him to death so plead that they were not permitted to execute the death sentence. [They had judged and condemned Jesus according to their own law, and Pilate, on their refusal to state their charges, requested them to proceed with the case according to their own laws. The power of life and death had been taken away from them and placed in the hands of the Roman authorities. Had this not been in their way, doubtless they would have already killed him.]

32 **that the word of Jesus might be fulfilled, which he spake, signifying by what manner of death he should die.**—Jesus had foretold that he would be crucified. This meant that he would be executed under the Roman law. That was the Roman method of executing the lowest criminals. The Jews stoned them. [Stephen was stoned to death in Jerusalem by a mob (Acts 7: 58, 59), and had the Jews been permitted to put Jesus to death, he would have been stoned to death also. But he had foretold what death he should die and that he would be crucified. (12: 32; Matt. 30: 18, 19.)]

33 **Pilate therefore entered again into the Praetorium, and called Jesus, and said unto him, Art thou the King of the Jews?**—Luke (23: 2) says: "And they began to accuse him, saying, We found this man perverting our nation, and forbidding to give tribute to Caesar, and saying that he himself is Christ a king." So Pilate asks him of his claims to be king of the Jews. This was another effort to make him condemn himself. [Before Pilate returned to the courtroom, where Jesus had been taken, the Jews had made a formal charge that Jesus was seeking to overthrow the Roman government.

Sayest thou this of thyself, or did others tell it thee concerning me? 35
Pilate answered, Am I a Jew? Thine own nation and the chief priests
delivered thee unto me: what hast thou done? 36 Jesus answered, My king-

(Luke 23: 2.) This, of course, demanded the attention of the Roman governor. Jesus did claim that he would establish a kingdom and that he would be a king. He had been hailed as king of the Jews on entering Jerusalem. It was not expected that Pilate would understand that his kingdom was spiritual but political, especially when a band of dishonest priests were perverting every fact to give color to their accusation. They had charged against him a triple accusation: (1) seditious agitation; (2) prohibition of the payment of the tribute money (taxes); and (3) the assumption of the suspicious title of "King of the Jews." (Luke 23: 3.) The last accusation amounted to a charge of treason—the greatest crime known to Roman law. Of the three points of accusation, the second was utterly false; the first and third, though in a sense true, were not true in the sense intended by his enemies.]

34 **Jesus answered, Sayest thou this of thyself, or did others tell it thee concerning me?**—Jesus asked him whether this charge was originated with himself, or was it made by others. [Jesus did not ask the question for information, but it strikes the heart of the charge. Who made it? Did you or any Roman citizen ever see me breaking the Roman law? If a Roman preferred the charge, it might be examined, but when did the Jews ever find fault with a man seeking to free them? Pilate knew how restive the Jews were under the Roman yoke, and how ready they were to rebel, and the very hate shown Christ by them was proof that Jesus was not aiming to be such a king as they desired. Pilate comprehends the point.]

35 **Pilate answered, Am I a Jew? Thine own nation and the chief priests delivered thee unto me:**—The Jews, not he, were accusing him. [The Romans had nothing to do with bringing the accusation. This disproved their charge.]

what hast thou done?—To stir up his people against him.

dom is not of this world: if my kingdom were of this world, then would my [4]servants fight, that I should not be delivered to the Jews: but now is

[4]Or, *officers:* as in ver. 3, 12, 18, 22

36 **Jesus answered, My kingdom is not of this world:—** While Jesus, in the thirty-fourth verse, had not said he was King of the Jews, he had no purpose of denying that he was their lawful king by descent from the kingly race; but explains to Pilate that his kingdom is not an earthly kingdom.

if my kingdom were of this world, then would my servants fight, that I should not be delivered to the Jews: but now is my kingdom not from hence.—In earthly kingdoms their subjects fight to deliver their king from their enemies. He did not do this as he had shown in forbidding Peter to use the sword. He said this to satisfy Pilate that he in no sense laid claim to earthly power or was a rival to Caesar. [His kingdom was not of this world, for the reason it did not spring from it, was heavenly in its origin, and hence his servants would not fight that he should not be delivered to the Jews. The fact that no resistance was made to his arrest was a proof that his servants did not propose resistance to worldly governments. His kingdom is supernatural, not of human origin. It is in the world, but not of the world. It is established and maintained, not by carnal weapons, but by spiritual and moral means. All attempts to propagate Christianity by the carnal sword are prohibited by the Prince of Peace. The only sword the Christian is authorized to use is "the sword of the Spirit, which is the word of God." If servants of Christ cannot fight for their Master, it stands true that they cannot fight for one not their Master; yet they have duties to perform. It is their duty, by example and teaching, to restrain the evil and angry passions, to teach moderation and self-restraint, to inculcate forbearance and mercy, and to pray earnestly and faithfully for kings and rulers and all that are in authority, that we may lead quiet and peaceable lives in all godliness and honesty. When war does come, it is their duty to act the part of the good Samaritan and do good to all that suffer and that are in need.]

my kingdom not from hence. 37 Pilate therefore said unto him, Art thou
a king then? Jesus answered, [5]Thou sayest that I am a king. To this end have I been born, and to this end am I come into the world, that I should bear witness unto the truth. Every one that is of the truth heareth
my voice. 38 Pilate saith unto him, What is truth?

And when he had said this, he went out again unto the Jews, and saith
unto them, I find no crime in him. 39 But ye have a custom, that I should release unto you one at the passover: will ye therefore that I release unto

[5]Or, *Thou sayest* it, *because I am a king*

37 **Pilate therefore said unto him, Art thou a king then?**—With the explanation given that it was not an earthly kingdom, he answered Pilate directly:

Jesus answered, Thou [rightly] sayest that I am a king.—In confessing this truth concerning his being a king which sealed his death warrant, he added:

To this end have I been born, and to this end am I come into the world, that I should bear witness unto the truth.—And he had done it in confessing that he was a king, even though it brought suffering to himself. And those who accepted this truth would listen to Jesus. He not only told the truth in this, but his mission in the world was to proclaim truth.

Every one that is of the truth heareth my voice.—[They "hear" in the sense of heeding to what he says. They follow his instructions.]

38 **Pilate saith unto him, What is truth?**—This he asked as though skeptical as to the claims or existence of truth. He was a timeserver. Such have little faith in truth, or any being faithful to truth.

And when he had said this, he went out again unto the Jews, and saith unto them, I find no crime in him.—[He testified unto the Jews that he found no fault in him worthy of condemnation.]

39 **But ye have a custom, that I should release unto you one at the passover: will ye therefore that I release unto you the King of the Jews?**—To conciliate the favor of the Jews, the Romans had adopted the rule of releasing to them some one guilty of some act of rebellion against the Roman authorities as friends of the Jews. Pilate proposed to release the King

**you the King of the Jews? 40 They cried out therefore again, saying, Not
this man, but Barabbas. Now Barabbas was a robber.**

of the Jews to them. This was said in ridicule of them and the claims of Jesus to be the King of the Jews. [By a comparison of other records of this incident, we find that in the interval, before Pilate's effort to release Jesus according to the custom of the passover feast, he sent Jesus to Herod in order to shuffle off the responsibility, but Herod had sent him back to Pilate. Then he asks whether I shall not release him according to the custom. He was placed in a very trying position. Jesus was accused of treason against the Roman emperor; he declared that he was not guilty; the priests then accused Pilate of not being Caesar's friend, intimating that they would accuse him to Caesar. Had he been accused of letting a man go free who claimed to be King of the Jews, it would have gone hard with him—probably would have been the cause of being put out of his office. This had much weight in his final cowardly decision.]

40 **They cried out therefore again, saying, Not this man, but Barabbas. Now Barabbas was a robber.**—Barabbas had excited an insurrection against the Roman authorities and had in the insurrection been guilty of both murder and robbery. They demand him in preference to Jesus. The difficulty of the Jews in formulating charges against Jesus, and the utter disregard of the Jews of justice arose from this: the crimes against the Roman law were not crimes under their law. What the Romans regarded as high crimes the Jews at heart approved. The crime against the Jewish law was that Jesus claimed to be the Son of God. The Jews at heart would gladly have accepted a king that would deliver them from Roman rule. In his trial, the singular thing was: sins of a man tried in the lower court for blasphemy in making himself the Son of God and in the appeal to the higher court the charge of claiming to be a king as treason against Caesar is substituted. It is not strange that a specific charge was not made against him, although it is once stated that he made himself obnoxious to their law by making "himself the Son of God." (19: 7.)

1 Then Pilate therefore took Jesus, and scourged him. 2 And the soldiers platted a crown of thorns, and put it on his head, and arrayed him
in a purple garment; 3 and they came unto him, and said, Hail, King of
the Jews! and they struck him [6]with their hands. 4 And Pilate went out
again, and saith unto them, Behold, I bring him out to you, that ye may

[6]Or, *with rods*

1 **Then Pilate therefore took Jesus, and scourged him.**—The scourging was a severe beating upon the naked flesh. It was a degrading punishment, one to which the Roman citizen could not be subjected. (Acts 22: 25.) Paul claimed exemption from it because he was a Roman citizen. The citizen differed from the subject who belonged to some of the provinces subjected to the Roman government. It was customary to scourge those who were crucified. It is thought that Pilate scourged him, thinking that this would excite the sympathy of the Jews and that they would be satisfied without his crucifixion.

2 **And the soldiers platted a crown of thorns, and put it on his head, and arrayed him in a purple garment;**—This was done in ridicule of his claims to be a king. The crown of thorns was not an instrument of torture, but of ridicule. The thorns were brambles, not thorns that would pierce.

3 **and they came unto him, and said, Hail, King of the Jews! and they struck him with their hands.**—They hailed him as King of the Jews, yet smite him with their hands, as much as to say, a poor king that may thus be smitten with impunity. A reed was placed in his hands to ridicule his claims to kingly power. (Matt. 27: 29.) [The Jews had already demanded his death by crucifixion. (Luke 23: 20, 21.) If condemned to this death, scourging must necessarily precede it. The scourge was made of rods or thongs with pieces of bone or lead fastened to one end. The condemned person received the blows while fastened to a post so as to have the back bent and the skin stretched. With the blows the back became raw and the blood spurted out. The punishment was so cruel that the condemned person very often succumbed to it immediately.]

4 **And Pilate went out again, and saith unto them, Behold, I bring him out to you,**—Seeing Jesus thus mocked and ridi-

know that I find no crime in him. 5 Jesus therefore came out, wearing the crown of thorns and the purple garment. And *Pilate* saith unto them, Behold, the man! 6 When therefore the chief priests and the officers saw him, they cried out, saying, Crucify *him,* crucify *him!* Pilate saith unto them, Take him yourselves, and crucify him: for I find no crime in him.

culed, when he knew he was innocent of crime, seemed to arouse his sense of justice, and the sympathy of Pilate for Jesus, and he brought him forth and showed him to the Jews and said:

that ye may know that I find no crime in him.—In this Pilate shows that he had some sense of justice and right, and that he preferred to let him go free. He had an apprehension too that Jesus was more than human. The trouble with Pilate was that he was not willing to suffer for the truth. He saw justice, acknowledged it, but was lacking in the devotion and manhood that made him willing to suffer for the truth and do justice at all hazards. There was nothing of the true hero in Pilate.

5 **Jesus therefore came out, wearing the crown of thorns and the purple garment.**—Jesus was serious, solemn, earnest; bore the buffetings and the ridicule of the soldiers; and with the crown of thorns and the mock robe Pilate brought him out and showed him to the Jews.

And Pilate saith unto them, Behold, the man!—He no doubt said this, thinking to appease their wrath, excite their sympathy, and induce them to be satisfied to let Jesus go free. [Look at him in this pitiful condition! Does he look to be dangerous to you or to me, to your ecclesiastical or my secular power, thus to be treated, and no friends to speak for him?]

6 **When therefore the chief priests and the officers saw him, they cried out, saying, Crucify him, crucify him!**—Instead of appeasing or satisfying them, it seemed the more to infuriate them and with increased wrath. Pilate knew they had no right to crucify him, neither did Pilate, when he was innocent. So they demanded that he should be crucified without cause.

Pilate saith unto them, Take him yourselves, and crucify him: for I find no crime in him.—His crucifixion on these

7 The Jews answered him, We have a law, and by that law he ought to die, because he made himself the Son of God. 8 When Pilate therefore heard this saying, he was the more afraid; 9 and he entered into the [8]Præ-

testimonies is unlawful, you demand it, you do the deed. [Pilate's patience was evidently giving out. As they were disregarding all law and justice in demanding that he should crucify him, they might just as well disregard law and crucify him themselves. Perhaps he meant to intimate that as governor he would not hold them responsible; but they were too wily to take such a risk.]

7 **The Jews answered him, We have a law, and by that law he ought to die,**—As justification for their course, they now bring forth their law that makes blasphemy against God ground for inflicting death on him. Pilate could not condemn them for respecting their own law, and the Roman government gave them the right to enforce their law on their subjects, modified by the requirement that death could not be inflicted without the sanction of the Roman government.

because he made himself the Son of God.—The statement that he claimed to be the Son of God and according to their law he should die possibly palliated their course in demanding his death, but it involved Pilate in a greater difficulty. He had been impressed by the hearing of Jesus that he was a superior being, and now if he claims to be the Son of God, it increases the importance of the case and greatly increases Pilate's responsibility. He may be dealing with God and not man. [They repudiate Pilate's intimation of illegality in their demand, and undertake to demonstrate that it is legal and just. Jesus was guilty of blasphemy, if a mere man, which by Jewish law (Lev. 24: 16) incurred the penalty of death. As Pilate had taken away from them the legal power of death, he was bound by general Roman policy to recognize their decision, and give the sentence that he only could give. This is the argument implied. Here is the Jewish testimony to the fact that Jesus claimed to be the Son of God, and thus far it is true. Pilate was in close quarters.]

8 **When Pilate therefore heard this saying, he was the more afraid;**—The idea that he might be God made Pilate afraid.

torium again, and saith unto Jesus, Whence art thou? But Jesus gave him no answer. 10 Pilate therefore saith unto him, Speakest thou not unto me? knowest thou not that I have [1]power to release thee, and have [1]power to crucify thee? 11 Jesus answered him, Thou wouldest have no [1]power against me, except it were given thee from above: therefore he that de-

[1]Or, *authority*

At this time came the message from Pilate's wife, "saying, Have thou nothing to do with that righteous man; for I have suffered many things this day in a dream because of him." (Matt. 27: 19.) By this Pilate's fears were more aroused. [Pilate had not heard this before. Up to this time the whole accusation before him was that claiming to be Messiah, he claimed to be a king, and was therefore a rival of Caesar, and, as such, ought to die by Roman law. They realize now that this plea has failed, and so enter another, that of verse 7. He realized that Jesus was something out of the common order of men, and these words aroused in his mind a weird questioning as to who or what he might be. The fear he had felt in connection with him was now intensified.]

9 **and he entered into the Praetorium again, and saith unto Jesus, Whence art thou? But Jesus gave him no answer.**—[All the interviews with the Jews had taken place outside, because these eminently religious (?) gentlemen feared to be defiled on this sacred day by entering a Gentile room. Pilate took Jesus with him for a private audience, but Jesus made no reply to his question, and why should he? His silence was answer enough—that, if he did not make this claim, he would certainly have denied it.]

10 **Pilate therefore saith unto him, Speakest thou not unto me? knowest thou not that I have power to release thee, and have power to crucify thee?**—This was said half as a threat and half as a promise to him. Neither the fear nor the hope moved Jesus. The peace of God was his that no fear or promise could disturb.

11 **Jesus answered him, Thou wouldest have no power against me, except it were given thee from above:**—Jesus was perfectly composed, realizing that he was guarded and guided by God. Judas was chosen of God to betray Jesus

livered me unto thee hath greater sin. 12 Upon this Pilate sought to release him: but the Jews cried out, saying, If thou release this man, thou art not Cæsar's friend: every one that maketh himself a king [2]speaketh against

[2]Or, *opposeth Caesar*

into the hands of his enemies. He was chosen because he was suited in character to do the work. [In reply to Pilate's arrogant boast, Jesus asserts the supremacy of God, perhaps with a significant gesture pointing up. God allows him to exert this power.]

therefore he that delivered me unto thee hath greater sin.—Judas and the Jews who accused and delivered him were greater sinners than Pilate. [Some think it no greater sin than Pilate, but greater sin on his own part on account of delivering him to Pilate.]

12 **Upon this Pilate sought to release him:**—Pilate showed a disposition to release him. He shows none of the marks of a bloodthirsty, vicious, or cruel man. He presents the character of a placable man, approving right and truth, but no strength of character to maintain right and enforce justice. Of the characters who dealt with Jesus in his personal ministry only Judas surpasses in turpitude and shame that of Pilate. Christendom has reechoed this judgment of God. To get the benefit of this judgment of God and man, we must recognize the sins for which they were condemned. Judas for the love of money betrayed Jesus, the embodiment of truth, justice, and mercy of God into the hands of his enemies. Pilate, with the power to rescue and save Jesus in his hands, for fear of losing his place, incurring the ill will of the Jews, bearing testimony to his innocence, yet turned him over to his enemies to be crucified. The same truths and interests then embodied in the fleshly body of Christ are now embodied in his spiritual body. Why is it not as great sin to betray the spiritual body as it was the fleshly? Why is the man who knows the truth and for the sake of popularity refuses to maintain it as guilty as was Pilate for so treating the fleshly body?

but the Jews cried out, saying, If thou release this man, thou art not Caesar's friend: every one that maketh himself a

Cæsar. 13 When Pilate therefore heard these words, he brought Jesus
out, and sat down on the judgment-seat at a place called The Pavement, but
in Hebrew, Gabbatha. 14 Now it was the Preparation of the passover: it
was about the sixth hour. And he saith unto the Jews, Behold, your King!
15 They therefore cried out, Away with *him,* away with *him,* crucify him!

---

king speaketh against Caesar.—Pilate made a show still of desiring to release Jesus. The Jews seeing his hesitating, temporizing spirit directly threatened him with Caesar's displeasure since Jesus claimed to be a king and the rival of Caesar.

13 **When Pilate therefore heard these words, he brought Jesus out, and sat down on the judgment-seat at a place called The Pavement, but in Hebrew, Gabbatha.**—Under this threat of the Jews, Pilate cowardly brought Jesus out and took his seat in the hall where he was accustomed to deliver his judgments and decisions.

14 **Now it was the Preparation of the passover: it was about the sixth hour.**—There is disagreement between this statement and that of Mark (15: 25), who says he delivered him to them the third hour of the day. Most critics think it should be the third hour or nine o'clock. Some think it was six o'clock in the morning, counting six hours from twelve o'clock. Mark uses the Hebrew count and makes the crucifixion begin at nine o'clock. Pilate yielded to them, released Barabbas, scourged Jesus, and delivered him to the Jews to be crucified. He did this against his judgment of what was right and just to appease the Jews. He had made cowardly surrender to their demands for fear that he might be accused to Caesar as encouraging treason against him.

[There is no contradiction between the statement of John and that of Mark regarding the time that Pilate gave sentence against Christ. The Jews divided the day into four quarters, which they called hours. The first was called the third hour, which answers to our ninth; the second, called the sixth hour, answering to our twelfth; the third, called the ninth hour, answering to our three in the afternoon; the fourth, called the twelfth hour, which was the time of their retirement from

Pilate saith unto them, Shall I crucify your King? The chief priests answered, We have no king but Cæsar. 16 Then therefore he delivered him unto them to be crucified.

labor, and the beginning of the first watch. The whole time from the third hour to the sixth, that is, from nine to twelve, was called the third hour; and the whole intervening time from the sixth to the ninth, that is, from twelve to three, is called the sixth hour. John does not say it was the sixth hour, but *about* or *near* the sixth hour. So when he says *about* the sixth hour, and Mark the third hour, we are to understand that Mark takes in the *whole* time of the third hour, from nine to twelve, and that John puts it near twelve. So in either case our Lord was sentenced between the hours of nine and twelve.]

And he saith unto the Jews, Behold, your King!—Like cowardly spirits after yielding in the important matters, they show spite and tyranny in small ones, so he tantalizes them by calling Jesus their King.

15 **They therefore cried out, Away with him, away with him, crucify him!**—Aroused and excited by their success, with more bitterness they cry out thus. Pilate still taunts them with demanding the crucifixion of their King.

Pilate saith unto them, Shall I crucify your King? The chief priests answered, We have no king but Caesar.—The Jews were anxious to be free from the dominion of the Romans, but to meet Pilate on grounds that condemn him, they claim Caesar as their only king. Men maddened with wicked fury profess anything to carry their ends.

16 **Then therefore he delivered him unto them to be crucified.**—Pilate yielded and gave Jesus to be crucified by the Roman soldiers at the behest of the priests and Pharisees and they took him away from the court of Pilate.

[We should note how careful the Holy Spirit is to record the time when Pilate gave sentence against Christ. In general, it was on the day of the preparation for the Passover; that is, the day immediately before it, when they prepared everything needed for the solemnization; and, in particular, it was about the sixth hour of that day. We should also observe the great love and condescension of Christ in stooping so low to expiate our guilt, which deserveth eternal sufferings.]

SECTION FIVE.

DEATH, BURIAL, AND RESURRECTION OF JESUS.
19: 17-42; 20: 1-25.

1. JESUS BEARS THE CROSS.
19: 17-24.

17 They took Jesus therefore: and he went out, bearing the cross for himself, unto the place called The place of a skull, which is called in Hebrew Golgotha: 18 where they crucified him, and with him two others, on either side one, and Jesus in the midst. 19 And Pilate wrote a title also,

---

17 **They took Jesus therefore: and he went out, bearing the cross for himself,**—They went forward in the work with all haste, wishing to get through with it before the Passover. Jesus started to the place of crucifixion without the gate, bearing his own cross. From some cause, supposed to be exhaustion on the part of Jesus, before he reached the place, Simon of Cyrene coming along was compelled to bear it for him.

unto the place called The place of a skull, which is called in Hebrew Golgotha:—The location of this place is not known. Some think it was the common place for executing criminals.

18 **where they crucified him,**—The crucifixion consisted in nailing him to a cross. The hands were stretched out and a nail driven through the fleshly part of each hand into the crossbar nailed across the upper end of the post. The feet were then nailed to the post. A pin was put into the upright post between the legs to support the body. The person thus nailed to the cross frequently lingered four or five days before death relieved their sufferings.

and with him two others, on either side one, and Jesus in the midst.—[Matthew and Mark say they were "robbers," and Luke "malefactors." Probably they were accomplices of Barabbas, who had escaped occupying the place of Jesus through the determined malice of the chief priests. (See Isa. 53: 12.)]

19 **And pilate wrote a title also, and put it on the cross.**—Over the head of the person the crime for which he was executed was written that all that saw might know the

and put it on the cross. And there was written, JESUS OF NAZARETH, THE KING OF THE JEWS. 20 This title therefore read many of the Jews, [a]for the place where Jesus was crucified was nigh to the city; and it was written in Hebrew, *and* in Latin, *and* in Greek. 21 The chief priests of the Jews therefore said to Pilate, Write not, The King of the Jews; but, that he said, I am King of the Jews. 22 Pilate answered, What I have written I have written.

[a]Or, *for the place of the city where Jesus was crucified was nigh at hand*

crime. Pilate wrote this title as if resentful to the Jews for pressing on him to crucify him against his wishes.

And there was written, JESUS OF NAZARETH, THE KING OF THE JEWS.—[It is impossible to resist the impression that there was a grim humor in the writing of Pilate. The Jews had humiliated him in forcing him to assent to the crucifixion. He now gets even with them by conceding the alleged claim of Jesus, and crucifying thus their king. Had he been acquainted with the prophecies, he might have realized a still more profound significance in the inscription.]

20 **This title therefore read many of the Jews, for the place where Jesus was crucified was nigh to the city;**—The cross was erected in a public place that it might be seen.

and it was written in Hebrew and in Latin, and in Greek.—This was written in the three languages spoken by the people that all might be informed of the charge against him. It is rather singular that each of the evangelists record this and no two of them give it in exactly the same language. If there were only three variations, these might be explained as translations from the three languages in which it was written. As it is, the copying was not exact, although all the writings are substantially the same. [The biting taunt of Pilate was made as public and accessible as possible. It was felt too as shown by next verse.]

21 **The chief priests of the Jews therefore said to Pilate, Write not, The King of the Jews; but, that he said, I am King of the Jews.**—The priests were chagrined at his saying, "The King of the Jews," and suggested that he change it. [Pilate evidently had his revenge.]

22 **Pilate answered, What I have written I have written.**—Pilate, like many other cowardly men who allow themselves

23 The soldiers therefore, when they had crucified Jesus, took his garments and made four parts, to every soldier a part; and also the [4]coat: now the [4]coat was without seam, woven from the top throughout. 24 They said therefore one to another, Let us not rend it, but cast lots for it, whose it shall be: that the scripture might be fulfilled, which saith,

[5]They parted my garments among them,
And upon my vesture did they cast lots.

[4]Or, *tunic*
[5]Ps. 22. 18

to be drawn into wrong, after he had committed the main crime, becomes courageous in some minor point so he refuses to accommodate them. [Pilate's natural stubbornness once again had sway now that he had deprived them of all ground of accusation in appeal to Caesar. So, to all time, Calvary proclaims the truth, the reality of the claims of Jesus and the same of the apostasy of the Jews.]

23 **The soldiers therefore, when they had crucified Jesus, took his garments and made four parts, to every soldier a part; and also the coat: now the coat was without seam, woven from the top throughout.**—The garments of the victim were the prerequisites of the soldiers who executed him. There were four of these soldiers. They stripped Jesus of his clothing. There were four pieces of his inner garments. Each soldier took a piece. His coat or outer garment was seamless, woven throughout. To divide it would destroy its value so they cast lots for it.

24 **They said therefore one to another, Let us not rend it, but cast lots for it, whose it shall be:**—[Some see in this a symbol of the unity of the church and superintending providence that the symbol might be preserved.]

that the scripture might be fulfilled, which saith, They parted my garments among them, and upon my vesture did they cast lots.—These soldiers knew nothing of this prophecy, yet fulfilled it in following their own idle fancies. The Jews fulfilled the scriptures and proved him to be the Son of God while gratifying their bitterness toward him by crucifying him. [The quotation is from Psalm 22: 18, according to the Septuagint. Luke records that the soldiers mocked him, offering him vinegar, and bidding him to save himself. Here we may mention the prayer of Jesus for his enemies, given only by Luke, the derision of chief priests, scribes, elders, people and robbers, and the episode of the penitent thief.]

2. JESUS COMMITS HIS MOTHER TO JOHN.
19: 25-27.

25 These things therefore the soldiers did. But there were standing by
the cross of Jesus his mother, and his mother's sister, Mary the *wife* of
Clopas, and Mary Magdalene. 26 When Jesus therefore saw his mother,
and the disciple standing by whom he loved, he saith unto his mother,

---

25 **These things therefore the soldiers did. But there were standing by the cross of Jesus his mother,**—It had been foretold to his mother that a sword would pierce through her own soul. This was now fulfilled as she beholds her son and the Son of God nailed to the cross.

and his mother's sister,—[Named Salome (Mark 15: 40), the mother of John and James. (Matt. 27: 56.)]

Mary the wife of Clopas,—She is supposed to have been a near kinswoman.

and Mary Magdalene.—Out of Mary Magdalene he had cast seven demons. Her gratitude led her to follow him, minister to him, and led her to come near him while he is nailed to the cross.

26 **When Jesus therefore saw his mother, and the disciple standing by whom he loved, he saith unto his mother, Woman, behold, thy son!**—The disciple whom Jesus loved was John the writer of the book of John. He is supposed to have been a kinsman of Jesus and his mother. His love for his mother and his desire to provide for her wants during her remaining days on earth led him to forget his own sufferings on the cross in the home of one noted for his tenderness and love. [The relationship in the flesh between Jesus and his mother was about to close, hence he commends her to another who should care for and protect her during old age. A son, who will not provide for his mother, is not worthy to be called a son. The last time the mother of Jesus is mentioned she was with John in Jerusalem, which would indicate that John was true to his trust. This was as great a compliment as Jesus could have given John as pertaining to this world.]

Woman, behold, thy son! 27 Then saith he to the disciple, Behold, thy mother! And from that hour the disciple took her unto his own *home.*

---

27 **Then saith he to the disciple, Behold, thy mother! And from that hour the disciple took her unto his own home.**—This expressive language shows his tender love and the willingness of both his mother and John to comply with his wishes. This circumstance would seem to indicate that Mary at this time had no other children to whom she could look for kindness and support. This would indicate that Joseph her husband was dead. No mention of his life or death has been made after Jesus began his public ministry.

3. HIS LAST SUFFERING.
19: 28-30.

28 After this Jesus, knowing that all things are now finished, [6]that the scripture might be accomplished, saith, I thirst. 29 There was set there a vessel full of vinegar: so they put a sponge full of the vinegar upon

[6]Ps. 69. 21

---

28 **After this Jesus, knowing that all things are now finished, that the scripture might be accomplished,**—[All things preceding his death which were necessary to complete his work and to the fulfillment of prophecy were finished. He now realizes his intense physical suffering, which had been forgotten in the more awful mental anguish of abandonment by his Father as he bore the burden of the world's sin.]

saith, I thirst.—Jesus had completed his work and the end was near. The suffering and bleeding he had undergone produced thirst. [The increasing inflammation of the wounds, the unnatural position, the forced immobility and the rigidity of the limbs which resulted from it, the local congestions, especially in the head, the inexpressible anguish resulting from the disturbance of the circulation, a burning fever and thirst tortured the condemned without killing him.]

29 **There was set there a vessel full of vinegar:**—[Sour wine, or vinegar and water, the common drink of the Roman soldiers, but probably a vessel of this specially placed for the use of those crucified.]

so they put a sponge full of the vinegar upon hyssop, and brought it to his mouth.—Jesus was too high on the cross

hyssop, and brought it to his mouth. 30 When Jesus therefore had received the vinegar, he said, It is finished: and he bowed his head, and gave up his spirit.

likely for them to reach his mouth with the hand so they dipped the sponge in vinegar and raised it to his mouth. [It is said that hyssop stalks grew to the height of eighteen inches. As the cross was not very high, this would be length sufficient to reach his lips with the sponge.]

30 **When Jesus therefore had received the vinegar, he said, It is finished:**—[The work of the suffering Savior is accomplished, all the prophecies embodying it are fulfilled, the price of redemption is paid, hencceforth will be the work of the conquering, triumphant, and glorified Savior.]

and he bowed his head, and gave up his spirit.—After drinking the vinegar all was completed and he let his head fall upon his breast and surrendered his spirit to God. Luke says (23: 46): "And Jesus, crying with a loud voice, said, Father, into thy hands I commend my spirit: and having said this, he gave up the ghost." [Consult Matt. 27: 51-56; Mark 15: 38-41; Luke 23: 47-49; John 19: 31-37 for the accomplishment of his death.]

4. THE BODIES PREPARED FOR REMOVAL.
19: 31-37.

31 The Jews therefore, because it was the Preparation, that the bodies should not remain on the cross upon the sabbath (for the day of that sabbath was a high *day*), asked of Pilate that their legs might be broken, and

31 **The Jews therefore, because it was the Preparation, that the bodies should not remain on the cross upon the sabbath (for the day of that sabbath was a high day), asked of Pilate that their legs might be broken, and that they might be taken away.**—The death of Jesus occurred on Friday, the day for preparing for the Sabbath. This Sabbath falling in the week of the Passover was a day of special sanctity, and is called a "high day." The Jews did not wish the bodies to hang on the cross to mar the sanctity of this Sabbath. They besought Pilate that their legs might be broken. This was to hasten death, so they would be taken away and buried. [Not only

that they might be taken away. 32 The soldiers therefore came, and brake the legs of the first, and of the other that was crucified with him: 33 but when they came to Jesus, and saw that he was dead already, they brake not his legs: 34 howbeit one of the soldiers with a spear pierced his side, and straightway there came out blood and water. 35 And he that hath seen hath borne witness, and his witness is true: and he knoweth that he saith

---

did they prepare for the Sabbath, but it was also preparation of the Passover. (Verse 14.) Breaking the legs was a barbarous method to hasten death. Something like a sledge hammer was used crushing the legs and the shock would bring speedy death.]

32 **The soldiers therefore came, and brake the legs of the first, and of the other that was crucified with him:**—This was a cruel method of hastening death. It would have been much less cruel to pierce the heart and let them bleed to death. But the purpose of crucifying was to prolong torture and cruel methods were used when from any cause it was desired to hasten the death.

33 **but when they came to Jesus, and saw that he was dead already, they brake not his legs:**—The speedy death of Jesus removed the occasion for breaking his legs. God's providence so overruled that the prophetic type of the passover lamb should be fulfilled in that not a bone of Jesus was broken.

34 **howbeit one of the soldiers with a spear pierced his side,** —Why the side was pierced by the soldiers is difficult to tell save God had so ordained and foretold, and the soldier did it to fulfill the prophecy unconscious to himself.

and straightway there came out blood and water.—Many suggestions have been made as to the significance of the blood and water. As the scriptures give none, it is safe to follow their example, and conclude that it is the natural result of piercing the side at this state of a dying body.

35 **And he that hath seen hath borne witness, and his witness is true: and he knoweth that he saith true, that ye also may believe.**—John the writer was an eyewitness of the occurrences and states them as he saw them. [It is conceded that John the apostle was this eyewitness and that modesty kept him from identifying himself plainly. What he saw estab-

true, that ye also may believe. 36 For these things came to pass, [1]that the scripture might be fulfilled, A bone of him shall not be [2]broken. 37 And again another scripture saith, [3]They shall look on him whom they pierced.

[1]Ex. 12. 46; Num. 9. 12; Ps. 34. 20
[2]Or, *crushed*
[3]Zech. 12. 10

lishes the death of Christ. His testimony kills the argument of modern skepticism that Jesus fainted and was taken from the cross and restored by his disciples.]

36 **For these things came to pass, that the scripture might be fulfilled, A bone of him shall not be broken.**—This prophecy was made in the passover lamb, a type and prophecy of the lamb of God that takes away the sins of the world, repeated in Psalm 34: 20. The fulfillment that a bone should not be broken was the more significant, as Pilate had commanded that they should be broken, and the legs of the others were broken.

37 **And again another scripture saith, They shall look on him whom they pierced.**—The scriptures had not only foretold that a bone of him should not be broken, but that he should be pierced. (Psalm 22: 16; Zech. 12: 10.)

5. JESUS IS BURIED BY JOSEPH AND NICODEMUS. 19: 38-42.

38 And after these things Joseph of Arimathæa, being a disciple of Jesus, but secretly for fear of the Jews, asked of Pilate that he might take away the body of Jesus: and Pilate gave *him* leave. He came therefore, and took

38 **And after these things Joseph of Arimathea, being a disciple of Jesus, but secretly for fear of the Jews, asked of Pilate that he might take away the body of Jesus: and Pilate gave him leave. He came therefore, and took away his body.**—It is singular that one who had failed to confess him while alive and manifesting his power should now do it when he was dead and all seemed lost. It is pretty sure that it was a modesty and shyness that shrank from publicity rather than a cowardly fear of the opposition it would have incurred. Persons moved by the personal timidity, rather by cowardice often when the issue can no longer be evaded, make the best and trusty friends of the truth. Joseph and Nicodemus both

away his body. 39 And there came also Nicodemus, he who at the first
came to him by night, bringing a [4]mixture of myrrh and aloes, about a
hundred pounds. 40 So they took the body of Jesus, and bound it in linen
cloths with the spices, as the custom of the Jews is to bury. 41 Now in the
place where he was crucified there was a garden; and in the garden a new

[4]Some ancient authorities read *roli*

seem to be of this class. They shrank from prominence until all friends seemed to forsake, then they put themselves upon the side of truth and justice. So he took charge of the body so as to give it sepulture.

39 **And there came also Nicodemus, he who at the first came to him by night, bringing a mixture of myrrh and aloes, about a hundred pounds.**—Nicodemus was of a similar temperament, and now declared himself the friend of the dead Savior by bringing the mixture for embalming the body of Jesus. [This is the third time Nicodemus is mentioned. First in 3: 5, the second 7: 50 where he protested against the injustice of the Sanhedrin, and here he is assisting in the burial of Jesus. Joseph of Arimathea is not mentioned save in connection with the burial of the body of Jesus. The Sanhedrin condemned Jesus to death, but here we learn that two of its members were minority voters in the Sanhedrin's decision to crucify the Savior. This shows that the majority rule is not a safe rule.]

40 **So they took the body of Jesus, and bound it in linen cloths with the spices, as the custom of the Jews is to bury.**—They wrapped the body in linen with the spices and laid the body away. [Here is fulfilled another prophecy that though Jesus was "numbered with the transgressors," he was "with a rich man in his death." (Isa. 53: 9, 12.)]

41 **Now in the place where he was crucified there was a garden; and in the garden a new tomb wherein was never man yet laid.**—Joseph of Arimathea owned a garden close by the place of crucifixion. He had hewn out of rock what we call a vault rather than a grave. This vault was large enough to contain a number of bodies and for persons to pass out and in. This sepulchre or vault had never been used. The body of Jesus was laid in this vault. It was a convenient place to deposit

tomb wherein was never man yet laid. 42 There then because of the Jews' Preparation (for the tomb was nigh at hand) they laid Jesus.

the body, as the Sabbath was now at hand and other arrangements for his sepulchre had not been made. It is not probable that it was intended that his body would permanently remain in this vault.

42 **There then because of the Jews' Preparation (for the tomb was nigh at hand) they laid Jesus.**—It was a convenient place to deposit the body of Jesus until the Sabbath had passed when the women intended a more thorough embalming and sepulchre. [In the tomb of Jesus the Jews supposed his works to be buried forever. In it were buried the hopes of his disciples who had "hoped that it was he who should redeem Israel." In it, had he not risen, would have been buried the gospel, Christian civilization, and the hopes of the world. The future of the world was sleeping in this tomb.]

6. MARY, JOHN, AND PETER FIND THE TOMB EMPTY.
20: 1-10.

1 Now on the first *day* of the week cometh Mary Magdalene early, while it was yet dark, unto the tomb, and seeth the stone taken away from the

1 **Now on the first day of the week**—The body of Jesus had been hastily buried on Friday evening to avoid breaking the Sabbath. The care in embalming him had not been as carefully done as the women who followed him desired. They had bought perfumes on Friday afternoon. (Mark 16: 1; Luke 24: 1.) The approach of the Sabbath caused them to delay the completion of their kind offices until Sunday morning. With the first dawn of the morning they appeared with the spices to complete the work. [This was our Sunday, here called "The first day of the week." The Sabbath ended at sunset so that Jesus had been dead and buried Friday night, Saturday, and Sunday morning, beginning at the previous sunset, three days according to Jewish reckoning. (1 Sam. 30: 12, 13; 2 Chron. 10: 5, 12.)]

cometh Mary Magdalene early, while it was yet dark, unto the tomb,—John mentions only Mary Magdalene; Matthew (28: 2) and Mark (16: 1) mentions also Mary the mother

tomb. 2 She runneth therefore, and cometh to Simon Peter, and to the other disciple whom Jesus loved, and saith unto them, They have taken away the Lord out of the tomb, and we know not where they have laid him. 3 Peter therefore went forth, and the other disciple, and they went toward

of Jesus, and Salome. John gives prominence to Mary Magdalene. She had been possessed of seven demons, most likely quite a sinner. The demons had been cast out of her, her many sins forgiven her, and she loved much—was much devoted to her Lord. For this devotion special mention is made of her service. [They had prepared spices to anoint and embalm the body.]

and seeth the stone taken away from the tomb.—They had anticipated difficulty in rolling away the stone from the door of the vault that they might enter. They found it rolled away, saw the angels and empty tomb, and went and told the disciples. (Matt. 28: 2-4.)

2 **She runneth therefore, and cometh to Simon Peter, and to the other disciple whom Jesus loved,**—They find Peter and John and tell the strange discovery. No thought of a resurrection seems to have entered the minds of either of the apostles or the women, notwithstanding Jesus had so often told them he would rise. The women were not led by faith, but by love, to the tomb to perform the last rites of respect and love for one who had been their true friend and helper while alive. [Mary Magdalene left the other women and ran to carry this news to the apostles. The others walked on and had the experience described in Matt. 28: 5-8; Mark 16: 5-8; Luke 24: 3-9 and left the tomb.]

and saith unto them, They have taken away the Lord out of the tomb, and we know not where they have laid him.—The only thought that came to their minds was that he had been taken away and they knew not where to find his body. This shows how difficult it is to see and accept things that are contrary to our fixed convictions and desires. [She had jumped at this conclusion from the sight of the open sepulchre, for none were expecting a resurrection.]

3 **Peter therefore went forth and the other disciple, and they went toward the tomb.**—Peter seems to have led in the

the tomb. 4 And they ran both together: and the other disciple outran Peter, and came first to the tomb; 5 and stooping and looking in, he seeth the linen cloths lying; yet entered he not in. 6 Simon Peter therefore also cometh, following him, and entered into the tomb; and he beholdeth the linen cloths lying, 7 and the napkin, that was upon his head, not lying with the linen cloths, but rolled up in a place by itself. 8 Then entered in therefore the other disciple also, who came first to the tomb, and he saw, and

start with his characteristic promptness. John first reached the tomb, but went not in. His timidity likely caused him to pause at the entrance, but he looked in and saw the cloths lying.

4 **And they ran both together: and the other disciple outran Peter, and came first to the tomb;**—[Their emotion would not allow them to walk.]

5 **and stooping and looking in, he seeth the linen cloths lying; yet entered he not in.**—[He was too timid to enter the tomb immediately. He went close enough to see the linen in which Jesus had been wrapped.]

6 **Simon Peter therefore also cometh, following him, and entered into the tomb; and he beholdeth the linen cloths lying,**—[How characteristic this is of Peter who twice plunged into the sea to meet Jesus. He hesitates not a moment, like the timid John, but springs at once into the tomb.]

7 **and the napkin, that was upon his head, not lying with the linen cloths, but rolled up in a place by itself.**—Peter, coming up without hesitation, entered the tomb and found the cloths folded carefully, showing deliberation and care in disposing of them. [This napkin doubtless held the mouth closed. Its position and condition shows a calm preparation to leave the tomb instead of a hasty removal of the body.]

8 **Then entered in therefore the other disciple also, who came first to the tomb, and he saw, and believed.**—[Doubtless believed that Jesus had risen from the grave.] John, after Peter had entered, also entered, saw and believed. It is not clear as to the extent of his belief. As yet they had not understood what he meant when he said he would rise from the dead. Now the truth began to dawn on their minds that he had been made alive and had risen from the dead.

believed. 9 For as yet they knew not the scripture, that he must rise again from the dead. 10 So the disciples went away again unto their own home.

9 **For as yet they knew not the scripture, that he must rise again from the dead.**—[Scriptures mentioned include Psalm 16: 10; Isa. 53: 10, 11. John desires to emphasize the fact that his faith was founded on what he witnessed with no previous expectations founded on scripture.]

10 **So the disciples went away again unto their own home.**—Finding the tomb empty, the body gone, these two disciples went away to their places of abode in Jerusalem.

7. JESUS APPEARS TO MARY.
20: 11-18.

11 But Mary was standing without at the tomb weeping: so, as she wept, she stooped and looked into the tomb; 12 and she beholdeth two angels in white sitting, one at the head, and one at the feet, where the body of Jesus had lain. 13 And they say unto her, Woman, why weepest thou? She saith unto them, Because they have taken away my Lord, and I know not

11 **But Mary was standing without at the tomb weeping: so, as she wept, she stooped and looked into the tomb;**—Mary, with her feelings wrought up, disappointed and supposing that some one had moved his body to a permanent resting place, lingered near the grave and relieved her overburdened feelings by weeping. She again stooped down and looked into the sepulchre. [Jesus had been everything to Mary in a spiritual way. He had freed her from the influence of seven devils. Around him all her hopes had centered, and now to be deprived of the privilege of embalming his body, the last sad rite of affection to his lacerated body seemed to be greater than she could bear.]

12 **and she beholdeth two angels in white sitting, one at the head, and one at the feet, where the body of Jesus had lain.**—[Two angels known by their bright attire sat, one at the head, the other at the feet, of where Jesus had lain.]

13 **And they say unto her, Woman, why weepest thou? She saith unto them, Because they have taken away my Lord, and I know not where they have laid him.**—They ask the question doubtless to open the way to say unto them: "Why

where they have laid him. 14 When she had thus said, she turned herself back, and beholdeth Jesus standing, and knew not that it was Jesus. 15 Jesus saith unto her, Woman, why weepest thou? whom seekest thou? She, supposing him to be the gardener, saith unto him, Sir, if thou hast borne him hence, tell me where thou hast laid him, and I will take him away. 16 Jesus saith unto her, Mary. She turneth herself, and saith unto him in Hebrew, Rabboni; which is to say, Teacher. 17 Jesus saith to her,

seek ye the living among the dead? He is not here, but is risen: remember how he spake unto you when he was yet in Galilee, saying that the Son of man must be delivered up into the hands of sinful men, and be crucified, and the third day rise again." (Luke 24: 5-7.) "Go quickly, and tell his disciples, He is risen from the dead; and lo, he goeth before you into Galilee; there shall ye see him: lo, I have told you." (Matt. 28: 7.)

14 **When she had thus said, she turned herself back, and beholdeth Jesus standing, and knew not that it was Jesus.**—Jesus was standing near and as she turned from speaking to the angels she beholdeth him. She was so troubled in spirit that she did not look with care and did not discern that it was Jesus.

15 **Jesus saith unto her, Woman, why weepest thou? whom seekest thou? She, supposing him to be the gardener, saith unto him, Sir, if thou hast borne him hence, tell me where thou hast laid him, and I will take him away.**—When Jesus spoke to her she still did not recognize him, but took for granted it was the keeper of the garden who would know of the removal and so asked if he had removed it to let her know and she would take charge of the body. [Observe the realistic touch in the use of the pronoun *"him"* as though she knew that the gardener understood who she meant. In her intense love for, and grief of the body, she seems to forget womanly physical weakness, and proposes doing the work of men.]

16 **Jesus saith unto her, Mary. She turneth herself, and saith unto him in Hebrew, Rabboni; which is to say, Teacher.**—Jesus, in a tone of tender reproach for not recognizing him, spoke her name with emphasis in a tone she well knew. She recognized the voice, and turned and called him, Rabboni.

[6]Touch me not; for I am not yet ascended unto the Father: but go unto my brethren, and say to them, I ascend unto my Father and your Father, and my God and your God. 18 Mary Magdalene cometh and telleth the disciples, I have seen the Lord; and *that* he had said these things unto her.

[6]Or, *Take not hold on me*

[All the former richness of tone of Jesus who spake as never man spake was in that single name that she had heard so often from his lips, and she recognized him immediately and addressed him as Teacher.]

17 **Jesus saith to her, Touch me not;**—She ran to him, prostrated herself at his feet, and as Matthew (28: 9) says "took hold of his feet, and worshipped him." They did touch him as he afterwards had Thomas to do.

for I am not yet ascended unto the Father:—It is difficult to determine what is meant here. Was this done before the final ascension? Some interpret it to "cling to" instead of "touch," and that he meant to tell them not to cling to him, for he would not leave them immediately, but go and tell his disciples that he would meet them in Galilee. This was an assurance that the time had not yet come for him to leave them.

but go unto my brethren, and say to them, I ascend unto my Father and your Father, and my God and your God.—[Why did he not say *our* Father and *our* God since he included both himself and them? For the reason he is not *our Father, our God* in the same sense that he is his Father and God.]

18 **Mary Magdalene cometh and telleth the disciples, I have seen the Lord; and that he had said these things unto her.**—Mary went to make his resurrection known to his disciples and to deliver his message to them. Peter and John had seen the empty tomb and were prepared somewhat for the information of his appearance, but Mark (16: 11) says, "And they, when they heard that he was alive, and had been seen of her, disbelieved." [John does not mention their unbelief because he himself believed (verse 8), and he could not mention their unbelief without an invidious distinction. Mary Magdalene was the first to tell the story of the resurrection.]

8. HE APPEARS TO THE ELEVEN.
20: 19-23.

19 When therefore it was evening, on that day, the first *day* of the week,
and when the doors were shut where the disciples were, for fear of the
Jews, Jesus came and stood in the midst, and saith unto them, Peace *be* unto
you. 20 And when he had said this, he showed unto them his hands and
his side. The disciples therefore were glad, when they saw the Lord. 21

19 **When therefore it was evening, on that day, the first day of the week, and when the doors were shut where the disciples were, for fear of the Jews,**—The crucifixion of Jesus filled his disciples with fear as to their fate. So at evening they were met together to discuss the wondrous reports they had heard during the day. They did it within closed doors lest they should attract the attention and incur the hostility of the Jews.

Jesus came and stood in the midst, and saith unto them, Peace be unto you.—[He suddenly appeared among them. How he did it, by miracle, or otherwise, it is useless for any one to discuss, since it is an untaught question. It is enough for us to know and accept the fact.]

20 **And when he had said this, he showed unto them his hands and his side. The disciples therefore were glad, when they saw the Lord.**—While his wounds did not now create the suffering and pain that such wounds would in other persons, else he could not have been able to walk around as he did, still the gaping wounds were there into which they could thrust their fingers and these he showed to his disciples to produce perfect assurance that he was the same Jesus that they had seen nailed to the cross. The effect was to fill their hearts with gladness to see their Lord. [Seven days later Jesus shows his wounds to Thomas. The resurrected body still carried these proofs of his suffering and love. Sixty years later, when the apostle at Patmos saw the Lion of the tribe of Judah, he beheld "a Lamb standing, as though it had been slain." Whether our Lord in glory will continue to bear the marks of the cross and whether these will forever, as we live with him in glory, remind us of the story of our redemption, I shall not discuss. Suffice it to say, that when the apostles saw Jesus they were glad.]

Jesus therefore said to them again, Peace *be* unto you: as the Father hath sent me, even so send I you. 22 And when he had said this, he breathed on them, and saith unto them, Receive ye the Holy Spirit: 23 whose soever sins ye forgive, they are forgiven unto them; whose soever *sins* ye retain, they are retained.

---

21 **Jesus therefore said to them again, Peace be unto you:** —He again pronounces the benediction of peace upon them and announces

as the Father hath sent me, even so send I you.—For the same purpose and end. He was sent by the Father. By the same authority Jesus sends them. The authority of the Father and of the Son was to be present with the apostles. [The apostles are the executors of the New Testament that comes into force after the testator dies (Heb. 9: 15-17) and are to be sent forth to declare its provisions to a lost world. This is the first development of the Great Commission, which is more fully developed in Galilee a little later, and finally completed on Mount Olivet, just before he ascended.]

22 **And when he had said this, he breathed on them,**—This verse presents difficulties. Does it mean he blew his breath on his eleven disciples here assembled and that they were at once authorized to forgive or retain sins, to proclaim terms of pardon to the world. This would not be in harmony with his telling them to tarry at Jerusalem until they were endued with power from on high. (Luke 24: 49; Acts 1: 7.)

and saith unto them, Receive ye the Holy Spirit:—Meaning when the Spirit should come. They showed no indication of having received the Spirit until received on the day of Pentecost. [Breath is the symbol of life. When God created man, he breathed into him the breath of life. (Gen. 2: 7.)]

23 **whose soever sins ye forgive, they are forgiven unto them; whose soever sins ye retain, they are retained.**—It was a promise that the Holy Spirit would come to them and when he came they would be authorized to lay down the conditions on which they could be forgiven. God alone forgives sin, and the apostles proclaimed the conditions as he gave them on which sins could be forgiven and which they could not be forgiven.

9. THE INCREDULITY OF THOMAS AND ITS REMOVAL.
20: 24-29.

24 But Thomas, one of the twelve, called [1]Didymus, was not with them
when Jesus came. 25 The other disciples therefore said unto him, We
have seen the Lord. But he said unto them, Except I shall see in his
hands the print of the nails, and put my finger into the print of the nails,
and put my hand into his side, I will not believe.
26 And after eight days again his disciples were within, and Thomas
with them. Jesus cometh, the doors being shut, and stood in the midst,
and said, Peace *be* unto you. 27 Then saith he to Thomas, Reach hither thy
finger, and see my hands; and reach *hither* thy hand, and put it into my

[1]That is, *Twin*

24 **But Thomas, one of the twelve, called Didymus, was not with them when Jesus came.**—Thomas always appears incredulous and slow to believe, given to looking on the dark side. He was not present when Jesus appeared to the disciples at night, nor any of the appearances of Jesus on the day of his resurrection. When told that they had seen Jesus, he firmly protested that he would not believe.

25 **The other disciples therefore said unto him, We have seen the Lord. But he said unto them, Except I shall see in his hands the print of the nails, and put my finger into the print of the nails, and put my hand into his side, I will not believe.**—When told by the other disciples that they had seen Jesus, he protested that he would not believe either them or his own senses. In addition to seeing and hearing him he should put his fingers in the nailprints and thrust his hand into the pierced side.

26 **And after eight days again his disciples were within, and Thomas with them. Jesus cometh, the doors being shut, and stood in the midst, and said, Peace be unto you.**—After eight days they were all again assembled and Thomas was present. The doors were shut and Jesus again stood in their midst and again spake peace to them.

27 **Then saith he to Thomas, Reach hither thy finger, and see my hands; and reach hither thy hand, and put it into my side: and be not faithless, but believing.**—He at once addressed himself to Thomas and proposed to meet the conditions he demanded. He held out his hands and his feet, asked him to place his finger in the nailprints, and presented

side: and be not faithless, but believing. 28 Thomas answered and said unto him, My Lord and my God. 29 Jesus saith unto him, Because thou hast seen me, [a]thou hast believed: blessed *are* they that have not seen, and *yet* have believed.

[a]Or, *hast thou believed?*

his side, and asked him to thrust his hand into the wound, and believe.

28 **Thomas answered and said unto him, My Lord and my God.**—Thomas was not so hard of belief as he had thought. When he saw Jesus he believed without thrusting in his fingers or his hand and exclaimed, "My Lord and my God." The evidence came, and his conclusion was that he was both Ruler and God.

29 **Jesus saith unto him, Because thou hast seen me, thou hast believed: blessed are they that have not seen, and yet have believed.**—While he presented these evidences to the senses of the apostles, he expected the world through all the ages to come to believe in him through the testimony of these apostles and other evidence that God would give to the world. So he reproved the lack of faith of Thomas by pronouncing a blessing on all who should believe without seeing him.

10. OTHER SIGNS AND PURPOSES OF THE RECORD.
20: 30, 31.

30 Many other signs therefore did Jesus in the presence of the disciples, which are not written in this book: 31 but these are written, that ye may believe that Jesus is the Christ, the Son of God; and that believing ye may have life in his name.

30 **Many other signs therefore did Jesus in the presence of the disciples, which are not written in this book:**—Jesus did many other miracles after his resurrection beside those mentioned in this book. "This book" means the book written by John. [Much that Jesus did both before and after his resurrection is not recorded. Each historian recorded some features of his work that the others omitted, and each of them reveal the fact that they only outlined his work.]

31 **but these are written, that ye may believe that Jesus is the Christ, the Son of God;**—These mentioned in the book

were written to the end that those who read the book may believe.

and that believing ye may have life in his name.—The faith is based on the testimony given in the writings concerning Christ, his work, and teaching. The faith leads to put on Christ, enter into his name, and as a servant of Christ, as a member of the body of Christ, might so act as to attain to eternal life. [Producing faith in Christ is the object of all gospel history. They so reveal Christ as to produce faith in him. "So belief cometh of hearing, and hearing by the word of Christ." (Rom. 10: 17.) "Here, with these words, John ends the great argument that he entered upon with the first chapter and which continues with unbroken connection until it reaches its culmination in the remarkable declaration of the purpose which he had written. The chain of argument embraces the testimony of Moses and the prophets, the witness of John the Baptist, whom the Jews acknowledged as a man of God, the wonderful life of Christ, the supernatural wisdom and authority of his teaching, his supernatural works, and last and greatest of all, the fact of his death, burial and resurrection. The last is the crowning argument, and it is after he has established it beyond a doubt, if such a wonderful fact can be proven by human testimony, that he closes with the declaration: *These are* written, that ye may believe that Jesus is the Christ, the Son of God, etc."]

11. JESUS APPEARS TO SEVEN AT THE LAKE OF TIBERIAS. 21: 1-14.

1 After these things Jesus manifested himself again to the disciples at the sea of Tiberias; and he manifested *himself* on this wise. 2 There were

---

1 **After these things Jesus manifested himself again to the disciples at the sea of Tiberias; and he manifested himself on this wise.**—Jesus had promised to meet his disciples in Galilee. All the apostles that are now faithful to him were Galileans. Jesus was reared in Galilee, and the greater portion of his public life had been spent in that country. The greater number of his following were Galileans. So he had promised to meet them in Galilee. He showed himself to

together Simon Peter, and Thomas called [1]Didymus, and Nathanael of
Cana in Galilee, and the *sons* of Zebedee, and two other of his disciples. 3
Simon Peter saith unto them, I go a fishing. They say unto him, We also
come with thee. They went forth, and entered into the boat; and that night
they took nothing. 4 But when day was now breaking, Jesus stood on the
beach: yet the disciples knew not that it was Jesus. 5 Jesus therefore
saith unto them, Children, have ye aught to eat? They answered him, No.

---

over five hundred brethren at one time in Galilee, but now he meets a few fishermen at the Sea of Galilee or Tiberias.

2 **There were together Simon Peter, and Thomas called Didymus, and Nathanael of Cana in Galilee, and the sons of Zebedee, and two other of his disciples.**—Five apostles are mentioned by name, and two others not named who may have been other than apostles.

3 **Simon Peter saith unto them, I go a fishing. They say unto him, We also come with thee. They went forth, and entered into the boat; and that night they took nothing.**—Simon Peter was a leader. He determined to go fishing. The others said they would go with him. They fished all night and caught nothing. [Although the night was considered the most favorable season they caught nothing. Doubtless a symbol of the utter failure of fishers of men without Christ, and verse 6 illustrates their abundant success with Christ.]

4 **But when day was now breaking, Jesus stood on the beach: yet the disciples knew not that it was Jesus.**—The disciples consisting of Peter, Thomas, Nathanael (supposed to be Bartholomew), James and John (sons of Zebedee), and the others not named had spent the night fishing in the Sea of Tiberias, or Galilee. They caught nothing. When morning came Jesus stood on the shore. The disciples did not know him. Whether it was yet too dark to distinguish a person, or they were too far from shore, or whether he transformed himself, as Mark (16: 12) intimates, so they could not know him, is not told. That he was near enough to talk with them as he did would indicate either the first or the last was the truth.

5 **Jesus therefore saith unto them, Children, have ye aught to eat?**—He calls them "children," an affectionate and familiar style of address. Still they did not recognize him. [He

6 And he said unto them, Cast the net on the right side of the boat, and ye shall find. They cast therefore, and now they were not able to draw it for the multitude of fishes. 7 That disciple therefore whom Jesus loved saith unto Peter, It is the Lord. So when Simon Peter heard that it was the Lord, he girt his coat about him (for he [8]was naked), and cast himself

[8]Or, *had on his undergarment only.* Comp. ch. 13. 4; Is. 20. 2; Mic. 1. 8, 11

meant have you caught any fish? His manner was that of a householder, desiring to purchase for the morning meal.]

They answered him, No.—[Evidently without a suspicion of his identity. There was nothing in his question that made the disciples suspect who he was.]

6 **And he said unto them, Cast the net on the right side of the boat, and ye shall find. They cast therefore, and now they were not able to draw it for the multitude of fishes.**—They did as he directed, and caught as many as their net could hold. A similar occurrence took place in the early part of his ministry. (Luke 5: 1-10.) The command was so done that they obeyed without inquiring why. [They were fishing on the wrong side to catch fish; you must fish where fish are. The fish were on the right side of the boat and Jesus knew it; not by natural signs, for the disciples would read these as well as he, but by his supernatural insight.]

7 **That disciple therefore whom Jesus loved saith unto Peter, It is the Lord. So when Simon Peter heard that it was the Lord, he girt his coat about him (for he was naked), and cast himself into the sea.**—This was John, who, on several occasions, speaks of himself in this way. (13: 23; 20: 2.) Doubtless the similarity of this to what had been done before suggested to John, "It is the Lord." The number of fishes after the night of fruitless toil, and the voice of Jesus, impressed on John the idea that it was Jesus, and he so told Peter. It is to John's credit that he was reminded of Jesus. While John first thought of him, Peter as usual is the first to go to him. He had nothing on the upper part of his body, but threw his coat about him and left the fishermen's vessel, and went through the water to the land. The water was doubtless shallow so he waded to the shore.

into the sea. 8 But the other disciples came in the little boat (for they were
not far from the land, but about two hundred cubits off), dragging the net
full of fishes. 9 So when they got out upon the land, they see [4]a fire of

[4]Gr. *a fire of charcoal*

8 But the other disciples came in the little boat (for they were not far from the land, but about two hundred cubits off), dragging the net full of fishes.—They were about one hundred yards from shore. The ships were boats, or canoes. In one of these they came to the shore, dragging the net with fishes. Their fishing vessel was a small one. The net likely had one end fastened to the shore. The boat with the other end made a circuit and caught all the fish in the circuit.

9 So when they got out upon the land, they see a fire of coals there, and fish laid thereon, and bread.—Jesus had "a fire of coals there, and fish laid thereon, and bread." Whence the fire and the fish we do not know. This shows that Jesus ate bread and fish when he was in the state between the resurrection and the ascension as recorded in Luke. (24: 41.) He had risen from the dead, seemed at will to assume the invisible state, and would seem to be immaterial in appearing and disappearing from houses, yet he ate material food. The angels did the same who appeared to Abraham, and we find it difficult to gain clear conceptions of beings in the spirit-land. Jesus said "a spirit hath not flesh and bones, as ye behold me having." (Luke 24: 39.) We take it that Jesus suffered hunger else he had not eaten. Nor is it clear that Jesus was clothed with an immortal body at this time. His hands had the prints of the nails in them, and his side the spear thrust. But it is possible he was changed at the moment of ascension. "It is not yet made manifest what we shall be. We know that, if he shall be manifested, we shall be like him; for we shall see him even as he is." But in the time before the fall, when not subject to death, they ate and drank. But our ignorance of the future state is so dense that we cannot think about it intelligently.

coals there, and [5]fish laid thereon, and [6]bread. 10 Jesus saith unto them,
Bring of the fish which ye have now taken. 11 Simon Peter therefore went
[7]up, and drew the net to land, full of great fishes, a hundred and fifty and
three: and for all there were so many, the net was not rent. 12 Jesus saith
unto them, Come *and* break your fast. And none of the disciples durst
inquire of him, Who art thou? knowing that it was the Lord. 13 Jesus

[5]Or, *a fish*
[6]Or, *a loaf*
[7]Or, *aboard*

10 **Jesus saith unto them, Bring of the fish which ye have now taken.**—Jesus asked them to bring of the fish they had caught to cook and eat. This, we take it, was to cook for a meal for the disciples. [The articles of food offered by Jesus must be made completely of the product of their own fishing. This detail would be absolutely incomprehensible unless this whole scene had a symbolic sense. Jesus wishes to tell them that he will occupy himself with their wants, but that their faithful labor must cooperate with his benediction and his aid.]

11 **Simon Peter therefore went up, and drew the net to land, full of great fishes, a hundred and fifty and three: and for all there were so many, the net was not rent.**—Peter ashore could pull the net more easily than those in the boat. He did it. The number, one hundred and fifty-three, even if very large fish, would not at all strain such nets as are now used. But then the material and workmanship of boats, nets, and all things requiring mechanical skill were of an inferior order. [We take it that he went to the water's edge on the shore. The net was not a large one, as our people count large, on the fishing shores, else it would have held more than one hundred fifty fishes, and it would have been no wonder that it did not break. Now nets are dragged frequently that draw to the shore thousands of fishes.]

12 **Jesus saith unto them, Come and break your fast. And none of the disciples durst inquire of him, Who art thou? knowing that it was the Lord.**—It is presumed that some of the fish they caught were cooked on the fire, and Jesus as host invited them to come and eat. It was so manifest to them all that he was Jesus that they did not ask who he was.

cometh, and taketh the [8]bread, and giveth them, and the fish likewise. 14
This is now the third time that Jesus was manifested to the disciples, after
that he was risen from the dead.

[8]Or, *loaf*

13 **Jesus cometh, and taketh the bread, and giveth them, and the fish likewise.**—He helped them to bread and fish. We know not whence the bread came. Possibly Jesus provided it by his power. As leader he took the bread he had and distributed to his disciples and the fish likewise. They all ate as they had done before his death while traveling around together.

14 **This is now the third time that Jesus was manifested to the disciples, after that he was risen from the dead.**—Jesus appeared to the eleven disciples the night after he arose from the dead. On the night of the eighth day following he met with them again. (19: 8.) This is the third time, showing that while he met with them on the first and eighth days after he was raised, he did not meet with them during the interim. He seems to have designed this to sanctify the first day, the day of his resurrection as the day for his disciples to meet with the assurance that he would meet with them to bless them. Thomas, failing to be with them, followed by a sense of doubt and uncertainty that may be a significant lesson to us. Where he was when not with the disciples we know not. Since his body seemed subject to the law of the natural world, we do not even know that he was in the body when not with the disciples.

12. REMARKS OF JESUS TO PETER.
21: 15-23.

15 So when they had broken their fast, Jesus saith to Simon Peter,
Simon, *son* of [1]John, [2]lovest thou me more than these? He saith unto him,

[1]Gr. *Joanes.* See ch. 1. 42, margin

15 **So when they had broken their fast, Jesus saith to Simon Peter, Simon, son of John, lovest thou me more than these?**—Peter, with self-confidence, had declared that though all others, including his fellow disciples, should deny him, he would never deny him. But he had been the first to deny him, and

Yea, Lord; thou knowest that I [3]love thee. He saith unto him, Feed my
lambs. 16 He saith to him again a second time, Simon, *son* of [1]John, [2]lovest
thou me? He saith unto him, Yea, Lord; thou knowest that I [3]love thee.
He saith unto him, Tend my sheep. 17 He saith unto him the third time,
Simon, *son* of [1]John, [3]lovest thou me? Peter was grieved because he said

[2] [3]*Love* in these places represents two different Greek words

had denied him three times in succession. This occurred before the crucifixion of Jesus. This seems to have been done as a reproof to this falling away of Peter and to result in the restoration to the favor of Jesus. After the restoration, Jesus asked Peter this question. Peter had boasted, if all "shall be offended in thee, I will never be offended." The usual interpretation given to it is that *these* refer to the other apostles and disciples who were with him, and attribute his asking such a question to Peter's bold declaration, "If all shall be offended in thee, I will never be offended." But we are sure from the structure of the sentence both in English and in Greek that it refers to the fishes and things of like character. Peter, do you love me more than you love these things of the flesh? We think fishes stand as the antecedent of *these*. The Greek more clearly indicates this than the English.

He saith unto him, Yea, Lord; thou knowest that I love thee.—This response was an appeal to the knowledge of Jesus. Some think he meant to imply, I do not know myself. He was careful not to say, "More than these," but the modest affirmative, "thou knowest that I love thee."

He saith unto him, Feed my lambs.—The tender ones of the flock. It was an assurance of the restoration of the Master's confidence.

16 **He saith to him again a second time, Simon, son of John, lovest thou me? He saith unto him, Yea, Lord; thou knowest that I love thee. He saith unto him, Tend my sheep.**—[In repeating the question, he leaves off "more than these." Peter gives the same answer. If there was special significance in changing from lambs to sheep, I do not know what it is.]

17 **He saith unto him the third time, Simon, son of John, lovest thou me?**—This corresponds to the number of times that Peter denied him. Jesus desired to assure him of his full

**unto him the third time, [3]Lovest thou me? And he said unto him, Lord,
thou knowest all things; thou [4]knowest that I [3]love thee. Jesus saith unto
him, Feed my sheep. 18 Verily, verily, I say unto thee, When thou wast
young, thou girdedst thyself, and walkedst whither thou wouldest: but
when thou shalt be old, thou shalt stretch forth thy hands, and another
shall gird thee, and carry thee whither thou wouldest not. 19 Now this he**

[4]Or, *perceivest*

and complete forgiveness. That he might do this fully, he must repent fully. So he repented.

Peter was grieved because he said unto him the third time, Lovest thou me?—Peter was grieved because of his apparent distrust of his statements.

And he said unto him, Lord, thou knowest all things; thou knowest that I love thee. Jesus saith unto him, Feed my sheep.—His profession of love without self-confidence or boast was thus apparently equal to the number of denials, and Jesus repeats the admonition. [Peter, pierced to the heart by these repeated questions, throws himself on the knowledge the Lord has of his heart. The third time the Lord charges him to act as a shepherd under him and to take care of the sheep. Three times Peter had denied the Master; three times the Master questions his love; three times he gives him courage concerning his work. The questioning was painful, Peter was grieved, but the grief was wholesome and Peter's whole subsequent life bore proof of the discipline. His rashness was forever gone.]

18 **Verily, verily, I say unto thee, When thou wast young, thou girdedst thyself, and walkedst whither thou wouldest: but when thou shalt be old, thou shalt stretch forth thy hands, and another shall gird thee, and carry thee whither thou wouldest not.**—This was added by way of illustrating Peter's lifework. When one is young he feels buoyant and self-confident, but when the infirmities of age come, he feels dependent and stretches out his hands for help and is led whither he would not go. ["Peter had denied his Master to save his own life. Now that he is reinstated in the old confidence and charged with the Master's work, he is told that he will be called on to die for it. He will be girded, not with a girdle,

spake, signifying by what manner of death he should glorify God. And when he had spoken this, he saith unto him, Follow me. 20 Peter, turning about, seeth the disciple whom Jesus loved following; who also leaned back on his breast at the supper, and said, Lord, who is he that [5]betrayeth thee? 21 Peter therefore seeing him saith to Jesus, Lord, [6]and what shall this man

[5]Or, *delivereth thee up*
[6]Gr. *and this man, what?*

but with bonds, and he shall be led where he would not, unto death."]

19 **Now this he spake, signifying by what manner of death he should glorify God.**—Peter would be taken and slain in his old age for the name of Christ. Jesus foretold it by this method.

And when he had spoken this, he saith unto him, Follow me.—As much as to say, while the future had good in store for him, all would depend on his fidelity to Christ. [I take the two verses that, though Peter was weak and ungrounded at first, he will increase in faith and courage sufficiently to die a martyr. The universal testimony of the historians of the early church is that he thus died—that he was crucified. He was to follow Jesus until he had drunk the cup that his Master had drunk, and thus "glorify God."]

20 **Peter, turning about, seeth the disciple whom Jesus loved following; who also leaned back on his breast at the supper, and said, Lord, who is he that betrayeth thee?**—Jesus did not conceal his love for John. John leaned on his breast at the supper. This did not seem to excite envy or animosity of the other disciples, but brought John into prominence among them.

21 **Peter therefore seeing him saith to Jesus, Lord, and what shall this man do?**—As Jesus had foretold the future of Peter, Peter asked what should become of John. Jesus seems to reprove the curiosity that made Peter seek to know the end of John. [Three years before on the banks of the same sea, our Lord had called Peter and Andrew, and the sons of Zebedee to become fishers of men. Peter seems to fully understand the prophecy with regard to himself, and is anxious to know what shall be the fate of his friend and colaborer.]

do? 22 Jesus saith unto him, If I will that he tarry till I come, what *is that* to thee? follow thou me. 23 This saying therefore went forth among the brethren, that that disciple should not die: yet Jesus said not unto him, that he should not die; but, If I will that he tarry till I come, what *is that* to thee?

---

22 **Jesus saith unto him, If I will that he tarry till I come, what is that to thee? follow thou me.**—So he gave an evasive answer with the hint that it did not concern him. [John did literally tarry until Jesus came, until he saw him, heard him speak and recorded in the last revelation from the Lord to the world in the book of Revelation. About sixty years from the time that Jesus uttered these words, John was an exile in Patmos. There, on a Lord's day, Jesus came and revealed to him the message he addresses to the seven churches of Asia.]

23 **This saying therefore went forth among the brethren, that that disciple should not die: yet Jesus said not unto him, that he should not die; but, If I will that he tarry till I come, what is that to thee?**—From this indefinite answer they drew the conclusion that John would not die, but remain till Jesus comes again. [John corrected the error that had spread among the disciples without accusing any one of lying. It is a pity that such a spirit does not prevail among brethren today.]

13. CONCLUSION OF THE NARRATIVE.
21: 24, 25.

24 This is the disciple that beareth witness of these things, and wrote these things: and we know that his witness is true.
25 And there are also many other things which Jesus did, the which

---

24 **This is the disciple that beareth witness of these things, and wrote these things: and we know that his witness is true.**—John who heard these things wrote them down and affirms their certainty.

25 **And there are also many other things which Jesus did,**—The writer of this affirms that only a small portion of the works performed by Jesus are recorded. They are recorded that those who read them may believe in Christ Jesus the Lord. (20: 30, 31.) The record made is sufficient to produce faith in all who read with the desire to do the will of God. More would be cumbersome.

if they should be written every one, I suppose that even the world itself would not contain the books that should be written.

A man then to believe must know and accept the things written concerning Christ in the scriptures; he must receive the seed into a good and understanding heart; he must hear and attend to the things written in the word of God. No example is found in the scriptures of a man believing, save as he heard the word of God, the testimonies given in it concerning Christ and his teaching and work. God gives us food by giving us the means of producing food. He gives the soil, the seed, the ability to plant and cultivate the seed so as to multiply it an hundredfold and to use this for food. He gives to man a heart to believe Jesus as the object of our faith, the testimony on which our faith in him must rest, and he gives the mental ability to understand and believe upon those testimonies, and then he requires us to use these means to produce faith. We have the power to use them or not as we like. The duty of the unbeliever is to faithfully and candidly study the word of God to see if these things be so with the desire of knowing and doing the truth. The testimonies are sufficient to convince every honest and true heart that Jesus is the Christ the Son of God.

the which if they should be written every one, I suppose that even the world itself would not contain the books that should be written.—In this strong expression, he clearly means that all the books in the world would not hold the record of the things said and done by Jesus. In the things revealed are the words of life eternal. ["The ministry of Christ was so busy, his teaching so voluminous and his deeds of mercy so numerous that the verse states that it would be impossible to make a minute record, and in order to convey this idea forcibly an oriental hyperbole is employed." I take it that he does not mean this material world, but that the mind of man would not be able to understand and comprehend all that Jesus said and did were all these things recorded in books.]

INDEX TO SUBJECTS.

A

Abraham, before, was, I am, 137.
Abraham rejoiced to see Christ's day, 136.
Abraham's seed, 131.
Abraham's children do the works of, 132.
Adultery, woman taken in, 120.
Agents, water and Spirit are the, in producing new birth, 44.
Angel hath spoken, 194.
Angels, ascending and descending, 34.
Angels, Mary saw two, in the tomb, 309.
Anointed, Mary, feet of Jesus, 184.
Apostles given power to remit sins, 313.
Appearance, judge not according to, 113.
Arise, let us go hence, 235.
Ask and ye shall receive, 259.
Ask, in my name, that I do, 225.
Ass, Jesus sat on a young, 188.
Authority, Jesus given, to execute judgment, 79.
Authority over all flesh, 262.
Away, I go, and I come again, 233.

B

Baptized, John, in water, 27.
Baptized, Jesus, 51.
Baptized, Jesus, more disciples than John, 54.
Baptized, Jesus, through agents, 55.
Baptizing, these things were done where John was, 27.
Baptizing in Ænon because there was much water, 51.
Baptizeth, Jesus, in the Holy Spirit, 29.
Baptizeth, Jesus, and all men come to him, 52.
Baptizest, why, thou? 27.
Barabbas, Jews demand the release of, 289.
Beginning, in the, was the Word which was God, 15.
Begotten, the only, of the Father, 22.
Believe, can't, when we receive glory one of another, 83.
Believe, this is the work of God that ye, on him, 94.
Believe, some believe not, 104.
Believe not, because not my sheep, 160.
Believe me not if I do not the works of my Father, 163; believe the works I do, 163.
Believe, all men will, on him if let alone, 179.
Believe, they could not, 198.
Believe, I have told you before it come to pass that ye might, 234.
Believe, that the world may, 269.
Believe, them that, on his name, he gave the right to become children of God, 22.
Believed, many, on Jesus, 41, 114, 129.
Believed, many, because of the word of the woman, 68.
Believed, many, through Christ's teaching, 69.
Believed, if ye, Moses, ye would believe me, 84.
Believed on Jesus from the testimony of John, 164.
Believed not on him, 197.
Believed, blessed are they that have, 315.
Believeth, whosoever, in him should not perish, but have eternal life, 49.
Believeth, he that, hath eternal life, 54.
Believing, the result of testimony, 48.
Betray, Jesus knew who would, him, 104.
Betrayed by one of you, 212.
Betrayal of Jesus, 205.
Birth, coming forth is the, 45.
Blind man healed, 137.
Blinded eyes, 199.
Blood, eat my flesh and drink my, 101.
Body of Christ, the temple, 41.
Body, spiritual, took the place of the fleshly, 162.
Bones, Joseph's, brought from Egypt, 55.

Bondage, seed of Abraham not in, 131.
Bondservant, every one committeth sin is the, 131.
Books, the world would not contain the, 326.
Born anew, to see the kingdom of God, 43.
Born, how can a man be, when he is old, 44.
Born of water and the Spirit, 44.
Born, that which is, of the flesh is flesh; and that which is, of the Spirit is spirit, 45.
Born, not of blood, etc., 22.
Bread of God cometh from heaven, 95.
Bread, Jesus the, of life, 97.
Bread, he that eat this, shall live for ever, 101.
Bread of life, 101.
Bride, he that hath the, is the bridegroom, 53.
Bridegroom, he that hath the bride is the, 53.
Branch that beareth not fruit he taketh away, 236.
Branch cannot bear fruit except it abide in the vine, 237.
Branches of palm trees strewed in Jesus' path, 187.
Branches, ye are the, 238.

C

Caiaphas, Jesus sent to, 281.
Cæsar's, thou art not, friend, 294.
Capernaum, the home of Jesus, his mother and brethren go with him to the city, 38.
Cause, they hated me without a, 248.
Children, as many as received Jesus, he gave the right to become the, of God, 21.
Christ, John said I am not the, but sent before him, 52.
Christ the seed of David, 117.
Christ abideth for ever, 106.
Christ is the way, the truth, and the life, 221.
Christ, grace and truth came through, 24.
Christ, John not the, 25.
Church exposes evil, 162.
Circumcision on the Sabbath, 113.
Clay is put on eyes of blind man, 141.
Commandment is life eternal, 203.
Commandment given me, 203.
Commandment, a new, 216.
Commandments, if ye love me, ye will keep my, 226.
Commandments, he that keepeth my, loveth me, 229.
Commandments, if ye keep my, ye shall abide in my love, 240.
Cock shall not crow, till thou hast denied me thrice, 218.
Comforter, he shall give you another, 226.
Comforter, even the Holy Spirit, Father will send, 232.
Comforter, when the, is come, 248.
Comforter, will convict the world of sin, righteousness, and of judgment, 253.
Choose, ye did not, me, but I chose you, 243.
Created, Jesus was one of the Godhead when matter was, 16.
Creation, the original, 15, 16; Jesus was with God in the, 16; Godhead one in creation, 16.
Crime, I find no, in him, 291.
Cross, Jesus bore the, 297.
Cross, mother of Jesus stood by the, 300.
Crown of thorns put on Jesus' head, 290.
Crown, Jesus came out wearing the, of thorns, 291.
Crying, John the voice, in the wilderness, 26.
Crucify him yourselves, for I find no crime in him, 291.
Crucified, Pilate delivers Jesus to be, 296.

D

Dark, I have spoken unto you in, 259.
Darkness, the light shineth in, 18.
Draw all men unto me, 195.
Day, the great, of the feast, 116.
David, Christ seed of, 117.
Dead, Father raiseth the, and giveth them life, 78.
Dead faith will not produce life, 49.
Dead shall hear and live, 79.
Death, Jews not permitted to inflict, 283, 285.

Death, took counsel to put Jesus to, 180.
Death, passed from, into life, 78.
Decrease, John must, and Jesus increase, 53.
Demon, can a, open the eyes of the blind? 158.
Denied, Peter, Christ, 281.
Desolate, I will not leave you, 228.
Destroy this temple and in three days I will raise it up, 40.
Devil, the, abideth not in truth, 134.
Devil, the, is your father, 133.
Devil, the, put into Judas' heart to betray him, 205.
Die, expedient that one man should, for the people, 278.
Disciple reclining on Jesus' bosom, 213.
Disciples, two, follow Jesus, 30.
Disciples, their faith increased, 38.
Disciples marveled that Jesus was talking with a woman, 64.
Disciples, many of his, went back and walked no more with him, 105.
Disciples, ye are my, indeed, 130.
Disobedient, God's wrath abideth on the, 54.
Division over Christ, 118.
Division over his words, 157.
Do these things and be blessed, 211.
Dove, the Spirit descending as a, out of heaven, 28.

E

Easter, Abib, the first month of the Jewish year corresponds with our, 38.
Eat my flesh and drink my blood, 101.
Economy, Jesus teaches a lesson of, 87, 88.
Eternal life is through faith in Christ, 49.
Evil exposed by church, 162.
Evil, he that doeth, hateth the light, 51.
Example given by Jesus, 210.
Expedient, it is, for you that I go away, 252.
Eyes blinded, 199.

F

Father, the only begotten of the, 22.
Father raiseth the dead and gives them life, 78.
Father draws by teaching, 99, 100.
Father, the, is greater than all, and not one able to snatch them out of his hand, 161.
Father, the, honor those who serve Jesus, 192.
Father, save me from this hour, 193.
Father gave me a commandment, 203.
Father, if ye had known me, ye would have known my, also, 222.
Father, no one cometh unto the, but by me, 222.
Father, I in the, and the, in me, 224.
Father is greater than I, 234.
Father, glorify thy Son, 261.
Father's, Jesus came in his, name, 82.
Father's voice not heard nor has he been seen, 81.
Father's, in my, house are many mansions, 219.
Faith, a dead, will not produce life, 49.
Faith of disciples increased, 38.
Faith grows from weak to strong, 41.
Faith produced by signs, 315.
Fast, come and break your, 320.
Fault, I find no, in him, 288.
Feast of tabernacles, 107.
Feast, Jesus refused to go to the, but later went, 109, 110.
Feast, the great day of the, 116.
Feast of the Dedication, 159.
Feast of the Passover, 204.
Feed my lambs, 322.
Feeding five thousand, 86-88.
Feet, ought to be washed by one another, 210.
Feet of disciples washed by Jesus, 206.
Feet of Jesus anointed by Mary, 184.
Feet of Peter washed, 209.
Fell, they went backward and, 274.
Fields are white already unto harvest, 66.
Fight, if my kingdom were of this world, then would my servants, 287.

Finger, Jesus with his, wrote on the ground, 121.
Fire, officers and Peter standing by the, 280.
First-born of the Egyptians slain, 38.
Fishing, Peter and others go, 318.
Flesh, the teaching of Jesus does not destroy the ties of the, 31.
Flesh, the Word became, 22.
Flesh, that which is born of the, is flesh; and that which is born of the Spirit is spirit, 45.
Flesh and blood, eat my, 101.
Follow me, 192.
Found, we have, the Messiah, 31.
Food, work for the, that brings eternal life, 93.
Foot washing, 206.
Fruit, good tree cannot produce evil, 162.
Fruit, every branch that beareth not, he taketh it away, 236.
Fruit, beareth much, 238.
Fruit, Father glorified if ye bear much, 239.
Free, truth makes one, 130.
Friends, ye are my, if ye do the things which I command you, 242.
Fullness, of his, we all received, 24.

G

Gate, sheep, 73.
Glory, Jesus received not, from men, 82.
Glory, we beheld his, 22.
Glorify thy Son, 261.
Glorified, both Father and Son, 215.
Glorified, Jesus not yet, 116.
God, no man hath seen, 25.
God, the Lamb of, that taketh away the sin of the world, 28.
God, the originator and provider of all things, 17; he gave them the right to become children of, 21; born of, 22.
God with those working signs, 42, 43.
God loved the world, and gave his Son to save it, 49.
God sent not the Son to judge the world, but that the world through him might be saved, 50.
God is true, 54.
God is a Spirit; worshipers must worship him in spirit and truth, 63.
God, this is the work of, that ye believe on him, 84.
God heareth not sinners, 147.
God, all good things come from, 162.
Godhead, three distinct personages composing the, yet one in nature, 16.
Good, can any, thing come out of Nazareth? 33.
Grace and truth came through Christ, 24.
Grafts, human, on the church does evil, 162.
Graves, J. R., on the new birth, 45.
Greater, thou shalt see, things, 34.
Greater works shall he do, 224.
Greeks went up to worship at the feast and asked to see Jesus, 189.
Grain of wheat must die to produce a new stalk, 190.
Ground, they fell to the, 274.
Guile, an Israelite indeed, in whom is no, 33.

H

Hates, world, Christ, 109.
Hated, the world, them, 266.
Hateth, he that, me hateth my Father, 247.
Harvest, fields white unto the, 66.
Heard, those who have, cometh to Jesus, 100.
Heart, worship must come from the, 63.
Heart, let not your, be troubled, 219.
Heart, let not your, be troubled nor be fearful, 233.
Heaven, the Spirit descending as a dove out of, 28.
Heaven, ye shall see, open and angels ascending and descending, 34.
Hireling seeing the wolf coming fleeth, 155.
Hospital, no, nor asylum for the unfortunate that was not built by the influence of Jesus, 31.
House, make not my Father's, a house of merchandise, 39.
House, in my Father's, are many mansions, 219.

I

Idea, men's, is to keep their works before the world, 108.
Increase, Jesus must, but John decrease, 53.
Influence of Jesus in building hospitals and asylums for the unfortunate, 31.
Influence of Andrew in bringing Peter to Christ, 32.
Isaiah saw the glory, 200.

J

Jacob's well, 56.
Jesus and his disciples invited to a marriage, 35.
Jesus attends a feast at Jerusalem, 73.
Jesus accused of being mad, 157.
Jesus appears after the resurrection to the disciples, 312.
Jesus again escapes from the Jews, 163.
Jesus again appears to the disciples, 316.
Jesus appeared the third time to the disciples after rising from the dead, 321.
Jesus baptizing in the land of Judæa, 51.
Jesus baptizeth in the Holy Spirit, 29.
Jesus bearing the cross, 297.
Jesus converts water into wine, 35-37.
Jesus cleanses the temple, 39.
Jesus converses with Nicodemus, 42.
Jesus came to the ground that Jacob gave to Joseph, 55.
Jesus cures the nobleman's son, 70-72.
Jesus came in his Father's name, 82.
Jesus came to do his Father's will, 98.
Jesus challenges the Jews to convict him of sin, 134, 135.
Jesus called the parents of man born blind, 144.
Jesus came not to condemn, but to save, 202.
Jesus came a light in the world, 202.
Jesus did not withdraw from all social relations, 35.
Jesus don't accuse you but Moses, 83.
Jesus delivered to be crucified, 296.
Jesus dies, 301.
Jesus forgets his hunger in the desire to save souls, 66.
Jesus feeds five thousand, 86-88.
Jesus feeds the disciples, 319.
Jesus goes to the Passover, 38.
Jesus gave his life freely, 156, 157.
Jesus glorified, 193.
Jesus gave Pilate no answer, 293.
Jesus heals a man at the pool of Bethesda, 73-75.
Jesus hid himself, 137.
Jesus heals a blind man, 137.
Jesus healed blind man on the Sabbath, 143.
Jesus hid himself, 197.
Jesus is the only one competent to teach these things, 48.
Jesus, prophesied that, should die for the nation, 180.
Jesus knew what was in man, and needed no witness, 42.
Jesus knew all were not clean, 209.
Jesus knew whom he had chosen, 211.
Jesus knew all things coming upon him, 274.
Jesus lifted upon the cross that people might believe, 48.
Jesus must increase, but John decrease, 53.
Jesus made and baptized more disciples than John, 54.
Jesus must die to bring life, 190.
Jesus made provision for the care of his mother, 301.
Jesus never brought evil to a single soul, 162.
Jesus not seeking privacy, 186.
Jesus of Nazareth, the King of the Jews, written on the cross, 298.
Jesus, pre-existence of, 15, 16; the glory he had with the Father before the world was, 15; he was with God in the creation, 16; he existed before his conception and birth of the virgin Mary, 16; he is not called the Son of God or the Son of man except prophetically before his conception and birth of the virgin, 16; he is nowhere called Jesus or the Savior until he came to save his people

from their sins, save as prophecy foretold this would be his mission, 16; he was called the Christ after being anointed with the oil of gladness, 16; he was one of the Godhead when matter was originally created, 16; he was the creative agent of the Godhead, 17; he made all things, 17; life was in Jesus, 17; he is the true light, 20; he was no intruder, 20; he came to his own and his own received him not, 20, 21; John bore witness of him, 23.
Jesus possessed superhuman knowledge, 34.
Jesus persecuted by the Jews for healing on the Sabbath, 75-77.
Jesus put clay on eyes of blind man, 141.
Jesus prayed for unity, 270.
Jesus received not glory from men, 82.
Jesus speaketh the words of God, 54.
Jesus sat on the well, 56.
Jesus seized and bound, 277.
Jesus struck by an officer, 281.
Jesus sent bound unto Caiaphas, 281.
Jesus scourged, 290.
Jesus saith, I thirst, and they gave him vinegar, 301.
Jesus said, it is finished, bowed his head, and gave up his spirit, 302.
Jesus sends out the apostles, 313.
Jesus said, follow me, 324.
Jesus, the length of his public ministry determined from the Passover, 38.
Jesus trusted himself to the power of no man, 41.
Jesus testifies what he heard in heaven, 53.
Jesus teaches in the temple, 110, 111.
Jesus, they sought to take, 114.
Jesus the light of the world, 123.
Jesus tells Peter how he will die, 323.
Jesus works his first miracle, 37.
Jesus was a witness from God, 46.
Jesus walking on the sea, 90, 91.
Jesus walked no more openly among the Jews, 180.
Jesus washed the disciples' feet, 206.
Jesus' body buried by Joseph and Nicodemus, 304.
Jesus' garments divided, 299.
Jesus' legs not broken, 303.
Jesus' supremacy over John, 53.
Jews accuse Jesus of having a demon, 135, 136.
Jews cast man born blind out, 148.
Jews have no dealings with Samaritans, 57.
Jews, many of the, believed on him, 178.
Jews not permitted to inflict death, 283.
Jews persecute Jesus for healing on the Sabbath, 75-77.
Jews purposed to stone Jesus, 137.
Jews request Pilate to allow the bodies to be takken from the cross, 302.
Jews, salvation is from the, 62.
Jews sought to kill Jesus, 107.
Jews stone Jesus for blasphemy, 162.
John baptized in Ænon because there was much water there, 51.
John bore witness unto the truth, 80.
John must decrease, and Jesus increase, 53.
John not cast into prison, 51.
John, sent from God, 19; he was a witness of the light, but not the light, 19, 20; he beareth witness of Jesus, 23; this is the witness of, when the Jews sent unto him priests and Levites, 25; he confessed, I am not the Christ, 25; he is not Elijah nor the prophet, 26; he is the voice of one crying in the wilderness, 26.
John was a lamp, 81.
Joseph and Nicodemus bury body of Jesus, 304.
Joy, I have spoken unto you that my, may be full and that your, may be full, 241.
Joy, my, is made full, 53.
Judged by the word, 202.
Judas complains of the waste of ointment used on feet of Jesus, 184.
Judas cometh with lanterns and weapons, 273.

Judas had the bag, 214.
Judas should betray him, 106.
Judge, Jesus not sent to, the world, but to save it, 50.
Judge not according to appearance, 113.
Judge, ye, after the flesh, 124.
Judged, he that believeth on him is not, 50.
Judgment, all, given to the Son, 78.
Judgment of the world, 194.

K

King cometh sitting on an ass, 188.
King, people desired to make Jesus, by force, 89.
King, art thou the, of the Jews? 285.
Kingdom, if my, was of this world then would my servants fight, 287.
Kingdom, Jesus states the leading conditions of entrance into the, 43.
Kingdom, my, is not of this world, 287.
Kingdom of God entered by the spiritual birth, 43.
Kill, Jews sought to, Jesus, 107.
Kill, some knew their purpose to, Jesus, 113.
Kill, ye seek to, me because my word hath not free course in you, 132.
Kill, will he, himself? 127.
Kill, why seek to, me? 112.
Killeth you, 249.
Knowledge, Jesus had superhuman, 34.

L

Lamb, behold the, of God, 29.
Lamp, John was a, 81.
Lanterns, Judas cometh with, 273.
Law of Moses commanded to stone such, 121.
Law, the, was given through Moses; grace and truth come through Christ, 24.
Laws, the Spirit dwells in and works through the, he has given, 104.
Lazarus ate after being raised from the dead, 183.
Lazarus sickens, dies, and raised to life, 164-177.
Lazarus' death sought by chief priest, 186.
Legs of Jesus not broken, 303.
Letters, Jesus never learned, 111.
Life, eternal, 78.
Life, God gave his Son that the world might have eternal, 49.
Life, he that believeth on Jesus hath eternal, 54.
Life, he that loveth his, loseth it, 191.
Life, he should give eternal, 262.
Life, it is the Spirit that giveth, 103.
Life principle in seed, 104.
Life eternal is his commandment, 203.
Life, must come to Jesus to have, 82.
Life, my words are spirit and, 103.
Life, passed from death into, 78.
Life, thou hast the words of eternal, 105.
Life, this is eternal, 263.
Life, work for food that brings eternal, 93.
Life, was in Jesus, 17; the life was the light of men, 18.
Light, he that doeth truth cometh to the, that his works may be made manifest, 51.
Light, he that doeth evil hateth the, 51.
Light in the world, 202.
Light, Jesus is the, of the world, 123.
Light, Jesus the, of world, 140.
Light remaineth a little while, 196.
Light, was in Jesus, and was the light of men, it shines in darkness, darkness apprehended it not, 18; John sent to bear witness of the light, 19, 20; Jesus the true light, 20.
Live, dead shall hear and, 79.
Live, he that eateth this bread shall, for ever, 101.
Living water, 58; give me this, water, 59.
Loaves, seeking Jesus for the, 92.
Lost, none is, but the son of perdition, 266.
Lord greater than the servant, 210.
Lord, make straight the way of the, 26.
Love, abide ye in my, 240.

Love, if ye, me, ye will keep my commandments, 226.
Love, if a man, me, he will keep my words, 230.
Love, men, darkness rather than light, 50.
Love one another, 216.
Love, the test of, 235.
Love, this is my commandment, that ye, one another, 242.
Loved glory of men more than the glory of God, 201.
Loved, if ye, me, ye would rejoice, because I go unto my Father, 233.
Loveth, he that keepeth my commandments, he it is that, me, 229.
Loveth, he that, me not keepeth not my words, 231.
Loveth, the Father, the Son, and hath given all things into his hand, 54.

M

Mad, Jesus accused of being, 157.
Man born blind healed, 37.
Man, how can, a, be born when he is old? 44.
Man, some said he was a good, others denied it, 110.
Man look at the outward appearance; God at the heart, 64.
Man, sent from God to bear witness of the light, 19, 20; no, hath seen God, 25.
Mary anoints feet of Jesus, 184.
Mary reports the resurrection, 311.
Mary Magdalene stood by the cross, 300.
Mary Magdalene came to the tomb, 306.
Mansions, in my Father's house are many, 219.
Manna in the wilderness, 95.
Marriage in Cana of Galilee, the mother of Jesus was there, 35.
Meat, my, is to do the will of my Father, 66.
Men, the life was the light of, 18.
Measure, he giveth not the Spirit by, 54.
More murmuring, 101.
Moses gave the law, and why seek to kill me? 112.
Moses, if ye believed, ye would believe me, 84.
Moses lifted up the serpent in the wilderness, 48.
Moses, not Jesus but, accuses you, 83.
Moses, the law came through; grace and truth came through Christ, 24.
Mother of Jesus attended a marriage in Cana of Galilee, 35.
Mother of Jesus stood by the cross, 300.
Miracle, the first worked by Jesus, 37.
Miracles produced faith, 41.
Miracles, the object of, 43.
Murderer, devil is a, 134.
Murmur, people, 98.
Murmuring, more, 101.

N

Name, another came in his own, 83.
Name, Jesus came in the Father's, 82.
Nations, the beginning of breaking down wall of separation between the, 69.
New commandment, 216.
New birth, J. R. Graves on the, 45.
Nicodemus and Jesus discuss the new birth, 42.
Nicodemus and Joseph bury body of Jesus, 305.
Nicodemus came to Jesus by night, 42.
Night cometh when no man can work, 140.

O

Obeyeth, he that, not the Son shall not see life, 54.
Officer strikes Jesus, 281.
Officers sent to take Jesus, 115.
Olives, Jesus went unto the Mount of, 120.

P

Parable of the sheep, 150-152.
Parables, two in one, 150.
Parents of man born blind called by the Jews, 144, 145.
Passover, eating the, 284.
Passover feast, 204.
Passover, Jesus goes to the, 38.
Passover, the preparation of the, 295.
Pasture, he shall go in and out and find, 154.

Pathway of duty, 197.
Peter and John go to the tomb, 307.
Peter and others go fishing, 318.
Peter brought in, 279.
Peter drew his sword, 276.
Peter denied Christ, 281.
Peter followed Jesus, 217.
Peter grieved, 323.
Peter's death foretold, 323.
Peter, originally called Simon, 32.
Peter warming himself, 281.
Peace I leave with you, 233.
Peace, in me ye may have, 261.
Persecuted, if they, me, they will also persecute you, 243.
Pharisees inspect the man born blind, 143.
Pharisees expected to kill Jesus at the feast, 181, 182.
Pilate delivers Christ to be crucified, 296.
Pilate proposes to release Jesus, 288.
Pilate said take and judge him according to your law, 284.
Pilate said I find no fault in him, 288.
Pilate said what I have written I have written, 298.
Pilate scourged Jesus, 290.
Pilate sought to release Jesus, 294.
Place, I go to prepare a, for you, 219.
Power, Pilate had no, except as given by the Father, 293.
Poor ye have always, 186.
Prison, John not in, 51.
Pray, I, not for the world, 264.
Pray, neither for these alone do I, 268.
Pray the Father, and he shall give you another comforter, 226.
Pray, if ye ask anything in my name, 225.
Prepare, I go to, a place for you, 219.
Preparation of the Passover, 295.
Prince of the world shall be cast out, 195.
Prince of this world cometh, 234.
Prophet has no honor in his own country, 70.
Prophet, no, from Galilee, 119.
Prophecy of Isaiah fulfilled, 198.
Purify, many went to Jerusalem to, themselves, 181.
Purifying, question about, 52.

Q

Question, ask me no, 259.

R

Receive, whom the world cannot, 227.
Receive you unto myself, 220.
Received of his fullness, 24.
Receiveth, he that, Jesus, receiveth God, 54.
Receiveth, whom I send, me, 212.
Revealed, God, the Son, 25.
Reap, Jesus sent disciples to preach and, what had been sown by others, 67.
Reapeth, one soweth, and another, 67.
Reapers and saved souls rejoice together, 67.
Resurrection, all in the tomb shall come forth unto the, 79.
Resurrection, Mary reports the, 311.
Resurrection of Lazarus produced faith, 187.
Rivers of living water, 116.
Romans will take away both our place and nation, 179.
Rulers, many, believed, but did not confess him, 200.

S

Sabbath, Jesus healed blind man on the, day, 143.
Salvation is from the Jews, 62.
Samaritan woman and Jesus contact each other, 57.
Sanctify them through thy truth, 267.
Sanctify, I, myself, 268.
Sayings, I have spoken unto you in dark, 259.
Satan entered Judas after the sop, 213.
Scattered, ye shall be, 260.
Scourged, Jesus, 290.
Scripture, these things done that the, might be fulfilled, 304.
Scriptures, coat not divided that the, might be fulfilled, 299.
Scriptures, search the, 82.
Sea, Jesus walked on the, 90, 91.
Search the scriptures, 82.
See me no more, 257.

See, thou shalt, greater things, 34.
Seed, Christ the, of David, 117.
Seed, life principles is in the, 104.
Seek, glory from God ye, not, 83.
Seek, Jesus, Father's will, not his, 80.
Seek, what, ye? 30.
Seek, when Jesus would reach the Samaritans he did not, the great, the noble, the intellectual, but an humble, ignorant woman, 64.
Seek, whom, ye? 275.
Seek, ye, me, and shall die in your sin, 127, 128.
Seeking Jesus for loaves, 92.
Seen, Father hath not, 81.
Seen, no man hath, God, 25.
Self-righteous, it is more easy to reach the poor, simple-minded, open sinners than the, 64.
Separated from God by our own sin, 151.
Serpent, Moses lifted up the, in the wilderness, 48.
Servant not greater than his Lord, 210.
Servant's ear cut off, 276.
Servants, my, would fight if my kingdom was of this world, 287.
Servants, no longer do I call you, 243; the, know not what his Lord doeth, 243.
Servant's, Peter cut off high priests's, ear, 276.
Sheepfold, 151.
Sheepgate, 73.
Sheep hear my voice, 160.
Shepherd of the sheep, 151.
Sin, he that is without, cast the first stone, 122.
Sin, if I had not spoken unto them, they had not, 246.
Sin no more, 123.
Sin remaineth, 150.
Sin, the Lamb of God, that taketh away the, of the world, 28.
Sin, ye shall die in your, 127, 128.
Sins, apostles had power to remit, 313.
Sins of our own separate us from God, 161.
Sinners, God heareth not, 147.
Simon, called Cephas or Peter, 32.
Signs, Jesus began his, in Cana of Galilee, 37.
Signs produced faith, 41.
Signs recorded to produce faith, 315.
Signs worked by those whom God is with, 42, 43.
Skull, the place of a, 297.
Slain, the first-born of the Egyptians, 38.
Snatch, no one, them out of my hand, 160.
Social relation, Jesus did not withdraw from all, 35.
Soldiers divide his garments, 299.
Son, all judgment given to the, 78.
Son, he made himself the, of God, 292.
Son of man glorified, 190, 215.
Son, the only begotten, who is in the bosom of the Father, 25.
Sorrow turned into joy, 258.
Sound, thou hearest the, of the wind, etc., 45.
Soul of Jesus troubled, 192.
Soweth, one, and another reapeth, 67.
Spake, never man, as this man, 118.
Speak, I, not of myself, 223.
Speaketh, Jesus, the words of God, 54.
Spoken, I have, unto you in dark sayings, 259.
Spirit, born of water and the, 44.
Spirit, descending as a dove out of heaven, 28.
Spirit dwells in and works through the laws he gives, 104.
Spirit, he giveth not the, by measure, 54.
Spirit, it is the, that giveth life, 103.
Spirit, Jesus baptizeth in the Holy, 29.
Spirit, Jesus received the, without measure, 16; the, organized the material, 17.
Spirit not given, 116.
Spirit of God abide and rule in the kingdom of God, 44.
Spirit of truth, whom the world cannot receive, 227.
Spirit, the essential of the, is to bring others to Christ, 33.
Spirit, that which is born of the flesh is flesh; and that which is born of the, is spirit, 45.
Spirit, worship in, and truth, 62.

Spirit will teach you all things, and bring to your remembrance all that I said, 232.
Spiritual body exposes the evil, but it never produces it, 162.
Spiritual healing, 72.
Storm, a great, 90, 91.
Stream can rise no higher than its fountain, 162.
Stumble, that ye should not be caused to, 249.
Stones, Jews pick up, to stone Jesus, 161.
Straight, make, the way of the Lord, 26.
Supremacy of Jesus over John, 53.
Sword, Peter drew a, 276.
Synagogues, I have spoken openly in the, 280.
Synagogues, they shall put you out of the, 249.

T

Teach, the Spirit will, you and bring to your remembrance all that I have said, 232.
Teach, no one but Jesus competent to, these things, 48.
Teaching, the Father draws by, 99, 100.
Teaching, if any man willeth to do his will, he shall know of the, 111.
Teaching, my, is not mine, but the Father's, 111.
Teaching of Jesus does not destroy the ties of the flesh, 31.
Temple, Jesus cleanses the, 39.
Temple, destroy this, and in three days I will raise it up, 40.
Temple was forty-six years in building, 40.
Temple, the body of Christ the, 41.
Temple, Jesus teaches in the, 110, 111.
Temple, Jesus goes into the, early, 120.
Temple, Jesus taught in the, 126.
Test of love, 235.
Thorns, Jesus came out wearing the crown of, 291.
Thorns, a crown of, platted and put on Jesus' head, 290.
Thomas doubted, 314.
Thief comes to steal and kill, 154.
Thief and a robber, 151.
Thundered, some thought it, others an angel had spoken, 194.
Title, Pilate wrote a, and put it on the cross, 297.
Title on cross written in Hebrew, Latin, and Greek, 298.
Tomb, all in the, shall come forth, 79.
Tomb, women came to the, 306.
Touch me not, 311.
Truth, grace and, came through Christ, 24.
Truth, he that doeth, cometh to the light, 51.
Truth, I tell you the, 251.
Truth shall make you free, 130.
Truth, Spirit will guide you into all, 255.
Truth, sanctify them through thy, 267.
Truth, whoever worships God according to the, will be accepted of him, 61.
Truth, worship in spirit and in, 62.
Troubled, let not your heart be, 219.
Travail, a woman in, 258.
Trying Jesus, 121.
Treasury, Jesus spake in the, 126.
Twelve, all of the, save Judas seem to have lived on the Sea of Galilee, 33.
Twelve, Jesus said to the, will ye also go away? 105.
Type, serpent on the pole, a, of Jesus on the cross, 48.

U

Unity, Jesus prayed for, 270.

V

Vine, I am the true, 236.
Vine, I am the, ye are the branches, 238.
Vinegar, they gave him, 301.
Voice, the, crying in the wilderness, 26.
Voice, thou hearest the, of the wind, 45.

W

Wages, he that reapeth receiveth, 67.
Walk while ye have light, 196.
Walked, many disciples went back and, no more with him, 105.

Wash one another's feet, 210.
Water, born of, and of the Spirit, 44.
Water converted into wine, 35-37.
Water, John baptized in, 27.
Water, John baptized in Ænon because there was much, there, 51.
Water, rivers of living, 116.
Way, how know we the? 221.
Way, Jesus is the, the truth, and the life, 221.
Way, make straight the, of the Lord, 26.
Way, ye know the, 221.
Well, Jacob's, was sixty-five feet deep and dry in 1879, 56.
Week, first day of the, Jesus came from the dead, 306.
Weep, ye shall, but the world rejoice, 257.
Wine, Jesus converted water into, 35-37.
Witness, Jesus bears, of himself, 125.
Witness, Jesus was a, from God, 46.
Witness, John sent to bear, of the light, 19, 20; John's, when the Jews sent unto him priests and Levites, 25.
Witness, one's testimony of himself is not accepted, but Jesus is true, 124.
Witness of the Father is found in the prophets, 126.
Witnesses, two, 80.
Witness, works of Jesus was his, 81.
Wind, the, bloweth where it will, 45.
Will, Jesus seeks the Father's, not his own, 80.
Word, the, was in the beginning, part of the Godhead, made all things, was made flesh, was Jesus, 15-23.
Word which ye hear, is not mine, but the Father's, 231.
Word, they have kept thy, 264.
Word, believe through thy, 269.
Word that I speak shall judge in last day, 202.
Words, thou hast the, of eternal life, 105.
Words, my, are spirit and life, 103.
Work, I have accomplished the, thou gavest me to do, 263.
Work not for food which perishes, 93.
Work of each person of Godhead in creation, 16, 17.
Work, this is the, of God that ye believe on him, 84.
Work while it is day, 140.
Works, for which of these, do ye stone me? 161.
Works, greater, 77, 78.
Works I do bear witness of me, 159.
Works, Jesus left his, to declare that he is the Son, 64.
Works, men's, were evil, 50.
Works of Jesus was his witness, 81.
Works that I do shall ye do, and greater works than I do, 224.
World cannot hate you, 109.
World, God loved the, and gave his Son for it, 49.
World hated them, 266.
World is gone after Jesus, 189.
World, if the, hateth you, 244; if ye were of the, 244; ye are not of the, 245.
World, I came unto the, 260.
World, I sent them into the, 268.
World, Jesus sent not to judge the, but to save it, 50.
World, Jesus the light of the, 123, 140.
World, Jesus not of this world, 128.
World, my kingdom is not of this, 287.
World, the Lamb of God, that taketh away the sin of the, 28.
World, they are not of the, 267.
World, that the, may believe that thou didst send me, 269.
World, whom the, cannot receive, 227.
World would not contain the books, 326.
World's idea is to keep its work before people, 108.
Woman in travail, 258.
Woman taken in adultery, 120.
Woman with five husbands, 60.
Women came to the tomb, 306.
Worship, must, God in spirit and in truth, 63.

Worship, the hour cometh when neither in this mountain, nor in Jerusalem shall ye, the Father, 61.

Worshiped, our fathers, in this mountain, 60.

Worshipers, true, worship the Father in spirit and truth, 62.

Writings, if ye believe not Moses', how can ye believe my word? 84.

Wrote, Jesus with his finger, on the ground, 121.

Wrath of God abideth on disobedience, 54.

Wilderness, Moses lifted up the serpent in the, 48.

Wilderness, the voice crying in the, 26.